Artificial Minds

Stan Franklin

A Bradford Book
The MIT Press
Cambridge, Massachusetts
London, England

This book was set in Sabon by Graphic Composition, Inc., Athens, Georgia and was
printed and bound in the United States of America.

Library of Congress Cataloging-in-Publication Data

Franklin, Stan.
  Artificial minds / Stan Franklin.
  p. cm.
  "A Bradford book."
  Includes bibliographical references and index.
  ISBN 0-262-06178-3
  1. Artificial intelligence. 2. Cognitive science. 3. Brain. I. Title.
Q335.F733 1995
006.3—dc20   94-38796
                                                                    CIP

Dedicated to the memory of Lil Franklin and of Paul Byrne

Contents

Preface

For thousands of years humans have struggled with the relationship between the mental and the physical, with the mind–body problem. Our efforts have been rewarded with a clear understanding of some of the alternatives and a great respect for the difficulty of the problem, but with no satisfactory solution. At long last, pieces of a solution seem to be on the horizon. Researchers in many fields are producing possible mechanisms of mind. Some are theoretical, some algorithmic, some robotic. Together they are leading us to a very different way of thinking about mind, a new paradigm of mind. This work is an exploration of these mechanisms of mind, and of the new paradigm of mind that accompanies them. It's intended to change your mind about mind.

Though the research involved is highly technical, this exploration of it is not. Technical concepts have been purposefully made accessible to the lay reader. Though I hope and expect that artificial intelligence researchers, computer scientists, cognitive psychologists, ethologists, linguists, neurophysiologists, philosophers of mind, roboticists, and such can learn of activity in the other fields from this multidisciplinary tour, it's not designed only for them. I also hope that anyone interested in how mind arises from brains, or from machines, can enjoy accompanying us on this exploration. Finally, I hope to have achieved accessibility without damage to the many powerful and elegant ideas, concepts, models, and theories to be explored.

Preparations for this exploration of mechanisms of mind began with a series of lectures titled "Artificial Minds." Even before the lectures began, it was becoming clear that my role was to be as much that of hawkster as of tour guide. I had my own goods to sell to the audience, an emerging new way of thinking about mind. The tenets of this new paradigm helped guide the selection of the mechanisms to be explored. Each mechanism is to provide background for understanding the new paradigm, or evidence to support it. I wanted to report on these mechanisms and to have a hand in shaping this new paradigm.

Little did I realize the magnitude of this endeavor. It's now four years later, and the end is in sight only with the help of more people than I would have believed. Appreciations are in order.

Thanks to Don Franceschetti for suggesting the title "Artificial Minds."

My heartfelt thanks to the participants in the Cognitive Science Seminar during the summer and fall of 1991 for listening to my "Artificial Minds" lectures and arguing with me about them. Thanks also to the students in the "Artificial Minds" class in the spring of 1994 who listened to and commented on these same lectures, and a few more.

The University of Memphis, through its College of Arts and Sciences and its Department of Mathematical Sciences, has been supportive throughout, by providing a sabbatical during the fall of 1991 and a faculty research grant during the summer of 1994.

Thanks to Elizabeth Bainbridge, to a second typist I never met, and to Helen Wheeler for transcribing the recorded lectures. Thanks also to the Institute for Intelligence Systems and to the Mathematical Sciences Department for supporting this work. Also thanks to Jarek Wilkiewicz for helping me to obtain permissions to reprint, for proofreading, and for indexing, all supported by the Institute.

For invaluable conversations over many years about this material, my thanks to Kaveh Safa, Daniel Chan, and Art Graesser.

And many, many thanks for stimulating conversations over the years to participants in the weekly AI lunch: Bill Baggett, Paul Byrne, Max Garzon, Art Graesser, David Kilman, Jim Michie, Joel Neely, Lloyd Partridge, Bob Schreiber, Shane Swamer, and many others. So often I tried ideas out on you first. And so often they came away improved, or discarded.

Perhaps my deepest indebtedness is to those friends (and relatives) who read and commented on chapters as they were produced: Bob Sweeney, Art Graesser, Phil Franklin, Dan Jones, Bill Boyd, David Kilman, Pat Patterson, David Lee Larom, John Caulfield, Nick Herbert, and Elena Franklin. Though I revised assiduously in the light of their comments, as the book goes to press, I find myself wishing I'd heeded even more of what they said. That would surely have improved the work, but perhaps would have required a second volume.

And thanks also to several reviewers—Mark Bedau, John Caulfield, Janet Halperin, John Holland, Chris Langton, and others who remain anonymous—for their helpful comments and suggestions.

My appreciation to Larry McPherson and to Eric Ehrhart for encouragement and badgering, to Brian Rotman for encouragement and for discussions about writing and publishing, and to Ralph Randolph for advice about how to look for a publisher.

Thanks to Fiona Stevens and to Harry and Betty Stanton for encouraging this project, and getting it through the door at the MIT Press. Additional gratitude to Fiona for so patiently dealing with my many questions and concerns, and for prodding me actually to finish (stop) the manuscript. I'm sure the phone company appreciates her also. And my appreciations to Katherine Arnoldi for gently guiding me through the copyediting process, and to Beth Wilson for a superb job of copyediting.

Much appreciation to Arthur Goodman for such fine work on the illustrations.

Finally, and most important, I'm so grateful to my wife, Jeannie Stonebrook, for support and encouragement, for sage advice, and for assuming many of my chores to give me time for this project.

Artificial Minds

1

Mechanisms of Mind

Phase Transitions and Fascinating Questions

The title *Artificial Minds* has a strange ring to it, almost oxymoronic. Are there any artificial minds? Could there possibly be artificial minds? What would make you think there might be such things to begin with? Why would one want to ask such a question? Let's take a brief detour by way of putting these questions in broader perspective.

Recall the notion of phase transition from that almost forgotten physics course. Common phase transitions occur when ice melts to water, shifting from solid to liquid, and when water boils to steam, shifting from liquid to gas. The properties of systems change quite rapidly at these phase boundaries. Some would say that all the interesting stuff, including life itself, happens only at phase boundaries (Langton 1992a). But that's another story.

Three questions seem to be inherently interesting, even fascinating, to many people:

1. How did the universe come to be?
2. How did life originate?
3. What is the nature of intelligence?

Each of these apparently has to do with a phase transition. For the cosmological question, there's the phase transition between being and not being, or between pre- and post-big bang, if you're of that persuasion. The origin of life question focuses on the phase transition between living and nonliving matter. Asking about the nature of mind leads to the phase transition between the physical and the mental.

These phase transitions are not as sharp as those bounding solids and liquids, or liquids and gasses. Some might argue that no phase transition occurs between being and not being, because the class of nonbeing has nothing in it. Also, the dividing line between the living and the nonliving isn't easily agreed upon. Biologists might argue about whether viruses are alive. How about the boundary between the physical and the mental? That question is the major issue of this book.

Here we will be primarily concerned with mechanisms of mind, with how mental activity arises from physical substructure. Don't miss the underlying assumption of the last sentence. It takes a currently fashionable position on the mind–body problem. More on that a little later, and in chapter 2. For now, I hope that our detour into the natural questions arising from phase transitions has begun the booklong process of putting the nature of intelligence in context.

Life Itself

Mind, until now, has been associated with life, usually only with human life. If we're to explore the mechanisms of mind, it would be well to trace a little of their history and development. Focusing a wide-angle lens on life, as we know it on Earth, may help. This goal gives me a perfect opportunity to tout you onto a marvelous little book by the DNA decoder, Francis Crick, titled *Life Itself* (Crick 1981). A wag of a reviewer referred to it as "Life Itself by Crick Himself."

Figure 1.1, taken from *Life Itself*, displays a time line of the universe. The Age of Humans is not explicitly mentioned. Why not? Well, from this view we're hardly visible. If the life span of the Earth to date, roughly 4.5 billion years, was represented by the Eiffel Tower, our "dominion" would occupy the thickness of the uppermost coat of paint. Compare this with what Crick calls the Age of the Prokaryotes, the simplest kind of single-cell organism, including bacteria and blue-green algae, which have had the Earth to themselves for well over half its lifetime. Some would say that neither humans nor ants nor cockroaches dominate the Earth today. It's the Age of Bacteria. It always has been, and always will be, as long as there's an Earth (Margulis and Sagan 1986).

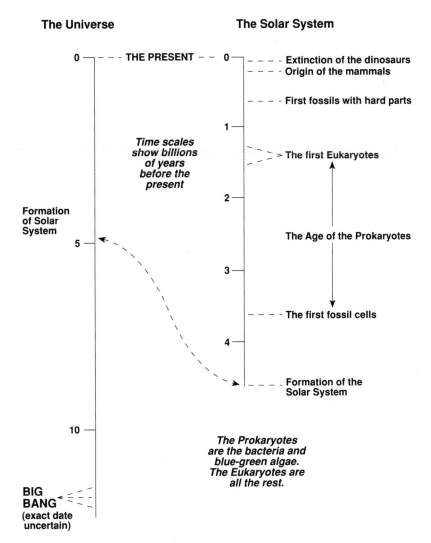

Figure 1.1
Life in time (redrawn from Crick 1981)

Bacteria are small, one to a few microns in diameter. They can sense food concentrations and toxic chemicals, and move toward or away from them by means of tiny flagella. They exercise efficient control of their metabolism, and enjoy a tenuous sex life without being dependent on sex for reproduction. Bacteria thrive in every ecological niche on Earth, inhabiting even nuclear reactors. Their combined biomass probably exceeds that of all other living things. Loose talk of humans wiping out life on Earth by nuclear warfare is just that: loose talk. Bacteria will survive quite nicely, thank you.

Amid all this glorifying of the infinitesimal, let's ask if in any sense bacteria could be said to partake of mind. (This is not the most ridiculous question we'll pose, but it's close.) The knee-jerk answer of "Certainly not!" may be less satisfying than you would think, after we've finished our exploration.

Next up on Crick's chart we find the first eukaryotes. These include all cells containing a well-defined nucleus and organelles surrounded by a membrane. Some eukaryotes are single-celled, like amoebas. All multicell organisms, like you and me and the grass on your front lawn, are colonies of eukaryotic cells.

At long last we arrive at the stuff of paleontology, the first fossils with hard parts. Our brief tour of the Earth's time line à la Crick ends with the origins of mammals and the extinction of the dinosaurs. (Don't tell the birds, who are widely believed to be the descendants of the dinosaurs.)

What strikes me most in Crick's chart is that mind, as we're accustomed to think about it, evolved from bacteria very much as a latecomer, even as an afterthought. Mind, in this view, has had no affect on life except during this last coat of paint atop the Eiffel Tower. Some trivial chance fluctuation along the way could easily have resulted in no humans[1] and, hence, no mind according to the *Oxford English Dictionary*.[2]

Crick makes two other points that may well prove germane to our exploration. One has to do with natural selection, and the other with what he calls the "combinational principle." Let's look first at Crick's combinational principle. Here's the argument. All life as we know it is complex. Nothing but natural selection produces such complexity.[3] This complexity requires the storing and replication of much information. The only efficient mechanism is the combinational principle: express the information by using a small number of standard units combined in very many different ways. We use the alphabet in this way to produce written language. Perhaps a more pertinent example is DNA, whose constituents form the "alphabet of life." If one wants artificial minds to replicate, this combinational principle doesn't seem like such a bad idea.

Here's Crick's most interesting view of natural selection: what natural selection does is to make rare chance events become common. Suppose you have a genome with a mutation in it, a rare, improbable event. If the mutation is successful, which would also be rare, it can influence organisms down the eons and eventuallly become quite common. Given enough time, organisms become finely tuned to their environment. This works as long as the environment stays fairly constant, but major environmental changes can lead to extinctions.

Crick points out that there's no mechanism to direct changes in the genes so that favorable alterations are produced. You don't know which mutations are going to be successful and which are not. This point has recently become controversial. There's new evidence that some bacteria (what else?), when placed in a sugar solution, mutate in the direction of metabolizing sugar at greater than chance rates. Some people are beginning to think there might indeed be mechanisms directing evolution. The issue of mechanisms directing evolution provides a bridge to get us back on track from our detour.

Stubbs's Great Leaps

Most evolutionists staunchly deny any direction or progress in evolution, any mechanism providing direction. Nonetheless, Monday morning quarterbacks often discern direction in the evolutionary record. One such is Derek Stubbs, a physician-turned-computer scientist, who publishes a newsletter now titled *Sixth Generation Computing*. Stubbs maintains that the evolution of life has made several "great leaps" when judged by "the criterion of adaptability and particularly the speed of adaptability" (1989).[4] A more precise criterion might be rate of adaptability. Keep in mind that "adaptability" is commonly used in several senses in this one context. You can speak of evolution as adapting species to their environments. You can also think of an individual adapting its behavior during its lifetime via learning. You may also talk of an individual adapting its behavior to short-term changes in its surroundings without new learning. These three meanings of the word are quite distinct. Watch out for the potholes.

So what are the "great leaps"? Stubbs identifies seven.

Life itself is the first great leap. First came the ability to reproduce, the basic definition of life.[5] Mutations are blueprint errors that, along with transcription errors,[6] allow for variation from which to select on the basis of fitness.

Second, sexual reproduction "allowed organisms to swap great chunks of adaptive blueprints from their selected-as-fit mating partners."

Third, multicell organisms developed for "safety in numbers" and for "the enhanced productivity of division-of-labor." (Each of the eukaryotic cells comprising our multicell organism contains organelles that some think derived from independently living prokaryotic ancestors [Margulis and Sagan 1986; Gould 1989]. These were incorporated into the eukaryotic cell. Perhaps they were parasitic to begin with, and evolved some sort of symbiosis. Hence we might view each eukaryotic cell as multicellular.)

The fourth leap was the development of specialized nerve cells that allowed the organism to "find food and mates and escape predators more rapidly."

Fifth was "Invention of a central nervous system. This allowed the organisms to more rapidly adapt to the highly nonlinear dynamics of the outside world and to store memories."

So far these "great leaps" seem uncontroversial, keeping in mind the criterion of rate of adaptability. But hang on to your hat for the next one. Stubbs says:

Then nothing happened for half a billion years until one creature invented computers . . . and shortly thereafter, the sixth step of evolution was invented as artificial neural networks: artificial learning machines. Life was becoming a going concern and was really in business to start shaping the Universe. Competitors such as rocks and gravity and earth, wind, and fire were taking a distinctly second place.

We'll hear a lot more about artificial neural networks in this and subsequent chapters. For now, suffice it to say that they are computing devices based loosely on biological models. You may or may not agree with

Stubbs's assessment of artificial learning machines as a great leap in evolution. But it's clear that such machines must partake in at least one aspect of what we call mind: learning.

At this point Stubbs leaves the past and leaps into the future: "From here onwards, life was guiding its own evolution, since the seventh step is genetic engineering, environment engineering and life-computer symbiosis." One might infer the coming of artificial minds from "life-computer symbiosis," or one might dismiss the whole notion as science fiction. Some competent scientists are predicting artificial minds. As a mathematician, like me, is wont to do, let's look at one of the extremes.

Mind Children

Among the competent scientists who, after serious study, expect to see artificial minds and then some, is Hans Moravec, a roboticist at Carnegie Mellon University. The following quote from his book *Mind Children* sets forth his expectations clearly:

Today, our machines are still simple creations, requiring the parental care and hovering attention of any newborn, hardly worthy of the word "intelligent." But within the next century they will mature into entities as complex as ourselves, and eventually into something transcending everything we know—in whom we can take pride when they refer to themselves as our descendants. (1988, p. 1)

Keep in mind that Moravec is a serious scientist expressing a thoughtful judgment backed by a book full of arguments. He may well be wrong, but he's not to be lightly dismissed. Toward the end of this volume, we'll have a look at some of his arguments. In the meantime, let's look at one more quote from Moravec to remove all doubt about exactly what he's predicting.

We are very near to the time when virtually no essential human function, physical or mental, will lack an artificial counterpart. The embodiment of this convergence of cultural developments will be the intelligent robot, a machine that can think and act as a human. (1988, p. 2)

We now have an existence proof. There is at least one serious scientist who thinks it's reasonable to talk of artificial minds. There are others.[7] I hope there will be many more after this book has been widely read. (Moravec shouldn't be allowed a monopoly on wild predictions.)

Moravec has also engaged in Monday morning quarterbacking, discerning a direction through prehistory leading (inevitably?) to mind children (1988, p. 2). A graphical version appears as figure 1.2. Notice how what each of us sees depends so heavily on our interest and concerns—that is, on the ax we're grinding. Figures 1.1 and 1.2 overlap almost not at all. Such time lines, like statistics, can be bent to almost any will.

What Is Mind, and Why Study It?

We started out asking if there were any artificial minds, or if there even could be. So far, our best answer is that some respectable scientists believe there can be. That's not very convincing. Some respectable scientists can

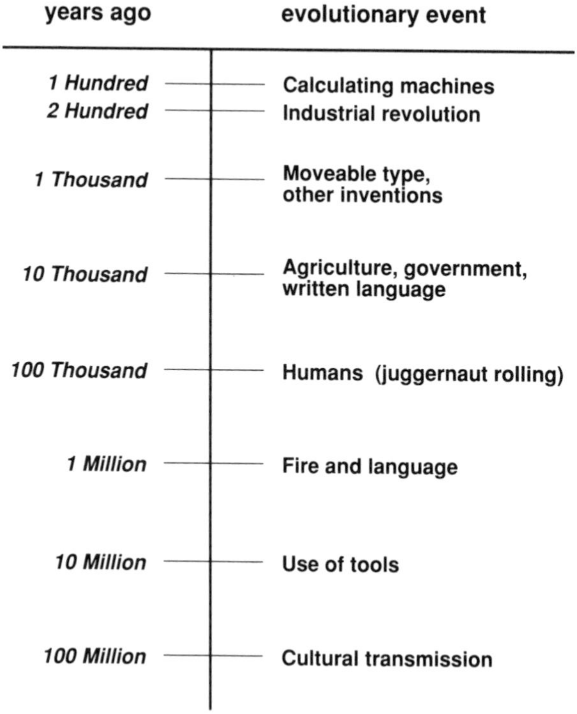

years ago	evolutionary event
1 Hundred	Calculating machines
2 Hundred	Industrial revolution
1 Thousand	Moveable type, other inventions
10 Thousand	Agriculture, government, written language
100 Thousand	Humans (juggernaut rolling)
1 Million	Fire and language
10 Million	Use of tools
100 Million	Cultural transmission

Figure 1.2
Evolution of mind children

be found who believe almost anything. I hope we can do better before the end of our exploration.

But even if we could be more convincing about the possibility of artificial minds, there's still the question of why we should study them. Why explore the mechanisms of mind? The preceding sections have provided answers, at least one of which, the first, is convincing to me. The three reasons are:

1. Questions of the nature of intelligence are inherently fascinating. The study of artificial minds may well throw light on this question.
2. Stubbs might well suggest that we study artificial minds, at least artificial learning machines, to better understand the coming man-machine symbiosis.
3. If we give credence to Moravec's predictions, we would be well advised to study artificial minds to prepare to give birth to our upcoming mind children, and to deal with them more effectively.

Now suppose we are at least marginally convinced by these arguments and, therefore, bent on exploring mechanisms of mind. What does this mean? What is mind? How can mental events occur in a physical world? Do mental events arise from the physical, or are they some kind of spiritual or mental stuff of their own? If they do arise from the physical, how do they do it? And if they don't, where do they come from? Later in this chapter we'll take a brief excursion into the philosophy of mind and the mind–body problem. Chapter 2 is devoted to these issues. For now, let's make what is known as the physicalist assumption: *Mind is what brain does, or something very like it in relevant ways.*

I want to assume so, not because it's the only reasonable alternative but because it allows a scientific approach to the mind–body problem.[8] Let's act on the physicalist assumption and see how far we can get. Let's ask how mental events arise from the physical, and what the mechanisms of mind are. Can they be simulated, or even implemented?

Having focused on these questions, how can we hope to answer them? There are approaches to the study of mind from various disciplines. Figure 1.3 displays some of them via their top-down versus bottom-up and their synthetic versus analytic dimensions.

You can start from *cognitive psychology,* which is a *top-down* approach. By and large it studies high-level concepts. It also takes an *ana-*

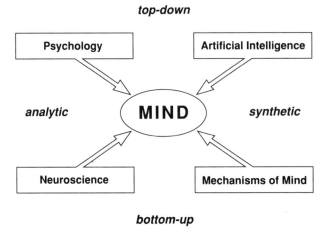

Figure 1.3
Approaches to mind

lytic approach in that it looks at existing minds and tries to understand them. *Artificial Intelligence (AI)* takes a top-down approach as well, but is *synthetic* in that it tries to build minds. *Neuroscience,* particularly cognitive neuroscience, studies mind from the *bottom up* and analytically. It looks at individual neurons and at groups of neurons and their activity. It's not trying to build things; it's trying to analyze what's already there, to take it apart to see how it works. Finally, some people are beginning to take a bottom-up and synthetic approach. They are trying to build what I like to call *mechanisms of mind,* artificial systems that exhibit some properties of mind by virtue of internal mechanisms. Later, and after some preparation, we will see this same figure with "mechanisms of mind" replaced by "robotics."

Let's not leave our discussion of figure 1.3 without pointing out its major deficiency. There's no mention of culture. How can one hope to understand mind while ignoring the cultural factors that influence it so profoundly? I certainly have no such hope. I clearly recognize that the study of culture is indispensable to an understanding of mind. I simply don't know how to gently include culture in the diagram. It's certainly top-down and analytic. Perhaps anthropology and sociology should share a corner with cognitive psychology.

So far, we've put our proposed exploration of mechanisms of mind in some context, we've at least feebly rationalized the endeavor, and we've looked cursorily at several approaches to the study of mind. Let's now try for something of an overview of where this exploration is likely to lead us.

Itinerary

I view myself as a tour guide for this exploration of mechanisms of mind. What should a tour guide do? He or she should keep the touring group more or less on course; make the way as easy, as comfortable, and as enjoyable as possible; and, above all, point out the interesting sights along the way, pausing to recount their stories. I hope to do all this.

But where are we going? Every tour should have its itinerary. Each tourist should look at it before embarking. After all, you might not want to go. It's only meet that I provide you such a look.

The upcoming itinerary will touch lightly on some of the major landmarks of the tour. More detailed views will appear in subsequent chapters, along with other sights of interest. For the most comprehensive understanding, the tourist is invited to live a while with the original sources, which will always be referenced. The itinerary begins here. Let's look briefly at some important specific approaches to creating mechanisms of mind. Concepts only alluded to here will be treated more fully later.

Symbolic Artificial Intelligence

AI is sometimes defined as the art of making machines do things that would require intelligence if done by a human—for example, playing chess, or speaking English, or diagnosing an illness. AI systems typically confine themselves to a narrow domain; for example, chess-playing programs don't usually speak English. They tend to be brittle, and thus break easily near the edges of their domain, and to be utterly ignorant outside it. I wouldn't want a chess player speculating as to the cause of my chest pain. AI systems tend to be designed and programmed, rather than trained or evolved. They tend to be propositional in nature, that is, based upon rules or some other data structure expressed in some language. AI systems are typically implemented on ordinary serial computers, often referred to in the trade as von Neumann machines. This dependence on serial computing will be less true in the future because of a move to parallel processors.

Artificial Neural Networks

These are cognitive and/or computational models based roughly on the structure of nervous systems. One such system is the sniffer, a device used to scan neutron reflections from airline baggage for plastic explosives. A straight expert system model (symbolic AI) couldn't quite get it right, but an ANN seems to have succeeded. Another example is Nettalk, a system that learns to pronounce English text. ANN systems can also perform higher-level cognitive tasks such as changing active sentences to passive ones. Typically, ANNs are trained rather than programmed. That's what Stubbs meant by "learning machines." Learning machines are crucial to full artificial minds. It would be utterly impossible to specify everything a human needs to know, as one would have to do when writing a computer program. There has to be some kind of learning involved.

ANNs operate in parallel rather than serially. Faulty units or connections result in graceful degradation rather than in sudden collapse (as occurs in symbolic AI systems). ANNs are particularly useful for pattern recognition and/or classification problems, although they are theoretically capable of anything any computer can do (Franklin and Garzon, to appear).

Silicon Nervous Systems

Having traveled downhill from high-level cognitive skills to pattern recognition and classification, let's go even further down to sensation via silicon nervous systems. This gives me a chance to quote from one of my heroes, Carver Mead: "If we really understand a system we will be able to build it. Conversely, we can be sure that we do not fully understand the system until we have synthesized and demonstrated a working model" (1989, p. 8). That's the engineering view. It's also the critical issue that separates cognitive scientists from cognitive psychologists. Cognitive scientists have a lust to build models, and hence their understanding is likely to be far more sophisticated. I think of this quote as justifying the bottom-up, synthetic approach of mechanisms of mind.

Artificial neural network chips are now on the market. I view these as the forerunners of components from which you might hope to contrive a silicon nervous system. Mead and his group have produced a silicon retina and an electronic cochlea (Mead 1989; Mahowald and Mead 1991). The enabling principle for these creations is wafer scale integration. This means using an entire silicon wafer, say 4 inches in diameter, for a single circuit.[9] The fault tolerance (graceful degradation) of ANNs makes this possible. Mahowald and Douglas have produced a "silicon neuron" sufficiently realistic to fool neurobiologists with its real-neuronlike output (1991a).

Artificial Life

Moving from concrete implementations to abstract simulations leads us to artificial life (AL). This is the study of man-made systems that exhibit behaviors characteristic of natural living systems. One AL example is Reynolds's boids, a computer model of flocking behavior in, say, birds or fish (1987). The flock will, for example, divide to pass on either side of an obstacle, then reassemble beyond it. There's no executive guiding this behavior. Each boid follows relatively simple local rules: keep a minimum distance from neighbors and obstacles, match your speed with that of your neighbors, and move toward what looks like the center of mass of the nearby boids. Yet they produce this emerging, global, birdlike behavior.

Computer viruses provide another AL example (Spafford 1992). They exhibit reproducing behavior as well as make trouble. So far, they tend not to evolve. Let's hope they never do! There are, however, populations of algorithms or programs that do evolve (Hillis 1992; Ray 1992).

These artificial life systems are typically concerned with the formal basis of life, not how it's made but how it behaves. Such systems attempt to synthesize lifelike behavior, focusing on the emergent behavior. Most such systems are highly distributed and massively parallel. Populations often evolve and sometimes coevolve.

Computational Neuroethology

The next stop on our itinerary refers to some relatively simple ideas with a not so simple name, computational neuroethology (CN). Ethology is the study of animal behavior within a dynamic environment. Neuroethology is the study of the neural substrates of such behavior. Computational neuroethology is concerned with the computer modeling of this behavior, including its neural substrates.

CN systems work within a closed-loop environment. That is, they perceive their (perhaps artificial) environment directly rather than through human input, as is typical in AI systems. They act upon their environment in ways that affect their next perceptions, thereby closing the loop. After the simulation or robot is running, there is no human in the loop to provide semantics. This is a central tenet of CN. The CN people both insist on a closed-loop environment and claim that traditional AI got untracked by failing to heed this dictum (Cliff 1991).

CN systems may model individual animals (Beer 1990; Wilson 1985) or populations (Ackley and Littman 1992). They tend to evolve genetically[10] and to learn neurally. They behave adaptively, which means they change their behavior depending upon the circumstances in which they find themselves. CN simulations tend to consume enormous computational resources. CN practitioners claim you'll learn more by building complex models of simple animals than you will by making simple models of complex animals, the traditional AI approach. My view is that we should do both. Here's another Mead quote that can be viewed as supporting the computational neuroethologists' position: "The nervous system of even the simplest animal contains computing paradigms that are orders of magnitude more effective than those systems made by humans" (1989, p. xi).

The next segment of our itinerary will mention only briefly several individual, and quite distinct, mechanisms of mind. Winograd has something to say about the necessity of such variation: "I predict we will not find a unified set of principles for intelligence but rather a variety of mechanisms and phenomena some of which are close to the current symbolic paradigm in AI and others that are not."

Subsumption Architecture

Brooks pushes what he calls subsumption architecture: the old brain that we share with the alligators controls much of our lower-level functioning, such as breathing (1989, 1990a, 1990b). We have built higher-level functions on top of that. For instance, we can suppress the old brain and hold our breath. If something happens to the higher-level operation, the lower-level stuff reemerges and is no longer suppressed. Conscious control of breathing works until you pass out. Then the old brain takes over.

Brooks has built robots on this principle, giving them a sequence of competencies, some subsuming and/or using others. His robots are built incrementally; new competencies are added one at a time, without disturbing older ones. For example, he hardwired a mobile robot to avoid stationary objects, so that it would stop or turn when about to run into something. On top of that he built the capacity of avoiding moving objects. Its next competence was to scan across the room, find an object, and move toward it. The object avoidance abilities remained. On top of all this he created a mechanism for exploration. All these competencies are hardwired. Nothing is learned. The robot seems to have goal-directed behavior but, according to Brooks, it has no representations of anything at all. This issue will be treated in some detail when we explore the necessity of internal representation to intelligence. There's some controversy here, to which I refer as the third AI debate. Among the protagonists are Brooks, who says nay to representations, and Simon and Newell, who maintain that symbolic representation is necessary for general intelligence.

Dynamic Representations

Another very different mechanism of mind, or more specifically, mechanism of perception, is Freeman's notion of dynamic representations[11] (1983, 1987; Freeman and Skarda 1990). Briefly put, consider patterns of firing rates of the neurons in the olfactory bulb of a rabbit as state vectors in the state space of a dynamic system.[12] This view makes visible various attractors and their basins. Freeman shows that rabbits classify smells depending upon the basin in which the state vector falls. I suspect that this mechanism underlies much of our perception, regardless of mode, and that it will prove to be a useful mechanism for artificial minds.

Other Mechanisms

Piaget discussed the *when* of children acquiring "object permanence," without speculating on the *how*. Drescher's *schema mechanism* provides a computer model of one way that object permanence could occur in children or in artificial minds (1986, 1987, 1988). It allows representations of objects to be created, recognized, and classified, but at a considerable computational cost. Drescher defends this cost, saying he sees no reason to expect that intelligence at the human scale can be achieved with significantly less powerful hardware than we have.

At a higher cognitive level than object recognition lies the use of language. Two related mechanisms for language processing are Pollack's *RAAM* (1990) and Chalmers's *passivization network* (1990). These mechanisms are both embodied as artificial neural networks. How can you take something complex and of varying length, like a sentence, and represent any such by a fixed-length vector? Pollack's RAAM does just that. Chalmers uses the RAAM mechanism to build a network for changing active sentences to passive. Both are examples of mechanisms of mind implemented as ANNs. There are, of course, many other such examples (e.g., St. John and McCelland 1990). I want to introduce you to the Chalmers work because of its implications concerning the second AI debate on symbolic versus subsymbolic models.

Moving from artificial neural networks to biological neural networks, we come to Gerald Edelman's theory of *neuronal group selection* (1987, 1988, 1989; Reeke and Edelman 1988). The key idea here is that individual groups of neurons aren't wired genetically or developmentally for specific purposes but, rather, are selected for specific tasks according to their suitability. Each of these neuronal groups, and collections of them as well, can be thought of as mechanisms of mind.

For any mind, biological or artificial, and at any given time, there is a single overriding issue: *how to do the right thing*. This includes what to do next as well as how to go about it. Don't think of "the" right thing as implying there is only one; for any organism or agent in any given circumstance there may be many possible "right things." And don't think of the "right" thing as being in some sense the optimal thing. Rather, think of it as a "good enough" thing. With these caveats, the control issue is central for any mind. The next two "mechanisms of mind" stops on our itinerary are control mechanism stops.

Maes's *reactive-plus-planning algorithm* puts control in the hands of a network of nodes, each node representing some competence, that compete for the chance to take the next action via spreading activation in the network (1990). She's after a control mechanism that can make quick, good enough decisions in a dynamically changing environment—say, exploring the surface of the moon. John Jackson's *pandemonium theory* has competence demons in a sports arena screaming to be chosen for action by spectator competence demons sitting in the stands (1987). We have, of course, visited other control mechanism stops at other points on our itinerary—Brooks's subsumption architecture, for example.

Our itinerary ends with the notion of a *society of mind:* mind is best viewed as a commonwealth[13] of more or less autonomous agents or competencies that have some intercommunication. They both compete for the right to act and cooperate to serve common needs. Ornstein, a psychologist, says in *Multimind:* "Some small minds are more encompassing than others; they may well control many smaller small minds" (1986, p. 74). He constructs a hierarchical kind of structure with a single decision-making "talent" at the top. Minsky, a computer scientist, says in his *Society of Mind:* "you can build a mind from many little parts, each mindless by itself. Each mental agent by itself can only do some simple thing that needs no mind or thought at all. Yet when we join these agents in societies . . . this leads to true intelligence" (1985, p. 17).

Having perused the itinerary, you now have some idea of where this tour will take us, and of whether you want to embark. Before you decide, however, I feel obliged to warn you: THIS TOUR MAY BE INJURIOUS TO YOUR PRESENT CONCEPT OF MIND. In particular, it's not an unbiased tour. The stops have been carefully chosen to strengthen certain positions your tour guide wants to sell. Here are some of these positions.

1. *Mind is better viewed as a continuous as opposed to a Boolean[14] notion.* That is, it should not be a question of whether something has mind or it doesn't. It's more useful to think about degrees of mind, and what capabilities of mind a particular organism, system, or agent displays.

2. *Mind is aggregate rather than monolithic.* All but the most simple minds are comprised of relatively independent competencies or agents with only limited communication bandwidth between them. Communication must be limited because, with so many different systems, it would be impossible for each system to be in contact with every other. Also, there is typically no need for one agent—say, the one that contracts your

right thumb—to dialogue with another—say, your respiratory control mechanism. On the other hand, it's useful to hold your breath when you go underwater. So it's useful that the goal agent for swimming underwater communicate with respiratory control.

3. *Mind is enabled by a multitude of disparate mechanisms.* There is a role for all the various modalities and mechanisms we have discussed so far and, no doubt, many, many more. I'm not a fan of unified theories of cognition (Newell 1990).

4. *The overriding task of mind is to produce the next action.* This is what minds, natural or artificial, are about. A few cautions seem in order. Don't be misled by "next." Mind may well operate in parallel, producing more than one action simultaneously. Also, "next" doesn't imply discrete, rather than continuous, action. Finally, don't read purpose into the word "task." Producing actions is just what minds do. A consequence is that *minds are properties of autonomous agents.*

5. *Mind operates on sensations to <u>create</u> information for its own use.* I don't think of minds as information-processing machines in the sense of taking information from the environment and processing it to arrive at the next action. Rather, I think of information as not existing out there in the environment at all. Information comes into being when minds process sensations (Oyama 1985). The same scene can provide quite different information to different minds.

6. *Mind uses prior information (memories) to produce actions by a reconstructive process rather than by retrieval.* Memories are not stored as if in a folder in a filing cabinet; rather, they are rebuilt when triggered by appropriate associative cues.

7. *Mind, to some degree, is implementable on machines.* The question is, how much—and, more important, how do we do it?

Thus ends the warning label. On with our exploration of the mechanisms of mind. Our tour begins with an attempt to put the nature of mind and the mind–body problem in perspective.

Notes

1. Stephen Jay Gould (1989, p. 291) put it thus: "Homo sapiens, I fear, is a 'thing so small' in a vast universe, a wildly improbable evolutionary event well within the realm of contingency."

2. During our "Nature of Mind" tour stop, we'll see that the *OED* ascribes mind only to humans.

3. To get some hands-on experience with analogous complexity, there's software for the Mac by Richard Dawkins, titled "The Blind Watchmaker," that accompanies his book of the same name (Dawkins 1987). Highly recommended!

4. All the quotes and paraphrases from Stubbs are from this source.

5. It seems to me that the ability to reproduce should not be taken as the essence of life. There are many things that are alive—say mules or sterile humans—that cannot reproduce. There are also nonliving things, like crystals, that can reproduce. And then there are viruses. Note that I'm falling into the trap of assuming there is some essence of life, some sharp distinction. That this is, indeed, an insidious trap will be made clear on a later tour stop when we meet Sloman's ideas on free will.

6. A mutation might occur, for example, when a cosmic ray strikes a gene. A transcription error occurs during the duplication of the DNA.

7. Biologists Margulis and Sagan (1986, p. 261) speculate that "Perhaps within the next few centuries, the universe will be full of intelligent life—silicon philosophers and planetary computers whose crude ancestors are evolving right now in our midst."

8. My friend and colleague Art Graesser pointed out to me that science, as an activity, can proceed assuming a dualist or even an idealist position on the mind–body problem. He gives cognitive science as an example. I'll say more about my stubborn insistence on a tentative physicalist position in chapter 2.

9. In producing typical computer chips, these wafers are cut into dozens of, hopefully, identical squares, each about the size of the nail of your little finger. Many of these will prove useless due to imperfections that are in the original wafer or are acquired in processing.

10. These systems evolve using John Holland's genetic algorithms (1975), of which more in chapter 9.

11. Freeman would no doubt object to my use of the term "representation" in this context. The issue of the need for representations is at the heart of the third AI debate, a topic to be met later in the tour.

12. A discussion of dynamical systems and their state spaces, attractors, and basins will be found in chapter 12.

13. I am indebted to my friend and colleague Lloyd Partridge, a neurophysiologist, for this metaphor.

14. In computer science a Boolean variable, or just a Boolean, is one that can take one of only two values. These values are most often represented as 1 and 0, but can be interpreted as "yes" and "no" or "true" and "false."

2

The Nature of Mind and the Mind–Body Problem

Science's biggest mystery is the nature of consciousness. It is not that we possess bad or imperfect theories of human awareness; we simply have no such theories at all.

—Nick Herbert, *Quantum Reality*

Perhaps the problem is the seeming need that people have of making black-and-white cutoffs when it comes to certain mysterious phenomena, such as life and consciousness. People seem to want there to be an absolute threshold between the living and the nonliving, and between the thinking and the "merely mechanical," . . . But the onward march of science seems to force us ever more clearly into accepting intermediate levels of such properties.

—Douglas Hofstadter, *Metamagical Themes*

Well, it's amateur night on the "mechanisms of mind" tour; Stan Franklin is going to talk about philosophy. Professionals make a living at what they do. And besides that, they usually have some professional training, and surely some professional experience. Well, I don't, and I have neither.[1] I worried about this, particularly at the thought of philosophers reading this chapter. But then the truth struck. Essentially every stop on the tour is going to be amateur night.[2] My training is in mathematics, my professional experience is in math and computer science, and I earn my living at the latter. The next chapter is about animal minds. I'm surely an amateur. And so it goes with almost all the rest.

But there's an upside to being an amateur. In an endeavor like exploring mechanisms of mind, being an amateur is a necessity. So many fields are involved that no one can be professional in them all. There's also a case to be made for what the Zen people call "beginner's mind." An amateur can, at least theoretically, view a field without being so enmeshed in its prevailing paradigms as to be blind to what's outside them. If this sounds like rationalization to you, it does to me, too. We'll see if there is any truth in it.

The Nature of Mind

In any event, being an amateur, and wanting to know about the nature of mind, what would you do first? You can't look mind up in the current literature; you wouldn't even know where to find it. But our amateur does know where to find the dictionary, so let's start there. Figure 2.1 describes mind according to the *Oxford English Dictionary* (*OED*). It starts with definition 17, passing by those having to do with "Do you mind?" or "mind the store" or any of those things. Definitions 17 and 18 are the ones that seem to suit the particular context of mind with which we're concerned.

Do notice that according to the *OED*, only humans have minds. It says very clearly "of a person" and "of a human being." There is nothing in

17. Mental or psychical being or faculty.
· The seat of a person's consciousness,
  thoughts, volitions, and feelings.
· The system of cognitive and emotional
  phenomena and powers that constitutes
  the subjective being of a person.
· Also the incorporeal subject of the
  psychical faculties, the spiritual part of
  a human being.
· The soul as distinguished from the body.

18. In more restricted applications.
· The cognitive or intellectual powers, as
  distinguished from the will and
  emotions. Often contrasted with *heart*.

Figure 2.1
Mind according to the OED

the definition that has anything to do with anything except people. I will argue that a vastly broader notion of mind is useful. I even want to talk about whether "mind" might, in some sense, be usefully ascribed to a bacterium or a Coke machine. I hope this won't sound so crazy later on.

Do note several features of "mind according to the *OED*":

1. Mind is essentially identified with the *conscious mind*. It's almost as if Freud had never existed. But much of what I want to call mind can lie outside of consciousness.

2. Mind is subjective. And that raises the question of whether artificial minds have subjective experience. More on this later in this chapter, and in chapter 5 on the first AI debate.

3. The mind is incorporeal, and is to be distinguished from the body. This leads to the mind–body problem, the subject of much of this chapter.

4. Definition 18 describes what I think of as the *rational mind,* a deliberative mind.

A number of different kinds of minds have come up. Let's take an organized look at some of these varieties of minds before getting into the mind–body problem. Figure 2.2, a Venn diagram with boxes, may help. Note that all the boundaries are fuzzy; they are intentionally so.

The largest class is labeled *agents*. An agent, roughly speaking, is anything that acts. Agents are typically described as having motives. The class of agents surely should include anything with mind, including subconscious mind. Agents with minds must include agents with conscious minds. And then there are agents with rational minds. It may be that rational minds are always conscious, but that's not clear to me just now.

Among the conscious agents are those that are also self-aware. Humans and some of the great apes are examples, according to Gallup (1970; Suarez and Gallup 1981) and Patterson (1991). In these studies, evidence of self-recognition in a mirror was taken as sufficient to conclude self-awareness. Apparently, baboons, gibbons, and some monkeys can't be shown to be self-aware in this way (Gallup 1977a, b).

At least one well-respected developmental psychologist, Barry Gholson, views agents with rational minds as lying completely in the class of self-conscious agents (personal communication). I'm open to this possibility. The containment relations expressed in figure 2.2 are speculative at best. This is necessarily so because the classes are by no means well

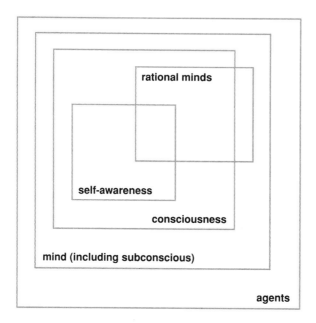

Figure 2.2
Varieties of mind

defined. But these various usages of the word "mind" are going to come up. We'll certainly want to distinguish between them.

The Mind–Body Problem

There's a tension between the physical and the mental over which one is going to have the ascendancy. Does the mental arise from the physical, or is it the other way around? How does consciousness occur in a physical universe? Or is the physical universe simply *maya* (illusion) and everything really mind? The desire for a resolution of this tension, for an explication of the relationship between the mental and the physical, gives rise to the mind–body problem, an active area of philosophical thought for millennia.

Here's what David Chalmers says about the significance of the mind–body problem: "The problem of consciousness, also known as the Mind–Body Problem, is probably the largest outstanding obstacle in our quest to scientifically understand reality" (1991). The thought that a solution to the mind–body problem may at long last become conceivable led me to this exploration of mechanisms of mind. My hope is that understanding the physical mechanisms leading to mind, and being able to model them, will lead to a fuller understanding of the relationship between mind and body.

To provide a context for the "physicalist" theory we'll tentatively adopt, let's spend a few minutes looking at traditional mind–body theories. There are essentially three.[3] The *mentalist theory* maintains that the mind is everything, and that it produces the material world as its sensation. The *materialist theory* asserts that mind is only a physical process. The *dualist theory* holds that the mental and the material have existences of their own.

How do we decide which of these views to accept? By rational thought, the traditional philosophical mode? Scientifically, by appeal to empirical facts? One may well argue that philosophers have tried their methods at least since the time of Aristotle without conspicuous success. Therefore, let's turn to science. Putnam is not optimistic about this approach: "The various issues and puzzles that make up the traditional mind–body problem are wholly linguistic and logical in character: whatever few empirical 'facts' there may be in this area support one view as much as another" (1981).

Later I'll argue that, for the purposes of this exploration of mechanisms of mind, we should tentatively accept a form of materialism. For the moment, let's have a quick glance at each of the three major mind–body theories, and some of their subtheories. (See figure 2.3.)

The *dualist* view asserts that minds and bodies are both substances. The body consists of extended or material substances; it occupies space. The mind is unextended, or spiritual. And (now for the kicker) the dualist view asserts that mind is subject to completely different principles of operation than body. That is, mind and body are essentially different and distinct.

The *mentalist* (or idealist) view says that mind is a spiritual substance, meaning that it occupies no space, and bodies are sensations of minds. Although Western philosophers these days aren't so high on mentalism, it must be mentioned, if only because most of the peoples of Asia profess religions based on mentalism.

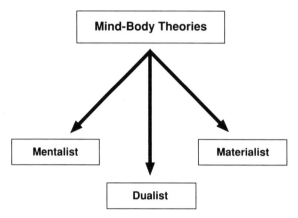

Figure 2.3
Mind-body theories

The *materialists* maintain that physical principles can account for mind as well as for body. This doesn't refer only to naive physical principles; they allow anything derived from physics, up to and including quantum mechanics.

Branchings of the dualist view are shown in figure 2.4. *Cartesian duality* postulates mind and body as substances, one extended and material, the other unextended and spiritual. A second view came from Hume, who looked around and said he couldn't find anything like mind, only bundles of perceptions. That's the *bundle theory,* partitioning the mind into bundles while leaving the physical world intact. I don't think these two will concern us greatly. Then there is *interactive duality,* which says that the mind affects the body and the body affects the mind. It seems obvious when separated from its dualist context. *Parallel duality* holds that the mind and body run in parallel, with neither having anything to do with the other. This seems not at all believable to me. Finally there's the *epiphenomenalist view* that the body affects the mind but not conversely. That is, our subjective experience is an epiphenomenon, and everything we do would go on in just the same way, even if we didn't have this subjective experience.

The following quote by physicist Eugene Wigner offers motivation for mentalism and its offspring, neutral monism, to be discussed below: "It is not possible to formulate the laws of quantum mechanics in a fully consistent way without reference to the consciousness." This is not an

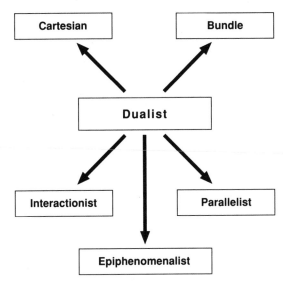

Figure 2.4
Branchings of the dualist view

unusual point of view for a quantum mechanic. Similar assertions go back as far back as Niels Bohr. The consciousness referred to is, of course, that of the researcher.

Recall that the mentalists hold mind to be a spiritual substance, with the body as its sensations. *Neutral monism* brings bundle theory into the mentalist camp. It views mind and matter as different ways of organizing and marking off bundles of the same constituents. This view is interesting in that it implies a single substance rather than two, with mind and body referring to different levels of observing this one substance. Chalmers takes a somewhat analogous position in a article we'll meet later in this chapter (1991).

Mentalism underlies the doctrine of two major religions, Taoism and Buddhism. The Buddhists believe that all is Mind, with a capital M. Mind in the Buddhist sense seems, superficially, like the Western notion of God but is vastly different in that there is no personification. The Taoists are also mentalists, but their view of the Tao is too subtle to talk about briefly.[4] I think a third major religion, Hinduism, could also fall in the mentalist camp, but I hesitate to make such a pronouncement. Hinduism is quite complex, and you can find all kinds of views within it. Still, I'm sure there are many Hindus who would agree that what appears to be physical reality is all *maya,* that is, illusion. The adherents of these religions add up to a lot of people. Even though you might not personally know many, it may well be that most people are mentalists.

Finally, there's the materialist view and its branchings, as shown in figure 2.5. *Behaviorism* maintains that mind is nothing more than sophisticated overt behavior. This is different, I've been warned, from psychological behaviorism, which is essentially methodological in nature. Here we have the ontological statement that certain types of behavior constitute mind. Next is the *identity view,* which identifies mental events with physical processes in the nervous system. There is only one substance, the physical, but mental happenings are allowed to interact causally with the physical body. Minsky adopts the *functionalist* view when he proclaims: "as far as I'm concerned, the so-called problem of body and mind does not hold any mystery: *Minds are simply what brains do*" (1985, p. 287). The functionalists view mind, the software, running on brain, the hardware. It could, of course, run on some other hardware, say computers. Hence, researchers in artificial intelligence are apt to be functionalists.

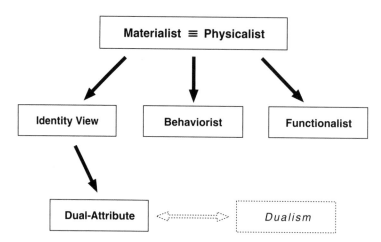

Figure 2.5
Materialist view and branchings

The *dual-attribute* position is that brain processes have both physical and nonphysical properties. Both mental and physical processes reside in the nervous system, but they're precisely the same. There's no distinction to be made. Brain processes have certain properties that are called physical, and others that are called mental. Different properties of the same processes, that's what it's about. For example, voltage across a membrane or the output of a cell would be physical properties. But there might also be some subjective sensation attached to a process that would be a mental property. The dual-attribute theory moves us to within a hairsbreath of dualism. Its ghost is depicted at the bottom of figure 2.5.

The dual-attribute theory also seems related to an issue within cognitive science. To what extent, if any, should cognitive scientists look to neuroscience for mechanisms and/or inspiration? Many would argue that brain processes are so complex, and their mental and physical properties so intertwined, that the study of physical properties is a hopeless entanglement for the cognitive scientist. Others would maintain that there is no hope of fully understanding the human mind until the neuroscientists and the cognitive scientists meet on middle ground.

Mind as Global Dynamics

The dual-attribute theory leads us directly to what I call the *global dynamics view of mind.*[5] A *continuous dynamical system* consists of a state space, X, and a mapping T: $X \times [0,\infty] \to X$, called the global dynamics. Each state vector, $x \in X$, represents a single, instantaneous, full state of the system. For example, a state vector of a working brain should include all relevant information about that brain's state or condition at some given time, perhaps a vector of voltages of individual neurons. The global dynamics, T, describes the way the system changes over time. For a given time $t \in [0,\infty]$, and a given initial state $x_0 \in X$, $T(x_0,t)$ represents the state of the system at time t when started from the initial state x_0. Typically, X is a subset of some very large dimensional vector space, and T is given as the solution of a different equation that describes the way the system changes. We'll encounter dynamical systems again while visiting connectionist models.

Let's look at Minsky's quote again: *"Minds are simply what brains do."* He and other people are saying that mind is the activity of the brain, the processes that carry brains from state to state. Here, as above, "state" refers to the global state, a full, instantaneous state of the system. The brain's process is mind. When viewed statically, you see the brain, the nervous system. When viewed dynamically, you see the mind.

Minsky's view of mind as process, surely not original with him, is now widely shared among people who talk about these things. It will serve admirably, I think, as a foundation for exploring mechanisms of the mind and the possibility of artificial minds. To explore mechanisms of mind is to look for ways that physical things give rise to mental events. For that enterprise we must, at least tentatively, adopt some sort of physicalist position and see how far we are able to proceed on that basis. We shall see that a dynamical systems view of mind as process will be just what we need.[6]

However, the global dynamics view is incomplete as an explanation of mind because it lacks any account of subjective experience. The next stop on our tour will be devoted to something that purports to be the beginnings of such an account.

Consciousness à la Chalmers

Chalmers (1991) talks about consciousness and takes two different approaches (see also Nagel 1974 and Dennett 1991). The *third-person approach* regards consciousness as a scientific problem, while the *first-person approach* treats it as a metaphysical issue. Under the third-person approach, consciousness is considered as a problem in science, like heat, life, or nuclear physics, and subject to the same methods. This approach, he says, leads to psychology, the study of behavior; to neuroscience, the study of brain functions; and to artificial intelligence, the study of cognitive modeling. Its essence is functionalism, that is, it understands mental processes by revealing the underlying abstract causal structure behind brain function. This structure can be understood objectively and duplicated in different materials—in computers, for example—in addition to carbon-chain chemistry. Thus Chalmers comes out explicitly for the possibility of artificial minds. Third-person consciousness is to be understood as an aspect of a complex system perhaps as that process by which "the system scans its own processing." This view of consciousness bothers me. I think a mouse is often conscious, but I can't imagine it spending much time scanning its own processes. On the other hand, existing self-diagnosing machines scan their own processing,[7] but surely could be conscious only at a rudimentary level if at all. Perhaps we should think of consciousness as synonymous with awareness, and "metaconsciousness" as scanning its own processing. There is, of course, the logical possibility of infinite regress here. It's a logical, but not a psychological, possibility because of the limitations of short-term memory. A brief thought experiment should convince you that watching yourself watching yourself . . . can only go on successfully for precious few levels. And defining consciousness as awareness still leaves us with the problem of understanding awareness. But on to the first person.

Chalmers claims that there are three hard problems concerning consciousness, and that they lie within the first-person approach. The first is the problem of *sensory qualia* (to be defined below): Why does red look like red? Why does red look like anything at all? The second is the problem of *mental content*: thoughts are about something, say white elephants. By our physicalist assumption, thought arises from neural firings. But what should neural firings have to do with white elephants? The third is the *existence of subjective experience:* Why should subjective states exist in the first place?

We've been on our tour only a short while, and already we've landed in a quagmire. Some people claim that we shouldn't bother studying subjective experience, that it's not scientific. Others point out that there's no other kind of experience. What else can you study? Still others say that nobody studies experience, unless it's his or her own. You may study behavior by observations, but you don't study anybody else's experience except by inference. As you can see, it's easy to get bogged down here.

But whether we study experience or not, we talk as if we do. We talk about other people's experiences. We talk about our own experiences. We talk about consciousness. Chalmers claims that consciousness itself is a mystery, but not what we say about it. According to our basic assumption, the physicalist view of mind, the third-person approach is sufficient, in principle, to yield a complete explanation of human behavior. Claims about consciousness are facts of human behavior. Facts about human behavior can be explained with the third-person, scientific approach. Therefore, the third-person approach, in principle, is sufficient to explain our claims about consciousness, the things we say about it. Claims about consciousness are not mysterious, but consciousness is, as a result of the three problems mentioned above.

We'll see that the third-person approach seems not sufficient to explain all first-person phenomenon. Let's start with qualia. Qualia are the qualitative aspects of our mental states, such as color sensations, the taste of chocolate, pleasure and pain. Looking at a red patch triggers a pattern of nerve firings. Why is there such a rich subjective sensation? Why this sensation and not green? And how personal that sensation is. I've often wondered if what I see as red is what you see as purple but refer to as red. There's no way to ever know.

Here's a little thought experiment that Chalmers provides[8] to highlight the problem of qualia:

A future scientist, living in a time when neuroscience is completely understood, might learn everything there is to know about physical brain processes. But if she has lived all her life in a black-and-white room, she will still not know what it is like to see red; when she sees red for the first time, she will *learn* something.

One might conclude that qualia cannot be understood in terms of physical brain functions, that something else is needed to explain them. That is, no matter how suitable the physicalist assumption is for our purposes, it can't hope to provide an adequate foundation for an explanation of conscious, subjective experience.[9] I would rather put it in a slightly different way. While a scientific approach cannot even in principle substitute for actual experience, it could allow for some explanation of that experience.[10] We may hope that starting with "mind is what brain does" may lead us to an explanation of qualia via an understanding of some of the mechanisms of mind. Now on to mental content.

Chalmers points out that thoughts have subjective content, that thinking about a lion has something to do with lions. Brain states must thus carry *intrinsic* content, not merely arbitrary attribution. Thoughts of a lion seem more like shared pattern than like reference, more like a picture of a lion than like the word "lion." This may well be because some of the same neural mechanisms are activated when thinking of a lion as when looking at one. Chalmers infers that "a completed theory of subjective mental content may end up having very little to do with reference."

I agree. The rational mind surely employs reference, but most of the rest of mind must get along quite well without it. Reference is needed for symbolic representation. Is this an argument against our using mental symbolic representations? Very much so. We certainly use them sometimes, but how much? Some people (Agre and Chapman 1987, 1988; Brooks 1990c, 1991; Chapman 1987, 1991; Freeman and Skarda 1990) claim that the rational mind is a thin veneer on top of all of the nonreferential, nonrepresentational activity that goes on in minds. In later chapters we'll look at their compelling arguments.

Finally, what of subjective experience? Why do I experience anything at all? Why don't I just go ahead and do what I'm doing without any experience? The epiphenomenalists maintain that subjective experiences are inconsequential, that only the physical processes really count. According to them, subjective states are purely epiphenomenal; they don't do anything. Chalmers doesn't subscribe to this view (and neither do I). Few people believe in zombies, that is, people exhibiting normal behavior but without any subjective mental states. However, functional zombies, androids with human functioning but without consciousness, are somehow more acceptable. Perhaps some of us tend to suspend disbelief because of our science fiction experiences.

This raises a question crucial to the study of artificial minds: To what class of entities may we ascribe subjective states? In chapter 3 we'll speculate on subjective states in nonhuman animals. Can any machine experience a subjective state? Some serious scientists think so (Moravec 1988). Answered affirmatively, this question gives rise to another, even more crucial, question: What are the mechanisms producing consciousness or facilitated by it? How is it done? But the issue of consciousness is surely not Boolean at all, not either present or absent. There must be many degrees of consciousness. This assertion may be more palatable after our tour has visited Sloman's dissolution of the freewill problem later in this chapter.

In any event, Chalmers is asking for some sort of explanation of subjective states, for some sort of a theory that explains the experience he's so aware of. What would satisfy him as an explanation? I don't know. I doubt that he knows. But we're going to see his beginnings of an answer, even though it doesn't satisfy him, and likely won't satisfy us either.

The key to Chalmers's beginnings of an answer to the problem of consciousness is his identification of pattern and information. His sequence of ideas runs like this:

Pattern and information, if they occur, always occur together.
All information is carried by some pattern in the physical world.
All patterns carry some information.
Patterns and information are two aspects of the same thing, PATTERN-INFORMATION.

One might object that some information might be carried in patterns over time, and hence not by a pattern in the physical world. But the physical world is a dynamical system varying over time. To me, a pattern in time qualifies as a pattern in the physical world.

One might also object that by this view, pixels darkened at random on a screen carry no information, and hence comprise no pattern. But this "random screen" provides information to a process that computes the average number of darkened pixels per line. Here we have a process for which the random screen would indeed carry information, even though the intent was that it carry none.

A pattern may carry different information, depending on the process that accesses that information. A text file may carry information about a new product for me, but quite different information for a word-processing utility program that simply counts the words. This observation led Chalmers to speak of *information as a difference that makes a difference,*[11] that is, a way things are to which some process is causally sensitive, leading to consequences that depend on that information (personal communication). Thus information must be relative to a choice of process. Different information makes a different difference.

Here's a synopsis of Chalmers's proposal for a step toward a solution to the mind–body problem. Third-person (objectively understandable) mental events are patterns of neural firings in the brain not all of which are conscious. Any corresponding subjective (first-person) mental events are information. Qualia are just information. Information is what pattern is like from the inside. My conscious mentality arises from the one big pattern that I am. This is a dual-aspect theory of mind–body. The aspects are information and pattern. Chalmers hopes that this view will focus attention on the relationship between pattern and information, and that whatever discoveries are made will illuminate the mind–body problem.

Let's consider several of the issues raised by this proposal. From Chalmers's viewpoint, one must conclude that any agent that uses information derived from pattern is conscious to some degree. This would be true even of a bacterium following a gradient in its ambient solution, or of a computer running a program. Chalmers can live with this. So can I. Mind, I maintain, is best viewed as continuous, not Boolean, not "there or not there" but "there to some degree, perhaps 0 degree." Our now imminent encounter with Sloman's views on free will should add plausibility to this contention.

The one–many relationship between pattern and information—that is, the same pattern providing different information to different agents— seems to account for the difference in subjective experience (information) of different agents when confronted by the "same" stimulus. This, of course, assumes that different agents can ever perceive the "same" stimulus. Here "the 'same' stimulus" must refer to two equivalent stimuli according to some relevant notion of equivalence.

This view of information as the one–many counterpart of pattern supports the contention of Oyama and many others that information doesn't simply reside within a pattern (Oyama 1985; Skarda and Freeman 1987; Winograd and Flores 1986; Maturana and Varela 1980). Rather, information is created by each agent according to its needs and goals of the moment, taking into account its present perception of the environment. Skarda and Freeman support this contention with physiological evidence, as we shall see in chapter 12. But for now, let's check out Sloman's view of free will as scalar rather than Boolean.[12]

Free Will à la Sloman

I'm rather taken with Sloman's notions about free will (1988). But how do I justify bringing up the freewill issue in a chapter entitled "The Nature of Mind and the Mind–Body Problem"? Well, we've just talked about an agent creating information according to its needs and goals. What if there are goal conflicts? Does our agent exercise free will? That's one connection. Recall that the central issue, always, for a mind is how to do the right thing. Does a mind exercise free will in deciding what is the right thing to do? That's a second connection.

But all this is rationalization. Sloman disposes of the freewill problem by showing it to be a pseudoproblem. He refocuses our attention away from the question "Does this agent have free will or not?" by exposing us to all sorts of degrees of free will. I want to convince you that it will be useful to think of all sorts of degrees of having mind, of all sorts of degrees of having consciousness. I hope Sloman's approach to free will serve as a formal analogy.

Sloman maintains that the basic assumption behind much of the discussion of free will is the assertion that "(A) there is a well-defined distinction between systems whose choices are free and those which are not." However, he says,

> if you start examining possible designs for intelligent systems IN GREAT DETAIL you find that there is no one such distinction. Instead there are many "lesser" distinctions corresponding to design decisions that a robot engineer might or might not take—and in many cases it is likely that biological evolution tried . . . alternatives.

The deep technical question, he says, that lurks behind the discussion of free will is "What kinds of designs are possible for agents and what are the implications of different designs as regards the determinants of their actions?"

What does Sloman mean by "agents"? He speaks of a "behaving system with something like motives." An agent, in this sense of the word,[13] operates autonomously in its environment, both perceiving the environment and acting upon it. What follows is a representative sample of Sloman's many design distinctions, taken mostly verbatim.

Design distinction 1

Compare

(a) *an agent that can simultaneously store and compare different motives* as opposed to

(b) *an agent that has only one motive at a time.*

I would say that the first exercises more free will than the second.

Design distinction 2
Compare
(a) *agents all of whose motives are generated by a <u>single top level goal</u>* (e.g., "win this game")
with
(b) *agents with several <u>independent sources of motivation</u>* (e.g., thirst, sex, curiosity, political ambition, aesthetic preferences, etc.).

If you're designing an autonomous agent, say a Mars explorer, here's a design decision you have to make. Will you design in only one top-level goal, or will you create several independent ones? If you choose the second, I'd say you must build in more free will.

This is going to get tiresome after a while because there are lots of these design distinctions. But that's Sloman's point! I have to show you lots of them, or you may miss it. Just skip ahead when you feel convinced.

Design distinction 3
Contrast
(a) *an agent whose development includes <u>modification of its motive generators in the light of experience</u>*
with
(b) *an agent whose <u>generators and comparators are fixed for life</u>* (presumably the case for many animals).

Design distinction 4
Contrast
(a) *an agent whose generators change under the influence of <u>genetically determined factors</u>* (e.g., puberty),
as opposed to
(b) *an agent for whom they can change only in the light of interactions with the environment and inferences drawn therefrom.*

In this case, I couldn't say which one exercises more free will. It's not much of an issue any more. The issue dissolves as we focus on whether to design in a certain decision-making property. And I think the issues of what has mind and what doesn't, or what's conscious and what's not, are going to dissolve in the same way when we get down to designing mechanisms of minds.

Design distinction 5

Contrast

(a) *an agent whose <u>motive generators and comparators</u> are themselves <u>accessible to explicit internal scrutiny, analysis and change</u>*

with

(b) *an agent for which <u>all the changes in motive generators and comparators are merely uncontrolled side effects</u> of other processes,* such as addictions, habituations, and so on.

In the first case we have an agent that not only can change its motive generators but also can change them consciously. That seems like quite a lot of free will.

Design distinction 6

Contrast

(a) *an agent preprogrammed to have motive generators and comparators <u>change under the influence of likes and dislikes, or approval and disapproval, of other agents</u>*

and

(b) *an agent that is only <u>influenced by how things affect it.</u>*

The agent has some social awareness. There's much more to designing agents than just the pseudo issue of free will.

Design distinction 7

Compare

(a) *agents that are able to extend the formalisms they use for thinking about the environment and their methods of dealing with it* (like human beings)

and

(b) *agents that are not.* (most other animals?)

Agents that can think about their paradigms and change them would seem to have a lot more free will.

Design distinction 8

Compare

(a) *agents that are able to <u>assess the merits of different inconsistent motives</u>* (desires, wishes, ideals, etc.) *and then decide which (if any) to act on*

with

(b) *agents that are always <u>controlled by the most recently generated motive</u>* (like very young children? Some animals?).

Design distinction 9

Compare

(a) *agents with a monolithic hierarchical computational architecture where subprocesses cannot acquire any motives (goals) except via their "superiors," with only one top-level executive process generating all the goals driving lower-level systems*

with

(b) *agents where <u>individual subsystems can generate independent goals.</u>*

In case (b) we can distinguish many subcases, such as

(b1) *the system is hierarchical and subsystems can pursue their independent goals if they don't conflict with the goals of their superiors*

(b2) *there are procedures whereby subsystems can (sometimes?) override their superiors.* [e.g., reflexes?]

Design distinction 10

Compare

(a) *a system in which all the decisions among competing goals and subgoals are taken on some kind of <u>"democratic" voting basis</u> or a <u>numerical summation</u> or comparison of some kind* (a kind of vector addition, perhaps)

with

(b) *a system in which conflicts are resolved on the basis of <u>qualitative rules,</u> which are themselves partly there from birth and partly the product of a complex high-level learning system.*

Here we have the distinction between connectionist systems (a) and symbolic AI systems (b). This distinction will occupy us during a later stop on our tour. Surely you've gotten the point by now and we can stop with ten examples, although Sloman did not.

It's a strange kind of argument. Sloman argues against free will not directly but by pointing out that free will is based on the assumption of a sharp distinction. He then says that if you look closely enough, you don't find this sharp distinction. The whole idea is to point out that free will is really a nonissue, that these specific design distinctions are the important issues. He's essentially taking the engineer's point of view rather than the philosopher's, even though he is a philosopher. When we explore the fascinating space of possible designs for agents, the question of which of the various systems has free will becomes less interesting.[14] Design decisions are much more fascinating.

Degrees of Mind

As we begin to make specific design distinctions concerning aspects of mind other than control, the question of mind attribution should dissolve as the freewill question did. Here are a few such distinctions couched in the style of Sloman. Note that all of them could and should be refined into finer distinctions, and that some of them may well turn out to be spurious.

Design distinction S1
Compare
(a) *an agent with several sense modalities*
with
(b) *an agent with only one sense* (e.g., a thermostat).

Design distinction S2
Compare
(a) *an agent only one of whose senses can be brought to bear on any given situation* (e.g., a bacterium [?]).
with
(b) *an agent who can fuse multiple senses on a single object, event, or situation.*

Design distinction M1
Compare
(a) *an agent with memory of past events*
with
(b) *an agent without memory.*

Does a thermostat have memory? It certainly occupies one of two states at a given time. One might claim that it remembers what state it's in. Allowing memory in such a broad sense makes it difficult to imagine any agent without memory. This distinction should be taken to mean memory in some representational sense, perhaps the ability to re-create a representation of the event.

Design distinction M2
Compare
(a) *an agent with short- and long-term memory*
with

(b) *an agent <u>with only short-term memory.</u>*

Do insects have only short-term memory for events, or can some of them recall the distant past?

Design distinction M3
Compare
(a) *an agent that <u>can add to its long-term memory</u>* (learn?)
with
(b) *an agent that cannot* (e.g., some brain-damaged humans).

I can imagine wanting to design an agent that remembers during its development period but not thereafter. An analogous situation is a human child's ability to learn a new language easily until a certain age and with more difficulty thereafter.

Design distinction M4
Compare
(a) *an agent that can <u>store sensory information from all its modalities</u>*
with
(b) *an agent that can <u>store sensory information from only some</u> of them.*

I think some of Rodney Brooks's robots satisfy (b), at least for brief periods (1990c). His work will occupy a stop on our tour.

Design distinction T1
Compare
(a) *an agent that can <u>operate only in real time</u>*
with
(b) *an agent that can <u>plan.</u>*

This is a graphic example of a coarse distinction that could be refined, probably through several levels. The ability to plan can range from a dog walking around an obstacle to get to food on the other side to a complex chess stratagem involving ten or more moves of each player.

Design distinction T2
Compare
(a) *an agent that can <u>"visualize" in all sensory modalities</u>*
with
(b) *an agent that can <u>"visualize" in none</u>*

with

(c) *an agent that can visualize in some but not others.*

I, for instance, can easily conjure up a mental image of my living room, but I cannot "hear" a melody in my head or imagine the smell of popcorn. Note that this is not simply a lack of memory for music or smells. I can readily recognize familiar melodies on hearing them, and familiar odors as well.

Design distinction T3
Compare
(a) *an agent that can create mental models of its environment*
with
(b) *an agent that cannot.*

The utility of mental models is a hotly debated issue just now, in the guise of "to represent or not." We'll visit this topic toward the end of our tour. Also, we have here another obvious candidate for refinement. There are surely many degrees to which an agent could create mental models, mediated by sensory modalities, type and capacity of available memory, and so on.

Could we say that agents with some of these abilities display a greater degree of mind than the counterpart with which they were compared? I think so. Surely it takes more mind to plan than to act, if only because planning—for an agent, not a planner—presumes acting.

Thinking of mind as a matter of degree may well make the task of synthesizing mind seem less formidable.[15] We can start with simple minds and work our way up. I expect a real understanding of the nature of mind to arise only as we explore and design mechanisms of mind. Let me remind you of a quote you've already seen in Chapter 1 by way of driving home the point: "If we really understand a system we will be able to build it. Conversely, we can be sure that we do not fully understand the system until we have synthesized and demonstrated a working model" (Mead 1989, p. 8).

The next stop on the tour is zoology, the animal kingdom. If we're to find minds and their mechanisms in other than humans, surely that's the first place to look.

Notes

1. Well, almost neither. Since writing the first draft of this chapter, I've published an article in a philosophy of computing journal (Franklin and Garzon 1992).

2. A kind reviewer suggested I clarify the "essentially" that begins this sentence. I have written several papers on artificial neural networks (in collaboration with Max Garzon, John Caulfield, and others), one on genetic algorithms (with David Kilman and others), and a couple in cognitive science (with Art Graesser, Bill Baggett, and others). A sampling can be found under these names in the references. All this is in order that you not take me for "a computer hack . . . spending his spare time writing speculative pop science/philosophy." Still, I stand by my claim to amateur status.

3. The following account is taken largely from Armstrong (1987).

4. The first verse of the *Tao Te Ching*, the Taoist bible, warns us that the Tao that can be spoken of cannot be the true Tao.

5. In the following description my mathematician self, who's gotten little exercise so far on the tour, slips out to provide a mathematical definition of a continuous dynamical system. This note is intended to explain some of the notation. $[0,\infty]$ denotes the set of all nonnegative real numbers, $t \in [0,\infty]$ says that t belongs to that set. $X \times [0,\infty]$ denotes the set of ordered pairs (x, t) with x in X and $t \in [0,\infty]$. The mapping T assigns to each such ordered pair some state in X. A vector space, in this context, can be thought of as all vectors, that is, ordered lists, of real numbers of some fixed length d, where d is the dimension of the space. Differential equations can be thought of as equations involving rates of change whose solutions are mappings.

6. My friend Art Graesser points out that cognitive scientists tend to view the mind as an "abstract information system." While this certainly seems a valid approach, the dynamical systems view might well prove more suitable for our endeavor of searching out mechanisms of mind. The dynamical systems view can hope to take us back to neural mechanisms for human minds, while the abstract information system view must stop at least somewhat short.

7. I'm indebted to Phil Franklin for pointing this out.

8. Due originally to Frank Jackson (1982).

9. This seems to be the conclusion drawn from the thought experiment by many philosophers of mind. An exception is Dennett (1991, pp. 398ff).

10. Science does study classes of subjective states. If a number of people were to experience a particular stimulus, you'd get a class of subjective states, which may have properties that you can study scientifically. Cognitive psychologists do just that. They build theories that try to predict the properties of such classes of subjective states resulting from the perception of a given stimulus.

11. Nick Herbert and Brian Rotman have kindly pointed out that this description of information dates back to Gregory Bateson. Chalmers also.

12. Computer scientists speak of a Boolean variable, or just Boolean, as one that assumes only two values, usually 0 and 1. A scalar variable, or scalar, assumes one of some finite set of values.

13. Minsky, in his *Society of Mind* (1985), uses "agent" to refer to a mental process with a certain amount of autonomy and some particular competence.

14. Not everyone will agree. Bob Sweeney comments as follows: "Free will has as much to do with the issues of accountability, ethics and 'sin'. These cannot be glossed over by reductionist arguments about design features."

15. I'm indebted to Dan Jones for this observation.

3

Animal Minds

Chuang Tzu and Hui Tzu were standing on the bridge across the Hao River. Chuang Tzu said, "Look how the minnows are shooting to and fro! How joyful they are!"
"You are not a fish," said Hui Tzu. "How can you know that the fishes are joyful?"
"You are not I," answered Chuang Tzu. "How can you know I do not know about the joy of the fishes? . . . I know it from my own joy of the water."

Animal Minds?

On this stop of our tour we'll visit not artificial minds but natural minds, animal minds. That is, if there are any. Recall that the *Oxford English Dictionary* ascribes mind only to humans. But I think it is important to our exploration of the mechanisms of mind to consider to what extent, if any, animals can be said to have minds. It is conceivable that artificial minds can exist while nonhuman animals experience mind not at all. Not that I believe this for a minute. I suspect that all animals can be ascribed some degree of mind, although there will surely be great variation from species to species. This suspicion of mine stems from adherence to a more general principle that was asserted as follows by Potts (1991, p. 42): "all distinctively human traits are extensions of the behavioral capacities of other primates." Diamond espouses this same principle in his *The Third Chimpanzee*.

Much of the material in this chapter is taken from, or motivated by, Griffin's *Animal Thinking* (1984). Griffin isn't looking for mechanisms of mind; rather, he is trying to make a case that it's reasonable to think that animals have minds. Some behavioral psychologists and anthropologists would argue against animal minds to this day (Griffin 1984, pp. 9ff.). Griffin reminds me of Chalmers in asserting that "It's a fundamental intellectual challenge to understand the nature of subjective mental experience" (p. 1).

Will the study of animals help us do that? I suspect it might. But Griffin gets right to grinding his ax, saying:

It is of great interest to inquire whether the important class of phenomena that we call thoughts and feelings occur only in human beings. If our species is unique in this respect, what endows us with this special attribute? Is the human brain different from all other central nervous systems in some basic property that permits consciousness? (p. 1)

I find this last hard to believe.

Can animals other than humans have minds? This question splits naturally into three subquestions according to our previous classification of mind. *Can animals be conscious, be self-aware, have rational minds?* Griffin focuses mainly on the first of these. During this stop on the tour we'll hear some of what Griffin has to say, as well as encounter thoughts of later workers.

The Mechanistic Alternative

Suppose we decide that animals don't have minds. What's the alternative? Here is what Griffin calls the *mechanistic alternative:* animal behavior is adequately explained by genetic instructions conveyed by DNA and molded by natural selection, or by learning during the lifetime of the individual animal, or by some combination of both.[1] That's all you need, it says. You don't have to postulate consciousness or self-awareness or rational thought. Programmed and/or trained specifications are enough. Postulating conscious thinking adds nothing.

Furthermore, the notion of animal consciousness seems unfalsifiable, and therefore unscientific. Let me remind you of a currently popular extention of Popper's view of proper scientific procedure. Accumulating evidence to support a scientific theory is not the appropriate way to test it. What you should do is try to falsify it, to challenge it with your best efforts at proving it false. A theory that withstands those best efforts can really gain some credibility, whereas a theory that only builds on confirmation isn't convincing. Theories that can't be so challenged, that are un-falsifiable, cannot be scientifically convincing.

As a final point in favor of the mechanistic alternative, there's the first commandment of ethology: *Thou shalt not anthropomorphize.* That is, don't attribute human feelings, capacities, and such to animals. Chuang Tzu was guilty of just that in the epigraph to this chapter.

Of course there are reactions against the mechanistic alternative. The critics of sociobiology like to point out that genes produce proteins, not behavior. It seems a little incongruous that these same people say genetics can't help to explain human behavior but often claim that genes suffice for animals. For one biologist's view of the relationship of genes and behavior, see Dawkins's *The Extended Phenotype* (1982), where he argues that the genes of one individual may conspire to produce behavior even in a member of another species.

Another argument against the mechanistic alternative points out that complex behaviors would require an impossibly lengthy genetic instruction booklet. How could you possibly encode genetically for all the behaviors of an individual animal? Ants perhaps. But chimps?

Griffin also claims that concepts and generalizations, being compact and efficient, would be useful to animals for the same reasons they're useful to humans. He asserts that conscious thinking is valuable when learning some new skill, when planning, and when the stakes are high. Another obvious use is for debugging. When routine unconscious procedures begin to go awry—say your tennis serve lapses into double faults—you will surely begin thinking. If consciousness has evolved in humans because of its utility, why not also in other animals?

One might well counter by proposing that categories and concepts evolve without consciousness, that they have third-person being as neural patterns but don't occur in first-person subjective experience. As we've seen, some people hold that consciousness is an epiphenomenon anyway. All this utility can be had without it, they say. Griffin doesn't take this argument seriously. You and I probably don't either. Griffin explicitly values the possibility of thinking ahead: "When the spectrum of possible changes is broad . . . then conscious mental imagery including explicit anticipation of likely outcomes and simple thoughts about them are likely to achieve better results than thoughtless reaction" (p. 41).

Finally, with regard to anthropomorphizing, Griffin simply wants to repeal the commandment. He claims that if you don't anthropomorphize, you're going to miss what's going on. To some extent, at least, he sides with Chuang Tzu. Cheney and Seyfarth, whose work with vervet monkeys we'll soon encounter, concur (1990, p. 303): "*anthropomorphizing works:* attributing motives and strategies to animals is often the best way for an observer to predict what an individual is likely to do next."

Other Minds

So how do we think about other minds? Well, there's a continuum with solipsism at one end and panpsychism at the other. The solipsist says "I'm the only one there is, and you guys are all just figments of my imagination." The panpsychist posits some mentality in everything. How do we judge this? How do we decide on some point between solipsism and panpsychism? How do we judge whether other humans have minds? What makes you think that I have a mind, or think that you have one? It's mostly by convention, I believe. I've been taught that. I look at my own experience and figure that you can't be all that different.

How about humans judging machines? How can you tell whether a machine has a mind, or to what degree? Turning offers one test (1950): Question it from a terminal, and see if it can fool you into thinking it's human.

This brings us to the issue at hand. How about humans judging animals? How can we tell whether an animal has a mind, or to what degree? Griffin offers some suggestions of behavior that might indicate an animal is thinking consciously.

Griffin's Criteria for Animal Consciousness

The following are to be interpreted as criteria in the sense that presence of any of them gives evidence of animal consciousness, not in the sense of necessary and sufficient conditions for animal consciousness.

His first criterion is *complex behavior.* He doesn't press this point. Suppose you look at an antelope running away from a cheetah, for example. It looks simple at first. The antelope simply runs as fast as it can, occasionally changing direction in an attempt to escape. But the more closely you look, the more complex this behavior seems. At a low level there are coordinated muscle contractions controlled by nerve tissue. At a higher level, there's the split-second timing required to take advantage of features of the environment. So Griffin concludes that complex behavior might be regarded as evidence but not as weighty evidence.

But why doesn't complex behavior constitute weighty evidence? The following passage, out of Wooldridge (1968) via Hofstadter (1985, p. 529), prompts caution:

When the time comes for egg laying, the wasp *Sphex* builds a burrow for the purpose and seeks out a cricket which she stings in such a way as to paralyze but not kill it. She drags the cricket into the burrow, lays her eggs alongside, closes the burrow, then flies away, never to return. In due course, the eggs hatch and the wasp grubs feed off the paralyzed cricket, which has not decayed, having been kept in the wasp equivalent of a deepfreeze. To the human mind, such an elaborately organized and seemingly purposeful routine conveys a convincing flavor of logic and thoughtfulness—until more details are examined. For example, the wasp's routine is to bring the paralyzed cricket to the burrow, leave it on the threshold, go inside to see that all is well, emerge, and then drag the cricket in. If the cricket is moved a few inches away while the wasp is inside making her preliminary inspection, the wasp, on emerging from the burrow, will bring the cricket back to the threshold, but not inside, and will then repeat the preparatory procedure of entering the burrow to see that everything is all right. If again the cricket is removed a few inches while the wasp is inside, once again she will move the cricket up to the threshold and reenter the burrow for a final check. The wasp never thinks of pulling the cricket straight in. On one occasion this procedure was repeated forty times, with the same result.

Griffin's second suggestion is *adaptability to changing circumstances.*[2] Some people are beginning to take adaptability as the very essence of intelligence (Beer 1990). But every animal adapts to changing circumstances to some degree, and thus would be intelligent to that degree. This seems right on to me. As an argument against adaptive behavior as a criterion for consciousness, Griffin notes conscious but nonadaptive behavior in humans. This point isn't at all clear to me. Why can't adaptive behavior be a sign of consciousness <u>and</u> some conscious behavior be nonadaptive? Where's the problem? Besides, my guess is that very little human behavior is really nonadaptive. As outside observers, we tend to see some behavior as nonadaptive. But if I had inside access to the person behaving, I might well realize that he or she was doing the best possible thing from his or her point of view. But what about suicide? Could the progeny benefit? Might suicide improve the gene pool? Ah, back to the fundamental issue facing any mind: how to do the right thing. Let's leave this digression, and get back to the issue of animal consciousness.

How about *obtaining food by a complex series of actions never before performed?* This would be a special case of adaptability to changing circumstances. Griffin gives, as an example, the tit, a small, chickadee-like bird of the English town and countryside, pecking through the aluminum foil cover of a milk bottle (circa 1930) to get at the cream inside. He speculates that this was done "with the conscious intention of obtaining food." I suspect that one smart tit discovered the behavior either by conscious ingenuity or by accident,[3] and was then copied by others. The behavior spread through the countryside until the dairies changed their packaging.

Another of Griffin's criteria requires *interactive steps in a relatively long sequence of appropriate behavior patterns.* The prototypical example is of the mama killdeer luring predators away from her eggs. I distinctly remember my wife's aunt showing me a little clutch of eggs lying on the ground just off her driveway. The eggs were so well camouflaged that at first I walked right past without seeing them. But on one occasion the mother was home. As I approached, she began slowly and inconspicuously to creep away from her nest. Once she'd moved some ten to fifteen feet, she squawked loudly and flapped her wings, apparently to draw my attention. She then limped off at an angle, giving every appearance of being injured. Sometimes she'd drag one wing, as if it were broken. When I followed her, she continued moving in this way until I was twenty or thirty feet from her nest. She then flew off and circled back to land even further from her nest. If I didn't follow her, she'd move back toward me and start this act over again, trying to lure me after her. Predators are well conditioned to go after a sick or injured animal. Mama killdeer has been observed acting out her drama with cats, with foxes, with weasels, and with skunks; it typically works.

You may think that this relatively long sequence of appropriate behavior patterns is all bred in. If a herd of cattle, rather than a human or a cat, is approaching, does mama perform the same routine? No; she behaves entirely differently. She stays where her eggs are, squawks loudly, and flaps her wings. It's as if she knows perfectly well the cows are not after her eggs, but might well trample them unintentionally.

This, to me, is a grand example of adaptability to changing circumstances. It is certainly interactive, since the behavior depends crucially upon who or what is approaching and whether the person or animal follows her. The sequence also satisfies me as long and consisting of appropriate behavior. It's not so clear how much of this behavior is built in genetically, how much is learned, and how much is due to conscious thought.[4] It's my guess that all of these come into play. There surely must be some evolutionary predisposition, some built-in capacity to make certain sounds and movements. In addition, Mama Killdeer may well have to learn which limp and which squawk work well. There must also be times when she has to think about it—for example, when individual differences come up. The standard routine does fine as long as the other guy's playing his role right. The minute he doesn't, she has to think up something else to do. As we'll see later on our tour, Agre and Chapman maintain that almost all of human activity is routine, requiring little or no conscious thought (1987; Agre forthcoming; Chapman 1991).

Still, many will maintain that all of this activity can be attributed to genetics. Some would also say that this behavior could be produced by a production system, an AI device we'll encounter early in the next chapter. Some would even say that all thought can be produced mainly by a production system (Newell 1990; Newell and Simon 1972).

Finally, Griffin points to *inventive behavior*, the kind of behavior that happens very rarely. The example he gives is one that he experienced. He was looking at a raven's nest on a cliff face. He climbed up a chimney for a view inside the nest. The raven, squawking loudly from above, dived at him a time or two as discouragement. When that didn't work, the raven began picking up stones in its beak and dropping them on him. Griffin had never seen this behavior before, and had never heard of another case of a raven dropping a stone on anything. Yet the raven dropped stones. He calls this inventive behavior, not typical raven behavior at all. How could this sort of behavior come from learning or evolution?

Let me reiterate that Griffin doesn't take these criteria as conditions conclusively demonstrating consciousness. He would argue that these are a few examples among many, lending support to there being some conscious activity going on, as well as the results of evolution and learning. One could, presumably, come up with a machine learning system leading to any of these sequences of behaviors. You could do that with any individual bit of any human behavior. That's exactly what the AI people, including the connectionists, have been doing, as we'll see in chapters 4 and 5. But that clearly doesn't mean that we're not conscious. As with free will and understanding in chapter 2, I'm going to argue that all sorts of design decisions result in consciousness to different degrees and of different types.

Brain and Consciousness

Like us, Griffin makes a physicalist assumption and, thus, presumes that consciousness comes from brain. The nervous system structures crucial to consciousness are, according to Griffin, the cerebral cortex and the reticular system. If you damage the reticular system, you do away with consciousness, as far as anyone can tell. It's not always easy to know. There are anecdotes of surgical patients under general anesthesia later recalling jokes told by operating room staff, or remarks like "We almost lost her that time."

Griffin asks what could be so different about human nervous systems as to allow consciousness there and not in other animals. Could there be consciousness neurons, or some kind of biological substances that are unique to human nervous systems? He doesn't believe either of these exists. Nor do I; there's simply no evidence of either. Griffin believes that "consciousness results from patterns of activity involving thousands or millions of neurons."

I'm not sure how much explanatory value this provides, but we've surely heard it before from Chalmers when he talked about the third-person view of consciousness as patterns of neural activity. On a later tour stop we'll hear a far-out version of the same theme from Hans Moravec.

Well, if not only humans can think, how far down the complexity ladder can thought be found? How about organisms with no central nervous system? Can they think? There's no evidence that they can, says Griffin, but also none that they can't. If we allow degrees of consciousness, a bacterium or a paramecium will be pretty far down on our list.

Griffin points out that there are only minor differences between the neurons and the synapses of insects and humans. As a result, he speculates that it's not the physical equipment, but the interactive organization, that distinguishes conscious thought. So, theoretically, consciousness could occur in the central nervous system of any multicellular animal. He doesn't see any reason to rule it out. He's not saying that every multicellular animal is conscious, but that there's no strong evidence against it at this point.

Are consciousness and thought the same thing? Well, we haven't defined either, and won't. Still, I'd like to distinguish between the two. I've been in a meditative state in which I was quite conscious but where there was nothing that I would call thought. There was nothing verbal going on, no beliefs, no desires, no visual images, none of the things that I would normally call thoughts. I think of this state as simple awareness. Thus it seems that thinking and consciousness can be different. I suspect that Griffin is equating them.

Griffin's next argument in favor of animal consciousness is interesting, if not completely convincing. He says that *small brains can store fewer instructions and thus have a greater need for simple conscious thinking.*[5] An insect, for example, has a tiny brain compared with ours. There's not much room for detailed instructions for each of its complex behavior patterns. Thus, it probably needs to think instead. That's the argument. But it's not clear that animals with small brains need as complex a repertoire as animals with large brains. The argument is not complete but might well have some truth to it. I believe that conscious systems exist because they are more efficient. They save both space and time by continuously using fresh data directly from the environment, as opposed to storing internal representations and executing detailed instructions. We'll encounter this idea again when our tour takes us to the work of Agre and Chapman. For now, let's move on to one of Griffin's most intriguing ideas.

Inherited Templates

Griffin proposes that genetically programmed behavior in an individual may be adaptive to changing circumstances. Suppose some neural mechanism responds selectively to a particular sensory pattern, that is, a template. Suppose also that the animal seeks to alter the sensory input to match its pattern. For example, suppose a beaver has a template of a pond in its head and that, at some stage in its life, it feels the urge to alter the environment so as to make a pond. If an animal is aware of such a "goal template," it might be capable of consciously behaving to match it.

Inherited templates might help to explain several different animal behavior patterns. Caddis fly larvae create clothing for themselves in the form of hard cases made of grains of sand, daubs of mud, cut pieces of leaf, and such, glued together with their own silk. All larvae of the same species of caddis fly construct cases of a particular, identifiable pattern. If a piece of the case breaks off, or is removed by an experimenter, the larva will go out and get or cut something else of the same shape with which to replace the missing piece. Inherited templates might help explain how individuals of a certain species of caddis fly build such similar cases, and how they choose particles or cut leaves of a particular size and shape so as to maintain the pattern of their case structure.

Individuals of some species of songbirds, raised apart from others of their species, will learn the songs of some alien species. Experiments show that they learn those of their own species much more quickly than those of another. There may, of course, be no template, but simply anatomy more suited to the songs of their species. The experimenters in this case didn't think so, because the range of sounds was the same in both songs.

Griffin devotes an entire chapter to examples of animal behavior patterns that might be explained by inherited templates. Most of his examples are taken from insect behavior. He says:

Can we reasonably infer from the varied, effective, and highly integrated behavior of leaf-cutter ants that they might think consciously about burrow construction, leaf gathering, fungus gardening, or other specialized activities? . . . The workers of leaf-cutter ants are tiny creatures, and their entire central nervous system is less than a millimeter in diameter. Even such a miniature brain contains many thousands of neurons, but ants must do many other things besides gathering leaves and tending fungus gardens. Can the genetic instructions stored in such a diminutive central nervous system prescribe all of the detailed motor actions carried out by one of these ants? Or is it more plausible to suppose that their DNA programs the development of simple generalizations such as "Search for juicy green leaves" or "Nibble away bits of fungus that do not smell right," rather than specifying every flexion and extension of all six appendages? (p. 105)

Presumably the "generalizations" to which Griffin refers are in the form of inherited templates. The argument seems to support some theory of action other than that of genetically determined routines for each possibly behavior.[6] Our tour will expose us to several such theories, my favorite being that of Agre and Chapman.[7]

Although Griffin sticks strictly to discussing other animals, how about inherited templates for humans? We apparently have built-in language capabilities. What form do these take? I suspect that some of it might be in the form of templates, but of course not visual templates. Such templates might, for example, somehow bias us toward the use of syntax, or toward attaching names to our categories.

The evaluation functions of Ackley and Littman (1992), which we'll encounter later on the tour, resemble a kind of template. Reinforcement learning takes place under the direction of these inherited evaluation functions. These evaluation templates do not change over lifetimes but do evolve over generations. They reward behavior that brings the environment in line with their values. This may be a little more sophisticated than what Griffin had in mind, but it seems to be the same sort of idea.

Can inherited templates be the basis of future-directed behavior in animals? Griffin thinks it might well be, but cautions against postulating thinking about the future:

Most of an animal's thoughts and subjective sensations are probably confined to the immediate situation rather than ultimate results. . . . When a female wasp digs a burrow . . . for an egg she has not yet laid, in a future she will not live to experience, it is unreasonable to imagine that she thinks about her eventual progeny . . . there is no way for information about the progeny to reach her central nervous system. But this inability to know the long-term results of her behavior in no way precludes conscious thinking about what she is doing. (p. 116)

Tool Use

One reason for ascribing intelligence and perhaps even consciousness to animals is their use of tools. We humans once considered tool use characteristic of our species. When Jane Goodall found chimps fishing for termites with straws, the response was either to redefine "tool" or redefine "tool use." But Griffin cites many examples of tool use among "lower" animals. Here are a few such.

Hermit crabs put their back ends into deserted snail shells with their claws out. You might say that's not really a tool; they've just found a home. All right, but they also attach anemones, those little creatures that sting, to their shells, so that other creatures will leave them alone. Darwin's finch, in the Galapagos, uses a cactus pine needle to skewer insects in crevices too small for its beak. The sea otter cracks shells on a flat rock balanced on its belly.

My favorite example of tool use is by the assassin bug, which feeds on termites. There are worker termites and warrior termites. He wants to feed on the workers, not the warriors, which are large and equipped with fierce pincers. In fact, he wants to avoid the warriors at all costs. So the assassin bug disguises itself with a coat made of material from the outer cover of the termite nest. He then stations himself by the entrance. The warriors don't notice him because of his camouflaged appearance, touch, and smell. When a worker happens by, the assassin bug grabs it and sucks out all the juice. He then places the remaining exoskeleton just inside the termite nest opening and holds on to one end of it, "jiggling it gently." Since the workers are compulsively neat, the first one that comes along picks the skeleton up to throw it in the trash. Our tool-using assassin bug reels this worker in, sucks her dry, and uses her skeleton as the next lure. Researchers have observed a single assassin bug consume thirty-one workers in a single feast.

Some tool use must be learned. Researchers noticed that young chimps fishing for termites weren't as successful as their more experienced companions. When humans tried it, they didn't do all that well. There's clearly a learning curve to be traversed. When humans learn a new skill, they pay conscious attention to what they're doing. Why should we believe that chimps don't?

Animal Architecture

Like tool use, we humans often consider architecture as characteristic of our species alone. Of course, there are spider webs, wasp's nests, and even beaver dams. But we dismiss these, saying that they are done instinctively and require no conscious thought. Human building is different. Griffin is not so sure.

Neither am I. I had the opportunity to witness one of Griffin's examples, the weaverbird. In the late 1960s, I visited at the Indian Institute of Technology, Kanpur, in northern India. My daily route across campus from home to office led past a weaverbird's nesting site. I was privileged to watch the construction of their nests by the males, and the subsequent courtships as well. Made of straw, their gourd-shaped nests hang from tree branches, affixed by a knotted strand of straw. It's amusing to watch a sparrow-sized bird struggling to tie a knot in a length of straw wrapped around a branch, and it's surprising when they succeed. The nest is then woven from foot-long strands of the same straw. The term "woven" is used advisedly. The finished nest is much like a woven basket. New strands are woven in and out among the old. An entrance hole protected by a narrow passageway is left in the floor. Although seeming much alike when viewed from a distance, the nests are quite individual in both location and construction. The nest, along with the male's display, is thought to determine the female's choice of a mate. Unsuccessful males often disassemble their unattractive creation and rebuild it. The colony of nests surely constitutes impressive architecture.

And then there are the bowerbirds of Australia and New Guinea, which build elaborate, decorated bowers for courtship, not for nesting. Made of leaves, moss, and branches, these bowers are decorated with all sorts of brightly colored objects, including colorful leaves, shells, feathers, pebbles, flowers, and fruits. Walls are sometimes colored with fruit pulp. Wilted flowers are replaced with fresh ones. Bits of plastic, tin cups, and car keys have been used. Not only might we reasonably suspect the bowerbird of thinking about "what he is doing, the males with which he is competing, and the females he hopes to attract," but we might well be seeing an instance of animal art.

Among the most impressive of the animal architects are species of termites in Africa whose nest height is to their length as a skyscraper a mile and a half high would be to a human. Their nests, which are air-conditioned by mazelike cooling passages in the basement, have numerous special-purpose rooms.

Finally, we must consider our fellow mammal, the beaver, which builds elaborate lodges and dams, requiring sometimes months of effort, which produce benefits only in the rather distant future. Experimenters have tricked beavers into piling branches on loudspeakers playing sounds of running water. This gives evidence that dam building may be a purely instinctive activity. But this theory doesn't explain the beaver, in natural settings, repairing an almost silently leaking dam, yet failing to dam a stream rushing noisily into its pond. Beavers also don't build dams when natural ponds are available, even when there is plenty of rushing water. Griffin speculates about an inherited template, and points out that the behavior of beavers "would be facilitated if the beavers could visualize the future pond." A behaviorist would maintain that the beaver's actions result from inherited tendencies augmented by reinforcement learning. On a later tour stop we'll encounter yet another view, called *participatory improvisation* by Agre and Chapman: "Improvisation, like Planning, involves ideas about what might happen in the future. Improvisation differs from Planning in that each moment's action results, effectively, from a fresh reasoning-through of that moment's situation" (1987, p. 2).

There are many other such examples of animal architecture among the social insects, say the leaf-cutter ants. Their behavior raises the issue of collective, versus individual, knowledge or competency. "Aunt Hilary," to use Hofstadter's term for an ant hill as a collective entity (1979), can build an arch. I doubt that any individual ant can even conceive of one. Yet it's difficult for me to imagine an arch emerging from the purely instinctive and local activities of an individual ant. There must be analogous situation involving humans. Probably no single human could build, say, a Boeing 747 or a space station.

Could dam-building beavers, and even arch-building ants, be conscious of what they're doing in something like the way a human aircraft builder is? Griffin suspects so. So do I, with the caveat that major aspects of their consciousness, particularly the ant's, may differ materially from that of the human. I also believe that the Agre-Chapman theory of situated activity (Agre forthcoming; Chapman 1991) will help to clarify our thoughts about animal architecture.

Communication Among Animals

Communication, interpreted broadly, is ubiquitous in the biological world. Some of this communication is clearly instinctive, genetically explained. Is all of it? Or does some communication between animals yield evidence for animal minds? Cooperative hunting, suggestive of planning, provides some evidence.

Lions, being large and often diurnal, are relatively easy to observe while hunting. I recently watched, via TV documentary, a male lion half-heartedly pursuing a wildebeest. After a short chase, the wildebeest found itself in the claws of a second male lion that had been lying in ambush downwind. The pair promptly began to feed.[8]

Schaller (1972) found that groups of four or five lionesses, hunting together, often approached their quarry starting in a line, with the center lionesses moving more slowly. In this way, at the time of the final rush, the lionesses were in a U-shaped formation surrounding the quarry on three sides.

Does either of these anecdotes give evidence of intentional cooperation? Reasonable opinions could surely differ. But Griffin was fortunate enough to witness a scenario even more suggestive of intentional cooperation. A group of five lionesses approached two groups of wildebeest separated by a road. Two lionesses mounted ant hills so as to be clearly visible but pose no threat. A third crept along a ditch paralleling the road until she was between the two bands of wildebeest. Then a fourth lioness charged out of the woods adjacent to the leftmost band, driving them across the road toward the other band. The lioness in the ditch easily killed one wildebeest as it jumped the ditch. All five then began to feed.

Griffin says:

This single observation cannot be taken as conclusive proof of intentional cooperation, but it was certainly very suggestive. Why should two lionesses climb to conspicuous positions where the wildebeest could easily see that they presented no serious danger? Why should a third sneak along the ditch to a position about midway between the two groups? Was it a pure coincidence that a fourth lioness just happened to rush out from an optimal point at the forest edge to chase the wildebeest over the ditch where one of her companions was waiting? . . . Considering the obvious advantages to cooperative hunting, it seems reasonable to conclude that lions are capable of planning their hunting tactics. (1984, p. 86)

It's hard for me to believe that the lionesses described by Griffin met as a committee to devise their plan. On the other hand, it's equally hard for me to believe that this scenario occurred unconsciously and without some sort of communication.[9]

The semantic alarm calls of the vervet monkeys provide an example of symbolic communication among nonhuman animals. These monkeys give three distinct calls in the face of predators, one for the presence of a leopard or other large carnivore, another warning of a large snake, and a third one saying "There is a martial eagle in sight." These are quite distinct calls, and specific in their meaning. The monkeys behave in quite different ways in response to the individual calls. The leopard call sends them into the high, small branches of a tree. At the eagle call, they move into thick vegetation near the trunk or on the ground. The snake call causes them to stand on their hind legs to locate the snake so they can avoid it. When researchers played the alarm calls over a concealed loudspeaker, the monkeys reacted in the appropriate way for the particular call. The experiment was carefully controlled to verify that the monkeys were responding only to the semantic content of the calls. Vervet monkeys are also known to use grunts with meanings.

Symbolic communication is not restricted to primates, nor to mammals, nor even to vertebrates. Honeybees use symbolic gestures to direct their companions toward food when they perform their waggle dance. *The direction to the food is signaled symbolically in relation to the current position of the sun!* The dance conveys not only the direction of the food but its distance and desirability as well. Pretty slick for an animal with such a tiny nervous system.

Perhaps an even more striking example of animal communication comes from the weaver ants, who not only communicate about events at a distance but also pass on hearsay evidence. Weaver ants are remarkable for other reasons. They build their nests of leaves high above ground. Sometimes chains of several ants reach from one leaf to the next to pull them together. They use their larvae as portable glue guns to join the leaves together. They also go out to search for food. When one returns with food, it will rub antennae with another worker in the nest, and make a side-to-side head movement. This tells the other what odor trail to follow to find the food. Some of the other workers will follow the trail, but not all. Some pass on the communication second hand to yet other workers. The news of the available food and where to find it is passed along a treelike route serving to recruit additional workers to bring it in. The news may not always be of food but rather of enemies. In this case, the head movement is back-to-front and jerky. Why a different movement? To help the other know what to expect? This is certainly an example of an animal passing on specific information the communicator obtained not directly but from another ant.

Is it possible that the weaver ants communicate consciously? Here's what Griffin says (1984, pp. 172–173):

The central nervous system of ants are minute compared to those of even the smallest birds and mammals. But how can we be certain about the critical size necessary for conscious thinking? Even the smallest insect brain contains thousands of neurons, each capable of exchanging nerve impulses with dozens of others. The content and complexity of conscious thought, and their range of versatility, might be roughly proportional to the volume of the central nervous system, but an absolute criterion of mass necessary for conscious thinking is not supported by anything we know about the nature and functioning of central nervous systems.

So animals can communicate. But do they have language? Here's where we can draw the line. Language must be characteristic of humans, of us. Or must it?

Animal Language

According to Zuckerman, a distinguished biologist, language is:

the critical evolutionary development that made man a unique primate, and one that released him from the immediate present within which apes and monkeys are tied, and by so doing opened for us human beings a world of our own creation, with a past, a present, and a future, one limitless in time and space. . . . it is what apes and monkeys do not share that makes us human—language. (1991)

Is there, in fact, no past and no future without language? Don't some animals (dolphins) exhibit memory of the past? Don't some (beavers) appear to plan for the future? How do we know that nonhumans don't imagine? I suspect that some nonhuman animals do imagine: lions lazing on a hot afternoon, for example. But that's merely a suspicion. I'm not as confident as Chuang Tzu was of his joyful fish. I am more confident, however, that the old silverback gorilla who leads his troop to a tree at the far side of its range, full of freshly ripened fruit, is both remembering having eaten that fruit before and how to get back to it. I'm almost equally confident that he's anticipating the pleasure of tasting the fresh fruit once

again. Similar tales are told of the matriarch of a band of elephants leading them to distant and seldom-used food sources. I don't believe that
past and present depend on language.

Still, I suspect that only humans are concerned with cosmology, the
origin of life, or the mind–body problem. On the other hand, I doubt that
bacteria either remember long term or plan. There must be many degrees
of past–future awareness in minds of many degrees. But back to language.

There doesn't seem to be any hard evidence of animals communicating
among themselves using what we would call language, although some
suspect dolphins and whales do. There have, however, been many studies
of animal communication with humans. In particular, there have been a
number of experiments with chimps being taught sign language. Some of
the people who worked with them for years—Terrace, for example—
turned out to be quite critical of the results, saying that it really wasn't
language at all (Zuckerman 1991). Critics point to a lack of syntax. Some
suspect the "clever Hans" phenomenon,[10] where the experimenter may
have been giving off subtle cues that were followed by the animal. The
chimps were communicating all right, but it was thought not to be language. And then there is Koko.

Koko is an adult female gorilla who after more than a decade of study,
or training if you prefer, has learned some 2000 words of American sign
language (Cohn and Patterson 1991). She regularly signs to herself, which
makes it hard for me to put much credence in the "clever Hans" phenomenon. She's been observed playing with her two dolls, signing a story between them. When the experimenter walks into the room, she puts them
aside as if embarrassed. (There we go, anthropomorphizing again.)
Koko's play with her dolls may well be evidence of animals imagining.
She also signs regularly with Michael, another gorilla, and has learned
new signs from him. When asked what she wanted for a Christmas (?)
present, Koko replied, "Kitten." After some months of having a kitten as
a pet, it was accidentally killed. On being asked how she felt, Koko replied, "Sad." It seems clear to me that Koko communicates by using primitive features of American sign language. She's pretty poor at syntax. One
can reasonably define "language" so as to exclude what she does.

And then there's Kanzi. Kanzi is a ten-year-old bonobo,[11] or pigmy
chimp, from equatorial Africa whose language abilities are said to com-

pare favorably with those of a two-year-old human child (Golden 1991). Kanzi communicates by pointing to lexigrams on a large keyboard. He asks for specific foods, for specific games, and even "announces his intentions, such as running off to visit another animal." Kanzi uses word order to distinguish between meanings, and so shows some understanding of syntax.

There are also animals that communicate using words of the English language. Pepperberg (1981, 1983) trained an African parrot named Alex to use some forty English words. Alex will name objects shown to him. He'll ask for an object with which to play by name. If offered something else, he will say "no." He also uses a few verbs, and adjectives for shape and color. There is no claim that Alex "has language." Still, it seems remarkable that a bird with a relatively small brain can communicate in this way.

The common assumption is that a larger body requires more motor neurons, more sensory neurons, and therefore a larger brain for the "same" degree of intelligence. More neurons are needed just to sense and control things because there's more to sense and control. So instead of comparing brain size as a measure of the intelligence of species, it would seem more sensible to try the encephalization quotient (EQ), the ratio of brain volume to body volume (or brain weight to body weight). Dolphins have the highest EQ of any nonhuman animal, approximately twice as high as the great apes (Wintsch 1990). So one would think that the likely place to look to falsify the theory of animal language is the dolphins.

Unlike Koko, there are dolphins, Phoenix and Ake, that apparently understand syntax (Herman et al. 1984). "Syntax is what tells us the venetian blind is not a blind venetian." [12] Presented sentences by means of gestures or of sounds, these dolphins can distinguish between PIPE SURFBOARD FETCH and SURFBOARD PIPE FETCH. In the first case the surfboard is taken to the pipe; in the second the pipe is taken to the surfboard. They are also able to substitute new lexical items without training. When taught the new symbol HOOK, the first time one was told SURFBOARD HOOK FETCH, he took the hook to the surfboard. Having learned the meaning of a symbol in one context, they are able to utilize what they have learned in another context. They refuse even to try to execute impossible commands. PERSON SPEAKER FETCH results in no movement by the dolphin. Anomalous commands such as PERSON SPEAKER HOOP FETCH are easily interpreted, resulting in the hoop being brought to the person. But are these really instances of language use?

Animal language critic and sea lion researcher Ronald Shusterman gives this necessary criterion for language: *For true language words and their reference should be interchangeable.* That is, words comprehended by an animal should have a symmetric relationship with their associated objects, as in human language. Shusterman claims that no nonhuman animal has passed this rigorous test, and that the apparent linguistic ability of these dolphins relies on paired associative learning and on conditional sequential discrimination. They simply learn to perform a different action depending on the order given. Herman claims the interchangeability test has been passed by his dolphins. Showing one of them an object and signaling the action yields the same response as if you had signaled both the object and the action. They treat the sign for ball and the ball itself the same in this context.

The use of learned symbols in new contexts gives further evidence of linguistic understanding. These dolphins generalize symbols to various exemplars of reference. Suppose they have been playing regularly with a large ball. If one day they have only a small ball to play with and someone says "Fetch the ball," they fetch the small ball. The dolphins can sometimes understand a symbol even when its referent is absent. They have been taught to answer questions about the presence of an object (e.g., Is there a ball in the pool?). They answer yes or no. It takes them longer to decide that there is no ball in the pool than to find one, which is exactly what you would expect. They can also answer "yes" or "no" to the question of whether a person swimming in the tank has performed a certain action. I'll leave to the linguists whether all this constitutes the use of language. But it certainly seems to support the possibility of linguistic competence in dolphins.

The communication between humans and apes, parrots, and dolphins described above was largely a result of training via classical behaviorist reinforcement. There is also one case of symbols coming to have referential quality for dolphins without the traditional training with food rewards. A keyboard with shapes representing an object or action was placed daily in the tank with two young dolphins. When one of them touched a key, the object symbolized on it, perhaps a ball, was placed in the tank. If the symbol represented an action, say a belly rub, that action was performed by the experimenter. Pressing the key also resulted in an auditory signal. The order of the keys was changed daily to ensure that the dolphins were responding to the symbols rather than their positions. What happened? First, spontaneous mimicry developed. A "ball" whistle was often emitted just before the "ball" key was pressed, or while playing with the ball. A "rub" whistle was often used during tactile interaction. A combination "ring and ball" whistle was invented for use while playing with both simultaneously. These vocalizations seem to have achieved referential quality. Amazingly, after two years of not seeing the keyboard, the dolphins were immediately able to use it again.

It seems that communication is ubiquitous in the animal world, and that some of it can be pretty sophisticated, using symbols for reference and paying attention to simple syntax. Whether any of this constitutes the use of language is a matter of how we want to use the word "language," and not a question of the abilities of nonhuman animals. Perhaps language, like free will and mind, is more fruitfully thought of not as a Boolean,[13] but as a matter of degree. Cheney and Seyfarth go to great experimental length to show ways in which communication between monkeys is languagelike and ways that it isn't (1990). They conclude, for example, that vervet monkeys' sounds for the various predators have semantic content, as do our words. On the other hand, they find that some monkeys fail to attribute knowledge to others and, hence, to "speak" accordingly.

Self-Awareness

Among the many claims of uniqueness for humans within the animal kingdom is that we are the only animal to exhibit self-awareness. Gallup (1970, 1977a, 1977b) subjected this claim to experimental testing with primates. His idea was that an animal that isn't self-aware, when looking in a mirror, would consider the image to be another animal of the same species. (I wonder if there has been experimental verification of this assumption.) A self-aware animal, on the other hand, would react to the image as one of itself. Gallup would allow a primate to play with a mirror over a period of time to become accustomed to it. He would then anesthetize the animal and put a red mark on its forehead. When the animal woke up and looked in the mirror, if it was self-aware, it would be expected to touch the spot, perhaps rub it, while observing its action in the mirror. Gallup's mirror experiments succeeded with chimpanzees and orangutans but failed with gorillas, gibbons, and several species of monkeys. He concluded that chimps and orangs gave evidence of self-awareness via the mirror experiments but no evidence of self-awareness was provided by the other species.

But Koko seems perfectly self-aware. She signs about herself, and even to herself. When asked who she is, the response is always multisigned, and each response is different. They all contain one of the signs KOKO, ME, GORILLA. Patterson performed her version of Gallup's mirror test on Koko (1991). She accustomed Koko to having her head rubbed with a soft, damp, lavender cloth. One day the cloth had lavender face paint on it, the kind a clown might use. When Koko looked in the mirror, she immediately rubbed the paint on her forehead.

There are other behaviors put forth as evidence of self-awareness. One is self-concealment, where the animal is trying to hide the whole body and not just a part of it. Another is avoiding leaving tracks, an action attributed to grizzlies. Stags are aware of the dimensions of their growing antlers. Rowan (1991, p. 287) proposes intentional deception, as Goodall reports of chimps (1986), as a sufficient condition for self-awareness. His reasoning is as follows: "For an animal to deceive intentionally, it must have the idea that the observer (the 'deceivee') thinks that it (the animal) is thinking and acting in a certain way. This necessitates a self-reflexive mental capacity and, hence, self-awareness."

Accepting Rowan's argument may entail conceding self-awareness to vervet monkeys. A member of one band, which is being bested by a neighboring band in an altercation, sometimes deceives the adversaries by emitting a "leopard" call. As a result, both bands scurry into the small branches, effectively breaking off the fight. Cheney and Seyfarth (1990, pp. 213ff.) argue persuasively that the call is intentional. They devote an entire chapter (1990, chap. 7) to deception by nonhuman animals. Trivers assumes that the practice of deception by animals is well known to biologists, and argues interestingly that it leads to self-deception (1991).

What is meant by self-awareness? Clearly, becoming the object of one's own attention. But there are so many and such varied forms of that attention. I believe there is no sharp distinction between animals that are self-aware and those that are not. Just as with free will, self-awareness is best looked at as a sequence of design decisions. Here's a list of competences that might or might not be built into a robot by its designer. Each might indicate some level of self-awareness. Contrast agents who can

- Conceal their bodies appropriately
- Observe their mental processing
- Attempt to modify (improve?) themselves
- Recognize themselves in a mirror
- Use personal pronouns
- Talk to themselves
- Talk about their own mental states
- Attribute mental states to others
- Practice deception

with those who cannot, Koko does the last six.

Well, there's another attempt at establishing human uniqueness down the tubes. How about rationality? Surely there are no rational animals other than humans.

Rational Animals?

As with mind, self-awareness, and so on, whether there are rational but nonhuman animals depends on what we mean by "rational." It would seem that one might draw a sharp distinction here. For instance, only humans can do mathematics, right? Well, that depends on what we mean by "mathematics."

Laboratory animals have been trained to follow rather abstract rules, for example, to distinguish the "oddball" among members of a set of objects presented. Shown three blue disks and a red one, they are trained to pick out the red one. A single such case isn't impressive, but whether you show them three blue disks and a red one, or three square disks and a triangle, they can still pick the odd one. They seem able to generalize. Chimps do rather well on such problems, pigeons less well, and cats and raccoons poorer yet.

Mathematicians often want to distinguish symmetry from asymmetry. So do trained pigeons and goldfish. A goldfish was trained to swim toward a square with a little triangle on top rather than toward a perfect square. When presented with a circle and a circle with a little semicircle on top, it swam toward the one with the semicircle on top. Again, it seemed to generalize, to follow an abstract rule.

There are also reported occasions of animals with some sort of number sense. Trained ravens can distinguish the number of objects in a group (up to seven) even when the objects change in size, color, and position. Even more remarkable are two rhesus monkeys who, when presented with five digits, chosen randomly and placed at random on a screen, can select them with the cursor in descending order (Washburn and Rumbaugh 1991). More recent results have chimps doing very simple additions.

Surely these chimps, monkeys, and goldfish won't compete with your eighteen-year-old for admission to her favorite college. Nor am I ready to attribute rationality to them. Still, their abilities suggest that rationality in humans had its roots in the animal world. Rationality, again, is probably better viewed as a matter of degree, of what design decisions were implemented.

Animal Humor?

The following anecdote concerns work by Gordon and Patterson (1990) with Koko's friend Michael, also a gorilla. They say, "Sometimes when we work with Michael using voice only, he responds with signs unrelated in meaning, but similar in sound when translated back into English" (p. 10).

Here's a transcript of one such conversation with Michael:

Penny: Can you work?
Michael: Work.
P: How do you sign stink? (voice only)
M: Stink ear eye.
P: Sign belly button? (voice only)
M: Bellybutton. Berry bottom.

My first impression on reading this transcript was that Michael was trying to be funny. Not very sophisticated humor, I grant you, but humor nonetheless. After some struggle to find a better explanation, I still view it as an attempt at humor. Perhaps humor is common but undetected in the animal world. I wonder if baboons tell jokes to one another. Or could it be that humor depends on language? In any event, it's no longer clear to me that we're the world's only comedians.

After all this recounting of experiments and anecdotes about the cognitive capabilities of other animals, it would be nice to draw some conclusions. Do animals have minds or not?

I believe, à la Sloman and free will, that there is no sharp distinction to be usefully made between animals with mind and those without. If we assume that other animals have no cognitive abilities, we're not likely to find any. If we assume they may have such abilities, we are more likely to recognize their occurrence. The evidence seems clear that many other animals can cognize to some extent. The questions of interest now are to what extent, and how do they do it?

I also see no sharp distinction between those animals with rational mind and those without, though this is a less strongly held belief. There seems to be no sharp distinction even between those animals with language and those without, unless one draws an arbitrary line. In each of these cases, I'd prefer to focus on the design decisions facing a robot engineer re mind, rationality, and language.

I also believe that a synthetic, bottom-up approach, a study of the "mechanisms of mind," will yield significant insights into cognition in humans and animals as well as in machines. Let me be clear that I am advocating this approach in addition to continuing work in the fields of cognitive psychology, artificial intelligence, and neuroscience. This sermon will be preached more than once before we complete our tour.

Next, let's visit the synthetic, top-down approach of symbolic AI.

Notes

1. Keep in mind that our physicalist assumption from chapters 1 and 2 implies that any consciousness results from some underlying mechanism. Such a consciousness mechanism would not fall within Griffin's mechanistic alternative.

2. Let me remind you again that the term "adaptive" is used in at least three different ways. We can say that the species has adapted by evolution, that individuals adapt by learning that changes their long-term patterns of behavior, or that an individual is behaving adaptively by changing short-term behavior in order to cope with short-term environmental changes.

3. Pop quiz: How many human discoveries resulted from accidents? Can you name some?

4. Does behavior due to conscious thought result from something other than learning or genetics? How else can it come about? Intuition, perhaps, or ingenuity? I think we're viewing the same elephant from different levels of abstraction.

5. We'll talk later in this chapter about the relationship between brain size and body size.

6. I say "seems to" because I'd prefer some quantitative estimate of the carrying capacity of the leaf-cutter's brain compared with a similar estimate of the information requirements of its behaviors. Maybe this is too much to ask for.

7. I apologize for repeatedly referring to Agre and Chapman's work without telling you about it. Unfortunately, it doesn't lend itself to brief encapsulation.

8. I specifically mention "male" lion because such stories are usually told of lionesses, who do almost all the hunting for a pride. These two males were indeed members of a pride containing females, but had wandered away from the rest of the pride and were hunting alone.

9. What motivates this lack of belief is, of course, the old watchmaker argument. On finding a watch with its many finely cooperating parts, one expects that, somewhere, there was a watchmaker. Dawkins (1987) goes to great lengths to demolish this argument in the case of complex natural creatures such as humans.

10. Clever Hans was a show horse who would tap out the answer to simple sums like 4 + 3, stopping after seven taps. People eventually concluded that Hans was taking cues from his master unbeknown to anyone, including his master. Seems pretty clever to me.

11. The bonobo is the primate whose sexual behavior most resembles that of humans. In particular, it prefers the missionary position for intercourse, and is anatomically suited for it. Also, the females are continuously in estrus.

12. The material in this section on dolphins, including this quote, is from Wintsch (1990).

13. A Boolean variable takes only two values, which may be interpreted as "yes" or "no."

4

Symbolic AI

Our artificial minds tour is billed as an exploration of the mechanisms of mind. But the first stop consisted only of a preview of coming attractions. The second was spent with philosophers discussing the nature of mind, and the third with ethologists speculating about animal minds. When are we going to explore anything that looks like a real "mechanism of mind"? Is there anything that even remotely resembles an artificial mind? If there is, let's stop there.

OK. On this stop we'll visit SOAR,[1] a prime candidate for the title of artificial mind. For some preliminary background we'll first take a peek at production systems, a possible mechanism of mind and the basic structure of SOAR. With some familiarity with SOAR as a foundation, we'll then eavesdrop on the first AI debate, an ongoing discussion of whether we can ever hope to see a system worthy of being called an artificial mind.

Productions systems, and SOAR, are a part of what is now called *symbolic artificial intelligence.* In chapter 1 we spoke of symbolic AI as the art of making machines do things that would require intelligence if done by a human, such as playing chess, speaking English, or diagnosing an illness. This rather engineering approach to AI will prove excessively narrow for our current purposes. Fortunately, Sloman (1986) gives a broader view that should be ideal: "AI is a very general investigation of the nature of intelligence and the principles and mechanisms required for understanding or replicating it." This view exhibits both the engineering side of AI and its cognitive science side. Both SOAR and the first AI debate are intimately concerned with each side.

Production Systems

Introduced in 1943 by Post, production systems were first employed to model intelligence by Newell[2] and Simon (1972). Since then, they've played a major role in several symbolic AI systems, including SOAR. They also underlie one AI programming language, OPS 5 (Forgy and McDermott 1977), and provide the theoretical foundations of rule-based expert systems (Buchanan and Shortliffe 1984).

To comprehend the structure of a production system more easily, let's keep a motivating example in mind. We'll use the eight puzzle, an abbreviated version of the familiar, cheaply constructed, plastic sixteen puzzle that children so often bring to their daddies, crying, "It's broken!" The eight puzzle (see figure 4.1) consists of eight numbered squares in a three-by-three grid, leaving one empty position. It comes in some initial state, and challenges the user to transform it into some goal state by successively moving squares into the blank position.

Suppose we have a system—anything that changes over time. The eight puzzle, together with someone or something trying to solve it, is a simple system. At any given instant in time, that system has a *current state* given as a description of its various parameters. For the eight puzzle, the collection of all the positions of the small squares would constitute its current state.

The *state space* of a system is the set of all possible current states, that is, the set of all the states the system could possibly assume. The state space of the eight puzzle consists of all possible arrangements of the eight small squares within the large one. In many cases one can represent the

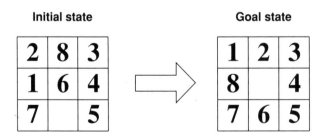

Figure 4.1
The eight puzzle (adapted from Laird et al. 1987)

state space geometrically, so that you can think of the states as points in some kind of a multidimensional space. For example, one might represent states of the eight puzzle as integer points in a nine-dimensional space. Thus a state would be represented by a vector containing the integers 1, 2, ... 8 in some order, with a 0 inserted to stand for the empty space.

Take the initial state of the system as a starting point in the state space and track the sequence of current states of the system as it moves toward its goal. You can think of this track as being a trajectory in a dynamical system. "Dynamical system"? Let's take a brief detour to view this important attraction.

In its most abstract form a *dynamical system* consists of a set X, called its state set, and a transition function, T, that maps X into itself.[3] If we think of the system's changing in discrete steps—a *discrete* dynamical system[4]—then T specifies for each state s in X its next state, T(s). Starting with some initial state s_0, as in the eight puzzle, the series of states through which the system steps before arriving at a goal state is called the *trajectory* of s_0. A trajectory need not lead to a *fixed point,* such as a goal state, which is always mapped by T to itself. It may be *periodic,* visiting each of several states in turn over and over again, as shown in figure 4.2.

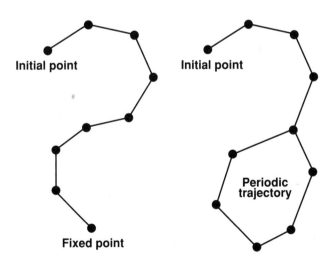

Figure 4.2
Trajectories in state space

A *production system* is a special kind of discrete dynamical system that consists of three components. One is the *global database*, which comprises the data of the system. Another is the set of *production rules*, the operations of the system that take it from state to state. Finally, the *control structure* acts as the executive of the production system, determining which production rule will fire next.

The global database is sometimes referred to as working memory, short-term memory, or the fact list. It's the system's representation of the current state of its world. In other words, the global database at a specific time can be thought of as a point in state space. The state space of a production system is the set of all possible global databases. Figure 4.3 uses our old friend the eight puzzle to illustrate a global database.

Production rules, often simply called *productions*, are condition/action rules: whenever a certain condition is satisfied, then a specified action is performed or may be performed.

Condition-action rules:
WHENEVER (condition) IS SATISFIED, PERFORM (action).

Note that something like pattern matching is required to tell whether the condition is satisfied. Figure 4.4 is an example of a production rule from a possible system trying to solve the eight puzzle.

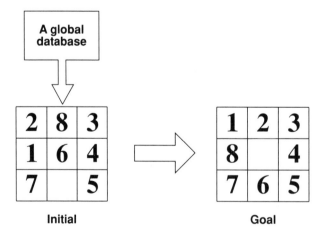

Figure 4.3
A global database

Example from the 8-puzzle:

**If the empty square isn't next to the left edge of the
board, move it to the left.**

Figure 4.4
Production rule

Procedure PRODUCTION SYSTEM
1. DATA <-- initial global database
2. **until** DATA satisfies halt condition **do**
3.   **begin**
4.   **select** some rule R that can be applied to DATA
5.   DATA <-- result of R applied to DATA
6.   **end**

Figure 4.5
Production system algorithm

Production rules can be thought of collectively as the long-term memory of the production system, that is, what the system knows: its knowledge base. This is the declarative view. From a procedural view, production rules are operators. As a collection, they constitute what the system can do.

Let's take a look at an algorithm for the production system itself (see figure 4.5). Our procedure is labeled PRODUCTION SYSTEM. First, we store the initial global database of the system in an appropriate variable named DATA. We then loop until a specified halt condition is reached, say a goal state. Inside the loop we select some applicable rule, one whose condition is satisfied by some fact in DATA. (Not every rule is applicable to every global database.) The selected production rule is then applied and the global database, in the variable DATA, is updated. Our new global database thus reflects the consequences of firing the rule.

What remains of our production system is its control structure, which performs the selection process in the PRODUCTION SYSTEM procedure. The control structure picks out the production rule to be fired next.

How does it do that? Via various heuristic search strategies. Search is required because typically not enough is known to point directly to the ideal rule. The search is heuristic in the sense that it's likely, but not guaranteed, to find the best choice. Nilsson (1980) describes several production system control strategies with such colorful terms as irrevocable, backtracking, graph-search and hill-climbing.

Let's see how the flow of control goes through a production system. Figure 4.6 may help. You start with some initial global database, a set of facts that defines the initial state of the system. Consulting that set of data, the control structure selects a rule to be fired. The rule is then fired. That firing results in some change in the global database. The system continues to loop in this way until a halt condition occurs. The system then stops. It seems pretty simple so long as we ignore the tricky part: choosing the next rule to fire.

While the human user of a production system may think of its global database as representing something in the outside world, to the production system its global database *is* its world. The control structure perceives this internal world in some unspecified way and then acts on it via the production rules. For it to be of use to us, some human must provide the initial global database and interpret the final global database. Relative to the outside world, a production system is purely a syntactic device manipulating symbols without regard to their meaning. Its relations to the out-

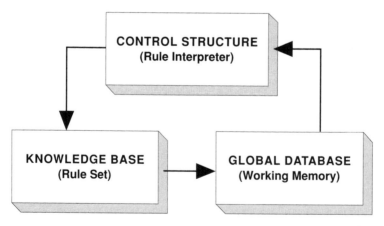

Figure 4.6
Control flow through a production system

side world, its meanings, its semantics, must be provided by a human. We'll confront this issue of connecting mechanisms of mind to the outside world frequently during our tour.

Now we've had a look at one possible mechanism of mind. (After all, such a device can solve the eight puzzle.) We know something about what a production system is and how it operates. The obvious and important next question is about its capability. What sorts of activities can a production system control? What problems can it solve? What can it compute? It's going to turn out that production systems can control, solve, or compute anything a computer can, no more and no less. To convince ourselves, we need to know what a computer can do, what it means to compute. Let's take a short side trip to visit an esoteric topic from theoretical computer science, Turing machines.

Turing Machines

Turing machines exist only in the way that numbers exist, as mathematical entities. But useful mathematical entities. You may think of a Turing machine as an abstract version of the kind of computer that you work with on your desk. That won't be quite right, but it's close enough to ease your way. Figure 4.7 may be helpful.

A Turing machine is composed of a tape, a read-write head, and a finite-state machine. The *tape* is essentially its input-output device, corresponding to the keyboard/monitor of your PC or Mac. The *read-write head* can read a symbol from the tape and can write one on it. The head also can move itself—change its position on the tape by one square left or right. The read-write head is analogous to a combination keystroke-reader/cursor-control/print-to-the-monitor routine. The *finite-state machine* acts as the memory/central processor. It's called a finite-state machine because it can keep track of which of finitely many states it is currently in; it has some finite memory. Knowing which state it's in, and knowing what symbol was just read from the tape, the finite-state machine will determine what symbol to write, what state to change to, and which way the head should move (left or right). It may, of course, rewrite the same symbol, remain in the same state, and/or keep the head where it is. Let me say all that again. The finite-state machine uses two pieces of

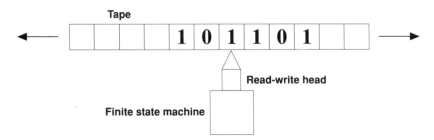

Figure 4.7
Turing machine

input, the symbol that's currently being read from the tape and its current state, to determine three actions. First, it can possibly write a new symbol on the current square of the tape. Second, it can possibly assume a new state. And third, it can possibly move the current position of the head one square to the left or to the right.

Input to a Turing machine and output from it come from some specified, but arbitrary, finite alphabet, which, in figure 4.7, is comprised of at least the three symbols 0, 1, and blank. A finite set of states, again arbitrary, must be specified. Finally, the action of the finite-state machine must be specified by a transition function that acts on a state/input-symbol pair and yields a state/output-symbol/head-move triple. With these three, the formal description of the Turing machine is complete. Its tape is assumed to be potentially infinite, that is, as large as need be for the current computation. Certain states are typically designated as *halt states*. Upon entering such a state, the machine halts, that is, it no longer changes state, writes symbols, or moves the head.

Why do this kind of thing? Why all the formality? Well, Turing, a British mathematician who is considered the grandfather of both computing and artificial intelligence, wanted to prove theorems about what could and could not be computed (1937). Some such formal definition was essential. During the 1930s, 1940s, and 1950s, many formal approaches to computability were offered. Each said something about what is computable and what isn't. All these approaches turned out to be equivalent in that they all gave you exactly the same things being computable. The Turing machine, being relatively easy to describe and amenable to a geometric illustration, became the standard representative of these equivalent approaches, and is now invoked in almost every discussion of computability.

So the question is, what can a Turing machine compute? Answer: anything that can be computed. This is one view of the Church-Turing thesis: *any effective procedure (algorithm) can be implemented via a Turing machine.* This is not simply a formal definition, nor is it a provable theorem. Rather, it's a statement that meets our intuition about what effective computability should mean. That's the reason it's called a thesis. It serves to make precise our rather intuitive idea of what computation is about. Any old-timers among you should keep in mind that we're talking about digital computation, not analog.[5] Now that we've seen enough of what's computable, let's get back to the question of what production systems can compute.

Production Systems vs. Turing Machines

As mentioned above, several formal approaches to computability were offered, all of which proved equivalent. One of these approaches was this very notion of a production system, introduced by Post in 1934. It was later shown that any computation on a Turing machine could be emulated by a production system and vice versa. Production systems today are typically simulated on digital computers and, hence, should be implementable by Turing machines. Here we're interested in the converse. How can production systems implement Turing machines?

Let's see how one might build a production system to implement some given Turing machine. Suppose someone gives us a Turing machine and says, "Can you emulate this with a production system?" What would we do? First, we'd define the global database. We would want to know the current head position, the symbols on the tape, and their positions. We'd write all this into our global database. We'd also have to assume that there's sufficient room to write it. If we're going to implement a Turing machine, our global database must be infinitely expandable, as is the tape on the Turing machine. Otherwise, there may be insufficient room in the global database to hold the arbitrarily long string of symbols on the tape. Remember, these are idealized notions of computability.

With global database in hand, where are we going to get our production rules? From the Turing machine. By definition, its finite-state machine knows what to do when presented with a given current state and a given input symbol. We may assume that this knowledge is in the form of a transition table whose rows each correspond to some state, and whose columns each correspond to some input symbol. Then for every cell in the transition table—that is, for each pair consisting of a state and a symbol—the corresponding table entry specifies the next current state, a symbol to be written, and possibly a head movement. Thus, the production rule extracted from the transition table cell corresponding to state 1 and symbol 2 will read something like "If in state 1 and reading symbol 2, then go to state 2, write symbol 4, move head 1 to the left." That's a perfectly good production rule. We have only to write one of those for every entry in the transition table of the Turing machine.

With our global database specified and all needed production rules created, we lack only a control strategy for our production system. How will we select the particular rule to employ at each time step? This is easy. At any given time, there will be only one rule whose preconditions are satisfied, because there's only a single current state and a single symbol read by the head at any time. So there's only one rule to choose from. The control strategy says to select that rule.

The production system thus defined will faithfully emulate the computation of the Turing machine. Since our Turing machine was arbitrary, any Turing machine can be emulated by some suitably defined production system. Given an algorithm, by Church's thesis, some Turing machine can execute it. But some production systems can emulate that Turing machine. Hence, some production system can execute any given algorithm. Thus, production systems can compute whatever is computable.

The point of all this is that production systems are powerful computing devices. They're not little toys, even though they may be used for toy problems like the eight puzzle. If you want a production system to guide a spacecraft to the moon, you can, in principle, have one. Researchers in symbolic AI use production systems to model cognitive processes. We've seen in this section that if such modeling can be accomplished by computers at all, it can, in principle, also be accomplished by production systems. If computers suffice to create intelligence, so do production systems. With that point made, let's visit a recent extension of production systems.

Parallel Production Systems

The era of parallel computing, that is, of computing simultaneously with multiple processors in a single machine, is fast approaching. Current parallel computers run from four to ten quite powerful processors, or up to 65,000 simple processors at once (Hillis 1985; Almasi and Gottlieb 1989, chap. 10). With this kind of hardware available, one can begin to think seriously of parallel production systems, that is, production systems where more than one production rule can fire simultaneously.

Suppose that instead of working with a serial computer, we had a parallel machine with many, many processors, all processing in parallel. Suppose also that it's a shared memory machine, meaning that a single block of memory is shared by all the processors. In a shared memory machine the processors communicate with one another by writing and reading to and from memory. When processor A wants to communicate with processor B, it writes a message to memory that can then be read by B. Shared memory machines are typically MIMD (Multiple Instructions Multiple Data) machines. Thus two processors may be simultaneously executing quite different instructions on quite distinct data.

Shared memory machines seem ideal for implementing parallel production systems. Common memory holds the global database; all facts are stored in memory. A few processors would be devoted to controlling input to the system and output from it. Each production rule, or a small set of them, is implemented by its own processor. Each processor is like a little demon,[6] who sits and watches memory. When he sees the conditions for (one of) his production rule(s) pop up, "Aha!" he says, and he fires. Some sort of conflict resolution strategy would be needed because you may very well have two demons who want to fire at the same time and write to memory. That's OK as long as what they write doesn't conflict. But if both of them want to change the same place in memory to different values, then someone's got to resolve the conflict.[7] In practice, this won't be much of a problem because a typical shared memory machine has only one path (called a bus) down which data can flow to be written to memory. The machine itself typically implements some sort of conflict resolution strategy when two processors want access to the bus simultaneously. I've glossed over timing problems here, but the major point holds: shared memory parallel computers seem ideally suited for parallel production systems.[8]

Note that no central executive rules here. Such a parallel production system is strictly a local operation. Each demon looks only to its own condition. No one has a global view, much less global authority. The closest thing to a central executive would be the conflict resolution device, but its powers are quite limited. A system like this is reminiscent of Minsky's *Society of Mind* (1985), which was mentioned in chapter 1 and will be visited at more length during a later stop on the tour. Each of the processor demons, ready to fire his production rules, can be thought of as an instance of a mechanism of mind, an agent in Minsky's terms. Each of these little rules would have its own enabling mechanism.

All this brings us at last to SOAR.

SOAR

All this talk of production systems was by way of background for visiting SOAR (Laird et al. 1987; Newell 1990; Rosenbloom et al. 1991). Why choose this one among the literally thousands of symbolic AI programs?[9] Because SOAR's designers, up front and unhesitatingly, declare it an architecture for general intelligence:

the goal is to provide the underlying structure that would enable a system to perform the full range of cognitive tasks, employ the full range of problem solving methods and representations appropriate for the tasks, and learn about all aspects of the tasks and its performance on them. In this article we present SOAR, an implemented proposal for such an architecture. (Laird et al. 1987, abstract, p. 1)

SOAR, then, should not be thought of as a mechanism of mind but, rather, as a collection of mechanisms of mind, well organized so as eventually to produce general intelligence. SOAR is also intended as the basis for a psychological theory that finds its expression in Newell's *Unified*

Theories of Cognition (1990). The above quote constitutes a high-level specification for SOAR and according to its authors, for general intelligence as well.

SOAR, they say, must be able to work on the full range of tasks, from the routine to extremely difficult open-ended problems. That's why they want to "employ the full range of problem solving methods and representations." Notice the assumption that representations are necessary for problem solving. We'll encounter controversy about the role of representations before our tour is done. The extent to which representations are necessary for general intelligence is the center of what I call the third AI debate.[10]

The *goal* of the SOAR project is to provide an architecture capable of general intelligence. There's no claim by its designers that it yet does so. They mention several necessary aspects of general intelligence that are missing:

1. SOAR has no deliberate planning facility; it's always on-line, reacting to its current situation. It can't consider the long-term consequences of an action without taking that action.

2. SOAR has no automatic task acquisition. You have to hand-code the task you want to give it. It does not create new representations of its own. And its designers would like it to. For Newell and company, not creating representations leaves an important gap in any architecture for general intelligence.

3. Though SOAR is capable of learning, several important learning techniques—such as analysis, instruction, and examples—are not yet incorporated into it.

4. SOAR's single learning mechanism is monotonic. That is, once learned, never unlearned; it can't recover from learning errors.

5. Finally, a generally intelligent agent should be able to interact with the real world in real time,[11] that is, in the time required to achieve its goal or to prevent some dire consequence. SOAR can't yet do this, but Robo-SOAR is on the way (Laird and Rosenbloom 1990; Laird et al. in press).

With many capabilities of general intelligence yet to be implemented, SOAR's architecture may not be stable. Some mechanisms may change; although SOAR's builders think it's roughly stable, they won't guarantee it. With all these caveats out of the way, let's explore SOAR's mechanisms.

SOAR's Mechanisms

At this stop on the tour we're concerned with symbolic AI, as opposed to other kinds of artificial intelligence. How is SOAR symbolic? How does it use symbolic representation? To begin with, the most elementary representation within SOAR is of objects as collections of attribute-value pairs. If SOAR's task is in the toy world of blocks (blocksworld), for example, it might represent *b13* as (*block b13 ^color red ^shape cube*). "*^color red*" and "*^shape cube*" are attribute-value pairs.[12] SOAR's goals are also represented symbolically, and progress toward them is accomplished by symbolic processes. SOAR's knowledge of the task environment is encoded symbolically in production rules and is used to govern its behavior. (Later, we'll struggle with the distinction between a system being rule describable vs. rule governed. You can describe the motion of the planets around the sun by rules, but it would be hard to say that your rules govern their motion.) SOAR, as any production system must, explicitly uses its knowledge to control its behavior. Symbolic representation is used explicitly and crucially.

SOAR's problem-solving activity is based on searching its *problem space* for a goal state. The state space of a problem-solving dynamical system, SOAR in this case, is called its problem space. Our old acquaintance the eight puzzle provides an example (see figure 4.8).

The triangle in figure 4.8 bounds only a small window into the problem space. There is much more to it. On the left is the initial state for some particular problem instance. Arrows out of a given state point to possible next states. A move is chosen, and then another. This continues until a goal state is reached. Task implementation knowledge and search control knowledge are used to choose the next move. For example, a task implementation production rule might allow you to move left if you're not already at the left edge of the board. But when should this rule be applied? There may be other production rules that encode your strategy for choosing which of the valid moves to act on. You may, for example, want to have a method of determining how far each of the possible moves leaves you from a goal. Using this method, you choose the operation that moves you closer to the goal. This strategy is called *means–ends analysis*. There are lots of such strategies.

Goals and subgoals represent what the system wants to achieve. Don't take this too literally. It's really what the designers of the system want it

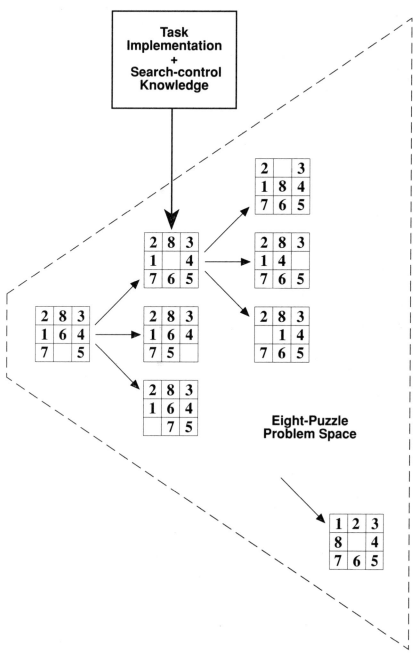

Figure 4.8
A problem space (adapted from Laird et al. 1987)

to achieve. The system has no intentionality in the ordinary use of the word, although it may well have in a philosophical sense (Dennett 1987). Goals and subgoals control the system's behavior. Newell and company chose the problem space as the fundamental organization for *all* goal-oriented symbolic activity. Every task for SOAR is formulated as finding a desired state in a problem space. As a consequence, every task takes the form of heuristic search. Symbolic AI is built around heuristic search.

Except for the current state, and possibly a few remembered states, the states of a problem space do not preexist as data structures. Except for toy problems, nobody has the whole problem space in front of them. Problem spaces are much too large. New states, although they exist theoretically as part of the problem space, must be generated for the system by applying operators to states currently existing within the system. This seems like an obvious point, even a trivial one, but I think it's important.[13]

At any given time SOAR occupies a *context* consisting of its current goal, the chosen problem space, its current state within that problem space, and perhaps an operator with which to move to the next state. All of these are represented explicitly and symbolically as objects with attribute-value pairs residing in working memory. A goal might look like (goal g3 ^problem-space p14 ^state s51). If asked to tell you about itself, it might reply, "I'm a goal. My name is g3. I'd like to move problem space p14 to its state s51." A problem space might look like (problem space p14 ^name base-level-space), a state like (state s51 ^object b80 b70 b64 ^input i16 ^tried o76), and an operator like (operator o82 ^name comprehended).

A production in SOAR is, of course, a condition-action rule. Its conditions require that certain objects be in working memory. These objects may be domain objects (e.g., a numbered square in the 8 puzzle), goals, a problem space, a state, an operator, and so on. Its action must add objects to working memory. No other action is allowed. Productions in SOAR serve only as memory, reacting to cues (conditions) by recalling associated facts to working memory (its action).

If productions act only as memory, who makes the moves? In the production systems we looked at previously, changes of state were effected by productions directly. The particular production to act was chosen by the control system. SOAR operates quite differently. Its control mechanism leads it through a *decision cycle* composed of an *elaboration phase* and a *decision procedure*. During the elaboration phase, each production whose conditions are satisfied acts to deposit objects in working memory. These new additions may then enable other productions that remember more objects. This procedure continues in a recursive forward chaining sort of way until, at last, no new memories are added. Thus ends the elaboration phase of the decision cycle. Note that conflict resolution is missing; any production with satisfied conditions fires. Note also the possibility of a parallel production system being employed to advantage. Working memory then contains, among other objects, operators, each clamoring to change the current state of some problem space.

To understand the second part of SOAR's decision cycle, the decision procedure, we'll need to meet yet another type of object, the *preference*. Some of these may have been deposited in working memory by the firing of productions. One such, represented symbolically by (preference o82 ^role operator ^value acceptable ^problem-space p14 ^state s51), finds operator o82, which moves problem space p14 to state s51, an acceptable next move. Other possible values of the ^value attribute of a preference are *reject, better, worse, best, worst,* and *indifferent*. The semantics are intuitive. They mean what you think they mean. One may prefer o82 to o16 (*better*). Another may *reject* o16 altogether, even though some other finds o16 quite *acceptable*. The rules for applying these preferences follow commonsense semantics closely. *Reject* takes precedence. If two are *acceptable* and the choice is *indifferent,* it is made at random. Preferences, like other objects, take part in both the condition and the action ends of productions, and thus accumulate in working memory during the elaboration phase. Preferences may be for or against operators, problem spaces, goals, or states.

Preferences also afford Newell an occasion for espousing a necessary condition for intelligence (1990, pp. 170–71):

An intelligent system must also be able to express its knowledge about what actions should be taken. It must be able both to represent an action, without taking it, and to represent that an action should be taken, again without taking it. This latter may be a little less obvious, but if it were not possible, how could deliberation of what should happen occur? Furthermore, since it is the architecture that finally actually takes an action (even an operator, which is an internal action), there must be an architecturally defined and understood communication about what action to take. *Preferences* are Soar's means of such communication.

One can agree with at least part of Newell's argument without joining the ranks of those who maintain that symbolic representation is necessary for all intelligent action. Later in the tour we'll meet the ideas of Maes on action selection (1990). She proposes a system that plans without representing its plans to itself, one that deliberates numerically, using spreading activation, rather than symbolically.

SOAR's decision procedure uses only preferences, and in a straightforward, commonsense sort of way. To be chosen for the new context, an object must be *acceptable*. No *rejected* object may be chosen, even if it is *acceptable*. Other things being equal, a *better* object must be chosen. And so on. An object may be proposed (*acceptable*) but rejected. Deliberation occurs. When all the decisions are made, SOAR's decision cycle starts again with another elaboration phase. The cycle continues until SOAR has solved its problem, that is, has reached a goal state in its problem space.

Will repetition of this decision cycle always lead to a solution? No. Sometimes it leads to an impasse so that problem solving cannot continue. For example, lack of preferences between task operators can create a tie impasse. This situation is detected by the architecture and a subgoal is automatically created for overcoming the impasse. In the case of the tie impasse, the subgoal might be to choose between the two operators. Goals other than initial goals are created only in response to impasses.

A new subgoal pushes a new context onto SOAR's *context stack*.[14] This new context contains only a goal state, that is, it looks like (g, —, —, —), with g representing the new goal and empty slots for problem space, current state, and operator. SOAR then may choose a problem space in which to search for this new goal state, a current state from which to begin its search, and the first operator with which to change state. Thus SOAR creates a dynamically changing hierarchy of subgoals to help it reach its initial goals. Newell conjectures that such a structure is necessary for intelligent action: "one of the main things that has been learned in AI is the effectiveness, and apparent necessity, of a goal hierarchy, with goals, subgoals, and alternative subgoals, for controlling behavior to achieve intelligent performance" (1990, p. 174). The truth of this assertion undoubtedly depends upon where we draw the line for intelligent action. At the high level of human problem solving, Newell must be right. On a later stop of our tour we'll see that Brooks's robots may be viewed by an outside observer as having a goal hierarchy. But internally, Brooks maintains, there are no such representations (1991).

Just as a new context is pushed onto the context stack in response to an impasse and its resulting new subgoal, so an existing context is popped from the stack whenever its subgoal is satisfied. More generally, an existing context reemerges whenever some decision changes a context further down the stack, making its subgoal irrelevant. SOAR's decisions are not constrained by the structure of its context stack but by the preferences in working memory. (For a more detailed exposition, see Newell 1990, chap. 4.)

Where do the initial goals come from? From the human user, of course. SOAR has no agenda of its own. Later we'll encounter Herbert, one of Brooks's robots (1990c), who wanders around an office collecting empty soda cans. Does Herbert have its own agenda, or Brooks's agenda? Do we have our own agenda, or one supplied by the Blind Watchmaker (Dawkins 1987)? Earlier I asserted that mind is a property of autonomous agents. One can argue that all agendas arise from outside the system, that SOAR, when supplied by some user with a problem to work on, is just as autonomous as Herbert, or as you and I. Perhaps "autonomous" should be understood not in the sense of supplying its own agenda but in the sense of pursuing that agenda without help or interpretation from outside the system. But having solved the eight puzzle means nothing to SOAR. Perhaps we'd best conclude that SOAR is not yet an autonomous agent and thus, so far, is devoid of mind.

Yet another SOAR mechanism is called garbage collection in computer science. Suppose it creates a subgoal to choose between two operators and, in the process of pursuing this, creates some local structures or some facts about it. The minute the decision is made, all these objects are discarded. The architecture cleans up after itself. The garbage is collected.

But having elaborated as much as machinely possible, having remembered all the potentially relevant facts, and still having reached an impasse, how does SOAR extract itself? How does it even begin to find a way out of its impasse? It uses *weak methods,* that is, methods of finding a trajectory through problem space to a goal. One such method, *means–ends analysis,* repeatedly finds some operator that reduces the distance from the current state to the goal state. Another is *hill-climbing*. Here the problem space is represented as a hypersurface in some high-dimensional Euclidean space[15] with goals at maximum points. A hill-climbing procedure moves the system uphill. Many such methods are employed. They are called weak methods because they don't require a lot of knowledge. They can be used in knowledge-lean situations. Typically these methods are implemented in individual procedures. In SOAR, they are uniformly implemented by search control productions instead. SOAR climbs hills because of productions that tell it that this operator has a higher evaluation than that operator. Nothing in SOAR implements hill-climbing directly, yet it is observed to climb hills. SOAR's weak methods are produced uniformly by productions.

SOAR also learns, and in a uniform way, by *chunking*. Suppose SOAR reaches an impasse and establishes a subgoal to clear it. Weak methods are used to find additional knowledge with which to arrive at a state satisfying the subgoal. If this is achieved, SOAR's chunking mechanism creates a production whose condition describes the state of affairs leading to the impasse, and whose action collapses into a single step the trajectory followed by the weak methods in clearing the impasse. If this same initial situation is encountered again, it's not an impasse anymore. The new production rule fires during the elaboration phase and the work continues. This is one-shot learning via collapsing the work of satisfying a subgoal into a single production. We'll meet other versions of this kind of learning along the tour.

Experimental evidence shows that learning during one task can result in increased efficiency in performing other tasks within the same domain. What's learned tends to generalize within a task domain. New productions resulting from chunking not only are theoretically available for other tasks but are actually so used.

SOAR's designers view weak methods as essential to intelligent action, being needed whenever a situation becomes knowledge-lean, say in new problem spaces or when all knowledge is used up. Weak methods drive learning, since chunking requires some way of attaining goals before knowledge is assimilated. Weak methods in SOAR are built into control productions (those producing preferences) that are part of the domain knowledge. There is no need to learn weak methods. This theme of the need for built-in weak methods will recur several times during our tour.

With all this said, we should now be able to appreciate a more global view of SOAR's architecture, as provided in figure 4.9. A few minutes spent contemplating it made SOAR's process more comprehensible to me. I recommend your doing likewise.

Applications of SOAR

SOAR has been under development for a decade with order of magnitude 100 published articles describing the work.[16] A number of these concern applications implemented in SOAR. Here, we'll look briefly at one such and mention a few others.

One of the more successful commercial expert systems is R1, written initially at Carnegie Mellon to configure VAXs for Digital Equipment Company (DEC).[17] Some years back I remember reading that DEC devoted seven person-years per year to the operation, maintenance, and further development of R1, and produced a net savings of some $25 million by its use. Based on some 10,000 rules, R1 was, at that time, already a large and complex system.

R1 has been partially reimplemented in SOAR. R1-SOAR implements 25 percent of R1. This is no toy problem. We've seen that SOAR is a general-purpose problem solver capable of working in knowledge-lean problem spaces by extensive search. By contrast, R1 is a knowledge-intensive, special-purpose expert system, carefully tuned to its specific task, that does as much direct recognition and as little search as possible. Much to my surprise, R1 proves to be only half again as fast as R1-SOAR when working on problems that R1-SOAR can solve. I'm impressed.

SOAR has been tried out on lots of other tasks. As would be expected, it performs well on knowledge-lean toy AI tasks and puzzles such as blocks world,[18] eight queens,[19] missionaries and cannibals,[20] tic-tac-toe, and tower of Hanoi.[21] It also has little difficulty with small routine tasks such as unification,[22] finding roots of equations, or correctly employing syllogisms. In addition to R1, SOAR has successfully mimicked other expert systems such as NEOMYCIN and DESIGNER. Small demos have been produced for miscellaneous AI tasks such as natural language parsing, concept formation, and resolution theorem proving.[23] A most

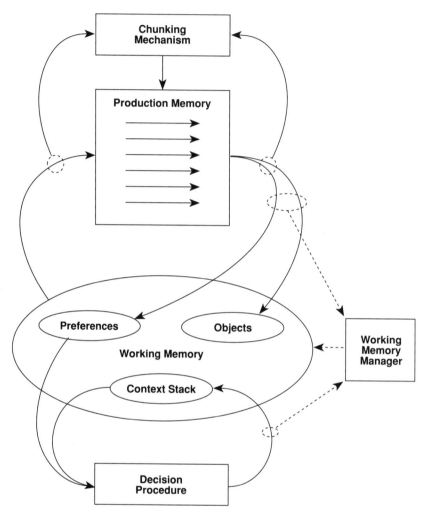

Figure 4.9
SOAR's architecture (redrawn from Laird et al. 1987)

interesting development is Robo-SOAR, which interfaces SOAR with the external world via a video camera and a robot arm to implement blocks world (Laird et al. 1989).

SOAR's Hypotheses

SOAR embodies some dozen basic hypotheses about the architecture required for general intelligence that are explicit enough to allow us to compare SOAR with some of the newer methods. Also, these hypotheses can be viewed as high-level specifications for mechanisms of mind. We will visit those that seem the most useful for our purposes. Their order is such that the latter hypotheses often depend on the former.

All lean on the first, the *physical symbol system hypothesis,* which says that *every general intelligence must be realized by a symbolic system.* This quite explicitly draws a line in the dirt for the second AI debate, which we shall encounter later on the tour. It seems clear to me that a rational mind must use some type of symbol system. How else would one do, say, mathematics? Thus a symbol system seems necessary for general intelligence. But this hypothesis claims more; every general intelligence operates only by means of a symbol system. The physical symbol system may well be implemented on top of some other, finer-grained architecture. But at some level, the physical symbol system hypothesis claims that there must be a symbol system that accounts for all the observed intelligence in every intelligent agent. This extends not only to rational intelligence but to every other sort as well, say image recognition.

It's this last that bothers me. I agree that a physical symbol system seems necessary for rational thought.[24] It even seems possible that physical symbol systems suffice for all intelligence, in that any intelligent behavior can be implemented by a physical symbol system, given sufficient time. This last is the rub. I doubt if physical symbol systems could ever implement in real time the mental activity of a basketball player during a fast break.[25] If this is true, there must be other, essentially different mechanisms of mind. Much of the rest of this tour will be spent exploring various proposals for such. Here's a foretaste of the views of one proposer (Maes 1991, p. 1):

Since 1970 the Deliberative Thinking paradigm has dominated Artificial Intelligence research. Its main thesis is that intelligent tasks can be implemented by a reasoning process operating on a symbolic internal model. . . . This approach has proved successful in . . . areas such as expert level reasoning. However, only poor results have been obtained in its application to research on autonomous agents. The few systems built show deficiencies such as brittleness, inflexibility, no real time operation. . . . They also spawned a number of theoretical problems such as the frame problem[26] and the problem of non-monotonic reasoning[27] which remain unsolved (at least within realistic time constraints). Some researchers view this as evidence that it is unrealistic to hope that more action-oriented tasks could also be successfully implemented by a deliberative machine in real time.

What Maes calls the deliberative thinking paradigm includes the physical system hypothesis as well as a second SOAR hypothesis, the *production system hypothesis: Production systems are the appropriate organization for encoding all long-term knowledge.* Here we have the "knowledge via rules" position. There are opposing views. Connectionists would prefer to encode long-term knowledge in the weights (synapses) of their artificial neural networks. Brooks would hardwire it into the layers of his subsumption architecture. We'll encounter each of these positions on later tour stops.

A third SOAR hypothesis is called the *goal structure hypothesis.* It asserts that *control in a general intelligence is maintained by a symbolic goal system.* It seems clear that any intelligent system must be motivated by drives or goals or some such, either inherited, learned, programmed in, or self-generated. The controversial point of this hypothesis is that they must be maintained symbolically. There are competing hypotheses. Here's one from Brooks (1991, p. 148): "Each layer of control can be thought of as having its own implicit purpose (or goal if you insist). . . . There need be no explicit representations of goals."

SOAR developers also promote the *problem space hypothesis,* which contends that *problem spaces are the fundamental organizational unit of all goal-directed behavior.* This approach emphasizes search and selection—search through problem space via operators and selection of the appropriate operator. Here's an alternative approach, again from Brooks (1991, p. 146): "Each activity, or behavior producing system, individually connects sensing to action." Connectionists offer yet another alternative—let your artificial neural net spread its activation so as to relax into an action. Maes (1990) offers a somewhat different version of spreading activation, and John Jackson (1987) suggests that various demons shout each other down, with the loudest allowed to act. We'll take more detailed looks at each of these during later tour stops.

You'll not be surprised to find here the *weak-method hypothesis*, asserting that *the weak methods form the basic methods of intelligence.* Arguments in favor were given above. I'm not aware of any against, although many symbolic AI researchers jump immediately to stronger methods, such as those of R1 (discussed above). Although this form of the hypothesis implicitly assumes symbolic representation and search through a problem space, weak methods can also emerge from the newer approaches that we've already mentioned and that we'll encounter later on the tour.

The last SOAR hypothesis we'll mention is called the *uniform learning hypothesis*. It insists that *goal-based chunking is the general learning mechanism.* Recall that chunking remembers an efficient path through a search tree. While something like chunking is included in every alternative system (J. Jackson 1987) or would seem a useful addition (Maes 1990), it's not clear to me how learning from observed examples, learning from an outside agent, or learning from reading can be accommodated within the concept of chunking.

Let me remind you that SOAR isn't the only symbolic AI system; it's not even the only one with pretensions to general intelligence. We might well have chosen Anderson's Act* (1983) or perhaps CAPS (Just and Carpenter 1987). My long-range goal in this discussion of SOAR was to provide you with some basis of comparison for the newer models we'll encounter as the tour progresses. The short-term goal was to create a target for the first AI debate. Could it be that the decade of work invested in SOAR is all for nought because artificial intelligence is inherently impossible?

Notes

1. I'm capitalizing SOAR because I think it was originally an acronym. Researchers developing the system sometimes write SOAR and sometimes Soar.

2. Allen Newell died in July 1992. The Earth is poorer.

3. That is, given any element x of X, T assigns to it another element, T(x), of X.

4. Dynamical systems that change continuously over time are even more common. In this case T is usually given as a solution of a differential equation. On this tour we'll mostly visit discrete systems.

5. Analog computation proceeds continuously by, say, voltage variation rather than by discrete steps, as does digital computation. Of course, analog computation can be approximated by digital.

6. This term is common computing jargon, referring to a process that waits watchfully for certain conditions to occur, at which time it performs its function.

7. Art Graesser kindly pointed out to me that if you make your rules specific enough, they'll rarely produce a conflict. But if you rely on more general rules, the implementation of conflict resolution strategies ends up being a major component of the system.

8. I'm not saying that a shared memory machine is necessary for parallel production systems. The DADO parallel production system machine built at Columbia (see Almasi and Gottlieb 1989, pp. 378–81 for a brief description and further references) spreads the global database among the leaves of a tree of processors.

9. There are, in fact, other reasonable choices, such as Anderson's Act* (1983), or perhaps CAPS (Just and Carpenter 1983).

10. In my terminology, the first AI debate is about whether computing machines can ever be intelligent, whereas the second questions whether connectionism (artificial neural networks) can add anything essential to what can be accomplished by symbolic AI. Both of these debates will be visited at length along the tour.

11. Consider a program capable of predicting weather with perfect accuracy twenty-four hours in advance. The rock in its shoe is the forty-eight hours it takes to make a prediction. Such a program does *not* operate in real time.

12. In spite of the superficial resemblance to Minsky's frames (1975) and to the objects of object-oriented programming (Goldberg and Robson 1983), SOAR's object representations are much simpler, lacking default values, attachment of procedures, and inheritance.

13. Analogously, memories don't exist in humans as data structures, but must be reconstructed as needed from cues currently existing in the system. The distinction is analogous to that of looking up a function value in a table as opposed to computing it.

14. A *stack* is a computer science data structure analogous to a stack of dishes. Some piece of information may be *pushed* on to the stack, that is, added to the top. Or some piece of information may be *popped* from the stack, that is, taken from the top. These are the only means by which information can be stored or retrieved in a stack.

15. The position of a point in the three-dimensional Euclidean space in which most of us think we live is given by a triple of numbers (x_1, x_2, x_3). In a Euclidean space of dimension n, points are n-vectors of numbers $(x_1, x_2, \ldots, x_n)$. State spaces are often subsets of some high-dimensional Euclidean space. A hypersur-

face is the high-dimensional analogue of a two-dimensional surface in three-dimensional space.

16. That is, closer to 100 than to 10 or 1000.

17. R1 has since been renamed XCON. VAX names a particular line of computers manufactured by DEC.

18. A simulation of a single robot arm capable of recognizing blocks of various colors and shapes, and of following a command to stack a certain one upon another even if several unspecified intervening moves must be first performed.

19. Place eight queens on a chessboard so that no one attacks any other.

20. Produce a plan to ferry three missionaries and three cannibals across a river by repeated crossings in a boat holding only two people, subject to the constraint that there must never be more cannibals than missionaries on the same side of the river.

21. A stack of disks of decreasing diameter is impaled on one of three stakes. The game is to transfer the stack to another specified stake by moving one disk at a time to some stake while never allowing a larger disk upon a smaller.

22. A process of formal logic useful in automatic reasoning and logic programming (e.g., PROLOG) that's a little complex to explain in a brief footnote.

23. Again part of automated reasoning and logic programming, and too complex for a brief footnote.

24. Although there is some lingering doubt. In my earlier life as a topologist, much of the mathematics I discovered came in the form of fragmentary visual images rather than as overt symbols.

25. This particular image is from Horgan and Tienson (1989), who give arguments for such a belief.

26. The intractable problem of tracking the side effects of actions of a complex system in the complex world by making corresponding modifications in the database representing the state of the world.

27. In ordinary logic, once an assertion is proved, it remains true regardless of subsequently acquired information. In the "real world" I assume that if Tweety is a bird, then Tweety can fly, until I learn that Tweety is a penguin. Nonmonotonic logics attempt to handle this type of reasoning.

5

The First AI Debate

With thought comprising a non-computational element, computers can never do what we human beings can.
—Roger Penrose, *The Emperor's New Mind*

Setting the Stage

With the above quote from Penrose, the battle is joined. *Can we, or can we not, expect computers to think in the sense that humans do?* This question invites an immediate rejoinder: On an already packed tour, why give time and space to a question that boils down to how we want to use the words "thought" and "computer"? The issue, though intriguing, lacks substance without agreed-upon definitions of the key words. Nonetheless, the ideas that arise during the debate will prove important to our understanding of the constraints on mechanisms of mind. So here we go.

The stage for the debate is set beautifully by John Haugeland (1985, p. 2). Speaking of artificial intelligence, he says:

The fundamental goal of this research is not merely to mimic intelligence or produce some clever fake. Not at all. "AI" wants only the genuine article: machines with minds, in the full and literal sense. . . .

Scoffers find the whole idea quite preposterous—not just false but ridiculous—like imagining that your car (really) hates you or insisting that a murderous bullet should go to jail.

Boosters . . . are equally certain that it's only a matter of time; computers with minds, they say, are as inevitable as interplanetary travel and two-way pocket TV.

This is the debate. Who's right, the scoffers or the boosters?

Opening Statements

Let's allow each side brief opening statements. A scoffer speaks (Penrose, 1989, pp. 447–48):

Consciousness seems to me to be such an important phenomenon that I simply cannot believe that it is something just "accidentally" conjured up by a complicated computation. . . .

. . . it is indeed "obvious" that the conscious mind cannot work like a computer, even though much of what is actually involved in mental activity might do so.

In the first sentence, Penrose is taking issue with the view of some AI proponents that consciousness will *emerge* in sufficiently complex machines. The second sentence requires some clarification. Penrose is drawing the line at consciousness, claiming that a computer can never be conscious. Don't take this as only a denial of first-person consciousness, the experience of qualia.[1] He's also denying the possibility of third-person consciousness[2] in a computer. Not only can computers not experience the things we experience consciously, they can't *do* the things we do consciously. Penrose is clearly a scoffer.

And now a booster (Moravec, 1988, pp. 1–2):

Today, our machines are still simple creations, requiring the parental care and hovering attention of any newborn, hardly worthy of the word "intelligent." But within the next century they will mature into entities as complex as ourselves, and eventually into something transcending everything we know—in whom we can take pride when they refer to themselves as our descendants. . . .

We are very near to the time when virtually no essential human function, physical or mental, will lack an artificial counterpart. The embodiment of this convergence of cultural developments will be the intelligent robot, a machine that can think and act as a human.

Here we have the strongest statement I've seen from an AI booster. But don't mistake it for wild science fiction. Rather, it's a conjecture about which a careful scientist[3] has thought seriously and has come up willing to bet his career. It can't simply be dismissed out of hand.

The Turing Test

How can we tell if a computer has really achieved AI? Turing (1950) offered us his "Turing test" as a sufficient criterion for machine intelligence,

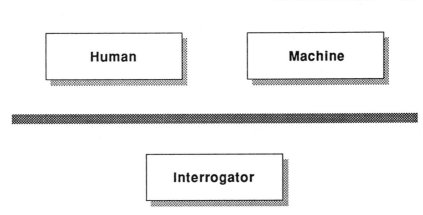

Figure 5.1
The Turing Test setup

though not a necessary one. A barrier separates an interrogator from a human and a machine as in figure 5.1. Allow the interrogator to question each via a terminal. The machine will be deemed intelligent if sophisticated interrogators, unconstrained as to subject matter, cannot reliably tell which responder is human and which is machine. To date, no machine has even come close to passing Turing's test in its full glory, although trials have been held at the Computer Museum in Boston with interrogators limited to questions from a narrow domain. The virtue of Turing's test lies in the general, but by no means universal, agreement that it is sufficient to establish the existence of computer intelligence. Thus it is at least theoretically possible to settle the first AI debate.

The Pro Position

Having heard the opening statements for and against a computer eventually being able to think, and having encountered Turing's suggestion of one way to settle the issue, we now turn to the arguments pro and con, mostly con. Why mostly con? Because the typical booster says, "Wait and see; we'll produce machine intelligence and show you." The scoffers, on the other hand, produce arguments purporting to prove the impossibility of artificial minds.

Let's narrow the issue and talk about the possibility of an artificial mind via symbolic AI. Recall that a physical symbol system uses physical symbols, symbolic structures (expressions) composed of these symbols, and operators that create, copy, modify, or destroy these symbols and/or structures. The system runs on a machine that, through time, produces an evolving collection of symbol structures. SOAR is one such physical symbol system.

Among the ardent boosters of symbolic AI are Herbert Simon and Allen Newell. The following quotes illustrate their views: "intelligence is the work of symbol systems" and "a physical symbol system has the necessary and sufficient means for general intelligent action. The computer is . . . [a] physical symbol system. . . . The most important [such] is the human mind and brain" (Simon 1981, p. 28).

They say that a physical symbol system can be intelligent, and that any intelligent agent must be implemented via a physical symbol system. That's a strong assertion, but one subscribed to by many on the cognitive side of AI[4]:

> . . . there are now in the world machines that think, that learn and that create. Moreover, their ability to do these things is going to increase rapidly until—in a visible future—the range of problems they can handle will be coextensive with the range to which the human mind has been applied. (Simon and Newell 1958)

Simon also made some predictions about how long all this would take. As is so often the case, his predictions proved overly optimistic.

With the booster's position in place, let's look at several different attacks on the possibility of artificial minds. We'll do so, not trying to decide who's right but to get acquainted with the arguments of the scoffers. First we turn to Dreyfus.

The Dreyfus Attack

Even its boosters readily admit that symbolic AI has stumbled over commonsense knowledge and reasoning. A typical human, in our society, would expect a dropped glass of water to break and splatter its contents. A typical AI program would expect no such thing unless specifically instructed. Dreyfus[5] (1988, p. 33) maintains that this situation is inevitable: "If background understanding is indeed a skill and if skills are based on whole patterns and not on rules, we would expect symbolic representations to fail to capture our commonsense understanding." Dreyfus (1988,

p. 37) specifically attacks the physical symbol hypothesis: "The physical symbol system approach seems to be failing because it is simply false to assume that there must be a theory of every domain."

A theory in this context is a collection of rules describing behavior within the domain. Dreyfus claims that not every domain is rule describable. Horgan and Tienson (1989, pp. 154ff.) offer basketball as such a domain. Imagine all the factors influencing a point guard's decision, during a fast break, to shoot or pass, and if the latter, to whom. They don't prove a description via rules to be impossible, but they clearly place the onus on proponents of rules to produce one.[6] Not likely!

But then, if not by rules, how are such decisions made? Dreyfus (1987, pp. 98ff.) identifies five stages of learning. As we view each stage, keep in mind some experiences of your own during which you became expert, say in learning to drive a car: (1) the *novice* uses rules, typically supplied by a teacher, applied to context-free features, also usually from the teacher; (2) a *beginner,* in addition, begins to recognize new situational aspects, such as using engine sounds to help determine when to shift gears; (3) a *competent* driver will examine only the situational features that are relevant to the selected goals or plan; (4) a *proficient* driver doesn't have to examine anymore but sees directly what is relevant— nonetheless, he or she decides consciously what to do at this point; (5) the *expert* just does it.

When things are going well experts do not solve problems or make inferences or figure out anything at all; they simply do what normally works and it normally works.
. . . experience-based, holistic, similarity recognition produces the deep situational understanding of the proficient performer. No new insight is needed to explain the mental processes of the expert. (Dreyfus 1987, p. 102)

Dreyfus maintains that similarity recognition says it all.

To illustrate this point, Dreyfus paired an international chess master (Julio Kaplan) with a slightly weaker master. Playing five-seconds-per-move chess, Kaplan was required to mentally add numbers presented orally to him once every second. Dreyfus intended to keep his conscious mind busy adding these numbers so that Kaplan would have no time to see problems or construct plans. Nevertheless, Kaplan played well and won. Deprived of the time necessary to think, he still "produced fluid and coordinated play." Although interesting and provocative, this experiment doesn't seem conclusive. Kaplan may have time-shared[7] his consciousness between the two activities.

To summarize, Dreyfus believes that human experts typically choose the behavior that usually works via similarity recognition, without resorting to problem solving by means of rules. This directly contradicts the physical symbol system hypothesis of Simon and Newell by denying its necessity. It also calls into question its sufficiency, since humans provide the only currently known example of general intelligence.

Scripts à la Schank

As background for our coming attraction, Searle's Chinese Room thought experiment, we'll pay a brief visit to Schank's notion of a script (Schank and Abelson 1977). Schank has been a leading exponent of natural language comprehension via machine. The data structure underlying several of his systems is called a *script*. Scripts are used for representing knowledge of common sequences of events, say those involved in going out to dinner. Such a script might record that you typically go into a restaurant, sit down (or are seated by a hostess), are brought a menu by a waiter who also takes your order and brings both your food and, later, the check. After eating, you leave a tip, pay the check, and depart. Scripts may contain entry conditions, results, props, roles, tracks, scenes, and so on.

One program uses scripts to answer questions about trivial stories. For example:

John went out to a restaurant last night. He ordered steak. When he paid for it, he noticed that he was running out of money. He hurried home since it had started to rain.

The question: Did John eat dinner last night? We would answer yes because we understand something about what happens in restaurants. The program also answers yes after consulting its restaurant script. Schank's program infers that John ate in spite of there being no statement to that effect in the story. This program is also supposed to understand something about what happens in restaurants. Well, not everyone agrees that it "really" understands, which takes us to our next stop.

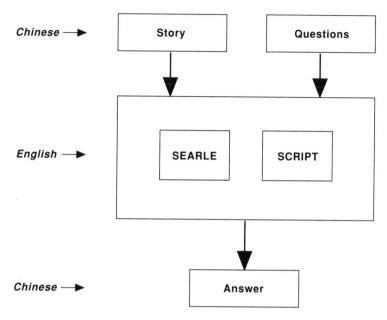

Figure 5.2
The Chinese Room

The Chinese Room

Philosophers, like physicists, often propose thought experiments designed to shed light on some issue. The famous Chinese Room experiment, offered by John Searle (1980), focuses on understanding. For the experiment Searle puts himself in a closed room (see figure 5.2). A story and a question about it, both written in Chinese, are slipped under the door to him. Searle understands no Chinese; the writing means nothing, just squiggles on paper. But he has been given a comprehensive script, written in English, that provides an algorithmic way of answering the question as a native speaker might. Thinking in English, and carefully following the directions contained in the script, Searle produces squiggles that form a native speaker's answer to the question. Searle slips the results of this purely formal transformation under the door as an answer. Searle, who understands English but no Chinese, has produced an answer giving the appearance of understanding. He actually understands nothing of the story, the question, or the answer. In the same way, Searle asserts, Schank's computer understands nothing of the stories even as it answers questions about them.

The Chinese Room experiment is certainly provocative and, in fact, has provoked any number of rejoinders. The first reply that occurred to me on hearing of the experiment is called the systems reply. Sure, Searle doesn't understand, but the entire system, including the script, must understand because it produces native speaker answers. To me that was almost a definition of understanding. How do we convince ourselves that some other person understands a story we've told? A common approach is to question that person and judge understanding by the quality of the answers. Searle counters the systems reply by supposing that he, Searle, memorizes the entire system. Then he is the system, and he still doesn't understand Chinese. But, you retort, it's preposterous to suppose that Searle could memorize that script. Of course it is. But it's no more preposterous than the existence of such a script in the first place. Thought experiments are often allowed this kind of license. After all, it's possible in principle, they say.

Another retort to Searle, at least as far-fetched as the thought experiment, is called the brain simulator reply. Suppose a computer program simulates the actual neural firings of a native Chinese speaker in order to answer questions posed about a simple story. To say that the system doesn't understand is to say that the native speaker doesn't understand, the argument goes. The system is doing exactly what the native speaker did. Searle counters thus: Have Searle calculate the answers using a system of water pipes and valves that simulate the native speaker's brain. Neither Searle, nor the water pipe system, nor their conjunction understands. The conjunction fails because the whole system could again be internalized. Searle could simply memorize all the workings of the native speaker's brain and go on from there. Thus, Searle maintains that the original script could have worked by simulating a native speaker's brain with the same lack of understanding. But how can a brain understand Chinese when a simulation of that same brain, neurally equivalent except for a slowdown factor, can't?

Comments on Searle's *Behavioral and Brain Sciences* article (1980) offer many other rebuttals, all of which Searle counters, at least to his satisfaction. Machines just don't understand, he maintains. But I've come to another view of understanding, as is illustrated next.

Quadratic Understanding

Discussions about whether a given system understands Chinese typically assume that there is a well-defined set of systems that understand, and that a system either understands or it doesn't. This is another instance of the "sharp boundary" fallacy we met in a previous chapter in connection with Sloman's treatment of free will. There we looked at many design decisions providing more or less free will. As with free will, there is no useful dichotomy between understanding and not understanding. Here we'll see degrees of understanding.

Arnie is a formal system (computer program) that solves quadratic equations. Feed it the numerical coefficients, a, b, and c of a quadratic equation $ax^2 + bx + c = 0$, and it pops out a solution. Arnie gives you right answers but understands nothing of the numbers it spews, and nothing else of algebra. In my view, it must understand something of quadratic equations because it can solve them correctly. It understands more than a program that produces incorrect solutions. But that's certainly very little understanding.

Bobby, by the ninth grade, has memorized some arithmetic facts and algebraic manipulations, and can solve quadratics. His teacher claims he does so by rote, and understands little of what he's doing. While this may well be true, he still understands more than Arnie, since he does understand something of the numbers and formula he's using.

Charlie not only can solve quadratics but also can derive the formula. But what that $i(= \sqrt{-1})$ is that crops up unbidden, he doesn't quite understand. Doris, however, is one up on Charlie, because she can derive the formula and she understands something about complex numbers. Elaine, whose mother is a mathematician, looks down her nose at Doris because Doris doesn't know the fundamental theorem of algebra,[8] which puts the quadratic formula in broader perspective. Elaine's mother, of course, views all this from the vantage point of algebraic field theory,[9] an extensive and detailed theory about how fields behave (see, e.g., van der Waerden 1953 for an introduction). She understands quadratics at a much deeper level than does her daughter.

A system's understanding of a concept, or of a collection of concepts, seems to vary with the complexity of its connections from the given concepts to other knowledge. Roughly, the more connections, the more understanding.

My colleagues Horgan and Tienson tell me that Searle anticipated this argument by degrees of understanding, and replied that computer systems have *zero* understanding, making them different in kind from the human systems with varying degrees of understanding. I disagree. Starting with a system having, say, Bobby's level of quadratic understanding, it should, in principle, be possible to dismember connections one by one. Thus one could approximate Arnie's level of quadratic understanding as closely as desired. Arnie has some connections, and therefore in my view, nonzero understanding. A system with more understanding can be reduced to Arnie's level connection by connection. I see no difference in kind.[10]

Chinese is many orders of magnitude more complex than quadratic equations. There must be at least as many levels of understanding Chinese, depending on the surrounding network of knowledge. It seems to me that the system comprised of Searle and his script does understand Chinese at some minimal level. Searle's argument doesn't lead me to doubt that artificial systems can be given, or can learn, ever increasing understanding of quadratic equations and of Chinese. Whether this artificial understanding must of necessity always fall short of that of humans, or whether the understanding of our "mind children" will eventually surpass ours, is the essence of this first AI debate.

Gödel's Incompleteness Theorem

Before visiting with our next participant in the AI debate, let's take a pilgrimage. A pilgrimage? Yes, indeed. I regard Gödel's theorem and its proof as one of the high points of human intellectual achievement, to be approached with respect, even with reverence.[11] As a professional mathematician, I often had occasion to read other people's theorems and their proofs. Usually I'd think to myself, "Well that's pretty clever, but if I had worked hard on that, I'd have gotten it." But when I read Gödel's proof I thought, "I would never have found this proof in a thousand years."

"That's enough adulation," you say. "Let's get to the theorem." Ok. But let me quickly provide some needed context. Around the turn of the twentieth century, logicians, pushed by Hilbert (1901), were trying to derive mathematics from logic. The idea was to develop a formal system, starting with finitely many axioms and rules of deduction, and from it to deduce all of mathematics. One major attempt was produced by Frege (1893, 1903). Whitehead and Russell spent decades writing their version, the *Principia Mathematica*[12] (1910–1913). Then, in 1931, along came an unknown Austrian, Kurt Gödel, who proved that their whole endeavor was hopeless to begin with.

After all this preamble, what's the theorem? Roughly, it says that *every sufficiently powerful formal theory allows a true but unprovable proposition* (Gödel 1931). Some elaboration seems in order. Let's suppose our formal theory to be consistent. (Inconsistent systems are uninteresting because every assertion is provable).[13] "Sufficiently powerful" means that the system can account for integer arithmetic. What is meant by allowing a true but unprovable proposition P? A formal theory will have symbols (variables, constants, and operators) as well as rules of syntax. P must be composed of some of these symbols arranged according to the syntax of the system. In technical terms, it must be a well-formed formula of the system. Furthermore, P is unprovable from the axioms and rules of deduction of the system.[14] On the other hand, the meaning of P is known to be true in the system. P, for example, might assert that P is unprovable in the system. This may be known to be true by an argument outside the system.

So, given any sufficiently powerful theory, Gödel's proof provides a method of constructing a proposition that you know to be true by the very nature of the beast, and that you also know to be unprovable within this very system. Gödel's theorem also has a computational form which asserts that every algorithm[15] for deciding mathematical truth must fail to decide some proposition correctly. An algorithm will tell you a proposition is true only if it can prove it. A true but unprovable proposition gets a wrong reading. The bottom line is that not all of mathematics can be produced algorithmically.

Some philosophers (e.g., Lucas 1961) have argued that as a consequence of Gödel's theorem, mathematicians must think nonalgorithmically. Our next scoffer, Penrose, makes much the same argument, and another besides.

The Penrose Attack

Penrose, a distinguished mathematician and mathematical physicist, joined the AI debate as a scoffer with his best-selling *The Emperor's New Mind* (1989). He's concerned with consciousness. Computers operate algorithmically. Brains also do algorithmic processing, but mostly unconsciously. Why, then, he asks, is anything conscious? Perhaps consciousness evolved to make judgments that cannot be made algorithmically. Penrose claims that humans make some judgments that cannot be made algorithmically, and that, therefore, cannot be made by a computer. His attack is two pronged: (1) the nonalgorithmic nature of mathematical thought and (2) quantum mechanical effects in the brain.

Penrose gives a reductio ad absurdum argument[16] in favor of mathematical judgments being nonalgorithmic (1989, pp. 417–18). He doesn't claim the argument constitutes a proof, but that it is convincing to him. Here is his argument. Suppose mathematical judgments are algorithmic. These judgments are communicable. Two mathematicians not only can discuss them but, unlike practitioners of many other disciplines, can eventually agree as to what's been proved, that is, agree in their mathematical judgment. Two such mathematicians can't be using different algorithms, Penrose says, or they wouldn't agree. Hence, a single algorithm must be universally employed. (This step in the argument bothers me. It is certainly possible for two different algorithms to give the same answer all the time. For example, the many different sorting algorithms all result in the same linear orderings.)

Now, he claims, this algorithm cannot be both *known* and the one used to decide mathematical truth. If the algorithm were known, the construction in Gödel's theorem would produce a proposition that it wouldn't handle correctly. Remember that our assumption is that mathematical judgments are algorithmic. Hence there would be an algorithm that would handle all such correctly. Thus, if there is an algorithm that is going to handle all mathematical judgments correctly, it can't be known; otherwise, you could contradict it by Gödel's theorem. Thus this algorithm must be "so complicated or obscure that its very validity can never be known to us." But mathematical truth is "built up from such simple and obvious ingredients." It is not a "horrendously complicated dogma whose validity is beyond our comprehension." Thus, the original assumption that mathematical judgment is algorithmic leads to an absurdity. Penrose proposes this as a convincing argument that mathematical judgments are nonalgorithmic.

Could the issue here be simply a case of confusion of levels of abstraction? In my AI classes we often stress heuristic programming, programs that usually yield the right answer but are not guaranteed to do so. In every class I disturb my students with the following question: How can this be a heuristic program when it runs on a computer that only acts algorithmically? The answer I want points to a difference in levels of abstraction. A running AI program performing a heuristic search in a problem space is simply executing an algorithm at the machine level. This algorithm is not guaranteed to find the goal state. At a higher level of abstraction it is performing a heuristic search. Is Penrose only denying an algorithm for mathematical judgment at a high level of abstraction? If so, we could probably agree. But in fact he seems to be denying such an algorithm at the network of neurons level.

I'm not persuaded. The essence of Penrose's argument, and its refutation, were captured in a review by Dennett (1989). Dennett counters not the particular form of Penrose's argument but the larger context of his argument against mathematical judgment being algorithmic. Here's Dennett's counter, almost verbatim (p. 1056):

For X read mathematician. *Premise one: X is superbly capable of achieving mathematical truth.* (Mathematicians have done so over the centuries.) *Premise two: There is no (practical) algorithm guaranteed to achieve mathematical truth.* (Gödel's theorem) *Conclusion: X does not owe its power to achieve mathematical truth to an algorithm.*

This argument, says Dennett, "is simply fallacious." Substitute Deep Thought for X. (Deep Thought is a chess playing program that has achieved grand master status.) And substitute "checkmate" for "mathematical truth." Let's read the argument again: *Premise one: Deep Thought is superbly capable of achieving checkmate.* (That's certainly true. Deep Thought can checkmate essentially everyone in the world except for perhaps a hundred or fewer of the finest human players.) *Premise two: There is no practical algorithm guaranteed to achieve checkmate.* (Perhaps an exhaustive search algorithm can guarantee checkmate. Unfortunately, the time required for any such process is prohibitive; under ideal conditions, it would take longer to make a single move than the age of the universe. Hence, no practical algorithm guarantees checkmate.) *Conclusion: Deep Thought does not owe its power to achieve checkmate to an algorithm.* (Not true, since Deep Thought runs on a computer.) Although both premises are true, the conclusion is false. Thus, the argument is formally fallacious; it simply doesn't hold. Here's Dennett's summary of this issue:

So even if mathematicians are superb recognizers of mathematical truth, and even if there is no algorithm, practical or otherwise, for recognizing mathematical truth, it does not follow that the power of mathematicians to recognize mathematical truth is not entirely explicable in terms of their brains executing an algorithm. Not an algorithm *for* intuiting mathematical truth—we can suppose that Penrose has proved that there could be no such thing: What would the algorithm be for, then? Most plausibly it would be an algorithm—one of very many—for *trying to stay alive*, an algorithm that, by an extraordinarily convoluted and indirect generation of byproducts, "happened" to be a superb (but not foolproof) recognizer of friends, enemies, food, shelter, harbingers of spring, good arguments—and mathematical truths. (1989, p. 1056)

Let's move on to the second prong of Penrose's attack: quantum gravity. One might argue that consciousness arises from brains. Brains are physical. The laws of physics provide an algorithm for computing what goes on in the physical world[17] (in this case consciousness). Hence consciousness is algorithmic. But, says Penrose, there are problems with the laws of physics:

There is actually a big gap in present understanding between classical physics, explaining the"big", and quantum mechanics explaining the "tiny". It is necessary to first bridge this gap. . . . That won't put everything into place immediately, but it is the first essential step to come to a scientific theory of consciousness. (1989, p.)

Who is this person claiming problems with the laws of physics? Penrose is a professor of mathematics at Oxford. His main scientific contributions have been to combinatorial mathematics (e.g., Penrose tiles) and theoretical physics (e.g., black hole theory). He's not some crackpot shooting from the hip at the laws of physics. He's an insider. All this is not to say that I agree with him, or that you should, or that he is right. It is to say that Penrose's claim of problems with the laws of physics is a serious proposal, not just hot air.

The kind of problem to which Penrose refers has to do with the collapsing of the many potentialities contained in a quantum description into a single actuality. It is best illustrated by a thought experiment known affectionately as the Schrödinger cat experiment (1935). A cat and a vial of cyanide are placed in a box insulated from any sort of observation of the condition of the cat. The vial is connected to a device that will break it (killing the cat) or not, depending on some atomic event happening one way or another.

One such device might be constructed as follows: An emitter of some sort sends a slow stream of photons toward a barrier with two parallel, closely spaced slits cut in it, until one photon passes through. A detector notes through which slit the photon travels. The device breaks the cyanide vial or not, depending on whether the photon travels through the right or the left slit. Since the box is so well insulated, we don't know whether the cat is alive or dead until we don gas masks and open the box.[18]

Quantum physicists, who deal with this sort of thing, maintain that which slit the photon went through is not decided until somebody looks at the detector, until the two potentialities collapse into a single actuality. But where does that leave the poor cat? Is it alive or dead? The mathematics of quantum mechanics seems to say that it is neither until some observer looks at the detector, at which time the potentialities collapse into an actuality and the decision is made.

The situation can be further muddied by placing a suitably protected observer in the box with the cat in view. From the perspective of this observer, the cat is deterministically either dead or alive shortly after the photon hits the detector, while simultaneously (whatever that means to these quantum mechanics) from the perspective of the first observer, the decision is not yet made. Weird stuff!

Don't look to me to defend any of this. I don't believe a word of it. And I'm in good company. Einstein argued until his death that quantum mechanics was incomplete because it was stochastic by nature and seemed inexplicable. He thought that new theories would make sense of all this. But quantum mechanics works. Its mathematics allows superbly accurate predictions of every type of particle reaction against which it's been tested, all this in spite of apparently allowing no sensible explanation whatever. Quantum mechanics, weird as it is, is the reigning, undefeated world champ. My favorite full account of all this is Herbert's *Quantum Reality* (1985). A clear but much shorter account can be found in chapter 12 of Davies's *The Cosmic Blueprint* (1988).

Penrose, along with Einstein but few others, expects new discoveries in physics—namely, a quantum gravity theory—to provide understanding and sensible explanations of these happenings. He postulates that a correct quantum gravity theory will be nonalgorithmic: "a common presumption is that if something acts according to the laws of physics, then it is computational. I believe this is false" (1989).

From this he concludes that brain processes involving frequent quantum decisions would be noncomputable. Hence, computers couldn't implement these processes, and artificial intelligence would be inherently limited. All this is based on there being such quantum mechanical decisions in the brain, for which Penrose argues in detail, and on a nonalgorithmic theory of quantum gravity, which so far is pure speculation, though he provides plausibility arguments.

Enough physics for now. Let's return to the philosophers.

The Horgan-Tienson Attack

Two philosophers, Horgan and Tienson, although not ruling out machine intelligence, claim that it cannot be produced via symbolic AI alone, via rule-based systems (1989). Theirs is a three-pronged attack, via multiple soft constraints, cognitive folding and the frame problem. We'll visit each in turn.

Many activities requiring intelligence seem to involve the satisfaction of multiple soft constraints. For example, suppose I want to shop for running shoes at a certain store in a shopping mall. Let's ignore the multiple soft constraints to be satisfied in getting to the mall. After arriving at the mall, I must search out a parking place following prescribed traffic patterns, modified by the actions of other vehicles, and occupy it. Next I must make my way to an entrance, taking care not to become a casualty on the way. Then I must find my way to the right level, perhaps traveling up or down escalators, all the time avoiding stationary obstacles (benches, potted plants, pillars, vendors' carts) as well as moving people and baby carriages. Surprisingly, I most often arrive at the shoe store without mishap.

There is a lot going on, many factors to take into account as I make my way along. Since these factors often interact with one another, the number of computations required expands exponentially with the number of factors.

Note a surprising contrast. Adding constraints makes the task harder for computers but easier for humans. For computers, every trial solution must be tested against all applicable constraints. But to decide which constraints are applicable means, essentially, to test against all constraints. For humans, having more constraints sometimes makes things easier. Suppose a guest of honor at a ball must choose a partner for the opening dance. Additional constraints (say having to choose someone from the head table, or the spouse of a founder of the sponsoring organization) may make the choice easier.

The constraints, in addition to being multiple, are usually soft. If the parking place I find is marked Handicapped, I'll have to search further. That is, unless I've recently pulled a hamstring and have a Handicapped sticker. I'm constrained to avoid those moving obstacles called other shoppers. That is, unless one of them happens to be one of my grown children looking the other way, whom I bump into accidentally on purpose. When I eventually find my way to the store, I'll buy shoes. Unless the store is late opening. These constraints are soft, and each of the innumerable possible exceptions to a constraint requires another rule. Horgan and Tienson point out that humans deal well with multiple soft constraints but AI programs do not. This, they claim, suggests that human intelligence is different in kind from computer intelligence.

Note that this is an argument not against computer intelligence but against symbolic AI. Brooks's robots seem to satisfy multiple soft constraints. Does this argument then imply that they cannot be viewed as physical symbol systems? Again we're back to the issue of rule-governed vs. rule-described systems.

The second prong is by way of cognitive folding. Horgan and Tienson claim that cognition cannot be partitioned into isolated domains. Any part of commonsense knowledge might be called upon in dealing with any of a vast number of cognitive tasks. Thus any fully intelligent agent must be able to see what is relevant in a given situation, and to recall the relevant information. For example, children easily fold together restaurant scripts and birthday party scripts to form reasonable expectations when they go to a birthday party at a restaurant for the first time. They don't get it all right, but they do have a fair idea of what to expect. They are able to fold the two scripts together. Nobody has the slightest idea of how to program a computer to know in general what's relevant to what. Is it because no one has tried? No. Schank and his colleagues have worked on the folding part of this problem for years (Schank and Abelson 1977; Schank 1980).[19] Or could it be that symbolic AI is inherently incapable of such folding? Anyway, for now, humans do it well; computers, almost not at all.

Horgan and Tienson also point out a relationship between folding and the Turing test. To pass the Turing test, a system must converse intelligently about many domains, individually and in every relevant combination. A sophisticated interrogator will see to it. But, say Horgan and Tienson, "there is little reason to believe that there are . . . domain independent rules[20] that govern the folding together of knowledge about any two . . . arbitrarily chosen domains" (1989, p. 153). This is reminiscent of the earlier comment by Dreyfus that there need not be a theory of everything.

The third prong of the Horgan–Tienson attack is via the frame problem, which they state as follows: to determine in an effective and general way, what to change and what to leave the same in a system of beliefs, when any new bit of information is added. Humans deal with this problem rather well; symbolic AI, with great difficulty and little success. A commonly used illustration of the frame problem has a system tracking, among many other things, a robot with a key in its hand. The system notes that the robot has passed from the office to the shop. Should it also note that the key is no longer located in the office? If so, how is it to do that? Building large systems that sensibly track such side effects seems an insurmountable problem. Whole conferences, even books (Brown 1987), have been devoted to the frame problem, without notable success. Humans, on the other hand, seem to handle the frame problem with relative ease. Could this be, in part, because we humans don't store representations of information but, rather, re-create those representations as needed? To a computer scientist, it's the difference between consulting a lookup table and running an algorithm.

Horgan and Tienson do not claim to have disproved the utility of symbolic AI as a model of general intelligence. They do assert that "the preponderance of evidence points to the conclusion that [symbolic AI] is a fundamentally mistaken paradigm for understanding human cognition" (1989, p. 153). I see the Horgan–Tienson attack as a challenge. If symbolic AI is to win this debate, it must successfully deal with at least these three issues: multiple soft constraints, the folding problem, and the frame problem.

What do we conclude? Will a descendant of SOAR someday discuss the early history of AI with one of our great grandchildren? The scoffers have not convinced me that it simply can't happen. They, particularly Horgan and Tienson, have made it clear that there are major obstacles to be overcome. A fully intelligent automaton surely must compile its procedural knowledge into automatically operating routines that don't consult explicit rules. It must make countless connections in order to understand. I'd like it well if it could prove a theorem or two, not within a formal system but as mathematicians do. And surely it must handle multiple soft constraints, the folding problem, and the frame problem. Will all this happen? To my mind, the jury's still out.

For those of you who are intrigued by the AI debate vistas and want to explore a little longer, let me recommend a detour through a few delightful pages in Crevier's history of AI (1993, pp. 263–77). For the rest of us, let's see what happens when one substitutes a brain model of mind for the computer model of mind we've been discussing.

Notes

1. My friend Art Graesser points out that first-person consciousness includes, in addition to the experience of qualia, the experience of relations, both subjective (e.g., more beautiful than) and objective (e.g., above).

2. Recall that we encountered the concepts of first- vs. third-person consciousness while visiting "Consciousness à la Chalmers" during our tour stop at chapter 2.

3. Moravec, director of the Mobile Robot Laboratory at Carnegie Mellon University, is a leading roboticist.

4. AI, like Janus, has two faces, one facing cognitive science, the other facing computer science. The cognitive face aims at increasing our understanding of intelligence via computer models. The computational face aims at smarter, and hence more efficient, computer programs. The computational AI people typically take no side in this debate.

5. "Dreyfus" actually refers to two people, Hubert Dreyfus and his brother Stuart. For linguistic convenience I'll refer to them in the singular. References are to the two of them.

6. Their account is too long for me to include as a quote. The next time you're in a university library, do take a few minutes to read it.

7. A computer serving several users, apparently simultaneously, allots a fraction of each second to each user. It time-shares.

8. Every polynomial equation with complex coefficients has a solution in the complex numbers.

9. Simply called field theory by mathematicians. I've added "algebraic" to distinguish it from a similarly named subdiscipline of physics.

10. The mathematically inclined among you may well be uncomfortable with this argument. After all, relative complexity of connection networks is not likely to comprise a linear order. What is the sense of "more understanding"? It's in the sense of the partial order defined by set inclusion of connections. "OK," you say, "but connections are discrete." "You can't approximate the complexity of a connection network 'as closely as desired.'" True, a connection network is a discrete system, but the sheer number of connections we're talking about makes approximation, as in continuous systems, a reasonable analogy.

11. A lengthy but extraordinarily rich approach with reverence is contained in Hofstadter's Pulitzer Prize-winning *Gödel, Escher, Bach* (1979). Highly recommended, but allow six months for a thorough understanding.

12. Pages of the *Principia* consist almost entirely of logical symbols seasoned with an occasional word. A favorite ploy has been to leave one thick volume on the coffee table, and to inform curious guests that it's for bedtime reading.

13. Suppose the proposition P and its negation ~P are both provable. Let A be any proposition whatever. Since P is provable, so is P or A. But P or A together with ~P implies A.

14. A more precise statement of Gödel's theorem asserts that both P and its negation are unprovable, that is, that P is undecidable.

15. An algorithm can be thought of roughly as a recipe for action, sufficiently detailed that it can be followed mechanically by the person or machine executing it. A lucid and detailed description is given in the first chapter of Harel's *Algorithmics* (1987).

16. Assume the contrary and deduce a contradiction.

17. One might well balk at this assertion, pointing out that algorithms are inherently discrete whereas most of the laws of physics are continuous. The retort might be that the continuous is approximable by the discrete to any desired degree of accuracy. Another might retort that the physical universe is discrete in both time and space, and that the laws of physics are only approximations.

18. Apparently this was a politically correct experiment in Schrödinger's day.

19. Thanks to Art Graesser for these references.

20. Here they are talking about hard (exceptionless), representation-level rules.

6

Connectionism

Connectionism—The Basic Ideas

The early stops on our mechanisms of mind tour have afforded us views only of symbolic mechanisms. Their general form is a program consisting essentially of rules of some kind, stored in memory along with appropriate data structures. The rules then operate on the data structures, producing, we hope, some semblance of intelligence.

Symbolic mechanisms, however, are far from being the only attractions available these days. In this chapter we'll visit another type: *connectionist models,* also referred to as *artificial neural networks* and sometimes by the general name of *parallel distributed processing.*[1] Yet another name for this class of models is *subsymbolic AI,* denoting an AI approach at the subsymbolic level. Connectionist models are often used to model cognitive functions at a level of abstraction below the symbol level, hence subsymbolic. Most connectionists still view themselves as contributing to AI.

Here's the basic idea from major contributors to this approach: "The idea of parallel distributed processing . . . intelligence emerges from the interactions of large numbers of simple processing units" (Rumelhart et al. 1986, p. ix). This idea actually encompasses more than connectionist models. Since the processing units are unconstrained, except for being relatively simple, networks of automata, with relatively simple finite state machines at each mode, would qualify. The statement also doesn't restrict the way nodes are connected. Other nonconnectionist models implementing this basic idea will appear later in the tour.

So far, we've dealt with symbolic AI, the computer model of cognition: brains work the way computers do. Connectionism can be thought of as the brain model of cognition. You model notions of cognition on how brains apparently do it. Here is the view of Lloyd, a philosopher (1989, p. 90): "The central idea of connectionism is that cognition can be modeled as the simultaneous interaction of many highly interconnected neuronlike units." Lloyd's version constrains the processors to be neuronlike and highly interconnected. "Highly interconnected" should be taken to require "many" connections from one unit to others in a human sense, and not necessarily connections from each unit to a large percentage of the others.[2]

A third and more detailed view is what Chapman (1991, pp. 35–40) calls "essential connectionism," that is, what he deems the essential development of the basic idea expressed by Lloyd. A connectionist model must be brainlike. But what does that mean? Certainly not that it weighs three and a half pounds, and is wet and pinkish-gray. Here's Chapman's answer:

The essential connectionist facts are that the brain
- is made up of a great many components (about 10^{11} neurons)
- each of which is connected to many other components (about 10^4)
- and each of which performs some relatively simple computation (whose nature is unclear)
- slowly (less than a kHz[3])
- and based mainly on the information it receives from its local connections. (p. 36)

Modeling a Neuron

So with all that, what are connectionist models? What are we talking about? Connectionist models are mathematical or computer models based roughly on the local structure of nervous systems of animals. "Roughly" cautions us that many of the features of nervous systems are suppressed and that several simplifying assumptions are made. We must carefully distinguish connectionist models from mathematical or computer models of some aspect of real nervous systems. The simplifying assumptions are much too great to allow these models typically to interest neuroscientists. With this caveat in mind, let's take a quick peek inside real nervous systems.

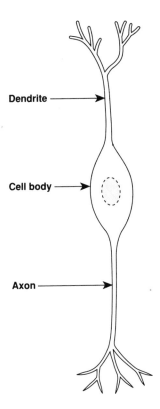

Figure 6.1
A neuron

The fundamental units of an artificial neural network (variously called units, nodes, neurodes) are modeled after individual neurons. Let's look at the principal parts of a typical individual neuron (see figure 6.1). Its dendritic tree collects excitatory and inhibitory inputs from other neurons, and passes these messages, as voltages, on to the cell body or soma. These voltages are added to its current voltage, if excitatory, or subtracted, if inhibitory. When a threshold is exceeded, an output voltage signal is transmitted down an axon to synapses that connect the leaves of the axonic tree to the dendrites of other neurons. Each synapse is a chemical connection between the axon in one neuron and a dendrite of the next. When the signal arrives at a synapse, vesicles of a chemical neurotransmitter are popped. The neurotransmitter then disperses across the

Formal neuron

Also called a linear threshold device or a threshold logic unit

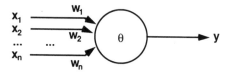

x_i -- the inputs
w_i -- the weights (synaptic strengths)
θ -- the threshold
y -- the output

$$y(t+1) = \begin{cases} 1 & \text{if } \sum_i w_i x_i(t) \geq \theta \\ 0 & \text{otherwise} \end{cases}$$

Figure 6.2
Formal neuron

synaptic gap, where it is picked up as an excitatory or inhibitory input on a dendrite of the postsynaptic neuron. And the process continues.

Neurons can be modeled formally, mathematically. Here is one such mathematical model, called a linear threshold device, that forms the fundamental unit comprising one kind of artificial neural network (see figure 6.2). First there are finitely many *inputs*, $x_1, x_2, \ldots, x_n$. Think of inputs as (possibly negative) numbers[4] in general, but restricted to the two Boolean values 0 and 1 for linear threshold devices. These inputs model both the excitatory (if positive) and the inhibitory (if negative) signals arriving at synapses from presynaptic neurons. The efficiency of a synapse in transmitting an incoming signal or, equivalently, the importance of this particular signal to the postsynaptic neuron, is represented by a number called its *weight* or synaptic strength. These weights are the numbers $w_1, w_2, \ldots w_n$, either positive or negative, one for each incoming synapse. The *threshold* that the voltage inside the cell body must reach in order to fire is represented by another number, θ, again possibly positive or negative. The *output* of a neuron is represented by yet another number, y, which takes on the Boolean value 0 or 1 at time t + 1, according to whether the weighted sum of the inputs, $\sum_{i=0}^{n} w_i x_i(t)$, is less than θ or not, where $x_i(t)$ is the ith input value at time t. Thus we have a formal model of a neuron, a formal neuron. Note that our formal neuron, or linear threshold device, is discrete both in time and in input/output values. It is discrete in time in that time proceeds in discrete moments enumerated by t = 0, 1, 2, 3, . . . , t, t + 1,. . . . The input and output values are restricted to the discrete set {0, 1}. Linear threshold devices are due to McCulloch and Pitts (1943). These ideas are not new.

Our formal neuron, or linear threshold device, seems to be a rather faithful model of a real neuron as described a few paragraphs back. The signals arriving at synapses are modeled by the inputs, the synaptic efficiency by the weights, the accumulation of voltages in the cell body by the weighted sum, the actual threshold by the formal threshold, and the voltage traveling down the axon by the output. Then why the caveat? Why is this a "rough," simplified model of a neuron? Let's tick off a few of the rough spots. In our model the output signal is represented by the magnitude of the output y, whereas in real neurons the significance of the signal most frequently is carried by the rate of firing, not the magnitude of a single firing. Another simplification allows a single neuron to excite one subsequent neuron via a positively weighted synapse, and to inhibit another via a negatively weighted synapse. In real nervous systems, individual neurons are either inhibitory or excitatory to all subsequent neurons to which they connect. And, of course, there are many details unaccounted for in the model, such as ion channels and neurotransmitters.

Computation with Formal Neurons

We've seen that a linear threshold device is a rough, simplified mathematical model of a neuron. So what? What can we do with such a simple model? With a single linear threshold device, not much. With networks of them, quite a lot! (McCulloch and Pitts 1943)

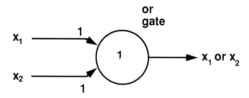

Figure 6.3
OR gate

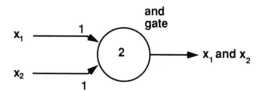

Figure 6.4
AND gate

A single linear threshold device can act as an *OR gate,* one of the standard devices used in microelectronics[5] (see figure 6.3): If either or both inputs are 1 (true), then the next output (x_1 or x_2) should also be 1 (true). Otherwise the output should be 0 (false). A linear threshold device with exactly two inputs, each with weight 1, and a threshold of 1 exhibits precisely this behavior. It is, by definition, an OR gate. Take a moment to check that this is so.

If you'd like an AND gate instead of an OR gate, one in which the output is 1 only when both inputs are 1, simply change the threshold to 2 (see figure 6.4). Or leave the threshold alone and change each weight to 0.5.

A NOT gate changes a 1 input to a 0 output and vice versa (see figure 6.5). A single input linear threshold device with weight −1 and threshold 0 does the job.

But these are trivial, you say, each involving only a single device. Yes, they are. But, as every computer architect knows, with AND gates, OR gates, and NOT gates, one can, at least theoretically, build any digital computer. Thus networks of linear threshold devices are computationally quite powerful. Such networks are, in fact, computationally universal.

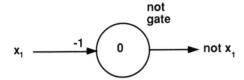

Figure 6.5
NOT gate

That is, they can compute anything that can be computed by a Turing machine.[6] Given a Turing machine and its initial input, Franklin and Garzon (1991) have provided a recipe (an effective algorithm) for building a network of these formal neurons that computes step by step exactly as the given Turing machine does. Thus, any computation that can be carried out by a Turing machine, and hence by a digital computer (Church–Turing thesis[7]), can be performed by an artificial neural network.

An Exclusive-Or Network

To begin to get a feel for these networks of formal neurons, let's look at one that's only a little more complex than AND gates and OR gates. It's called an exclusive-or device, or more commonly an XOR gate (see figure 6.6). An "or" becomes "exclusive" if we insist that one input, but not both, take on the value 1 in order to get an output of 1. I had cereal or pancakes for breakfast this morning, but not both. Put another way, the output of XOR is to be 1 only if the two inputs are different. An XOR gate is an anti-matching instrument. A little thought will convince you that a single formal neuron doesn't suffice to implement XOR. Just a few units will suffice, however.

In the figure, the leftmost circles represent *input units* that generate and pass forward the inputs. The two central units are called *hidden units* because they neither receive input directly nor produce output directly. The rightmost unit produces the output of the network. The hidden units and the *output unit* are linear threshold devices, formal neurons.

Let's spend a few moments watching this XOR net compute its output. Given two 0's as input, both weighted sums at the hidden units are below threshold, so that the output unit receives only 0 inputs, leading to a 0

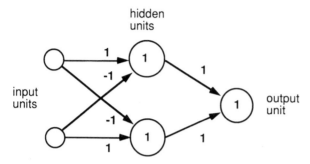

Figure 6.6
An XOR network

output as desired. Suppose the upper input unit receives a 1 and the lower a 0. At the next time step the weighted sum of the upper hidden unit is at threshold and that of the lower is below. Thus at the third time step the output unit receives an input of a 1 and a 0, leading to a weighted sum at threshold and, hence, an output of 1 as desired. If the 1 and 0 inputs are reversed, the situation is quite symmetrical and the result the same. The action is a little trickier when both inputs are 1. At time step two, both weighted sums of hidden units are 0, due to their excitatory and inhibitory inputs canceling one another. Thus at the third step the output unit receives 0's and produces a 0 as desired.

You might enjoy producing your own XOR net using one fewer hidden unit but allowing connections from the input units to the output units. Such a net would employ four units and five connections as opposed to the five units and six connections in the example above. The exercise is guaranteed to add to your understanding of how artificial neural networks work in specific cases, "understanding" in the sense of the quadratic understanding of chapter 5.

The XOR net we analyzed above is known as a layered, feed-forward network. Its composed of three layers of units, and all of the arrows point from lower-level layers to higher-level layers, that is, to the right. There is no feedback at all. But feedback can play an important role in computation via artificial neural networks, as we will see next.

Feedback and Word Recognition

Building an XOR device is a simple task. One might expect it to be easily accomplished using simple, artificial neural networks. How about something more challenging? One of the early connectionist models attempted a task that, although still a toy problem, required considerably more complexity in its network, including feedback.

McClelland and Rumelhart (1981; Rumelhart and McClelland 1982) tackled the problem of word recognition, at least for a small number of short words. Their network (see figure 6.7) is also layered but is not feedforward. Their units are not Boolean but, rather, take on values from an interval of real numbers.

Their idea for recognizing words is to begin by recognizing letters. Their idea for recognizing letters is to recognize the strokes that produced them. To keep the project computationally feasible, they restricted them-

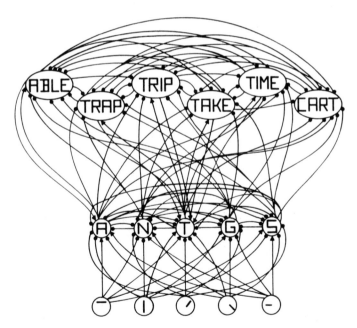

Figure 6.7
Word recognition network (reprinted from McCelland and Rumelhart 1981)

selves to four-letter words. For each of the four possible letter positions in a word, twenty-six letter units locally represent the letters of the English alphabet. (The representations are *local* in that each unit represents a letter in a one-to-one fashion. See the next section for more detail.) Thus the network uses 104 letter units. Only five of these are depicted in figure 6.7. Let's assume these represent five possibilities for the first letter position. The units in the lowest layer locally represent strokes. There must be four copies of the full set of stroke representing units. Note that there are more strokes than are depicted in the figure. For example, an N requires a long diagonal stroke that's not shown. In the topmost level, possible words are locally represented.

For the purpose of recognizing words, strokes are unrelated to one another. Hence, there are no connections between units in any of the stroke layers. The stroke layer and the letter layer, for each letter position, are *fully interconnected,* meaning that each stroke unit is connected to each letter unit. A stroke unit excites a letter unit if the corresponding stroke is used in forming the corresponding letter, and inhibits it otherwise. Excitatory connections are shown with little arrows and inhibitory connections end with small disks. Within the letter layer, for each letter position, a single unit must emerge victorious. Thus each letter unit within a given position inhibits every other letter unit, producing a *winner-take-all* situation. Similarly, each word unit inhibits every other word unit, resulting in another winner-take-all strategy that serves to recognize exactly one word.

Connections between the word layer and the four letter layers occur in both directions. A unit representing a word, say ABLE, with the letter A in the first position, is excited by the unit representing the letter A in the first position, and is inhibited by each unit representing some other letter in that position. And similarly for the B in the second position. Feedback occurs when the A in the first position unit is excited by the ABLE unit, as is the B in the second position unit, and so on.

Let's see how this network might behave if given noisy input like the one in figure 6.8. What word could this be? By some mysterious process you and I rather quickly conclude it has to be WORK. Perhaps we reason that the last letter must be either an R or a K, and that WORR isn't a word. McClelland and Rumelhart's network model reaches the same con-

Figure 6.8
Noisy input (reprinted from McCelland and Rumelhart 1981)

clusion, not in any obvious way by following rules, but rather by settling on the correct answer. Let's see if we can get some feeling about how this settling happens.

The units representing W, O, and R should rapidly gain ascendancy in their respective positions because each of their strokes is present and no others are. Units representing K and R should compete for ascendancy in the fourth position. Having the same strokes present, they should initially rise about the same amount. The feedback from the word level eventually distinguishes between them.

At the word level, units representing WORD, WORK, and FORK, among others (say WEAK, or WEEK), may be initially highly activated by virtue of several of their corresponding letter units running high. These letter units are, in turn, strengthened by the three word units. But D cannot win out in the fourth position because too little activation came from the strokes. Lack of input from D eventually weakens WORD. Similarly, FORK can't win out for lack of input from F in the first position. The network settles on WORK.

It's not the details of this process that are interesting but its ability to look at incomplete information and come to a correct conclusion. The popular computer maxim, "Garbage in, garbage out," seems to be violated here. From a cognitive science point of view, the network accomplishes word recognition, a form of categorization. From a computer science point of view, the network is acting as a *content addressable memory*, able to access the appropriate data record from part of its contents.

Also note that this process arrives at its correct conclusion via a form of statistical calculating, giving rise to a global dynamics that settles into some stable situation. This process apparently is not rule based. There's nothing that looks quite like the syntactic operators applied to symbols, unless one is willing to broaden the conventional meanings of these terms considerably.

Representation

Practitioners of symbolic AI often tout the importance of representation. Winston (1992, p. 18) raises this position to the level of a principle: "The representation principle: Once a problem is described using an appropriate representation, the problem is almost solved." Horgan and Tienson (1989), you'll recall, conclude that humans typically operate using representations but not rules. Later we'll visit cognitive cultures containing philosophers, psychologists, neurophysiologists, computer scientists, and roboticists who maintain that representation can be dispensed with altogether (Maturana and Varela 1980; Winograd and Flores 1986; Brooks 1991; Varela et al. 1991). The connectionist camp, for the most part, sides with the representationists.

Let's first distinguish between two forms of connectionist representation, local and distributed. *Local representation* employs one unit to represent one object, one concept, or one hypothesis. A one-to-one correspondence is set up between the units in the network and the items to be represented. Thus, with n units I could represent n objects; the ability to represent increases linearly with the number of units. The networks we've viewed so far all use local representation.

With *distributed representation*, on the other hand, each unit may participate in the representation of several items, and conversely, each item is represented by a pattern of activity over several different units. Thus you can represent as many items as you have subsets of units; n units can represent 2^n items. Theoretically, ten units, using distributed representation, can represent over a thousand items. The trade-offs are clear: distributed representation is much more computationally compact than local representation, whereas local representation is much easier to comprehend.

A third type of artificial neural network representation, *featural representation,* occupies a middle ground between local and distributed representation (Lloyd 1989, p. 104). Here individual items are represented distributively by patterns of activity over sets of units, and the individual units locally represent features of the given item. Featural representations can be programmed into a system or can occur with no human fore-thought during a training process, as we'll see shortly. Featural representation can lead to spontaneous generalization. For example, suppose you are "teaching" your network about the great apes, and you mention that chimps like bananas. If both chimps and gorillas are represented in a featured way, many of their features will be held in common, and may be very different from those of a gazelle or something else. If you then ask the network whether gorillas like bananas, it will probably tell you yes, on the basis of what it knows about chimps and on the similarity of their features. All this is likely to occur not via the application of rules but by the network settling on an answer.

Lloyd suggests classifying connectionist models according to their type of representation (1989, pp. 105–6). Locally represented systems model at the fully cognitive level. Since units represent concepts, the dynamics of the network would model the dynamics of thought itself. The distinction between the computational view of mind held by symbolic AI and traditional cognitive science, and a strong form of the connectionist view, is particularly clear here. In a locally represented connectionist model, there is nothing that looks at all like symbol manipulation via rules. There is no recognizable stored program. All this conflicts with the computer model of mind.

Featurally represented systems model at what Lloyd calls the microcognitive level At the conceptual level, patterns of activation interact in complex ways. Thoughts are then activation vectors. At the featural level, units can still be interpreted, inferences can sometimes be discerned, and the cognitive level is emergent.

Fully distributed systems model at the subcognitive level, since the individual units are uninterpreted. Cognition emerges only at the whole system level. Thus the connectionist model may be implementing some production system when viewed from a higher level of abstraction. These issues will come to the fore a little later in our tour. For now, let's have a look at some of the more pleasant features of artificial neural networks themselves.

Virtues of Artificial Neural Networks

Connectionists often claim that their tool of choice, the artificial neural network, will produce cognitive models superior to symbolic models because they enjoy inherent advantages in their architecture. In this section we'll look at some of these purported virtues. (A more extensive account of these issues was presented by McClelland et al. 1986.)

One of the most conspicuous properties of an artificial neural network is its lack of a central executive. Nobody's in charge. No one has the overall picture and makes decisions. Control is distributed. All decisions are made on local information. Each unit decides on its output solely on the basis of the input it gets from its neighbors, possibly including itself, and its internal state. It can't even tell one neighbor from another. Why is this a virtue? Because the network incurs no expense gathering global information and arriving at a global decision.

Another conspicuous benefit of the architecture is the automatic presence of default assignments. Give it an input, and you'll get an output. The network is going to do something, no matter what. That something is a default value for the situation at hand. With symbolic systems, a programmer laboriously builds in whatever defaults are to be present.

While visiting the word recognition example, we saw artificial neural networks complete patterns such as the corrupted word WORK. Pattern completion allows content addressability. Some of these networks have been designed as little databases (McClelland et al. 1986, pp. 23–29; McClelland and Rumelhart 1988, chap. 7).[8] If you want information out, just put part of it in.

Symbolic AI systems tend to be brittle. That is, a single, apparently small mishap often results in catastrophic failure. A widely circulated, but perhaps apocryphal, story illustrates this point graphically. A Venus lander, designed to land softly under the cloud cover, splattered unceremoniously due to a misplaced comma in its program. Connectionist networks using distributed representation, on the other hand, tend to degrade more gracefully. The failure of a small number of units is more likely to cause some degradation of performance rather than a catastrophic failure.

Note that spontaneous generalization, which we've previously encountered in connectionist networks, may well be considered a virtue. These networks also often exhibit global behaviors beyond the scope of any of their individual units. These are called emergent behaviors, and are considered by some to be a distinct advantage. And finally, there's the feature of artificial neural networks that brought them fame and fortune—learning. This virtue is definitely worth a more careful look.

Learning by Artificial Neural Networks

The output of a unit is often referred to as its *activation*. The pattern of this activation at a given time is called the network's *configuration* at that time. Think of a configuration as short-term memory, or what the network is representing at the moment. The pattern of weights, on the other hand, is more like long-term memory, representing what the network knows. This pattern of weights determines how the network will react to a given stimulus. In order for an artificial neural network to learn, it must change some of its behaviors, that is, it must respond differently to a given stimulus. For this to happen, weights must change. Thus *learning in artificial neural networks takes place via changing of weights.*[9]

Recall the example of an XOR network (see figure 6.9), this time with its units labeled with lowercase letters, and with its distinctive pattern of weights. This pattern is often represented in matrix form. Figure 6.10 shows the corresponding *weight matrix*.

Since there is no connection from a to a, a 0 occurs in the ath row, ath column of the matrix.[10] There is a connection from a to c with weight 1. Hence a 1 occurs in the ath row, cth column.

An artificial neural network is build on a directed graph, or digraph,[11] called the *architecture* of the network. The units of the network are the nodes of the digraph, and the weighted links are its arcs. Given a particular architecture, the set of all its possible weight matrices comprises its *weight space*. The architecture of the XOR network above is a digraph consisting of five nodes and six arcs. Thus its weight space will be composed of all 5×5 matrices containing 0's in all but perhaps the six positions specified by the existing arcs in the digraph. One could, for example,

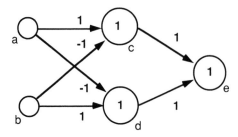

Figure 6.9
A labeled XOR network

$$
\begin{array}{c}
\quad\; a\; b\; c\; d\; e \\
\begin{array}{c} a \\ b \\ c \\ d \\ e \end{array}
\left[
\begin{array}{ccccc}
0 & 0 & 1 & -1 & 0 \\
0 & 0 & -1 & 1 & 0 \\
0 & 0 & 0 & 0 & 1 \\
0 & 0 & 0 & 0 & 1 \\
0 & 0 & 0 & 0 & 0 \\
\end{array}
\right]
\end{array}
$$

Figure 6.10
Weight matrix

enter weights at random in the positions not required to be zero and get a member of the weight space. You should not expect the corresponding network to behave like the XOR network.

As is so often the case with humans, a geometric view helps our understanding. A 5×5 weight matrix contains twenty-five weights (numbers), and thus can be thought of as a point in a 25-dimensional space.[12] The weight space can then be thought of as a subset of this 25-dimensional space. Learning, then, can be viewed as a search problem in weight space. You look from weight matrix to weight matrix, trying to find the one that will do your job best. Note the analogy between this view of learning and the view of problem solving as a search for a path through state space encountered during our visit to symbolic AI land.

Now we have some idea about what learning is, at least in artificial neural networks. The next question is how to make those networks learn. What heuristic strategies can we use to guide our search through weight space? There are at least five major strategies, or training styles, that can

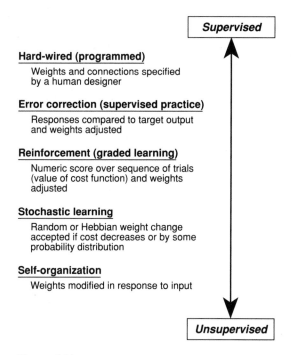

Figure 6.11
Training styles

be classified from the highly supervised to the highly unsupervised (see figure 6.11). Supervision is by humans, of course.

A hardwired, or hand-coded, network is the most highly supervised of all. The weights and connections are specified by a human designer. The word recognition model we've already visited is an example. Garzon and I specified all the weights and connections for a neural network implementation of a Turing machine (Franklin and Garzon 1991). Hardwiring is a reasonable strategy when you have a carefully thought-out model that works.

Error correction or supervised practice provides a somewhat less supervised training method. In this paradigm, responses are compared with targeted output and weights are adjusted so as to minimize the error. *Backpropagation* is by far the most common example of supervised practice. Here a layered, feed-forward network[13] is trained on a corpus of input-output exemplars. Each network output is compared with the desired output of the exemplar and the error is calculated. That error is then propagated back through the network and used to modify weights so as to reduce the error. Errors can be totaled over all the exemplars, defining an error surface in weight space. Back-propagation works via gradient descent (going downhill in the steepest direction) on that error surface. We'll encounter this popular and effective training method several times at future tour attractions.

Reinforcement or graded learning allows a still less supervised training paradigm for neural networks. This method reminds me of the child's game during which a blindfolded protagonist stumbles after a goal guided only by cries of "You're getting hotter" or "You're getting colder." For neural network reinforcement training, a numeric score, the value of a cost function, is calculated over a sequence of trials and the weights are adjusted so as to lower the cost. (A behaviorist might well jump at this method, protesting that this is how humans do it.) The interesting thing is the cost function. Where does it come from? From the designer, no doubt. Can such a cost function have evolved in us? I suspect so. We'll return to this issue during a later stop on the tour at the Isle of Artificial Life[14] (chapter 9).

Stochastic learning uses trial and error. Try out a random weight change and check the cost to see if it decreases. If it does, accept that change; if it doesn't, go back to the previous weights. Or follow this same procedure using Hebbian weight change. Hebb's rule (1949; or Anderson and Rosenfeld 1988, p. 50) says to increase the synaptic strength between any two connected neurons that fire almost simultaneously.

And finally, some neural nets self-organize, which is as unsupervised as you can get. Their weights are modified in response to input. How would you modify the weights in response to inputs? One possibility is to see which output was the strongest for a particular input and strengthen those connections even more while weakening neighboring connections a little. Repetition of this process can allow the net to categorize its inputs. We'll meet self-organizing systems again when we visit Edelman's work.

During the next major stop on our tour, we'll question the possible contribution of connectionism to cognitive science. Are there mechanisms of mind that can be modeled by artificial neural nets but cannot be modeled well via symbolic AI? Or can connectionism, at best, merely implement the symbolic paradigm without adding anything new? These questions spur the second AI debate.

Notes

1. "Connectionist" models are most often cognitive, whereas "artificial neural networks" often refer to purely computational models. Originally, "connectionism" referred to the Rochester school, which was distinguished by its use of local representation (an object or concept represented by a single node) vs. distributed representation (an object or concept represented by a pattern of activity over many nodes). "Parallel distributed processing" referred to the San Diego school, which relied on distributed representation. These distinctions have become blurred, with the term "parallel distributed processing" falling into disuse.

2. I can't resist including one more delightful quote from Lloyd: "the brain exemplifies the fact that it is all right to be very stupid if you're well connected."

3. That is, less than 1000 cycles per second.

4. I'm being deliberately vague about the kind of numbers being discussed. Mathematical readers can think of them as real numbers. However, most connectionist models are simulated on digital computers where "numbers" are restricted to finite subsets of the rational numbers.

5. In practice, NOR gates, the negation of OR gates, are commonly used, along with NAND gates.

6. To review the definition of a Turing machines, see chapter 4.

7. Again, see chapter 4.

8. The book referred to last comes with software illustrating many connectionist models in depth. It is highly recommended.

9. As so often happens when one tries to simplify, this assertion is not quite right. Learning can also occur via a change in the threshold. And, the threshold function that operates on the weighted sum of inputs to calculate the output of a linear threshold model is only one example of what is often called an activation function or a transfer function. There are many others. Presumably, an artificial neural network could also change its behavior, and thereby learn, by changing the activation functions of its units. This strategy is certainly not common.

10. Note that a connection with 0 weight into a unit has precisely the same effect on the weighted sum that unit produces as does no connection at all. Hence, for the purpose of constructing weight matrices, we shall assume that all connections are present but that some have 0 weights.

11. A directed graph consists of a set of nodes (often represented by dots) and a set of directed edges, or arcs (often represented by arrows), with each arc connecting two (not necessarily distinct) nodes in a fixed direction.

12. The physical space in which we live is traditionally regarded as being three-

dimensional, meaning that three numbers are required to specify the position of a point relative to some coordinate axis system. Mathematicians have generalized this notion so as to regard a sequence of n numbers as a point in n-dimensional space. These higher-dimensional spaces have proved useful in many fields, including physics, engineering, economics, and artificial neural networks.

13. The network is formed of layers of units. Each units sends output only to units in subsequent layers.

14. If you're impatient, see Ackley and Littman (1992).

7

The Second AI Debate

Setting the Stage

Two stops back on the tour, we visited the first AI debate. Philosophers, physicists, computer scientists, and others were arguing over whether there can be any such thing as AI, over whether artificial intelligence can exist in principle. Serious thinkers can be found on each side of the issue. As far as I can tell, the jury's still out.

Whereas the first AI debate pitted AI researchers against outsiders, the second is a family squabble between siblings. In one corner we find the symbolic AI people advocating a computer model of mind, and in the other corner the connectionists argue for a brain model of mind. Symbolic AI constructs its model of mind using computation as a metaphor; mental activity is like the execution of a stored program. Connectionism bases its model of mind on a nervous system metaphor; mental activity is like the settling of a network into a stable configuration. I refer to them as siblings for two reasons. First, both sides share the twin goals of understanding and implementing intelligence. And second, several of the practitioners of connectionism came from the ranks of disaffected symbolic AI researchers.

The symbolic AI people maintain that intelligence can be achieved only via symbol manipulation. (Recall the physical symbol hypothesis of SOAR's designers that we met in chapter 4.) Although admitting that connectionist models can implement symbolic structures,[1] and therefore intelligence, the symbolic AI corner denies that anything new can be obtained by doing so. That is, connectionism doesn't give us any information about cognition that isn't available from symbolic models. Connectionist models are at too low a level of abstraction to be useful, they say.[2]

In response, the connectionist camp claims to have made contributions. One such claim is from Lloyd (1989, p. 100): "The main contribution of connectionism to the science of the mind is the postulated formal treatment of highly interconnected networks of simple units." In other words, connectionist units don't have to work just like neurons. The basic idea is that intelligence and mind somehow emerge out of these highly interconnected groups of relatively simple units.[3]

The Connectionist Agenda

How do the connectionists see themselves? What are they all about? What do they want to do? Of the many people we might ask, McClelland, a founder of the field and an author of its "bible" (Rumelhart, McClelland, et al. 1986; McClelland et al. 1986), is an appropriate choice. His version of the connectionists' agenda, taken from an Internet message on the Connectionists List,[4] contains three major items:

· To find better methods of solving AI problems
· To model actual mechanisms of neural computation
· To explore mechanisms of human information processing.

Let's take them up one by one, since he has a little more to say about each.

McClelland's first purpose is "to find better methods of solving AI problems, particularly those that have proven difficult to solve by conventional AI approaches." This goal is by no means surprising, since McClelland is a cognitive scientist who became dissatisfied with symbolic methods. But have they succeeded? Well, yes and no. First the no. I personally know of nothing I would call a difficult AI problem that has been completely solved by connectionist methods. And now the yes. Connectionist models have proven particularly effective at visual pattern recognition, at learning to predict time series, at producing quick, good enough solutions to optimization problems. In many of these areas traditional computational methods still hold a slight advantage, but the connectionists have made remarkable progress in only a few years.

I think this comparison reflects the suitability of symbolic AI for mimicking rational thought. That is what symbolic AI does well, whereas connectionist models excel at pattern and information recognition. When a carpenter goes out looking for work, he looks for a door to put in or a deck to build. He doesn't look for a toilet to fix, because he has the wrong set of tools. The symbolic AI people have quite naturally looked for the kinds of problems their tools can help to solve. The connectionists are doing exactly the same. Of course, there is some overlap.

Also, keep in mind that until now, all connectionist models have been simulated on digital computers. Neural network chips are now on the market, with neural network boards and even neurocomputers not far behind. To reach their full potential, connectionist models depend on massive parallelism. Serial emulations hardly do them justice. I believe McClelland's first agenda item may well be achieved when connectionist models routinely run on massively parallel neurocomputers.[5]

Concerning his second agenda item, modeling mechanisms of neural computation, McClelland says:

There's lots of data on such things as the stimulus conditions under which particular neurons will fire, but there is little understanding of the circuitry that leads to the patterns of firing that are seen or the role the neurons play in overall system function. Connectionist models can help in the exploration of these questions.

Distinguish connectionist modeling carefully from computational modeling of neuronal function or neuronal group function. Connectionist models are greatly simplified. They're not detailed enough to model neuronal activity well at a low level of abstraction, but they can give useful information at higher levels. Although connectionist models have certainly proved useful, their promise is, in my view, still greater than their performance.

Finally, McClelland talks about human information processing:

The idea is that there is a set of putative principles of human information processing that are more easily captured in connectionist models than in other formalisms. The effort to determine whether these principles are the right ones or not requires the use of models, since it is difficult to assess the adequacy of sets of principles without formalization, leading to analysis and/or simulation.

Note that connectionism, as does symbolic AI, models the mind as an information processor. In that sense, they are siblings. This is the first time we've seen the connectionist brother saying to his symbolic AI sister, "Hey, I can do it better than you." Later on, we'll see that Edelman (1987, pp. 37–42) and others assert that brains are not information-processing systems in the sense that computers are. Information processing, according to them, is simply a metaphor that they are ready to throw out. This line of thought will lead us, in chapter 14, to the third AI debate, over the necessity of internal representations. In the meantime, let's visit a calculation argument against brains as computers.

The Hundred-Step Rule

Human reaction time is order of magnitude 500 milliseconds. That is, for a human to categorize a perception, retrieve a memory, disambiguate a word in a sentence, or perform some other single cognitive act requires something like half a second. "Something like" should be interpreted as within a factor of 10 more or less, that is, between 50 milliseconds and a few seconds. Consecutive neuron firing times fall within a narrow range around 5 milliseconds. Thus the number of firings per reaction is approximately 500 divided by 5, or about 100 neural firings. Feldman's *hundred-step rule*[6] is a consequence: *Human reactions are physiologically constrained to require roughly 100 serial steps to calculate.* Note that we are talking about reaction time, not decision time, not stopping and deliberating, but simply having an idea pop up.

But no serial computer computes anything worthwhile in 100 serial steps. Here we're talking about primitive steps corresponding, say, to single machine language instructions.[7] One concludes that nervous systems must depend heavily on their massive parallelism. One *mustn't* conclude that computers can't do useful work in the time it takes a human to process 100 serial steps. Remember that computers calculate much more rapidly than neurons do. Keep in mind also that serial computers can do informative, symbolic, cognitive modeling off-line,[8] often by simulating parallelism. What Feldman's argument does make clear is that serial computation, as a model for human cognition, has limitations.

Some may well object that some aspects of human cognition, say route planning or storytelling, are inherently serial, and thus may be modeled effectively by serial computers. Granted, but with a caution. Some apparently inherently serial processes can be performed more efficiently in parallel. For example, one of the most obviously serial tasks I can think of is to locate the end of a linked list, starting at the beginning. A linked list is

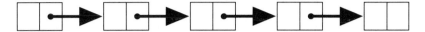

Figure 7.1
A linked list

a common data structure in computer science. It holds an ordered but unindexed list of items. Each item in the linked list (see figure 7.1) contains a slot for its content and a second slot for a pointer to (i.e., the address of) the next item in the list.

Each cell knows where its next cell is but cannot locate any other cell in the list. So suppose you want an algorithm to find the end of a linked list when given the beginning. Clearly, only from the first cell can you find the second, and only from the second cell the third, and so on. Thus, locating the end cell of a linked list seems to be a quintessentially serial process for which no amount of parallelism will help. More specifically, it seems absolutely and unmistakably clear to me that the time required to locate the end of a linked list is directly proportional to the length of the list, whether or not you're working with a parallel computer. If you've got a longer list, it's going to take you longer. However, in spite of being "absolutely and unmistakably clear," this belief is simply false. Hillis and Steele (1986) found a "data parallel algorithm" that finds the end faster. That is, with their algorithm, the time required to locate the end of a linked list increases quite slowly as the length of the list increases, not proportionally.[9]

The moral I draw from this story is not to trust my intuition as to what's usefully parallelizable and what's not.

Brain vs. Computer Model of Mind

Let's take a few minutes to make explicit the difference between the brain model and the computer model of mind. The computer model postulates symbolic internal representation, an internal language of thought. The brain model drops this idea. The computer model postulates stored programs in the form of production rules or some such. This idea is also dropped from the brain model, which postulates instead activity guided by connections in networks tuned by their weights.

In order to set the stage for a later visit to the "enactive" approach to mind during the third AI debate, let's view the distinctions between the brain and computer models of mind from the vantage point of their respective answers to three common questions. This formulation is quoted from Varela et al. (1991). First the questions and their symbolic AI responses (pp. 42–43):

Question 1: What is cognition?
Answer: Information processing as symbolic computation–rule-based manipulation of symbols.
Question 2: How does it work?
Answer: Through any device that can support and manipulate discrete functional elements—the symbols. The system interacts only with the form of the symbols (their physical attributes), not their meaning.
Question 3: How do I know when a cognitive system is functioning adequately?
Answer: When the symbols appropriately represent some aspect of the real world, and the information processing leads to a successful solution of the problem given to the system.

And now the same questions as answered by the connectionists (p. 99):

Question 1: What is cognition?
Answer: The emergence of global states in a network of simple components.
Question 2: How does it work?
Answer: Through local rules for individual operation and rules for changes in the connectivity among the elements.
Question 3: How do I know when a cognitive system is functioning adequately?
Answer: When the emergent properties (and resulting structure) can be seen to correspond to a specific cognitive capacity—a successful solution to a required task.

Though quoted from proponents of yet a third model of mind, the answers to these questions seem faithful to their respective camps, and highlight the distinctions between the symbolic AI and connectionist views.

One must carefully distinguish the use of the word "rule" in the symbolic AI answer to question 1 from the use of the same word in the connectionist answer to question 2. Once again we have a disparity of level. Symbolic rules (production rules) operate on high-level (representation-level) constructs, whereas connectionist rules operate locally on low-level (implementation level?) constructs.[10] The first is a rule in the sense of condition/action or premise/conclusion. The second is a mathematical rule (formula) for updating the activation of a unit or for changing the strength of a connection. This second use might well dig a pothole to trip an unwary traveler.

Note also that the answers to question 3 are alike in that each postulates an act of interpretation by a human. The problem mentioned in the symbolic AI answer is given by a human who, presumably, also decides whether it has been solved successfully. In the connectionist answer, the same may be said of the task and its solution. A human must also have "seen" whether an "emergent property" "corresponds to a "specific cognitive capacity." Later on our tour, we'll see pushes from several directions to get the human out of the loop.

Lloyd's Cautions

Connectionism offers a brain metaphor for the mind. Lloyd, whom we met earlier, cautions us about taking that metaphor too seriously. As philosophers are wont, he proposes a thought experiment to make his point. Suppose we're a century into the future and neurophysiologists have gone great guns. They've gotten more funding than the Human Genome Project and the Supercollider[11] combined, and have produced a complete wiring diagram of the brain. (Of course we know that not all brains are wired alike, but suspend disbelief. This caveat won't affect the argument.) Further, they've constructed a computer model that operates exactly as their wiring diagram of the brain prescribes. Now what? This model must be implemented as a computer program with 100 billion subroutines, one for each neuron. If that's not imposing enough, it must have a million billion subroutine calls, one for each synapse. Their number may have surpassed the national debt. What can you do with such a program? Even a simple cognitive act couldn't be simulated in a lifetime on any conceivable computer. Ignoring for a moment the problem of scale, suppose you *could* run it.

The model is, in essence, only a wiring diagram of the brain. That's not going to tell you much about cognition. Lloyd states the goal of cognitive neuroscience as "a principled interpretation of our understanding of the brain that transfigures it into an understanding of the mind" (1989, page 93). A total brain simulation does little to meet this goal. It does not "transfigure" our understanding. It provides no "principled interpretation." To use Lloyd's metaphor, it amounts no more to an understanding of mind "than photocopying an alien script amounts to translating it." Hence, let's be cautious. That connectionist models are based *roughly* on brains needn't, per se, add to their value as cognitive models.

Lloyd goes on to offer a second caution: "Just because we can describe the behavior of a complex system with cognitive language does not make the system cognitive and certainly does not make the system a mind." He presents the following thought experiment to illustrate his point (1989, pp. 93–94).

This time let us imagine a much simpler device, without biological pretensions. Call it a Computational Associational Reactive device, or CAR for short. It will be another simulation of the brain but greatly simplified: Just as brains receive many inputs at once, so will the CAR device, which will have about ten distinct simultaneous inputs. These inputs are processed in parallel as in the brain. CAR's outputs are also parallel and distributed, again varying along ten or so dimensions. All of this is mechanical; but under a suitable interpretation, CAR provides a model of a complex cognitive task—face recognition. Our interpretation of CAR maps facial features onto ten input dimensions and name features onto ten output dimensions. For example, perhaps one input variable will stand for the height of a forehead and one output variable for the first letter of a simple name. Though the interpretation scheme is not obvious, with patience we can find a consistent scheme, supporting the interpretation of CAR as a cognitive model. It may not work just as we do, but it does "recognize faces" in that when a face is encoded along the ten input dimensions, an (encoded) name pops out. Face recognition is a cognitive task, so CAR looks like a system to study for insight into the brain and the mind.

This is a cautionary thought experiment for the simple reason that CAR is an automobile. Its parallel inputs include specific quantities of air and gasoline, the state of the accelerator, gearshift, steering wheel, ignition system, and so forth. Its parallel outputs include exhaust, forward motion, direction of movement, and so on. One can also interpret it as a model of face recognition, but the unveiling of an old Ford Falcon ought to give us pause. We are warned against succumbing to the lulling rhythms of the language of cognitive science.

Lloyd has been evenhanded with his cautions, first warning us against taking connectionism to the extreme, and then warning us against following symbolic AI down the garden path to the junkyard. With these cautions in mind, let's meet one of the main protagonists in this second AI debate.

Fodor's Attack

A quick, and somewhat simplistic, view of Fodor's attack on connectionism follows (Fodor and Pylyshyn 1988; Fodor and McLaughlin 1991). Why quick, and why simplistic? Well, quick because I haven't the patience to devote as much time to this tour stop as it deserves. We could easily spend our whole tour on this one sight alone. And simplistic, because Fodor's arguments, as those of philosophers are wont to be, are both subtle and intricate, and can be presented only in overly simplified form if they are to be presented briefly. I'd like to give you the flavor of what Fodor and his cohorts are putting forth by describing one of their arguments.

Fodor says that thoughts have composite structure, which he refers to as compositionality. Put in linguistic terms, words are composed to form phrases, phrases are composed to form sentences, sentences to form paragraphs, and so on. In logical terms, constants, predicates, operators, and quantifiers compose to form propositions; propositions, operators, and quantifiers compose to form new propositions; and so on.[12] Thoughts may be expressed linguistically, logically, or in some other form, but can be composed to form new thoughts. Compositionality is an essential feature of thought.

Thus thoughts have composite structure. Cognitive processes are sensitive to the structure of the thoughts they process. Symbolic AI systems represent entities compositionally and process them in a structure-sensitive matter. On the other hand, connectionist processes operate via statistical association and are not structure-sensitive. Hence, connectionism, says Fodor, can add nothing to cognitive modeling beyond the contributions of symbolic AI.

Fodor does concede that connectionist models may provide *mere* low-level implementation of symbolic AI structures and processing. You can build symbolic models out of these connectionist models, but that is the best you can do. McClelland's "principles of human information processing that are more easily captured in connectionist models" simply don't exist, according to Fodor.

Of course, not many connectionists concur. Smolensky (1988), one of several physicists-turned-connectionist, prefers to treat connectionist models as subsymbolic rather than as implementing symbolic AI. The subsymbolic level lies between the neuronal level and the symbolic level, with individual connectionist units modeling neuronal groups rather than neurons. He views symbolic rules as approximations of what is really happening at this subsymbolic level, not exactly right but close.

Lloyd (1989, p. 126) claims that, lacking a stored program, "connectionist networks are manipulating representations noncomputationally": "That is, there are black boxes in [connectionist] systems which have representations as inputs, representations as outputs, but nothing representational in between." Computers operate on symbolic representations, by means of rules. Lloyd claims that connectionist models do it in some other fashion. But what other fashion? What other mechanism? Let's look at one candidate.

Chalmers's Defense

Chalmers asserts that despite Fodor's arguments to the contrary, connectionist models can process in a structure-sensitive way. And, in an absolutely unphilosopher-like manner, he proceeds to construct a neural network (connectionist model) that does so. But I'm getting ahead of myself.

Following van Gelder (1990), Chalmers (1990) distinguishes two versions of compositionality, the concatenative version that Fodor has in mind and a functional version. In the concatenative version, two symbol tokens are composed by concatenating them, that is, by placing one next to the other. In functional composition, on the other hand, functions[13] operate on symbol tokens, producing coded representations having a complex compositional structure. To appreciate distinguishing features of these two forms of compositionality, it helps to have a nodding acquaintance with the classical AI programming language, LISP. Being a longtime LISP hacker, I'll happily introduce you.

LISP, an acronym for LISt Processing, uses simple lists as its basic data structure. A left parenthesis signals the beginning of a list (a b c), and a right parenthesis ends it. The elements of the list are separately by spaces. LISP operates on lists by means of functions, typically producing other lists. These functions are asked to operate on their arguments using a list of the form (function-name argument1 argument2).

The fundamental constructor of lists in LISP, a function called cons, allows concatenative composition. It operates as the following example indicates: (cons d (a b c)) produces (d a b c), that is, cons inserts its first argument, d, as the new first element in its second argument, (a b c), yielding the expanded list (d a b c). That's how lists are put together. How are they taken apart? By functions, what else? The fundamental LISP extractor functions, first and rest, together act to undo what cons does: first returns the first element of its single argument, thus (first (d a b c)) returns d; rest returns its argument missing its first element, so (rest (d a b c)) returns (a b c).

Symbolic AI, Chalmers points out, allows exactly these classical symbol-manipulating operations of construction and extraction, *and no other.* You can put things together (compose them) and take them apart (extract them), and that's all. Symbolic systems have only compositional structure. Beyond this are only atomic components. They don't have any structure of their own. You can cons d into (a b c), but you can't get down into d itself. To change the tense of a sentence, say (stan is going on a tour) to (stan went on a tour), first extractions, and then concatenations, are required. Symbolic AI has no means of making that change directly. Concatenation and extraction are allowed, and that's it.

Connectionism is richer, says Chalmers. It allows you to operate holistically on functionally composed representations, that is, without first proceeding through the step of extraction. But this is precisely what must be proved to show that Fodor's argument is wrong. Cognitive models must use operations other than composition and extraction to go beyond mere implementations of symbolic AI models. Further, such models must operate directly on distributed representations—directly, in that extractions and compositions are not allowed. Chalmers wants to produce just such a model. As a major tool he uses another mechanism of mind—interest in its own right, which we'll visit next.

Pollack's RAAM

An often applied neural network architecture called recursive auto-associative memory, RAAM for short, was produced by Pollack (1990).[14] Let's pick this name apart as a first step in understanding what RAAM's all about. "Memory" refers to some sort of storage device. An "associative memory" stores input/output pair associations. Given an input pattern, it should produce the associated output pattern, or perhaps the output pattern associated with the closest match the system can find to the input. In an "auto-associative memory" each input pattern is associated with itself as the output pattern.

Associate a pattern with itself? Why would you want to do that? If you already have the input pattern, why go looking for it in an auto-associative memory? Ah, but such initial intuitions can be misleading. Why would one want a number that counts nothing? Because zero is of great utility. And then there's the infamous empty set, the set with no elements, that's indispensable in set theory. You'll soon see that auto-associative memory has much to recommend it.

A recursive procedure is one that calls itself during its operation. Since we're now slightly acquainted with LISP, let's look at a recursive LISP function as an example. Suppose I want a function that returns the number of elements in a simple list, that is, given the list (a b c), it would return the number 3. LISP code defining such a function, named length, follows:

```
(defun length (list)
       (if (null list) 0
           (+ 1 (length (rest list)))))
```

Here's a verbal description of what this code means. The first line says that we're defining a function named length with one argument named list. The second line says that if the list, list, is null (empty), then return a 0, else execute the next line. The third line finds the length of all of the list but its first element, and adds 1 to it. Note that the recursive

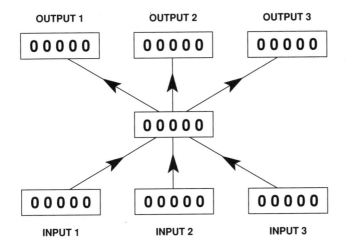

Train the output to the input.

Figure 7.2
RAAM architecture (redrawn from Chalmers 1990)

function `length` calls itself in the third line. Applying `length` to a small list such as (a b c) helps in understanding recursion. Take it as an exercise.

A recursive auto-associative memory, then, associates patterns with themselves in a recursive way. The ultimate goal is to store sentences[15] in a fixed amount of space regardless of their length, a kind of fixed-length compaction. Let's see how all this is done.

Imagine an artificial neural network with three sets of five input units, a single set of five hidden units, and another three sets of five output units (figure 7.2). Each input unit is connected to each hidden unit, and each hidden unit to each output unit. Train the network as an auto-associator via backpropagation, whose acquaintance we made in chapter 6. That is, train it so that its output pattern is identical with its input pattern. We now have an auto-associative memory.

Our trained artificial neural network has three layers: an input layer, a hidden layer, and an output layer. An input pattern of length 15, presented to the input layer, will induce a coded version of itself in the hidden layer at the next time step. This encoded pattern will induce the original input

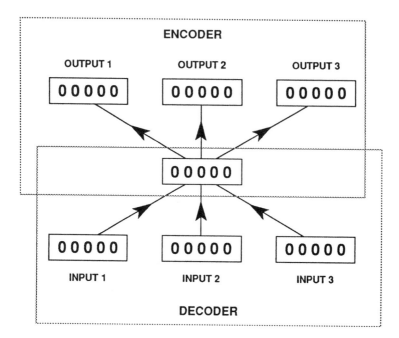

Figure 7.3
Encoder and decoder (redrawn from Chalmers 1990)

pattern on the output layer at the next time step. Thus we may regard the bottom two layers as an encoding device, and the top two as a decoding device. Taken together, they constitute the two necessary portions of a device for compressing data, an encoder and a decoder (figure 7.3). The compression device, in this case, compresses three to one.

In these days of graphical computing, compressors are useful devices. The computer screen I'm looking at right now displays almost a million dots (pixels, in computer science jargon). A single graphic image from this screen would occupy a goodly chunk of storage space. If we had an auto-associative memory with a million inputs rather than fifteen, we could compress that data to one-third size, using the encoder, and store the compressed version. The decoder could later serve to put the image back in its original form.[16]

So far we've talked about our encoder/decoder pair as being an auto-associative memory. But Pollack calls it a *recursive* auto-associative memory. How can this encoder/decoder pair be used recursively? Suppose that a word can be represented by five units. Take a sentence like "The vervet monkey fearfully screamed an eagle alarm." Using representations of the three words in the first phrase, "The vervet monkey," as input, encode the phrase as a five-tuple of values of the hidden units, called phrase 1. Adding a placeholder, nil, to the second phrase, "fearfully screamed," brings its word count to 3. Encode the extended phrase, "fearfully screamed nil," as phrase2. Then encode the third phrase, "an eagle alarm," as phrase3. Now comes the recursive part. Use the three encoded phrases—phrase1, phrase2, and phrase3—as input to the encoder, yielding a five-tuple encoding of the entire sentence, sentence1. To retrieve the original sentence, send sentence1 to the decoder as input, yielding codes for the three phrases as output. Each of these is then decoded separately, and the original sentence reconstructed. This is an overly simplified account in several respects,[17] but it illustrates recursive use of an auto-associative memory.

Pollack's RAAM, in principle, allows fixed-length representation of arbitrarily long sentences. The "in principle" caveat is included because computer systems are limited in the number of numbers they can discriminate, and because errors tend to accumulate as we recurse to deeper depths. With RAAM well in hand, let's see what Chalmers does with it.

Passivization of Sentences

As we've seen, Fodor claims that connectionist models are incapable of structure-sensitive processing because they operate purely statistically. Chalmers offers, as a counterexample, a connectionist system that converts active sentences to passive form without extracting and reusing parts of the active sentences (1990). His system works directly with representations encoded via Pollack's RAAM.

Chalmers first builds and trains a 3 × 13 RAAM (figure 7.4). (We previously looked at a 3 × 5 RAAM.) He then builds a second three-layer network with thirteen input and thirteen output units. This network is also trained via back-propagation to convert an encoding of an active sentence to an encoding of its passive form. To use the completed system to passivize a sentence, one just encodes the sentence using the RAAM,

Output: Distributed rep of passive sentence

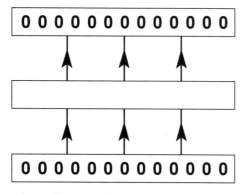

Input: Distributed rep of passive sentence

Figure 7.4
Transformation network (redrawn from Chalmers 1990)

then runs the encoded version through this second network, and finally decodes the resulting output.

Chalmers claims the encoded distributed representation of a sentence still maintains the structure of the sentence, because that structure can be recovered from the encoded version by decoding. This encoding illustrates functional rather than concatenative composition. The encoded distributed representation of the active sentence is then processed by the second network, the processing occurring holistically, without any kind of extraction.

For this plan to work requires a trained passivizer net. Chalmers used forty active sentences and their passive versions as training pairs. Both active and passive sentences were encoded via the RAAM encoder. These encoded representations were then used to train and passivizing net, with the active sentence RAAM encoding serving as input and its passive form as the target. After training, the entire system, RAAM and passivizer, worked perfectly on the training sentences. Training was successful.

But did the system really know how to passivize sentences, or had it simply memorized the appropriate responses to these forty sentences? When tested with forty active sentences other than those it was trained on, twenty-six decoded to the correct passive, thirteen produced one incorrect word, and one showed an incorrect sentence structure. Analysis showed that all the errors occurred during the encoding/decoding process, and not during passivizing. Not only did the system generalize, it generalized quite well.

Chalmers concludes that RAAM representations are well suited for direct structure-sensitive operations, and that they can be used directly to train connectionist models via backpropagation. He asserts the impossibility of describing this system at any level of functional abstraction as an implementation of a purely symbolic process. Compare this assertion to that of Fodor and McLaughlin: "... *the constituents of complex activity vectors typically aren't 'there' so if the causal consequences of tokening a complex vector are sensitive to its constituent structure, that's a miracle*" (1991, p. 347). These "complex activity vectors" are the encoded versions of active sentences. They have no constituents, so whatever structure-sensitive processing took place didn't depend on constituent structure. Something other than an implementation of a symbolic system must be going on. Hence, we have a counterexample to Fodor's attack. Maybe a "miracle"?

Is Connectionism Richer?

Earlier we noted Chalmers's claim that connectionist representations are inherently richer than symbolic representations. Symbolic representations have primitive atomic components and compositional structures, and that's all. Connectionist representations also have a compositional structure, as we've just seen. But instead of having primitive atomic components, they have a complex, distributed microstructure containing much more information. Let's look at an example to clarify what's meant here.

Suppose I'm going to represent animals by using a connectionist representation with microfeatures. One unit may represent the number of legs, another the number of horns, and so on. Each species of animal is represented by its vector of features. Each feature may take part in the representation of several different species, and each species is represented by a host of different features. This is distributed representation. Suppose we represent gorillas, and include a feature asserting that gorillas like bananas. If we now ask the system if chimps like bananas, without having included such a feature for chimps, it's not difficult for a connectionist system to respond yes because chimps and gorillas have so many features in common.

Still, I'm not convinced that connectionism is inherently richer than symbolic AI. Though symbolic systems all ultimately rest on primitive atomic elements, these can be chosen at as fine a grain size as needed. I can imagine, for example, a symbolic system that can handle the chimps and bananas question nicely, concluding that chimps probably like bananas because it knows that gorillas do and that the two species are similar in many respects.

Well, we've seen attacks on connectionism and defenses of it. Our next visit may be a little harder to interpret.

Representations Without Rules

Horgan and Tienson, philosophers and colleagues of mine, talk about representations without rules (1989). They come down strongly for the necessity of representations, and equally strongly in opposition to rules. It's not clear that they're wholly in the connectionist camp, but their arguments do seem to lend credence to a connectionist view.

They assert the need for representations as follows:

The cognitive system needs representations that can be processed in highly interactive, highly content sensitive, ways. That is, it needs representations that contain repeatable predicates applied to repeatable subjects, so that the relevant relations of co-reference and co-prediction can get encoded and thus can get accommodated during processing. In short, it needs syntactic structure, a language of thought. (1989, p. 155)

So far, Horgan and Tienson haven't strayed from the symbolic camp. The phrase "language of thought" derives from a book of that title by Fodor (1975).

And why are representations needed? How else, they ask, could one take into account all the relevant factors with which to make a decision, for example, about what to do next during a basketball game? Or for another, it seems clear to me that in planning a route from an unusual starting point in a city I know well to a familiar destination, I use semivisual representations. I conjure up a sequence of intersections, landmarks, and so on. It's hard for me to imagine planning such a route without some use of representations. A plan itself is a sequence of representations. This issue will pop up again when we visit the third (and last?) AI debate over the need for representations.

So much for representations. What do Horgan and Tienson say about rules? First, note that by a rule they mean a hard, high-level rule, hard in the sense of being exceptionless, and high-level in that it operates on high-level representations. The formula (rule) for computing the weighted sum of the inputs to a connectionist unit would be hard but not high-level. The rule asserting that birds fly would be high-level but not hard, since penguins are birds that don't fly.

Again basketball is a canonical example. Here you are, the point guard on a fast break. You have to decide whether to shoot or to pass off. What sorts of issues are relevant? Your position on the floor, the positions of the other players, both teammates and opponents. All their speeds and directions. The offensive and defensive strengths of these individual players. Who's hot and who's not? Who is guarding whom? Your center of gravity. How many points you have scored that night. Whether the guy you might pass to has a girlfriend who is watching and whom you are after. And the decision must be made in milliseconds. With this background, Horgan and Tienson build their argument:

> It seems very unlikely that this sort of thing [playing basketball] could be done by a program. . . .
> Any of these constraints can come into play in any combination—thereby threatening computation explosion. . . .
> All of these constraints are soft constraints. Any one of them can be violated while the system is working properly. . . .
> [Symbolic AI] can produce a semblance of this softness only by adding exceptions to its rules, which enormously compounds the computational problem. (1989, p. 156)

It is certainly hard for me to imagine a symbolic expert system that could play point guard in real time. It's true that Andersson's robot Ping-Pong player uses a symbolic expert system to choose its next stroke (1988), but the Ping-Pong player's task seems orders of magnitude less complicated than the point guard's.[18] The number and complexity of the issues to be considered during a fast break seem almost unlimited. Each of these issues imposes constraints on possible choices. Any constraint seems capable of combining with any other, so that the number of combinations of constraints would seem to increase without bound. And each of these constraints admits of a seemingly endless number of exceptions, with each exception requiring an additional rule. And we've considered only decision making, not the probably more difficult problems of perception and motor control. Animals are capable of amazing feats of computation in real time. Our computers seem much more limited. I'll believe in a robot point guard based on a symbolic expert system only when I see it.

(Art Graesser asks at this point, "What about a case-based system?" Cased-based systems decide on actions by analogy with previously experienced, similar situations. Brief accounts of such systems can be found in standard AI texts [Rich and Knight 1991] along with further references. We'll meet this concept again on a visit to the work of Brustoloni. But to answer Art's question, I'm less skeptical about a case-based point guard than I am about one that's rule based.)

In support of an essentially limitless supply of possible exceptions, Horgan and Tienson point out that all, or virtually all, psychological laws will be, ceteris paribus, generalizations, that is, of the form If A and nothing else is relevant, then B. As an example, they say, suppose Susie is thirsty for a beer. If she thinks there is a beer in the fridge, and if nothing else is relevant, then maybe she will go and get a beer. But maybe she doesn't want to miss a conversation that's going on. Or maybe she doesn't want to stop reading her book in the middle of a paragraph. Or maybe she doesn't want to drink a beer in front of her mother. Or maybe. . . . One could always dream up one more exception. The number must be endless. Hence a rule-based system, in the sense of hard, high-level rules, seems at best highly improbable.

Horgan and Tienson give connectionism something concrete to shoot at. How does one model decision making under myriad, simultaneous, soft constraints? Many connectionists would maintain that this kind of task is exactly what artificial neural networks do best. The problem is to make them do it best in a complex real-time domain comparable with basketball.

Their metaphor of basketball, with multiple competing and conspiring factors influencing every decision, as a goal of cognition also lends support to the notion of a multiplicity of mind. Thinking of these factors as independent agents, each "clamoring for attention," gives us a foretaste of Minsky's society of mind (1985) and of John Jackson's pandemonium theory of mind (1987), both of which we'll visit later on the tour.

So after all this debate, what are we left with? Perhaps a clearer picture of just where each contestant stands. Let's see if we can systematically catalog and contrast the positions (table 7.1). As is typical with such succinct comparisons, some caveats are called for. Here are some.

Not all symbolic rules are hard. Some receive hypotheses with confidence factors attached and assign confidence factors to their conclusions. But a single number can never do justice to all possible exceptions. I don't think confidence factors invalidate any of the arguments we've heard.

And not all symbolic systems are rule-based. Some newer systems are case-based and, as such, not subject to a combinatorial explosion of exceptions.

Since the arrival of parallel processors, symbolic AI has moved toward their use. Hence, not all multiple-constraint situations are handled sequentially, although almost all still are. And parallel actions can be taken on serial machines; it just takes longer.

Table 7.1
Symbolic AI versus Connectionism

Symbolic AI	Connectionism
Representations are syntactically structured.	Activity patterns over sets of units represent structure.
Cognition is accomplished via hard, representation level rules.	Problems are solved by networks settling into states fitting well with constraints.
Multiple constraints are handled sequentially.	All constraints are put into the hopper at once and allowed to do their work.
Representations of memories are stored.	Only active representations are present. Representation-forming dispositions reside in the weights.

The corresponding assertion about connectionist models handling multiple constraints in parallel is ideally, but not practically, true. Most connectionist models today are simulated on sequential digital computers. However, artificial neural network chips are now available, with boards allowing their use just around the corner. When real neurocomputers are common, this assertion will be true.

The last line of table 7.1 requires some additional comment. Symbolic models typically contain symbolic representations, often in encoded form. Connectionist models must reconstruct representations each time they are needed. The difference is analogous to that between looking up the current principal owed on your mortgage from a table versus calculating it from a formula. The table holds the representation you are looking for explicitly, whereas it is implicitly available from the formula. In connectionist models, and in human brains, representations are available only implicitly. Cues are required to trigger the calculating process that reconstructs them. Only currently active symbols are explicitly present. Representation-forming dispositions that serve to reconstruct symbols reside in the strengths of connections (synapses). Memories are not stored but reconstructed. The dispositions, the procedures for reproducing the memories, are stored in a distributed way, not as individual little files that you can label as a representation of a particular memory. Connectionist models, and humans, re-create their memories.

There are several reasons for optimism about connectionism. First, connectionist representations can have arbitrarily complex syntactic structure. They can be expected to do anything a symbolic model can, because they can do anything that a computer (Turing machine) can do (Franklin and Garzon 1991). Second, connectionist models are good at satisfying multiple soft constraints, at softly folding together multiple items of information. Third, the lack of stored information may help connectionist models bypass the frame problem. And fourth, from Horgan and Tienson, "Robust softness at the representational level is likely to rest upon a form of subrepresentational softness in which the causal links typically work collectively rather than singly" (1989, p. 166). Connectionist models may well be able to implement systems driven by multiple soft constraints. These are reasons for optimism.

Finally, a quote from Lloyd ends this stop on our tour: "connectionism is a study of great value even if connectionist models are poor shadows of brains" (1989, p. 126). They certainly are that.

During our next tour stops we'll visit genetic algorithms and classifier systems to get an evolutionary view of mechanisms of mind.

Notes

1. Connectionist models are computationally universal (Franklin and Garzon 1991), as we saw in chapter 6.

2. A similar level of abstraction argument is used against cognitive neuroscience, the attempt to understand cognitive function by studying activity in the nervous system. My friend Art Graesser uses a TV metaphor, asserting that one would be foolish to attempt to understand TV programming by studying electrical activity in the hardware of television sets.

3. Graesser's symbolic network model of human question answering, QUEST, (Graesser and Franklin 1980) can be seen as another step somewhat in this direction. Though his networks are not so highly interconnected as typical connectionist models (much less as nervous systems), there is an elegant formal theory behind them.

4. The Internet is a worldwide electronic communications network. On it one can send and receive electronic mail, download files, access distant computers remotely, and so on. Messages can be posted on lists on the Internet for the perusal of subscribers to those lists. That is, each posted message is automatically mailed to each subscriber. I subscribe to the Connectionists List. The agenda referred to above was posted by McClelland.

5. I take this prediction seriously enough to bet a fair amount of effort on it. The AMNIAC project (Garzon, Franklin et al. 1992), to produce a general-purpose neurocomputer, has reached the hardware prototyping stage. An optical version has been designed (Caulfield, Garzon, Boyd, and Franklin submitted). Proposals for funding of both optical and VLSI implementations have been submitted as of this writing.

6. I have no reference for this, having first heard Feldman lecture about it at the University of Memphis some years back.

7. Machine language is the primitive language of a computer, typically expressed in strings of zeros and ones. Even the most trivial chore useful to a human requires many machine-language instructions.

8. In computerese, off-line is the opposite of real time. A computer operating in real time responds to its sequence of inputs as they come in, dealing with one before the next arrives. A computer operating off-line stores its inputs and re-

sponds to them as it can. Real-time responsiveness will be necessary for implementing machine intelligence.

9. In technical terms, their algorithm is of order $\log_2 N$ rather than order N. For a clear explanation of these terms see Harel (1987, chap. 6).

10. Talk of a connectionist model operating at a *low* level of abstraction may well seem to contradict my recent warning about confusing these models with models of neuronal or neuronal group function. There I spoke of connectionist models as being at a *higher* level of abstraction. The apparent contradiction results from "higher" and "lower" being relative terms. Smolensky (1988) places connectionist models in a "subsymbolic" slot above low-level implementation (neurons) and below higher-level abstractions (symbol processing). We'll meet him briefly in just a bit.

11. Congress shot me down on this one by cutting off funding. Feel free to replace "Supercollider" with your favorite "big science" project.

12. Here's a brief glossary of logical terminology. Constants typically represent specific entities, such as Socrates. Predicates represent some assertion about entities, such as "Socrates *is mortal.*" Operators typically join predicates or propositions, such as "All men are mortal *and* Socrates is a man." Quantifiers assert the scope of an assertion, such as "*All* men are mortal."

13. Recall from your math classes that a function, say f, operates on one or more elements, say x and y, of its domain to produce an element, $f(x,y)$, of its range.

14. Pollack, a computer scientist by trade, is by avocation a hilarious stand-up comic. If you get a chance to hear him, don't miss it. I'm sorry that only his RAAM act can be part of this tour.

15. RAAMs actually store trees, but not biological trees. To a computer scientists, a tree is a particularly useful data structure. The organization chart of your favorite bureaucracy is no doubt an example of this sense of a tree.

16. I've given you a somewhat simplified account of this process. A single pixel might well take more than one unit to represent its current value.

17. That is, in the length of the representations and in the accuracy of the decoding. The original sources (Pollack 1990; Chalmers 1990) provide full accounts.

18. My friend and son-in-law, Bob Sweeney, was amazed to hear of a robot Ping-Pong player, and quite reasonably asked, "Is it any good?" It plays "robot Ping-Pong" on a slightly downsized table with shots over the net constrained to travel within a wire rectangle directly over the net. The human opponent always serves, since the robot has only one arm. The robot plays completely defensively, only attempting to get the ball back in play. Within these limits it plays well enough to consistently beat its maker, who looks like a middling amateur player. There's a video available, so judge for yourself.

8

Evolution, Natural and Artificial

It is raining DNA outside. On the bank of the Oxford canal at the bottom of my garden is a large willow tree, and it is pumping downy seeds into the air. There is no consistent air movement, and the seeds are drifting outwards in all directions from the tree. Up and down the canal, as far as my binoculars can reach, the water is white with floating cottony flecks, and we can be sure that they have carpeted the ground to much the same radius in other directions too. The cotton wool is mostly made of cellulose, and it dwarfs the tiny capsule that contains the DNA, the genetic information. The DNA content must be a small proportion of the total, so why did I say that it was raining DNA rather than cellulose? The answer is that it is the DNA that matters. The cellulose fluff, although more bulky, is just a parachute, to be discarded. The whole performance, cotton wool, catkins, tree and all, is in aid of one thing and one thing only, the spreading of DNA around the countryside. Not just any DNA, but DNA whose coded characters spell out specific instructions for building willow trees that will shed a new generation of downy seeds. Those fluffy specks are, literally, spreading instructions for making themselves. They are there because their ancestors succeeded in doing the same. It is raining instructions out there; it's raining programs; it's raining tree-growing, fluff-spreading, algorithms. That is not a metaphor, it is the plain truth. It couldn't be any plainer if it were raining floppy discs.

—Richard Dawkins, *The Blind Watchmaker*

Evolution of Mind

Our tour now takes a Darwinian turn. Many of the sights are chronicled by Dawkins in *The Blind Watchmaker* (1987). It's sobering to have him point out that "living organisms exist for the benefit of DNA rather than the other way around" (p 126). That's you and I he's talking about. "An individual body is a large vehicle or survival machine built by a gene co-operative for the preservation of [its members]" (p. 192). If we're our bodies, that's what we're all about. But what about minds? Since, for the duration of this tour, we've made the physicalist assumption that minds are what brains do (natural minds, anyway), minds must also serve the preservation of the genes. But what are minds for, anyway? They decide what to do next, which certainly affects the preservation of the genes. I sometimes think that we are allowed to choose the tactics while the genes provide the strategy. Within the strategy genes insist on, I can have some little choice about what I do. I can't choose to fly or to burrow, but within walking or running I can choose direction and speed. I can't choose to echolocate, but I can choose what to look at. Ah, but I can build a sonar device with which to echolocate, or an airplane in which to fly. But let's not pursue this issue of strategy vs. tactics too far, lest we bog down in the mire of nature vs. nurture.[1] That would require a whole other tour.

But this tour is about artificial minds. Why should we spend time on evolution? For several reasons. First, the evolution of simple animals, rather than complex ones, may help us better understand artificial minds. Also, a look at evolution may provide some perspective on philosophical issues, such as subjective experience. What about these artificial minds? Do they experience? And if they do, in what way? Natural evolution also provides background for genetic algorithms, which will be the second major attraction of this tour stop. Finally, a view of evolution will help with artificial life, the port of call of our next major tour stop.

Here is some of what Dawkins has to say about the evolution of brains:

Our brains were designed to understand hunting and gathering, mating and child-rearing; a world of medium-sized objects moving in three dimensions at moderate speeds. We are ill-equipped to comprehend the very small and the very large; things whose duration is measured in picoseconds or gigayears; particles that don't have position; forces and fields that we cannot see or touch which we know of only because they affect things that we can see or touch. (1987, p. 2)

How well designed are our brains for understanding mind? Probably not well at all. In particular, we are not well equipped to comprehend neurons and synapses, which are too small, or algorithms and mechanisms of mind, which are too abstract. That's not what we evolved for, and yet here we are struggling with them. By the very nature of things, our tour must be a struggle.[2]

Life's Timetable

With that warning, let's struggle a bit with gigayears to put life's time span (and mind's) on Earth in perspective. Here's a table that will help.[3] Let's start at the bottom (table 8.1). Current estimates mark the age of the Earth at about 4.5 billion years. The oldest sedimentary rocks show signs of organic molecules or organic activity. The oldest unmetamorphized rocks, the earliest that *could* contain any fossils, actually do. In geologic terms, life has been around a long time. For some 2 billion years only prokaryotes, the bacteria and blue-green algae, lived on Earth. Many call this period the age of bacteria. Margulis and Sagan argue that we still live in the age of bacteria and claim that it will always be the age of bacteria (1986). Eukaryotic cells, the kind you and I, and all living things except the bacteria and blue-green algae, are made of, first evolved about 1.4 billion years ago. All life on Earth consisted of single-cell organisms until some .7 billion years back. At roughly the halfway point of the expected span of life on Earth, multicellular organisms first evolved. Organisms with hard parts soon evolved to make life more enjoyable for the paleontologists.

We humans evolved only a coat of paint ago. What? A coat of paint? Recall the analogy from chapter 1. Suppose the time span from the Earth's

Table 8.1
Life's Timetable on Earth

	Billions of Years
End of life on Earth (Sun to explode)	5.0
Present time	0.0
Advent of humans	−0.000001
First fossils with hard parts	−0.5
Multicellular organisms	−0.7
Advent of eukaryotic cells	−1.4
Oldest unmetamorphized rocks (contain fossils of cells)	−3.5
Oldest sedimentary rocks (signs of organic activity)	−3.7
Earth's beginnings	−4.5

formation to the present were represented by the height of the Eiffel Tower. The time span of the human species would then be represented by the thickness of the topmost coat of paint.[4] Again, it's sobering to realize that Earth and its biosphere have gotten along perfectly well without us for all but a minute part of their existence and could, no doubt, have continued to do so. It is equally sobering to be told that all but an infinitesimal portion of the species that have occupied the Earth are now extinct (Margulis and Sagan 1986, p. 66). What's the probability that humans will be around to avoid being incinerated by an exploding sun? Approaching zero?[5]

Single-Cell Minds

I suspect you're wondering about more of this talk of prokaryotes and eukaryotes. What can they have to do with mechanisms of mind? This is biology. What does it have to do with artificial life? Well, I've often asked myself, and sometimes other people, how much mind a single cell has, if any at all. So we need to know something about single cells. All prokaryotes are single-cell organisms. They have none of the cellular structure we learned to expect in elementary biology class: no organelles, no nucleus, no paired chromosomes, no chloroplasts, no mitochondria. Eukaryotes can be single-cell (e.g., amoebas, paramecia) or multicell, and may well have evolved from colonies of prokaryotes. Prokaryotes are the simplest of living creatures. Nonetheless, they are highly successful. Measured either by number or by biomass, collectively they probably outnumber and outweigh all other living beings.

Well, what can they do? Lots! As we've seen, they can synthesize most vitamins. They can manufacture most of the essential amino acids that you and I have to eat to get. They are mobile. Some of them can detect and move toward food concentrations. They can avoid certain toxic substances. These last two are, perhaps, the most elemental natural behaviors. They can produce particular enzymes as needed. In other words, they can turn enzyme production on and off as needed, depending on their current state. So they preserve a certain homeostasis. They have a tenuous sex life. Although they don't need sex for reproduction, they do exchange genetic material. They can reproduce in twenty minutes to half a day. They live in a variety of habitats, apparently from the upper atmosphere down to 2000 feet below the Earth's surface. They even take up residence in nuclear reactors.

The assertions of the previous paragraph may well leave you concerned about quantifiers. Can *all* bacteria really do *all* these things? We typically talk of a species being capable of some function though not every member is. For example, we speak of chimps using tools to crack nuts, though not all bands know to do this. Being conspecific, in essence, means being able to usefully share genetic material, usually in the context of reproduction.[6] But "all the world's bacteria essentially have access to a single gene pool" (Margulis and Sagan, 1986, p. 18). Hence, "there are no true species in the bacterial world. All bacteria are one organism" (Margulis and Sagan, 1986, p. 89). Thus it seems reasonable to speak of bacteria being capable of these various functions though not all of them are.

All right, suppose we agree that bacteria are capable of all these functions. Does that imply they have minds? I'm inclined to answer yes, to come small degree. Minds control behavior. Bacteria behave. Whatever controls that behavior is usefully thought of as a smidgen of mind.[7]

What Is Life?

Well, here we are, caught in the trap of arguing about how to use the word "mind." Another word that often leads to such a snare is "life." Discussion about whether viruses are alive is not uncommon.[8] Some have been bold enough to attempt a definition. Here's one such, due to Crick (1981, p. 56), that will prove useful in preparing us for genetic algorithms to come. To be alive,

1. A system must be able to replicate directly both its own instructions and indirectly any machinery needed to execute them [instructions for its own replication].

2. The replication of the genetic material must be fairly exact, but mutations—mistakes that can be faithfully copied—must occur at a rather low rate.

3. A gene and its "product" must be kept reasonably close together.[9]

4. The system will be an open one and must have a supply of raw material and, in some way or another, a supply of free energy.

Note that sexual reproduction is not a basic requirement. Note also the requirement that mutations occur but at a low rate. Without mutation there is no new genetic material, at best myriad recombinations of the old. Too much mutation, on the other hand, leads to chaos, which is typically not viable. Here we have one instance of a general principle: interesting systems balance on the edge of chaos. Almost any dynamic organization exemplifies this principle. If the system is too static, too controlled, there is no interesting dynamics. If it's too chaotic, with things going this way and that, there is no interesting order. Interesting systems, including life, live on the edge of chaos.[10]

Crick's requirements for life omit not only sex but also that mysterious life force, that élan vital, that almost all of us would like to consider the essence of life. Where Crick leaves it out, Dawkins shoots it down. Here's his view, presaged by this chapter's opening quote: "What lies at the heart of every living thing is not a fire, not warm breath, not a 'spark of life'. It is information, words, instructions. . . . If you want to understand life, don't think about vibrant, throbbing gels and oozes, think about information technology" (1987, p. 112). Ah, but what is this information, and how is it processed?

Evolution as Information Processing

Recall that a *gene* is essentially a recipe for a protein. With it, a cell containing the necessary building materials can manufacture the protein. The gene provides information as to the protein's structure. The collection of genes of an organism is called its *genotype*. Every organism begins as a single cell containing such a genotype. Some organisms develop into multicellular creatures like ourselves. The organism's *phenotype* is the collection of properties or attributes it exhibits during development. What these properties will be depends on the properties and the abundance of the proteins produced, *and* on the properties of the environment.[11] The information in the genes is processed during development into the phenotype. How well the resulting organism fits its environment depends on both the organism and its environment.

But the processing isn't over. It continues via *natural selection*. Differentially successful reproduction among organisms results in expanding or contracting populations of certain genes in the gene pool. Natural selection has taken place.[12] Here is a brief sermon from Dawkins on what natural selection is, and isn't.

Natural selection, the blind, unconscious, automatic process which Darwin discovered, and which we now know is the explanation for the existence and apparently purposeful form of all life, has no purpose in mind. It has no mind and no mind's eye. It does not plan for the future. It has no vision, no foresight, no sight at all. If it can be said to play the role of watchmaker in nature, it is the blind watchmaker. (1987, p. 5)

Note the phrase "apparently purposeful form." We'll encounter this idea again when we visit with the roboticists, who sometime speak of robots exhibiting emerging behavior that is apparently purposeful. But Dawkins's, or rather Darwin's, essential message is that there is no progress in evolution. There's no goal to progress toward: "Having survived in an unbroken line from the beginnings of life, all organisms today are equally evolved" (Margulis and Sagan 1986, p. 16). Nothing in the information-processing mechanisms of evolution allows for combination or mutation of genes to achieve favorable changes.[13]

Darwin's basic idea is that order, and unbelievable complexity, incredible capabilities, result from selection operating cumulatively on chance events. Crick puts it this way: "When times get tough, true novelty is needed—novelty whose important features cannot be preplanned—and for this we must rely on chance. *Chance is the only source of true novelty*" (1981, p. 58).

If you are going to build artificial creatures with artificial minds, and you want them to survive and procreate, you will have to endow them with some way to produce novel behavior. Not all important contingencies can be predicted, on either an individual's or evolution's time scale. Crick is telling us that chance is the only source of the needed novelty.[14] This assertion certainly seems right when applied to natural evolution. The "only" part seems doubtful when applied to learning in an individual's lifetime, or to artificial evolution, which we'll visit soon. In the meantime, let's try to get a handle on subjective experience.

Us and Bats

Early on, I warned you to expect a sales job along with the sights on this tour. It's like being invited to spend two nights *free* in a condo at the newest lakeside resort. *All* you have to do is listen to a sales pitch. Here you have to somehow acquire access to this book *and* listen to a sales pitch. If the cost seems high, you can skip the next couple of paragraphs. Unfortunately, I don't promise to warn you of each approaching hawking.

Here's a quote from the first chapter of this book:

Mind operates on sensations to create information for its own use. I don't think of minds as information-processing machines in the sense of taking information from the environment and processing it to arrive at the next action. Rather, I think of information as not existing out there in the environment. Information comes into being when minds process sensations (Oyama 1985). The same scene can provide quite different information to different minds.

But, you exclaim, surely there's information in the environment. Either there's one dog barking at me or two. I don't create one event or the other. Of course, one or two dogs barking is information to the one being barked at, but it is only data to a squirrel high in a neighboring oak. Again I find myself, somewhat reluctantly, arguing about the use of a word. Consider a computer screen containing this very text. Its information content is very different to a human reader than to a word-processing utility that counts words. The information content will even differ from human reader to human reader. Yet the data from the environment are exactly the same. I think it useful to distinguish between data from the environment and information created from that data by and for its user. This point has important consequences. Ornstein, from whom we'll hear more on a later stop, states it thus: "Our world appears to us the way it does because we are built the way we are, not because of how the world is" (1986, p. 40). When we build artificial minds, their world is not going to appear to them the way our world appears to us. The same is true of other natural minds.

Still, there may be similarities based on function. Dawkins compares the subjective experience of humans and bats, noting that bats depend largely on echolocation, whereas humans are primarily visual animals as a result of our arboreal progenitors. Since we and the bats seem to need the same type of internal model for locating objects in space, he conjectures that bats see via echo in much the same way as we do via light (1987, p. 34). That is, their subjective experience might be similar to ours. I wonder how this might sort out among dolphins, who use both sight and echolocation. I also have some concern at the reliance on internal models. Certainly there are internal responses, but are they representational in nature? Are they models to be consulted or simply causal gears in some mechanism of mind? Later, we'll encounter proponents of this latter view.

All this discussion of bats leads to a highlight of the tour,[15] Dawkins's intelligent bat's view of humans. Please forgive me for quoting at such length, but the passage would only suffer under my paraphrasing.

I can imagine some other world in which a conference of learned and totally batlike creatures, flabbergasted to be told of animals called humans that are actually capable of using the newly discovered inaudible rays called "light," still the subject of top-secret military development, for finding their way about. These otherwise humble humans are almost totally deaf (well, they can hear after a fashion and even utter a few ponderously slow deep drawling growls, but they only use these sounds for rudimentary purposes like communicating with each other; they don't seem capable of using them to detect even the most massive objects. They have, instead, highly specialized organs called "eyes" for exploiting "light" rays. The sun is the main source of light rays, and humans, remarkably, manage to exploit the complex echoes that bounce off objects when light rays from the sun hit them. They have an ingenious device called the "lens" whose shape appears to be mathematically calculated so that it bends these silent rays in such a way that there is an exact one to one mapping between objects in the world and an image on a sheet of cells called a "retina". These retinal cells are capable, in some mysterious way, of rendering the light "audible" (one might say), and they relay their information to the brain. Our mathematicians have shown that it is theoretically possible, by doing the right kind of highly complex calculations, to safely navigate through the world using these light rays, just as effectively as one can in the ordinary way use ultrasound—in some respects even *more* effectively! But who would have thought that a humble human could do these calculations. (1987, p. 35–36)

Variations in built-in equipment have other possible consequences. Here's a delightful fantasy about dolphins taken from Dawkins (1987, pp. 96–97). Echoes from some object produce a particular pattern of sound. Dolphins have highly versatile voices, so why can't they mimic this pattern? By doing so, perhaps they could convey a mental picture of the object to other dolphins. Although there is no evidence that such communication actually occurs, it's an intriguing thought. It's as if we could produce holographic images via the activity of some internally produced and controlled light source. Maybe I could produce a holographic image to show you what I think it's like to be a bat.

Genetic Nuts and Bolts

Here are a few miscellaneous facts about genes and how they operate, to provide background for our visit to genetic algorithms. Dawkins measures the storage capacity of cells by the number of copies of the *Encyclopaedia Britannica,* all thirty volumes, that can be encoded in its DNA. Let's call this unit an eb. An individual human cell measures 3 or 4 ebs. Quite a lot! (A lily seed measures 60 eb, an amoeba 1000 eb and a bacterium 0.003 eb.) Human cells use only about 1 percent of their genetic material during their lifetime. There's no generally accepted explanation (1987, p. 116). At any time an individual gene may be on or off, that is, usable as a template or not.

Another important point is that development is local. Embryos grow by cell division, each cell splitting into two daughter cells. Genes affect bodies by local influences on cells. Everything is local. Large-scale form emerges from local cellular effects. There is no grand design (1987, pp. 52–53). Note that the maximum evolution rate occurs when mutation is unchecked. Natural selection acts as a brake by weeding out most of the mutations.

The world shows various levels of organization, ranging from the relative simplicity of a rock, a cloud, or a bacterium, to the highly complex organization of a bat or a human. The second law of thermodynamics tells us that in a closed system, increasing entropy moves the system from complexity to simplicity, from organization to heat death. But how do things organize in the first place? One answer is through cumulative selection, an iterated process of generation and selection (figure 8.1).

Cumulative Selection

Cumulative selection is the key to the evolution of complex, capable organisms. This process leads to what I like to call organized complexity.

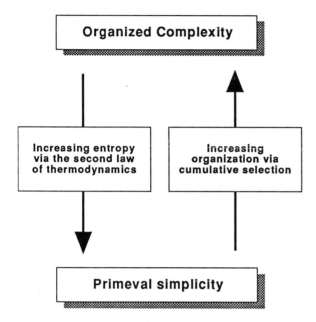

Figure 8.1
Cumulative selection

In some sense, cumulative selection can be thought of as an inverse of increasing entropy. We'll see it in action once again when we visit artificial evolution next.

Genetic Algorithms

Having paid homage to Darwin (and unjustly ignored Wallace), let's leave natural evolution and turn to an artificial version. Developed by Holland, his students, and his colleagues at the University of Michigan (Holland 1975, 1992; Goldberg 1989), genetic algorithms are search algorithms based on natural evolution. As we saw in our visit to symbolic AI, problem solving can be viewed as a search through the state space of a system for one of the goal states that solve the problem. Typically, we start our search at a single initial state, perhaps randomly chosen, perhaps not, and use various heuristics to guide a search trajectory toward a goal state. The better the heuristics, the more efficient the search. Genetic algorithms, instead of starting with a single initial state, begin with an initial sample population of usually randomly chosen states. Heuristics modeled on natural evolution are then iteratively applied, allowing the entire population to evolve toward an acceptable solution of the problem. Genetic algorithms, following multiple search paths simultaneously, run efficiently on parallel computers (Kilman et al. 1992; Collins 1992).

Now that we've had a view from the stratosphere, let's see what genetic algorithms look like from the treetops. Think of the population of states as a collection of potential solutions to the problem. The four basic elements of a typical genetic algorithm are mating, mutation, selection, and reproduction. Members of the initial population mate. Their offspring are subject first to mutation and then to selection. Those selected comprise the next iterate of the population, and start the process once again by mating. This process iterates until an acceptable solution to the problem is found or until the searcher gives up.

Now let's climb down out of the trees for a ground-level view. A state in the population is referred to as a genotype. Typically it is just a string of genes representing some possible hypothesis or solution. Sometimes a genotype can be more complex—a hierarchical structure, for instance. A gene, or rather its chosen allele,[16] is typically expressed as a character, or string of characters, in some alphabet, often a binary one. As is true for the genotype, an individual gene can have a more complex structure. Usually a gene codes for a particular feature or parameter value. You've no doubt noticed the juxtaposition of biological terms (gene, genotype) with computer terms (string, tree, codes for). A concordance (see table 8.2) may help keep things straight. This one introduces a little more complexity than I've mentioned. Thinking of a genotype as containing a single chromosome, as is typical in genetic algorithms, tames it quite a bit.

With this structure in mind, let's look at the steps in a simple genetic algorithm in more detail. Here's a version of the algorithm.

Initialize the population with random alleles.

Parallel repeat until a good enough solution is found.

Judge the fitness of each candidate.

Select candidate strings for reproduction in proportion to their fitness.

Mate pairs of selected strings via crossover.

Mutate the resulting new strings.

Table 8.2
Concordance of biological and computer terms

Natural	Genetic Algorithm
chromosome	string
allele	feature, character or detector
locus	position on string
genotype	structure
phenotype	parameter set, alternative solution, decoded structure

Modified from Goldberg 1989

A genetic algorithm first forms an initial population of trial solutions by randomly choosing values (alleles) for each of the features (genes).[17] The algorithm then cycles through four steps until it finds a good enough solution. Each of these steps involves operations on all members of the population or on a subset thereof. They can often be carried out in parallel for increased efficiency. Let's look at these steps one at a time.

First the fitness of each candidate is judged. "Fitness," as in "the survival of the fittest," is a troublesome term to some biologists: "['Fitness'] is actively confusing because it has been used in so many different ways" (Dawkins 1982, p. 179). For the artificial geneticist, fitness is simply a function in the mathematical sense. The fitness function assigns to each candidate solution some value, typically numerical, that measures how close the candidate comes to an "optimal" solution. Usually implemented as a procedure, the fitness function puts each candidate solution through its paces and returns how well each performed as its fitness. Since the fitness of one candidate solution is usually independent of that of another, the computation of a population's fitness can be done efficiently in parallel.

Once the fitness of each candidate is determined, the next step selects candidates for reproduction in proportion to their fitness. The fitter a candidate is, the better its chance of being selected. That doesn't mean that one who is not so fit might not be selected; it just has a smaller chance.

Once the lucky winners have been selected, they are paired at random. (To my knowledge, no one has yet tried arranged marriages.) Mating takes place via crossover. Suppose our genotypes are single strings of alleles of genes. One possible crossover mechanism lines up two mating strings, chooses a crossover point at random, and interchanges the portions of the two strings after the crossover point. There are other, more complex crossovers, say with two crossover points that interchange the segment between them. Once the pairings have been made, crossover can be efficiently implemented in parallel. Entirely different operators also can be inserted into the genetic algorithm just after (or even instead of) crossover. The choice of such operators is dictated by knowledge of the problem domain.

With crossover complete, it's time to mutate. It often works this way. Choose a small number of candidates at random. In each of these, randomly choose a single gene and, having done so, randomly choose a replacement allele for that gene. The candidate has mutated. Again, this mutation can be implemented efficiently in parallel. Some mutations are much fancier—changing, for example, the length of a genotype or the structure of a gene.

With all the operations complete, a new population is constituted and the process begins again. Most genetic algorithms keep their population at a fixed size. Sometimes all the parents are replaced by their children, so that each successive population is entirely new. Another possibility is to evaluate the fitness of the children, and to choose the new population from parents and children with the fitter having the better chance of being selected. As you can see, there are many different genetic algorithms.

As search procedures, say for optimization, genetic algorithms are generally useful and often effective. One typically needs to know little about the problem domain, other than enough to be able to code candidates as genotypes and to develop an appropriate fitness function. Often, however, a search procedure designed for the particular problem domain, and therefore requiring more knowledge, will prove more efficient than a genetic algorithm. But all this is quite abstract. How about something more concrete?

Genetic Search for XOR Weights

Let's look at a simple genetic algorithm in action. During our connectionist visit, we met an artificial neural network that implemented an exclusive or (XOR) net. Recall that an XOR neural net outputs a 0 if its

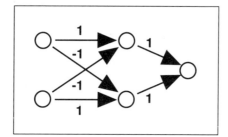

Figure 8.2
XOR net

two inputs are the same, and a 1 if they are different. Figure 8.2 illustrates a neural network handcrafted to behave in this way. Recall that each node of the network produces a 1 if the weighted sum of its inputs equals or exceeds the threshold (1 in this case), and yields a 0 otherwise. You can easily check that the network behaves as specified by the table.

What makes the network work? This choice of weights, of course. Some other choice of weights might also allow it to behave as an XOR, but most would not. Now suppose we didn't know those weights, that the 1's and −1's mysteriously disappeared. We're left with the problem of finding suitable weights for this network so that it becomes an XOR. Of course, they needn't be the same as those that disappeared. Let's choose to search for them using a genetic algorithm, so we can see how one is set up and put to work.

Our first task is to produce an encoding scheme for transforming nets into genotypes. To begin, let's label the diagram of nodes and arrows, the underlying directed graph. Figure 8.3 provides such a labeling. These numbers are simply labels by which we can refer to particular arrows. They're not weights but position markers. Using these position markers, a genotype can be simply a string of six numbers, each representing the weight at its position. Figure 8.4 provides an example of such a genotype. This genotype assigns, for example, a weight of −0.9 to the arrow labeled 4. Now that we know how to code a candidate set of weights into a string acting as genotype, how might we calculate its fitness? First construct its

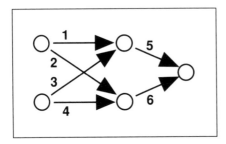

Figure 8.3
Labeled digraph

1	2	3	4	5	6
-1.2	2.4	0.4	-0.9	-0.3	3.0

Figure 8.4
Genotype for a neural net

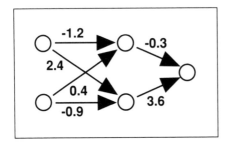

Figure 8.5
The phenotype net

phenotype, which the neural net the string determines. Figure 8.5 shows the net for the string we saw just above.

Next evaluate that net over each of its four inputs, that is, put in the four inputs one at a time, and see what you get out. Calculate the error for each input, and sum the errors thus produced. The lower the number, the higher the fitness. Here's an example of fitness evaluation, using the same string we looked at before (figure 8.6). It gives rise to these individ-

IN	OUT	ERR
0 0	0	0
0 1	0	1
1 0	0	1
1 1	1	1

Figure 8.6
Error calculation

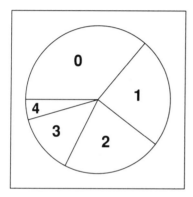

Figure 8.7
Fitness spinner

ual errors. With a total error of 3, where 4 is worst and 0 is best, this is certainly not a very fit phenotype, and would have only a small chance of mating.

With fitness determined it's time to select the lucky winners in the mating game. Use a spinner wheel with the central angles of the wedges roughly proportional to fitness to select a fitness level (figure 8.7). Then randomly select a string of that fitness for reproduction. (I warned you this was a simple version.) Continue this process until you've selected as many as your initial population size.

Now that we've selected the strings, we want to mate them. Choose pairs at random from among all of the selected strings. For each such pair

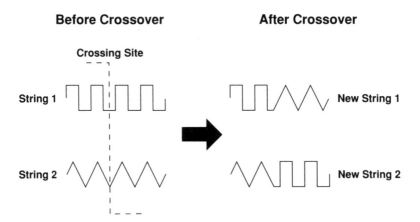

Figure 8.8
Crossover (adapted from Goldberg 1989)

choose a crossover point at random. If string₁ is paired with string₂, swap the segments after the chosen crossover point, to yield two new strings. Figure 8.8 illustrates one such crossover.

We're now ready to mutate. With small probability, choose a string. Randomly choose a site on that string, randomly choose a replacement allele for that site, and return the modified string to the population. In this simple genetic algorithm the genotype size (length) is kept constant. We want to change only the weights, not the architecture. Notice that what we've done is very much a parallel generate-and-test algorithm. We've generated possible solutions, tested them, and used the best candidates to generate again.

In summary, genetic search proceeds from a population of strings, not from a single point. After selection via some fitness function, they crossbreed, they mutate, and the search begins anew from (one hopes) a more fit (closer to the desired solution) population. Picture the space of possible solutions as a surface with hills and valleys, ridges and plains. Picture the problem as one of optimization; you want to find, say, the top of the highest hill. Starting with a sample population spread over the landscape, a genetic algorithm iteratively selects new populations whose members tend to cluster around the various hills. Success is attained when some solution sits atop the highest hill or, rather, high enough on a high enough hill. We humans (and nature also) are almost always satisfied with a good enough solution.

But what has all this talk of selection to do with mechanisms of mind? Surely individual minds don't evolve in this way. Well, that's not so clear. On a later stop we'll hear about Edelman's theory of neural Darwinism (1987), where just such a suggestion is made. But before that, let's look at artificial animals that learn by artificial evolution. We'll meet them in the context of artificial life, our next stop.

Notes

1. For a safe path through, or rather above, the nature–nurture quagmire, I recommend Oyoma (1985).

2. In my experience, both faculty and students struggle with almost everything that goes on in a university.

3. Much of this table comes from Crick's diagram, which we discussed in chapter 1.

4. I first heard this vivid analogy during a presentation by Stephen Jay Gould. It seems to go back at least to the humorist Mark Twain (1938, pp. 215–16).

5. Bob Sweeney cautions me about making analogies from past conditions to those of the future, and points out that some species have already survived for hundreds of millions of years. While acknowledging the truth of what he says, I'd still be loath to bet on human long-term survival. Though we are surely among the most adaptable of all species, which works in favor of survival, we are also the most dangerous to ourselves by virtue of the global effects of our actions.

6. Dawkins (1987, p. 118) puts it this way: "The thing that defines a species is that all members have the same addressing system for their DNA."

7. Bob Sweeney suggests that glaciers behave, and asks about ascribing mind to them. My first reaction was to deny that their motion is behavior, because it is unintentional. They don't sense the world and respond to it in the service of needs. But where are the boundaries of sensing? Does my thermostat have more of a need than a glacier? Here I am again, caught firmly in the quagmire of the fuzzy boundaries of word meanings.

8. Unable to create the components to be a true living system, viruses are little more than a stretch of DNA or RNA coated with protein" (Margulis and Sagan 1986, p. 50).

9. At least one biologist would disagree. Dawkins argues that genes can encode for behavior in a member of another species (1982).

10. For an example of this principle involving cellular automata, see Langton (1992a). For some cautions, and a pointer to earlier versions of the principle, see Mitchell et al. (to appear).

11. That "and" is crucial. Oyama (1985) expounds this theme.

12. A point of some moment is glossed over here. Natural selection is often constrained to refer to selecting out those who don't survive to reproduction age. Another form of selection, sexual selection, is exemplified by peahens choosing to mate with peacocks with more abundant tails. Also, there's genetic drift, the result of mutations that are neutral as to fitness.

13. I recall reading of some strain of bacteria that normally couldn't metabolize particular sugars but could mutate to do so. When placed in an environment rich in those sugars, this mutation occurred faster than expected, indicating a "direction" in the mutation. I can't recall the source of information about these experiments, nor do I know if they have been successfully replicated. The view expressed above is, to my knowledge, still current.

14. Chance need not be nondeterministic, as is believed of quantum mechanical events (Herbert 1985). Rather, it may mean unpredictable, such as a distant point in the trajectory of a chaotic dynamical system (see Gleick 1987 for a popular account or Devaney 1987 for a mathematical account).

15. It leads as well to a fascinating side trip for the philosophically inclined. See Negal's "What is it like to be a bat?" and Hofstadter's reflections on it Hofstadter and Dennett (1981).

16. Allele? An oversimplified version of the story has the human gene that codes for eye color containing either the allele for blue eyes or the allele for brown eyes.

17. In some cases one wants to start with random variations on a single, seed solution. I'm involved in a research project using recursive transition networks (RTN) to predict speech acts (Baggett et al. 1993), which uses this idea.

9

Artificial Life

So far on our tour of mechanisms of mind, we've visited mostly mechanisms aimed at high-level abstract tasks like configuring VAXs, solving puzzles, recognizing words, and turning active sentences to passive ones. This initial emphasis follows history. Early AI researchers worked from the perhaps unconscious, and culturally blessed, homocentric view that minds are a specifically human characteristic. Thus they concentrated their efforts on characteristically human tasks: chess playing, theorem proving, language translation. Recall the "Approaches to Mind" diagram (figure 1.3) we encountered as our tour began. It classified approaches to mechanisms of mind along two dimensions, analytic/synthetic and top-down/bottom-up. Symbolic AI occupied the synthetic, top-down corner by virtue of the high-level abstract tasks upon which it focused. Toy versions of these tasks proved relatively tractable, and much was learned. But most solutions scaled up poorly to real world problems.

Consequently, another group of researchers, including the computational neuroethologists (Cliff 1991; Wilson 1991), whom we've met briefly, propose to approach mind from the synthetic, bottom-up corner instead. They expect to learn more by building complex models of simple systems (such as simple animals) than by making simple models of complex systems (such as humans). Much of the rest of our tour will be devoted to mechanisms arising from models of relatively simple systems, such as autonomous vehicles, robots, and artificial agents living on computer monitors. The last of these examples brings us to the focal point of this tour stop, artificial life.

Artificial Life

We previously defined artificial life as the study of man-made systems that behave in ways characteristic of natural living systems. This definition comes from Langton, arguably the father of the field,[1] as do many of the ideas in this section (1989, pp. 1–6). Levy has produced a very readable account of the brief history of this new discipline (1992).

Artificial life researchers are "typically concerned with the formal basis of life." They ask what mechanisms produce lifelike behavior. They then build systems that synthesize such behavior. These are almost always computer systems; artificial creatures mostly "live" in artificial environments visible on computer monitors. Reynolds's boids (1987), whom we've met briefly, are such creatures. Intended to model flocking behavior, they live in an environment so simple that it contains, in addition to boids and space, only obstacles for the boids to flow around. Artificial environments, though typically simple compared with environments supporting natural creatures, are often more complex than this one.

Much of the lifelike behavior displayed by these artificial creatures is emergent, that is, produced without being specifically programmed in by the system's builder. A boid is instructed by Reynolds only to (1) maintain a minimum distance from obstacles and other boids, (2) to match its speed with the average speed of nearby boids, and (3) to fly toward the perceived center of the mass of the boids it can see. Flocking behavior emerges as the individual boids follow these instructions. Local behavior in artificial life systems is often built in, whereas global behavior is often emergent.

Many artificial life systems, like Reynolds's boids, are inhabited by a population of artificial creatures. Most such systems are highly distributed, in that no central executive controls behavior from a Godlike vantage. Rather, control is local and global behavior emerges. These systems are often implemented on massively parallel computers with many thousands of processors.[2] Populations often evolve, employing one or another of Holland's genetic algorithms. Sometimes, as natural creatures almost always do, they coevolve. The natural world arms race pits ever increasing offensive potency of the predator against ever improving defensive resiliency of the prey.

Other artificial life systems are home to a single artificial creature rather than a population. These range from rather simple creatures like Wilson's Animat (1985), which learns to find food, to considerably more complex creatures such as Johnson and Scanlon's Pacrat (1987), which according to its designers, both thinks and feels. Animat is one of the two major attractions of this tour stop; a population model due to Ackley and Littman (1992) is the other.

We'll meet several familiar mechanisms of mind. Animat learns via *classifier systems* (see below), an amalgam of production systems and genetic algorithms. Ackley and Littman's agents evolve via a genetic algorithm and learn using neural networks. These mechanisms, along with cellular automata,[3] are among the most common in artificial life systems.

Symbolic AI systems have been criticized for having their input preprocessed by humans and their output interpreted by humans. Critics maintain that this simplification sloughs off the hardest problems, those of perception and motion. Connectionist systems are often subject to the same criticism. Artificial life creatures, though designed and implemented by humans, sense their environments and act on them directly. Their actions affect the environment and, hence, the creature's future perceptions. All this without further human intervention. The human is taken out of the loop. Thus the semantics of the system are well grounded and "results are generated by observation rather than by interpretation. . . . the fruits . . . are 'hard' objective measurements rather than 'soft' subjective ones" (Cliff 1991, p. 29).

But all this is rather abstract. Let's have a close look at one such artificial life system, Animat.

Animat and Intelligence

The basic idea of an artificial creature that learns to cope with a simple environment by means of a classifier system is due to Holland and Reitman (1979). We'll visit with a version of such a creature designed by Wilson (1985).

For many years I've been meeting each Wednesday at noon for lo mein (soft noodles) and conversation with a diverse group whose initial common interest was AI. Before trying to define *artificial* intelligence, we thought it prudent first to say what we meant by *intelligence*. After almost two years of wrangling, we gave it up as hopeless.[4] But not everyone fails so miserably. Here's a definition from the physicist van Heerden, as adapted by Wilson: "Intelligent behavior is to be repeatedly successful in satisfying one's psychological needs in diverse, observably different, situations on the basis of past experience" (1985). Wilson was drawn to this definition because it is easily translated into computing terms. Let's examine his computational translation a clause at a time.

What does it mean "to be repeatedly successful in satisfying one's psychological needs"? On the level of simple animals, the somatic level, it means satisfying bodily needs. More specifically, it means a high rate of receipt of certain reward quantities, and a low rate of others. More pleasure, less pain. This should be easy to model computationally, perhaps as simply as by variations of a couple of variables.

How about "diverse, observably different, situations"? Wilson talks of "sets of distinct sensory input vectors with each having a particular implication for optimal action." In other words, the behaving creature faces different situations and best responds to them in obviously different ways. Computationally, it's no trick to produce meaningful variations in environmental states, that is, states requiring distinct responses. And it's no trick to observe the response of an artificial creature.

And finally, what does he mean by "past experience"? Wilson speaks of "a suitable internal record of earlier interactions with the environment, and their results." Now we've come to an interesting issue. Keep this statement in mind as we visit with Wilson's Animat. The "internal record" will be in the form of genetically produced production rules. This seems very different from the usual memory paradigm of data structures[5] recording past events. Production rules seem closer to procedures, recipes for action, than to data structures for memory. There will seem to be nothing that looks like a representation of any "earlier interaction" or of its "result." It will be well to bear all this in mind on a later stop, when we visit the third AI debate, over the need for representations. Anyhow, Wilson was able to satisfy himself that this part of the definition was computationally operational.

With van Heerden's definition of intelligence translated into computational terms, Wilson set himself the task of producing an artificial creature, Animat,[6] that exhibits intelligent behavior. Let's see how he goes about it.

Animat as a Simple Animal

As we've seen, there's much support for the idea of making complex models of *simple animals* rather than simple models of complex animals. So what can be said about simple animals? First, where do simple animals find themselves? In a sea of sensory signals, says Wilson. At any given moment only some of these signals are significant; the rest are irrelevant. The irrelevant signals typically far outnumber the significant ones. Our simple animal must figure out which is which, not absolutely but relative to its needs and circumstances. Second, simple animals are capable of actions (movements) that tend to change these sensory signals. Although they don't control the environment, they do affect it. Third, certain signals—those attendant on consumption of food for example, or the absence of certain signals, such as freedom from pain—have special status. We often think of pleasure and pain as being internally produced in response to external stimuli. Wilson simply treats them as sensory input. Fourth, simple animals act both externally and through internal operations so as to approximately optimize the rate of occurrence of the special signals. They tend to maximize their pleasure and minimize their pain.

From this vantage point, Wilson describes the *basic problem* of our simple animal as determining what to do next in order to maximize pleasure and minimize pain. I'd like to take this idea a little further. If we're willing to expand our range to include psychological pleasure and pain, and even if we're not, the same can be said of complex animals like us. Our only problem is what to do next. The same is true of any animal.

The life of the sea squirt makes this point crystal clear. During its larval stage, this creature swims about, for a few minutes to a few days, looking for sustenance and for a rock or a coral reef or a wharf onto which to permanently settle. During this stage it has a small but adequate nervous system. Its adult stage commences when it attaches itself permanently to a hard surface, thenceforth absorbing nutrients from the surrounding water. Early in this adult stage, the creature reabsorbs its unneeded nervous system. It no longer has the problem of what to do next, so it eats its brain (Dethie 1986). But back to Wilson and Animat.

Wilson rephrases this *basic problem* as one of generating rules that associate sensory signals with appropriate actions so as to achieve something close to optimization. Notice the assumption; it's going to be done with rules. As a result, Wilson constructs his Animat using a classifier system, à la Holland, that operates via rules.

I wonder if the rules will be hard or soft. Recall Horgan and Tienson's distinction, which we encountered on an earlier stop. A hard, or exceptionless, rule produces its action whenever its condition is satisfied. A soft rule, on the other hand, says that other things being equal, the action follows when the condition occurs. This is not a matter of probabilities but a means of allowing for exceptions. If the conditions hold, and no circumstance has occurred that suppresses the rule, then the action will be taken. That's the notion of a soft rule. Sometimes it's not so easy to distinguish a hard rule from a soft one.

I'm also curious as to whether these are going to be low-level rules, dealing more or less directly with sensory input and motor output, or high-level rules with more abstract conditions and actions.

Wilson poses the *major questions* for Animat as (1) how to discover and emphasize rules that work; (2) how to get rid of rules that don't work—your system has limited memory and won't survive a lot of noise; (3) how to optimally generalize the rules that are kept—a more general rule will operate in more situations and will take the place of several specific ones, thus using less memory. Animat must discover and emphasize rules that work, get rid of rules that don't, and generalize the rules it keeps.

Having defined intelligence, the *basic problem,* and the *major questions,* Wilson defines an *animat* in terms of these concepts as "a computer model of a simple animal in a simple animal's situation that solves the *basic problem* by satisfactorily answering the *major questions* and so satisfies the given definition of intelligence" (1985). Note that this is a functional definition of an animat. It allows for the possibility of many animats based on different solutions to the *basic problem,* even in the same environment. Here we'll continue to refer to Wilson's classifier-based animat as Animat.

Animat and Its Environment

Animat lives on a rectangular grid, eighteen rows by fifty-eight columns. Each row is circled back on itself, so that its two ends are identified, as are the tops and bottoms of the columns. Animat's world is toroidal,[7] a big doughnut. Objects populating this world are represented by alphanumeric characters located at various positions (squares) on the grid, for example a T for a tree, or an F for food. Animat himself is represented by *. Some positions, possibly many, are blank. These are represented by b's.

Since the *basic problem* is posed in terms of sensory signals, Animat must have sensory channels with which to sense its environment. Animat can receive signals from eight neighboring positions: the four cardinal directions and the diagonal ones. The positions surrounding Animat are mapped onto a string. The mapping begins above Animat and proceeds clockwise. For example,

```
TT
*F
```

maps into the string

```
TTFbbbbb.
```

Call this string a sense vector. It denotes that Animat has trees to its north and to its northeast, and food to the east. He senses equally well on all sides rather than when facing in a particular direction.

Note that Animat comes with built-in equipment for categorizing food and trees, and for distinguishing between them. Food is labeled as such, as are trees. Edelman, whom we'll meet on a later tour stop, points out that the real world does not come labeled (1987). Each individual creature must learn to categorize and to recognize anew. Providing a built-in labeling to Animat glosses over the difficult problems of perception. Animat doesn't have to figure out what's a tree, what's food, and so forth. They all come with meanings attached.

I prefer to think of objects as useful constructions of individual agents rather than as preexisting meaningfully in the outside world. A mite, crawling on a tabletop, would never construe that table as an object. But, you say, the table surely exists out there in the world. Of course it exists as a table to you and me, but not to a mite, nor to a newborn. We construct a category "table" and sometimes learn a name for it. And sometimes not. For example, you probably have a category for the plastic sleeve at the end of a shoelace but probably don't have a name for it. Names are most often culturally determined, and may well precede category construction. But we learn and retain such names only when they denote some category useful to us. Real objects, to me, are constructs of agents rather than denizens of a uniquely organized world. The real world comes neither labeled nor categorized. Animat is given something of an advantage because its world does come labeled.

Given this advantage, what kinds of things can Animat sense? Not many. Only food to be eaten and trees as obstacles. Animat and its world are pretty simple. But keep in mind that most living things sense not much more than this, since most living things are bacteria.

Animat senses by means of feature detectors. Each feature detector is Boolean; it produces 0 or 1. Either it senses that feature or it doesn't. If there are two detectors, each object (really each adjacent position) induces in Animat a two-bit binary string. A fancier Animat with some number $d > 2$ of features would induce a d-bit string, one bit for each of its d detectors. Either a feature is detected or it's not.

So each object (position) induces such a string. A sense vector translates into an 8 d-bit detector vector. Because the sense vector has eight directions, each one of which induces d-bits, Animat senses an 8d-bit detector vector at each instant of time. In our simple case Animat senses a 16-bit detector vector. Time for Animat, like space, is discrete, proceeding from one instant to the next.

Wilson encodes Animat's detector vector as follows. Let the first position detect edible or not, say a food smell and the second detect opaqueness (does light shine through?) (Alternatively, you may think of the second as detecting solidity.) Thus food in a particular direction would be represented by a 1 followed by another 1; a tree, by a 0 followed by a 1; and an empty location, by two 0's (table 9.1). Thus the string T T F b b b b b, which we looked at above, translates into the detector vector 01 01 11 00 00 00 00 00. Thus Animat senses its world. How does it act on that world?

Animat can move one square in any one of its eight directions in a single time step. A move to a blank square produces no response to An-

Table 9.1
Animal feature detectors

	edible	opaque
F	1	1
T	0	1
b	0	0

imat from the environment, other than perhaps a change in what he senses at the next time step from this location. A move into a location with food in it results in the food being eaten. Animat is a champion glutton; he never becomes sated. And his gluttony produces no ill health. The food object in the location moved to is considered to be eaten, and a reward signal is sent. The view taken here is of the environment instructing the agent by providing a reward. I'd much prefer to think of the environment as totally indifferent, and of the reward as being produced internally by Animat in response to his meal.

What if Animat moves into a location containing a tree? Such a move is not permitted, and a collision-like banging is displayed. Later we'll see that the Ackley–Littman agents have rocks against which they can bang their heads. These agents, more complex than Animat, have a certain store of health that is diminished with each such bang. When health passes below a threshold, the agent dies. By comparison, Animat is really very, very simple. But such a simple agent as Animat seems an ideal place to start studying artificial life.

Wilson characterizes the situation in which Animat finds himself as semirealistic. Animat's sensory signals carry partial information about the location of food, in that he can sense food only if it is right next to it. He can't sense food at any greater distance. The actions available to Animat permit exploration and approach to objects. Environmental predictability can be varied through the choice and arrangement of objects, that is, where you put the trees and the food. Food always being next to a tree yields a more predictable environment than food placed at random. Finally, the number of object types depends only on the number of feature detectors. If you have d detectors, you can, in principle, have 2^d types of objects. In this simple case we have only trees and food, and of course Animat itself.

But even with such a simple environment, Animat must learn to find food. This he does by means of a classifier system à la Holland.

Animat's Classifier System

Classifier systems use genetic algorithms to evolve rules (Holland et al. 1986). Animat's classifier rules consist of a *taxon*, an *action*, and a *strength*. (A fourth item will be added later.) A taxon is a template capable of matching any of a certain set of detector vectors. In particular, a taxon could *be* a detector vector, and in that case would match itself and nothing else. More commonly, 0's and 1's in certain positions in a detector vector are replaced by the wild card, or I don't care, symbol (#) to create a taxon. A taxon with a single wild card symbol would match either of the two detector vectors created by replacing the # with a 0 or a 1. The more wild cards a taxon contains, the more detector vectors it matches. A taxon with only wild cards will match every detector vector.

After the taxon comes an action, that is, one of the eight possible moves. Moves are labeled 0, 1, 2, 3, 4, 5, 6, 7, with 0 denoting a move to the north and the numbering proceeding clockwise. The strength is a numerical measure of the classifier's value to Animat. Here's an example of a classifier rule: .

```
0# 01 1# 0# 00 00 0# 0# / 2;
```

Its taxon matches thirty-two different detector vectors (2^5, because it contains five wild cards). Its action is labeled 2, signifying a move to the east. As yet no strength is assigned. What would this classifier's taxon match? A matching detector vector would have to be 0 in the first position, either 0 or 1 in the second, 0 in the third, 1 in the fourth and fifth, either 0 or 1 in the sixth, and so forth. Note that our classifier so far looks exactly like a condition/action production rule with the taxon playing the role of condition.

Animat has a population [P] of classifiers. Their number is a fixed parameter of the system. Initially Animat's classifiers contain taxons randomly filled with 0, 1, and #, and randomly filled with actions. The population evolves as Animat lives. At first classifiers don't know what they do. Later, they are pressed into service and modified. All this reminds me of Edelman's neuronal groups in the biological world that we'll meet on a later stop. How does Animat use these classifiers to answer the all-important question of what to do next? Here's his control algorithm:

Loop forever
  Calculate detector vector D
  Find the matching set [M] of D in the population [P]
  Select a classifier C from [M] with probability depending on strength
  Animat moves (or ties to) as indicated by the action of C
  The environment responds as indicated earlier.

Let's go over this one carefully, a line at a time. First note that Animat gets into his living loop and stays there. Living things do just that; we loop until we die. Here there's no provision for dying, although in actual computer implementations there'll be some means of stopping the action. The next line has Animat sensing his world by calculating the detector vector D. In other words, it looks around and sees what's happening. D is a detector vector. One hopes some classifiers in the population [P] have taxons that match. The next line has Animat collecting all such matching classifiers into the matching set [M]. Think of the matching set as containing all those rules that Animat thinks may be useful in this situation, that is, in the presence of this detector vector. We'll see in a bit what happens if there aren't any matching classifiers. (Note here that we're talking about a single Animat equipped with its own specific population [P] of classifiers.) Now Animat selects from the matching M some particular classifier. Those with greater strength have a greater probability of being chosen. Ah, shades of genetic algorithms, where genotypes are selected with probability depending on their fitness. Now Animat knows what to do next. He moves according to the action of the selected classifier. After the move, either Animat eats and is rewarded, or he bounces off a tree, or he simply moves into an empty position. We're now at the bottom of the body of the loop, so we loop back to the top and start anew by sensing this newly changed world.

In summary, after looking around, Animat asks which classifiers recognize the current sensory situation, which ones might help. He then picks its next move nondeterministically, with the probability of a given classifier's being chosen increasing with its strength. Animat then makes the chosen move. Now we know how Animat chooses to act. But do his actions vary only via the stochastic nature of the control mechanism? No. Animat can adapt to particular environments.

Animat adapts by learning. How does he learn? In three different ways that we'll explore individually. One is by *reinforcement* of classifier strength. Second, there are *genetic operators* that operate on classifiers, yielding new classifiers. Finally, *classifiers are created directly*. Let's visit each of these methods in that order.

Animat is reinforced whenever he eats—by the environment, according to Wilson; internally, in my view. Since one wants the strength of a classifier to reflect the quality of its performance, those that perform better should be stronger. Hence it seems reasonable to increase a classifier's strength after firing if its action has led to a desired result: eating. You reinforce it, make it stronger, when it has done well. But this leads to a difficulty. Typically, a desirable result stems not from a single action but from a sequence of actions. What we've suggested so far results in only the last classifier of the chain being strengthened, and that really doesn't do what we want.

Holland and company have devised a way around this problem that they refer to as the *bucket brigade algorithm* (Holland et al. 1986). The idea is to pass the strength along the sequence. Here's a brief summary of how it works. Classifiers make payments out of their strengths to classifiers that were active on the preceding cycle. Pay off those who helped you get where you are. Active classifiers later receive payments from the strengths of the next set of active classifiers. It works sort of like a Kwakiutl Indian potlatch.[8] External reward from the environment, when food is eaten, goes to the final active classifiers in the sequence. Let's take a slightly more detailed look.

Given an action A(t) selected at time t, let [A(t)] denote the set of matching classifiers pursuing that same action. The bucket brigade algorithm prescribes the following steps:

• Remove a fraction of the strength of each classifier in [A(t)]
• Distribute this strength among the classifiers in [A(t-1)]
• Animat then moves as instructed by A(t)
• If external reward is received, distribute it among the classifiers in [A(t)].

Every time a classifier becomes active, it loses some strength by paying off the classifiers that helped it become active. The strength of any individual classifier estimates its typical payoff. Since the payoff to classifiers in [A(t)] is shared equally, the more classifiers in [A(t)], the less each benefits. Wilson claims that "a given amount of external reward will eventually flow all the way back through a reliable chain." I take "reliable" to refer to a chain that typically finds food. And the operative word in the quote is "eventually." When one classifier and its matching set receive external reward, the redistribution of that wealth doesn't begin until one of these classifiers becomes active again. Wilson is noncommittal about how initial strengths are assigned. Small, randomly assigned strengths would probably do nicely, perhaps even 0 strengths.

This completes our look at how reinforcement learning takes place in classifier systems. We still have visits with genetic operators and with the creation of classifiers. First, genetic operators.

After having visited with genetic algorithms, Animat's genetic operators will seem quite familiar indeed. Classifier c_1 is selected with probability proportional to its strength. Two (later three) types of genetic operators may be applied. Cloning simply copies c_1; the child is identical to the parent except, possibly, for mutation. Cloning is asexual reproduction. Sexual reproduction occurs via crossover. This takes two. A second classifier, c_2, is selected, again with probability by strength, from among those classifiers having the same action as c_1. Only two classifiers with the same actions are allowed to mate. With two compatible classifiers in hand, the crossover operator randomly chooses two cut points, that is, two locations along the strings that comprise the taxons of the mating classifiers. The genetic material between the two cut points is interchanged to produce taxons for a pair of offspring. Each is given the common action of both parents. Both the cloning and the crossover operators add new classifiers to the population [P]. Since the size of [P] is fixed, other classifiers must be removed. Deleting at random works well for a large population. Removing the weakest classifiers does not work well, that is, is worse than random. (This rather counterintuitive situation probably resulted from a loss of genetic diversity). Deleting with probability proportional to the reciprocal of the strength works best. But enough of deletion. On to creation.

Occasionally, Animat may encounter a detector vector matched by no classifier. The matching set, M, may be empty. No existing classifier looks as if it might be useful in this situation. What does Animat do? He makes one up. He creates a new matching classifier whose taxon is derived from the unmatched detector vector by randomly adding a few # symbols to it, and whose action is assigned at random.

Well, so much for now on Animat's structure. What does he do? And how well?

Animat in Action

Figure 9.1 shows a sample environment for Animat. Wilson calls it WOODS7. Note that in WOODS7 every piece of food is next to a tree, but in no particular direction from the tree. In some other environment, things could be quite different. Perhaps food wouldn't grow in the shade of a tree, and so would be separated from any tree by a space. An environment could be more regular, say food always to the north of a tree, or trees occurring in a lattice structure like an orchard. WOODS7, while less regular, is far from random. It contains ninety-two distinct sense vectors. That is, Animat can encounter ninety-two distinct situations, not very many by human standards.

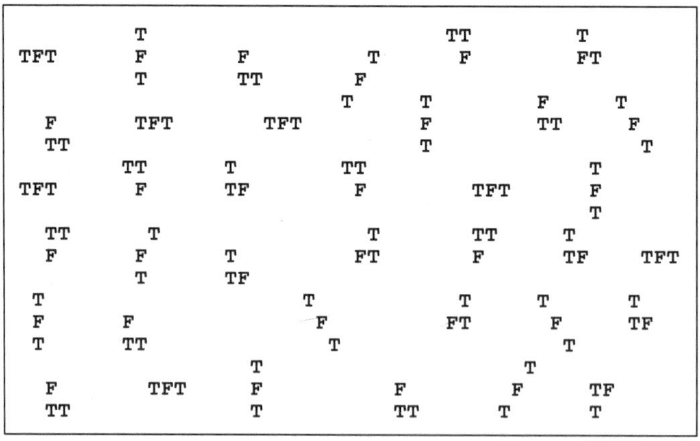

Figure 9.1
WOODS7 (redrawn from Wilson 1985)

How easy is it for Animat to find food in WOODS7? Starting at a random location unoccupied by a tree, and moving at random (a random walk), how long should it take Animat to bump into something to eat by pure chance? The answer is forty-one steps, on average. Animat might be pretty hungry by that time. But suppose instead that, again starting at a random location, Animat this time is endowed with sufficiently Godlike powers so as always to choose the quickest way to dine. Now how long should it take him? His time is reduced from 41 steps to only 2.2 steps, on average. Knowledge clearly pays off. Thus, if Animat learns to find food in about forty steps, he hasn't done much. On the other hand, if he learns to find food in something like half a dozen steps or anything close, he's done a lot.

Technically, a problem instance (food search) for Animat consists of starting in a randomly selected blank square and moving until food is found. The meal completes the instance, and the number of steps between starting and dining is recorded. The next instance starts again at a randomly selected blank square. Animat's performance on a single instance isn't much of a measure of how smart he is, since so much depends on the randomly chosen start. So a moving average of the number of steps required to find food over the last fifty instances is taken as a measure of performance. Since the environment doesn't change, and food replenishes itself immediately, Animat's situation is a particularly simple one. How well does he do?

Since Animat begins learning immediately, before the end of its first problem instance, he's already much better than chance. His early runs on this environment typically take eight to ten steps. By 1000 runs its average is down to about four steps, after which it levels off. (Wilson sees a continued slight improvement.) Not bad performance, I'd say! Though able to sense only neighboring squares, Animat learns to find food in only four steps, with a random walk requiring forty-one and the theoretical optimum a little over two. I'm impressed!

But what has Animat learned that lets him perform so impressively? Nothing very arcane. When next to food, Animat nearly always eats it directly. Occasionally he moves one step sideways before taking it. When next to a tree with no food in sight, Animat reliably steps around the tree and finds food if it's there. When out in the open with no information,

Animat tends to drift in one direction.[9] After several problem instances, the direction of drift may shift. This emergent behavior works well for WOODS7. It might not work at all for a different environment.

All of this is impressive—it may seem to be too good to be true. And in fact it is. The preceding account, although accurate, is not complete. Things weren't so easy.

Trouble in Paradise

The final results obtained with Animat have been described. The initial results weren't so good. Animat's algorithm didn't distinguish between long and short paths to food. In particular, even a path that looped before finding food would lend strength to its classifiers. Penalizing long paths wasn't a solution because sometimes the long path is the only path, a minimal long path.

To solve this problem, Wilson added a fourth element, mentioned previously, to each of Animat's classifiers: a distance to food estimate. Our tour schedule doesn't allow for a detailed description. Suffice it to say that with distance estimates in place, selection of a move is based on probability proportional to strength divided by distance. A move tends to be selected if it is short as well as strong. Competition is local in that path length need not be considered directly.

But even more tweaking was needed. Recall that when an action $A(t)$ was selected at time t, $[A(t)]$ denoted the set of matching classifiers pursuing that same action. Ah, but there may well have been other matching classifiers that prescribed some different action. This new tweak taxes each such classifier by some small amount, a kind of lateral inhibition. Now short classifiers, those with small distance estimates, tend to be picked even more often; long ones, less often. Wilson claims that this algorithm doesn't work against minimal long paths.

And additional tweaks. A small tax was imposed on $[A(t)]$ itself to discourage looping. A threshold was set on the total strengths of matching sets $[A(t)]$. Being below threshold caused creation of a new classifier. This also helped suppress looping, and improved performance. Some random creation was introduced at a very low rate, leading to new directions. Next a kind of heuristically guided creation of classifiers was used. Instead of randomly picking an action, an educated guess based on a few trial steps was used. Finally, a new genetic operator, called intersection, was included. Parent classifiers were selected as before. A range of loci (positions) was picked randomly. Outside the range the child's allele was the same as the mother's. Inside, if the parents' alleles were the same, that same one was passed on to the child. If they were different, an "I don't care" was passed on: By means of these tweaks, paradise was regained.

Some Conclusions

By now Animat's originally simple algorithm has gotten quite complex. On the other hand, his performance is truly impressive, requiring only four or so steps, on average, to find food, with forty-one steps needed by chance and a little over two as best possible. But Animat lives in a particularly simple environment. Animat need concern himself with but a single drive: to find food. He has no predators, no toxins, no competitors of his own or another species to worry about, no environmental hazards. Bumping into trees doesn't seem to hurt. His environment is unchanging. Yet for all these simplifying advantages, a relatively complicated control structure seems needed for good performance. How complex must the control structure be of a creature who faces all the difficulties that Animat needn't and more, say a bacterium or a paramecium? It's a sobering thought.

But is it true? How could a single-celled natural agent implement such complex control? Perhaps individual control is simple, and the species relies on large numbers for its perpetuation rather than on good individual performance. Or could it be that biological agents have some inherent advantage in producing complex controls with which computer-based agents can't compete? Or perhaps all control mechanisms for autonomous agents are destined to be highly complex, with those controlling natural organisms hiding their complexity under their microscopic size. On later tour stops we'll visit several control structures at least as sophisticated as Animat's, all of which allow for scaling up to highly complex systems.

Visiting with Animat provides a preview of Agre and Chapman's work on indexical-functional representations (1987, 1988). Note that Animat doesn't distinguish food at this place from food at that place. He's interested only in food-next-to-me. And he doesn't care which tree is beside him. It's just the-tree-I'm-going-around-just-now-searching-for-food. Animat has no specific representation of individual trees, TREE, or $TREE_{206}$, or of individual food items, $FOOD_{22}$ or $FOOD_{138}$. Also, he doesn't learn paths explicitly. Any such knowledge is emergent,[10] and neither programmed nor explicitly represented. Only reactions to local situations are programmed into or learned by Animat. Global behavior emerges. Later we'll encounter the third AI debate, which questions to what extent explicit internal representation of the environment is needed for intelligence.

As we conclude our visit with Animat, recall Wilson's interpretation of van Heerden's definition of intelligence. To qualify as intelligent, Animat must learn to be repeatedly successful in finding food in diverse, observably different situations, ninety-two of them in this case. From what we've seen of Animat's abilities, he certainly seems to fulfill the demands of the definition. Hence, if we accept the definition, we must accord Animat intelligence. Ah, you say, but the definition isn't stringent enough. That's what AI researchers have complained about for decades. They say they're shooting at a moving target, with people moving the definition of intelligence to just beyond what their machines can currently do. But here we go again, spinning our wheels debating the use of the word "intelligence." Let's move on to visit populations of artificial creatures with built-in value systems.

Learning and Evolution

Any tour guide on any tour can be expected to have his or her favorite sights. I'm no exception. One of my favorites on our mechanisms of mind tour is surely the work of Ackley and Littman (1992), whose artificial agents both evolve and learn to deal with an environment that is both dynamic and complex relative to that of Animat. Of course, one's reaction to any tour attraction is heavily dependent on the vantage point from which it's seen—for instance, the Taj Mahal viewed through the archway in its front gate or Hong Kong seen by night from atop Victoria Peak. In my view, the ideal vantage point from which first to view the Ackley–Littman work is via a videotape produced at Bellcore with Dave Ackley narrating. This twenty-minute segment is included on a video, "Proceedings of the Second Artificial Life Conference," a companion to the hard copy proceedings (Langton et al. 1992). If it's available to you, don't miss it.

Since we're stuck with a less than ideal vantage point, let's ease into this work slowly by first looking at the environment, compared with Animat's. Like Animat's, this world consists of a two-dimensional array of cells, 100×100, operating in discrete, synchronous time steps. Unlike Animat's, it isn't toroidal but is surrounded by walls. Like Animat's, cells may contain plants (food) or trees. Unlike Animat's, they may also contain walls or carnivores. Animat is replaced by a population of adaptive agents, the primary objects of study. Walls remain unchanged, and dangerous to bump into, until the end of time, that is, until the end of the current computer run. Trees also are static but afford a haven to agents, who can climb them to avoid carnivores. Plants serve as food for agents and regenerate themselves over time when eaten. Carnivores can move to a neighboring (north, south, east or west) cell during a single time step, and can see and recognize the nearest object no further than six cells away in all cardinal directions. They are hardwired to seek their prey, the agents, and eat them, and may also scavenge a dead conspecific. Carnivores typically die from starvation, or rarely from damage inflicted by an agent defending itself. They reproduce when sufficiently full of ingested agents, that is, when their energy level is high enough. They do not evolve; each carnivore is identical to its single parent.

Agents, as you no doubt anticipated, are more complex and more interesting. Like carnivores, they can move to a neighboring cell during a single time step, and can see and recognize the nearest object no further than four cells away in all cardinal directions. Note that carnivores have a longer range of vision than agents, and that an agent and a carnivore may occupy diagonally adjacent cells while remaining unaware of one another. Note also that the difficult problem of perception/recognition is solved here by the programmer. A few lines of code replace the complex mechanisms of mind required of natural organisms. Agents gain energy by eating plants, occasionally dead carnivores, and, rarely, one another. They can be damaged (lose health) by encounters with carnivores or, more rarely, with walls or with one another. They can climb trees to avoid carnivores. Agents are androgynous, reproducing when sufficiently ener-getic—sexually if another agent is nearby, asexually if need be. Well, you say, agents do seem slightly more complex than carnivores, but not enough to make them more interesting. Ah, it's not their range of behav-iors that makes these agents interesting to me, but how these behaviors are selected. Agents are adaptive.

Agents adapt on three different time scales. At a specific instant of time, the action selected by an agent depends on (adapts to) his current sensory input. During the course of his life, an agent learns. During evolutionary time, the species of agents evolves. How does all this occur?

Each agent is born with an action selector, unique to the individual, that chooses a behavior (move north, south, east, or west) at each time instant, based on what it sees in the four directions. The result of that behavior is the move and its consequences, which depend on who's occu-pying the cell. A wall, a carnivore, or another agent in the cell results in damage. A plant in a cell is eaten, a tree is climbed. A dead carnivore or agent is fed upon.

An agent's action selector comes in the form of an artificial neural net-work, called its action network, that learns by altering the strengths of its synapses (weights). Each agent is born with an action network capable of probabilistically selecting more or less desirable behaviors immediately. During the course of its life the agent learns, that is, it adapts its patterns of behavior. An agent may be born with a tendency to beat its head against a wall. With luck, he may learn not to do so before the tendency proves fatal. But how does this learning take place? Agents learn via back-propagation (which you may recall from our visit with Chalmers's active-to-passive network). But where do the target behaviors for training come from? Who's the teacher? The teacher is an inherited evaluation network that provides reinforcement, positive or negative, after each behavior. But reinforcement doesn't provide target behavior, you say. No, it doesn't. And Ackley and Littman's way of solving this problem is pretty slick.

Each agent, in addition to its action network, comes equipped at birth with a unique evaluation network, again an artificial neural network. An evaluation network compares the current circumstances in which the agent finds himself with the situation a moment before, and decides whether things have improved. No improvement results in a negative reinforcement to the most recent behavior. Technically, the action network learns by back-propagation, using the complement of the behavior as the target, or desired, behavior. The complement of a behavior simply moves in the opposite direction. An agent's evaluation network allows its action network to learn, but the evaluation network itself remains fixed for life. However, an agent whose evaluation function likes approaching carnivores probably won't live long enough to produce many offspring. Evaluation networks don't learn, but they do evolve. In Ackley and Littman's words, "the inheritable evaluation function . . . converts long-time-scale feedback (lifetime-to-lifetime natural selection) into short-time-scale feedback (moment-to-moment reinforcement signals)" (1992, p. 491).

The genetic code of an agent provides the initial weights for its action network and the lifetime weights of its evaluation network, as well as other parameters. An agent who reproduces asexually passes its genetic code to its offspring intact, except for rare mutations. Sexual reproduction uses random two-point crossover to combine the genes of the two parents, again with rare mutation. This procedure differs from the genetic algorithms we visited earlier in two important ways. First, there's no explicit fitness function; the environment acts as an implicit fitness function, deciding who lives long enough and eats well enough to have the energy to reproduce. This results in a second major difference: the population size varies.

Birth and death are independent phenomena dependent on internal health and energy levels and on what's happening in the external environment. Births can occur with no corresponding deaths, and conversely. Population size may increase or decrease. In fact, the environment we've described "is not an overly kind world. Most initial agent populations die out quite quickly." Some, however, persist for millions of time steps, eating, mating, fleeing from predators, learning, evolving, doing pretty much what you'd expect of a living population. After this tour stop, the term "artificial life" seems much less oxymoronic to me.

Having created this artificial world with its artificial creatures, Ackley and Littman proceed to seed it with initial agent populations, and carefully observe and experiment with the outcome. Experiments allow them to discover under what circumstances learning and evolution together are superior to either alone or to a random walk. In one run they observe cannibalism rampant in the southwest but making little difference in the long run. Surprisingly, one population of agents with carefully hand-crafted evaluation networks optimized to find food, avoid carnivores, and so on, performed less well than some "naturally" evolved agent populations. One exceptionally long-lived population lent support for the Baldwin Effect, in which inherited properties (e.g., an initial action network that avoids carnivores) mimic learned properties (e.g., an action network that learns to avoids carnivores) without violating the canons of Darwinism. It seems that artificial life may yet influence thinking about still controversial issues in evolutionary biology.

But to me the fascination of the Ackley–Littman work lies in the inherited evaluation network that provides a mechanism by which values influence the learning of behaviors. I suspect that culturally learned values may be constrained by and subservient to more fundamental (primitive?) inherited values in all species that learn. After all, the continual, fundamental problem of every autonomous agent, including us, is what to do next. Without some values, one action is as good as another. There's no basis for a decision. To me this is a fundamental issue. It will arise again when we visit Edelman's work, and even more vividly on a later encounter with Sloman's thoughts on motives and goals (1987).

Epilogue

Artificial life is a brand-new field of study whose first conference was held in 1987 (Langton 1989), and whose first professional journal (*Artificial Life,* MIT Press) has just appeared. As yet, there are no degrees in the field, and certainly no academic departments. It has attracted an interdisciplinary cadre of researchers including physicists and computer scientists but relatively few biologists. I'm told this trend is changing, and that the biologists are beginning to take note.

I can't leave artificial life without mentioning Ray's Tierra (1992), although it doesn't properly belong on a mechanisms of mind tour. Ray has produced a virtual computer environment, within a real computer, inhabited by snippets of self-reproducing code that evolve in the most amazing ways. Parasites evolve to infest hosts that evolve to con the parasites into reproducing the hosts. After the parasites are driven to extinction, the erstwhile hosts, all related, develop a cooperative culture that flourishes until cheaters evolve to take advantage of their unsuspecting nature. And so on. Here is artificial evolution of a complexity worthy of study, and sufficiently swift to allow study in a human lifetime. Although I can find no convincing connection to mechanisms of mind, a side trip to visit Tierra is recommended nonetheless.

But for the next stop on this tour, let's consider the issue of one mind or many per individual.

Notes

1. Langton organized the first three conferences on artificial life, edited (with some help) their proceedings (Langton 1989, 1994; Langton et al. 1992), and edits the first artificial life journal.

2. Thinking Machines Corporation's CM-2, with 16,000 to 64,000 quite simple processors, has recently become a favorite vehicle for artificial life systems. An earlier model was excitingly described by Hillis, its designer, in *The Connection Machine* (1985).

3. The most accessible example of a cellular automation is Conway's Game of Life (Berlekamp et al. 1982; Poundstone 1985).

4. That's not quite accurate. We briefly tried for a definition of stupidity but gave that up, too. Let's not hear any remarks about definition by recursion here.

5. Traditional data structures in computer science include lists, arrays, queues, stacks, and trees.

6. As we'll see, Wilson uses the term "Animat" generically to refer to any of a certain class of artificial creatures. One of his articles is titled "The Animat Path to AI" (1991). Here, "Animat" will refer to the particular artificial creature described by Wilson in "Knowledge Growth in an Artificial Animal" (1985).

7. The mathematical (topological) name for a doughnut-shaped object is "torus." "Toroidal" is its adjectival form.

8. A festival during which possessions are given away in return for status. Often possessions are received, in turn, during subsequent potlatches from earlier benefactors (Benedict 1934).

9. In general, drifting may not be the best strategy. A square search, that is, searching outward in a right-angled spiral, may be better.

10. David Lee Larom objects at this point, saying, "With such a complicated rule set in such a simple world, is [Animat's] behavior really emergent? He seems to me to have been jury-rigged to do what his creators wanted!" Yes, of course. Every autonomous agent is "jury-rigged," that is, designed and/or evolved to couple with its environment or to learn to do so.

10

Multiplicity of Mind

. . . we have come to recognize an ever increasing number of semi-separable mechanisms within the human brain. They are sensory and motor. There are also mechanisms that may be called psychical, such as those of speech and of the memory of the past stream of consciousness, and mechanisms capable of automatic interpretation of present experience. There is in the brain an amazing automatic sensory and motor computer that utilizes the conditioned reflexes, and there is the highest brain-mechanism that is most closely related to that activity that men have long referred to as consciousness, or the mind, or the spirit.

—Wilder Penfield, *The Mystery of the Mind*

Gazzaniga (1985) erects a straw man about "the strong subjective sense we all possess of ourselves . . . that we are a single, unified, conscious agent controlling life's events with a singular integrated purpose" and goes on to argue against it.[1] I don't know whether "we all" possess such a sense of ourselves, but I certainly do. Well, mostly. Occasionally, there seem to be two Stans in there with dialogue running something like this:

This is a perfect time to pop over to my office and spend a couple of hours working on the book. Yeah, but Jeannie wants to take the kids to visit their new cousin. In the interest of family harmony, I ought to go with them. Well, maybe I'll take a separate car and stay only for a little while. But that's a twenty-minute drive each way, and they won't stay long anyway. Why not just go with them? Hanging out with family is more fun than struggling over writing anyway. Maybe so, but I've got to finish the book. This project has been hanging over my head for years now.

We don't seem to be "controlling life's events with a singular integrated purpose." Note the "we." And sometimes there seem to be even more than two of us. But maybe I'd best leave this line of thought, before you begin to suspect me of harboring multiple personalities.

Although for the most part there seems to be one mind up there running the show, evidence is mounting for this view being illusory. More and more, I and many others are coming round to the position outlined by Penfield above. Gazzaniga (1988, p. 231) talks of "thousands, if not millions" of "independent modules . . . capable of affecting things like bodily movement as well as more subtle events like mood shifts." Mind is best thought of as multiple or aggregate, rather than as monolithic.

In this port of call, we'll visit the work of two proponents of this multiplicity view of mind, a psychobiologist (Ornstein) and a computer scientist (Minsky). Beginning from an abstract, functional level (Ornstein), we'll go on to explore various functional mechanisms (Minsky). But that won't be the last we'll see of multiplicity. Subsequent tour stops will put us in contact with several other such advocates (John Jackson, Edelman, Drescher, Calvin, Hofstadter).

Multimind

Ornstein's *Multimind* (1986) is the first major attraction on our multiplicity tour stop. Ornstein, a respected psychobiologist who has taught at Stanford, is also a student of Sufism[2] as well as a popular author to the New Age movement. He's a personal advertisement for the ideas he's trying to sell. Some of the major parts of his book are introduced by Sufi teaching stories that are more than just amusing. Here's a sample.

Nasrudin went into a bank with a cheque to cash.
"Can you identify yourself?" asked the clerk.
Nasrudin took out a mirror and peered into it.
"Yes, that's me all right." he said.
Idries Shah, *The Subtleties of the Inimitable Mulla Nasrudin*

I'm reminded of the experiments on self-consciousness in apes we encountered earlier. Would Nasrudin have convinced Gallup that he was self-conscious?

Ornstein claims "We are not a single person. We are many." Our "strong subjective sense" of a "single, unified, conscious agent controlling life's events with a singular integrated purpose" is only an illusion. It is illusory to think that a person has a single mind. Rather, we are many.

We are coalitions or, as my neurophysiologist friend Lloyd Patridge once said to me, "the mind is more like a commonwealth."

Well, if a single mind is an illusion, what's the truth? The truth à la Ornstein asserts that mind is diverse and complex, composed of a changeable conglomeration of different kinds of "small minds." "We have lots of minds that are specialized to handle different chores." Among them are fixed reactions, talents (procedures), and memories (data). These different entities are temporarily employed, wheeled into consciousness, then usually returned to their place after use, and put back on the shelf. Gazzaniga also postulates "a vast number of relatively independent systems in the brain that compute data from the outside world." Although the computer metaphor just expressed is losing adherents, the notion of multiplicity of minds is rapidly gaining them. Instead of "small minds," we'll hear Minsky speak of "agents," Brooks of "competencies," John Jackson of "demons." Competencies are talents, procedures. Agents and demons can be either procedures or data.

Ornstein talks about specialized memories for rote learning, for names, for people, for places, for conversations, and more, each of these a separate mental ability. His memories are more like data structures that are retrieved. We'll soon hear Minsky maintain that whatever memorization takes place, does so in the procedure that is using it. In his view, and mind, memory is best viewed as a reconstructive procedure rather than as retrieval of a static data structure, although a sharp line between the two is hard to draw.

Ornstein's *talents,* like his memories, are highly specialized. In addition to spatial, verbal and intuitive talents, there are talents for feelings, mathematics, and personal interactions, and bodily talents such as athletics and dance. "Talent" should be read not as some God-given superlative talent, such as Mozart's for music for Gauss's for mathematics, but as our normal procedures for doing things. Different groups of people, or segments within a society, or various cultures will put more emphasis on one skill or another. Thus two of us may have quite different sets of talents.

As most of us do, Ornstein tends to jump back and forth among the several meanings of "mind," depending on context to enable disambiguation. When he talks of the mind wheeling from one condition to another, from crisis to quiescence, from happiness to concern, he seems to be speaking of the conscious mind.[3] (Even the conscious mind has been split. Edelman [1992] talks of primary consciousness and higher-order consciousness, as we'll see on a later tour stop.) The conscious mind wheels in various *small minds,* which accomplish quite limited and specific purposes. When a small mind has done its job, it's wheeled out, and another is wheeled in. We'll postpone posing the obvious question of who's doing the wheeling, that is, who's deciding on which small mind to wheel in next.

This wheeling in and out of small minds allows for diverse centers of control. Ornstein speaks of centers of control at lower levels having developed over millions of years to regulate the body, to guard against danger, to organize and plan efforts, and so on. These various centers have different priorities; some are more important than others. The one that keeps you breathing, for example, has very high priority. Centers of control are often at cross-purposes with each other. One might say, "Let's go eat," while the other says, "I want to hear the answer to who's doing the wheeling." We humans share some sort of hunger control that gives us a taste for fats. When our progenitors led very active lives requiring lots of calories, and food was scarce, such a preference was only prudent. Today, the fat-loving small mind often conflicts with the stricture-hurling small mind that says, "That ice cream has too much fat in it."

Patterns of Behavior

Approaching mind from the top-down, analytic corner of psychology, Ornstein, identifies four strong tendencies, or patterns of behavior, of human minds. We'll meet them one at a time. He introduces each with a catchy sentence.

"*What have you done for me lately?*" This introduces our extreme sensitivity to recent information. For example, an airliner crashes, 240 people are killed, and suddenly people are expressing concern and interest, and there is movement toward improving safety procedures. Within a few months it's entirely forgotten. It's just gone. Nobody cares anymore. On the other hand, 80,000 auto accident fatalities over a year's time cause little comment or concern.

"Don't call me unless anything new and exciting happens." Unexpected or extraordinary events seem to enjoy a fast track into our consciousness. A sudden loud noise behind us will result in an abrupt turn to inspect. A rabbit may blend into the landscape so as to be essentially invisible, until it moves. The sentence that begins this paragraph found my fast track. It caught my attention, since I would have said, "Don't call unless *something* new and exciting happens." My expectation in that context was for "something" rather than "anything." When that expectation wasn't met, my attention was captured. Other people seem not to share my expectation. If you don't, perhaps you read right by that sentence and thought nothing of it. And then there's our urge to explain, a tendency Ornstein didn't mention. Maybe my version of the sentence is a southernism.

"Compared to what?" We constantly judge by comparisons and rarely make absolute judgments of any kind. In baseball, a batter swings two bats in preparation so that one will seem light when he steps to the plate. This morning (in September), 50-degree weather seemed a bit nippy to me when I went out for an early morning jog. In midwinter, 50-degree weather will seem balmy. I'd be quite appreciative of a 5 percent raise—unless, of course, I was expecting 10 percent. I can remember a 6-foot-5 student in one of my classes seeming so tall, but not so when I saw him as a shooting guard on the basketball team. And self-esteem is often measured by how I compare myself with others. Almost all of our judgments are relative to something.

"Get to the point." The meaning of any event, its relevance to the person (or the autonomous agent), is the point. As a police car pulls up behind you with siren blaring, it's not the siren that's frightening, it's the meaning of the siren. Having just made up, the meaning of a kiss may be even more pleasurable than the kiss. It's the meaning to the person that counts. More specifically, it's the meaning to the particular talent that has most recently been wheeled into consciousness. That talent will use the information.

Ornstein claims that we "throw out almost all the information that reaches us," asking how many of the billions of leaves you saw last summer you remember. At a lower level of abstraction, he claims that "the eye . . . transmits less than *one trillionth* of the information reaching its surface!"⁴ At this point I'd like to suggest more discriminating terminology. Let's use "data" for the light rays falling on the retina and, at a higher level, for the leaves. Let's reserve "information" for those meanings created by us (or any autonomous agent) because of their relevance to our current situation, including our needs and goals. In these terms we rapidly throw out all the data and hold on to the information as long as it's useful (and, sometimes, much longer).

About now, you may be wondering why I'm regaling you with these stories that sound more like pop psychology than serious science. Ornstein's not talking about mechanisms of mind, that's true. But he is proposing a high-level theory of the functioning of mind that I judge (comparatively, of course) to be useful. It's a high-level theory that will give us a framework within which to view the work on mechanisms of mind of Minsky, Brooks, John Jackson, and others during this and later tour stops. So let's continue our visit to multimind.

High-level perception produces organization and, thus, simplification. We extract (I'd say "create") meaning from our sensing. When something is meaningful, it is organized. When it is organized, it is simplified in the mind. Ornstein cites the example of the dalmatian. Do you recall having seen a black and white pointillist picture that at first sight seems like nothing but a bunch of dots? It looks very complex but has no meaning. Suddenly, there's an "aha" experience: "There's a dog!" You recognize a dalmatian. From that moment on, you can't see the complexity. At least I can't get it back. The feeling of wonder, of bafflement, seems unrecoverable. The image, instead of being complex, is simple. Meaning leads to organization leads to simplicity.

All this is in the service of making sense of our worlds. Ornstein maintains that we "hold in our minds" a well-organized and simplified version of our environment, of the nature of other people, of our personal histories, and of our beliefs. I'd quibble a bit and say "reconstruct" rather than "hold." I doubt that even a most microscopic examination of my brain would yield even one encoded picture of a dalmatian. Yet I can reconstruct one. I'm arguing against the filing cabinet metaphor for memory. The distinction is identical to the one computer scientists make between storing a table of the first fifty prime numbers in memory and storing a procedure that calculates any one of the first fifty primes on demand.

Ornstein sees the brain as a compendium of circuits piled atop one another, each developed over past millennia to serve a short-term purpose. Different circuits may have very different ideas behind them, rather than being guided by some unified conception of cognition. Here, Ornstein's view seems on the opposite side of the fence from Newell's unified theory of cognition. Although I tend strongly to the position of Ornstein and others, as you have seen and will see again, I'm not ready to rule Newell out. At a sufficiently high level of abstraction, we may yet discover a unified mechanism of mind. But for now, the picture is one of separate structures laid on top of each other, like a house being added on to. This picture is very much like Brooks's subsumption architecture, which we'll see later in some detail.

Ornstein talks about our having small minds, or talents, for alertness, for emotions, for danger, for comparing sensory information, for avoiding scarcity, and so forth. He points out evolutionary influences that have shaped these talents. We tend to prefer temperatures between 60 and 85 degrees Fahrenheit because our remote ancestors lived on the plains of East Africa. Similarly for the late afternoon work slump. East African plains get hot in the late afternoon, so that's a good time to sit under a tree and not do much. People in Norway in November also experience this same kind of slump because our archaic nervous system hasn't had enough evolutionary time to adjust. Another such example is the hackles that get raised when you're angry or afraid. A lion's mane stands out so he'll look larger to the encroaching lion he's threatening. Primates, too. Their hair stands up so they'll look larger and more threatening. I vividly recall the hair standing up on my wife's neck as we approached a mama rhino and her calf in southern Nepal.

Sensory experiences are relative. No change, no experience. Sitting in a room where everything is the same color and texture, no distinction whatever, you don't see anything. Constant noises disappear. Were you aware of your breathing until I mentioned it? Or your body against your chair? If you light a candle outside in the sunlight, it's hardly visible. But lit in a dark room, it illuminates the whole room. Context is everything.

·

The Creation of Information

Ornstein views the sense as filters, not windows. We have no need to reflect all occurrences. What difference does the angle between two particular blades of grass make? Or the fact that a particular leaf is falling? We want to convey (create) only relevant, important information, say changes in the state of an object. And only a minute fraction of available information is transmitted (or available data transformed into information). And then there are occurrences in the world for which we have no senses: radio waves, infrared, ultraviolet, sounds below 20 hertz, and a universe of microscopic organisms smaller than our best visual resolution. Here's the point of the matter: we obviously cannot see what is really out there. There is no point in arguing about it. Essentially, we create our worlds to meet our own needs.

We're not hallucinating and creating worlds out of whole cloth. Rather, we're constrained by what is actually out there. But appearances are built in. "*Our world appears to us the way it does because we are built the way we are*" (p. 40). Consider a cat looking at chocolate cake versus me looking at chocolate cake. I see it as brown, but the cat doesn't see in color. I can taste it as sweet, but the cat doesn't have any sweet taste buds. The appearances of chocolate cake are very different for each of us because we are built differently. It seems to me that dolphins or bats, which use echolocation, must see a very different world than we do.

The world we create is also affected by internal transformations. Referring to the graph in figure 10.1, the x-axis records actual stimulus magnitude as measured by instruments, and the y-axis lists the average estimate of magnitude, that is, what magnitude a person reports perceiving. For length, there's a linear relationship[5] between the actual length and the perceived length. The longer it is, the longer the person perceives it to be. Perception of brightness behaves differently. Early on, as an object begins to brighten, the apparent brightness increases quickly. Later, when the object becomes very bright, the apparent brightness tapers off. The relationships seems logarithmic.[6] Perception of pain behaves differently yet. Low levels of pain are perceived as being less than it "actually" is, that is, less than you would measure the magnitude of the stimulus causing the pain. As the magnitude of the stimulus increases, the perception of the

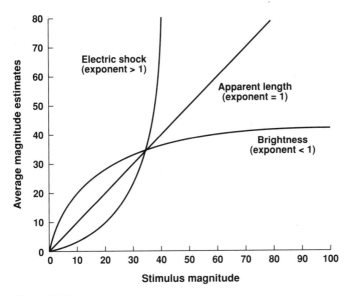

Figure 10.1
Power curves for different stimuli (redrawn from Ornstein 1986)

pain increases much more rapidly, an exponential[7] rush. As we sense through our window on the world, we filter, we transform, we create to fit our needs.

The Brain à la Ornstein

What do we use to do all this creating? Our brains, which are often partitioned into the brain stem, the limbic system, and the cortex. Our brain stem, says Ornstein, looks much like the brain of a crocodile. The basic design is about 500 million years old. It accounts for alertness and the basic mechanisms of life support, and is not the locus of many of the activities we heretofore have called mind. It would follow, then, that the crocodile doesn't have much mind. I would like to broaden the usage of "mind" to include these activities.

Penfield (1975), a neurosurgeon, says the indispensable substratum of consciousness lies outside the cerebral cortex, probably in the higher brain stem. Removal of even large portions of cerebral cortex doesn't affect consciousness, whereas "injury or interference with function in the higher brain-stem, even in small areas, abolishes consciousness completely." If consciousness is mediated by the higher brain stem, and crocodiles have brain stems, must crocodiles experience consciousness? They may well do so, but the argument is specious. As my friend Lloyd Partridge pointed out to me, removing the distributor cap from your automobile will turn off your motor, but that doesn't mark the distributor as the center of movement. There's been a long and unsuccessful search for the center of human consciousness. Penfield presents evidence that seems to rule out the cortex. My physician friend Dan Jones takes issue with this last assertion as follows:

> The great preponderance of evidence is that the neocortex is the "locus" of consciousness, but that input from the reticular activating system of the brain stem is required to activate it. . . . Since the neocortex is large, you have to destroy most of it on both sides to eradicate consciousness, but small ablations of critical areas can serious impair the quality of consciousness, e.g., destruction of the color-perception cortex prevents further "consciousness" (seeing or imagining) of color. (personal communication)

Dennett, a philosopher, makes a book-length argument that there is no such center in his immodestly titled *Consciousness Explained* (1991). I'm not sure Dennett and Jones would find much to argue about. Having a center of consciousness dispersed over the neocortex may well be the same as not having a center of consciousness at all.

Ornstein (1986, p. 48) credits the limbic system "with having presided over the transition from sea-dwelling animals to land animals." Its 200 million-year-old design regulates body temperature, thirst, hunger, and weight and controls emotional reactions and responses to emergencies. "We have pretty much the same basic emotional apparatus as our remote ancestors had."

In the quiltlike cortex covering the brain, decisions are made, schemes are hatched, language is produced and understood, music is listened to, mathematics is created, and so forth. It seems to be the home of the higher cognitive functions. Penfield (1975, p. 18) views the cortex not as "the 'highest level' of integration" but as "an elaboration level, sharply divided into distinct areas for distinct functions." But what does he mean by that? I picture sensory data coming in—visual, auditory, olfactory, tactile, proprioceptive, whatever. Somewhere along the line the data fuse into information. I think Penfield is saying that this highest level of integration is to be found not only in the cortex but also lower down. He proposes the cortex as an elaboration of a system already capable of fusing data into information, an elaboration composed of additional pieces with additional skills like language, that you wouldn't find at lower levels. (We'll soon meet this piling of skills level upon level in Brooks's subsumption architecture.)

In Ornstein's terminology, Penfield sees the cortex as composed of mechanisms for various talents. He also sees the cortex as "sharply divided into areas for distinct functions." Ornstein claims reasonably well identified areas of the brain associated with most of the following talents: activating, informing, smelling, feeling, healing, moving, locating and identifying, calculating, talking, knowing, governing. (I'll soon take issue with this last.) This question of the localization of function has been hotly debated. A recent correspondence thread on the connectionist list on the Internet found neurophysiologists reporting that localization is losing support.[8]

Structure of Multimind

Ornstein offers a hierarchy of mental structures as follows. At the lowest level of organization are the basic neural transformations. I picture these as groups of neurons acting cooperatively to perform a set function. Later on this tour stop we'll hear Edelman refer to them as neuronal groups. Next Ornstein talks of reflexes, set reactions. Then come domain-specific data-processing modules, the "quick and stupid analytical systems of the mind," one of which might produce "the consistent perception of red under bright sunlight and dusk." Slower, but smarter, more general, and more flexible, are the talents. Combinations of talents, useful in particular situations, comprise small minds. And finally, at the top of the heap, rests consciousness, into which small minds are wheeled (and wheeled out) as our goals and environment demand.

Ornstein talks of physiological evidence for many kinds of memory in many parts of mind—memory for faces, locations, smells, movements, sights. Further, he identifies memory and perception, saying, "There is little reason to think that perceiving and remembering are in any way different (1986, p. 76)". I think he means to assert that the two "faculties" use the same neural mechanisms, and that perceptions and memories are not reliably distinguishable. Experimental psychologists test subjects for recall ("Write down all the words you can remember from the list.") and for recognition ("Was the word 'hungry' on the list you just saw?"). Psychological models of memory are often expected to account for both recall and recognition, that is, for both memory and perception. But recent neurophysiological evidence casts doubts on the single-mechanism hypothesis. Here's a quote from the *Wall Street Journal* (September 30, 1993, p. A13):[9]

Until C.K. and one other brain-damaged person came along, it was thought that the brain used the same bunch of neurons for recognizing what the eyes are seeing and for remembering what things look like. Both abilities, it was thought, centered in a vast storehouse of images the memory had accumulated.

Recognition, or perception, it was believed, involved matching up the images flashing in from the retinas with those in the storehouse, while imagery involved calling up stored images on cue. This one-system idea was reinforced by the observation that many brain-damaged patients who had trouble recognizing what they were looking at also had trouble remembering what things look like.

But the case of C.K.'s bafflement with asparagus [he could draw asparagus nicely from memory but couldn't recognize a picture of one] suggests that visual perception and visual imagery involve separate patches of neurons. One possibility is that there are two storehouses of images, one for perception and one for mental imagery, and C.K.'s access to the first has been damaged but his access to the second is intact. The alternative is that there are two "routes" to the one big storehouse.

C.K. seems to have no trouble recognizing human faces, lending another bit of evidence to the argument for separate memories for faces.

And then there are feelings. Ornstein has us organized by our specific emotions to feed (hunger), fight (anger), flee (fear), and reproduce (lust), pointing out that strong emotions fix our memories and amplify our experiences. Sloman, whom we previously met regarding free will and will meet again on a later stop, believes emotions are essential to intelligent autonomous agents. More of this later.

Finally, Ornstein takes up the issue of will and volition. Who's minding the store? This control issue is, of course, central to any theory where multiple agents form a mind. We'll be concerned with it for much of the remainder of our tour. Ornstein doesn't believe that "the separate minds clamor and fight for control and the strongest wins, with no directing force" (p. 178). (John Jackson's pandemonium theory says something much like this. More later.)

Instead, he postulates a "governing self" that controls the wheeling of small minds in and out of consciousness: ". . . it is this component of the governing self that links many of the separate small minds" (p. 178). Not that everyone has a governing self, mind you. In most of us, which small mind gets wheeled in is decided automatically on the "basis of blind habit." But, says Ornstein, ". . . a person can become conscious of the multiminds and begin to run *them* rather than hopelessly watch anger wheel in once again" (p. 185).

Until now I've been quite taken with Ornstein's multimind theory. Here I begin to feel some discomfort. It's so easy to explain mind by inadvertently postulating a homunculus, a little "man," who sits up there and provides whatever intelligence is needed. This, of course, leaves open the problem of explaining how the homunculus works. The issue hasn't been dealt with, but simply pushed back. I fear that Ornstein, by introducing an unexplained governing self, has allowed the homunculus to sneak under the door.

As Minsky puts it (1985, p. 18), "Unless we can explain the mind in terms of things that have no thoughts or feelings of their own, we'll only have gone around in a circle." This introduces us to the next major attraction in this port of call.

The Society of Mind

One of the founders of symbolic AI, Minsky has also made seminal contributions to artificial neural networks, robotics, and theoretical computer science. Here we'll visit with his *Society in Mind* (1985). Minsky cannot be accused of being unambitious. His first sentence reads, "This book tries to explain how minds work." Well, surely this is right up our alley. Let's have at it.

Minsky motivates his theory of mind from evolution: "Each human cranium contains hundreds of kinds of computers, developed over hundreds of millions of years of evolution each with a somewhat different architecture" (1985, p. 66). But whereas Ornstein, as befits a psychologist, approaches mind from the top-down, analytic direction, Minsky, wearing his roboticist hat, takes a bottom-up, synthetic route. he wants to show how "you can build a mind from many little parts, each mindless by itself." He refers to these little parts as "agents." In Orstein's terminology, an agent might be a module, a talent, or a small mind. Minsky's agents run the gamut from low-level to clearly cognitive: "Each mental agent by itself can only do some simple thing that needs no mind or thought at all. Yet when we join these agents in societies . . . this leads to true intelligence" (1985, p. 17).

Note carefully that each agent can *do* something, as contrasted to Ornstein's talents, which *can* act as static data structures. Minsky's agents are all processes, even when they empower memory. Note also that Minsky is trying to sell the idea of intelligence implemented by a *society* of relatively unintelligent agents. (Remember the termite colony as architect of a remarkable edifice that no one member has any idea how to build.) Minsky proposes another instance of the multiplicity of mind idea, but with the term "society" carefully chosen to spotlight the importance of the interaction of agents.

To have something more concrete in mind, let's look at Minsky's example of the agent *builder*, who knows how to stack blocks into towers. *Builder* can call on his high-level buddies *begin, add,* and *end. Begin* finds himself a nice flat space on the table and decides, "We'll build it here." That is all he does. *Add* grabs a block and stacks it on top. *End* says to *add,* "Stop, that's enough, don't go any higher." How does *add* stack blocks? As *builder* uses *begin, add,* and *end,* so *add,* in turn, uses *find, get,* and *put,* who do just what you'd think they'd do from their names. And each of these three agents calls several other, still lower-level agents. Each of these has a hierarchy under him. *Add* uses *find* to find a block, and *find* in turn uses *see.* He wouldn't have to use *see.* Suppose blocks were smelly and better found by olfaction. *Find* could use *smell* instead. Once a block is found, *add* calls *get* to fetch it. *Get* then uses *move* to get to the block and *grasp* to get hold of it. Now *put* takes over, using *move* again. And so on.

Agents, according to Minsky, are the primitives of intelligence. Lower-level agents have no thoughts and no feelings, yet out of them emerge intelligent actions. They are mental procedures that do things. They are similar or equivalent not only to Ornstein's talents, which we've already met, but also to Brooks's behaviors, John Jackson's demons, Maes's actions, and Edelman's neuronal groups, all of which we'll visit on the tour. Agents have very limited abilities, but they can do one thing well. Agents can call on other agents as procedures can in a programming language. They have limited bandwidth[10] for communicating with other agents. In fact, it is mostly 0 bandwidth, because communications between agents is relatively rare. The chance of picking two agents randomly out of the human mind and their having anything whatever to say to one another is vanishingly small. Each agent uses only a small number of others with whom it can communicate. Typically, one agent doesn't know much about what another does. This lack of communication between agents seems biologically plausible. The human brain, with each neuron connected to 10,000 others on average, and with some 10^{15} synapses total, surely seems well connected, with plenty of opportunity for communication. But this is an illusion. Each neuron, or each group of 1000 neurons, for that matter, can communicate with only a tiny fraction of the remaining neurons.[11].

Minsky's Mechanisms

True to his promise, Minsky proposes many possible mechanisms of mind, most of them at a relatively high level of abstraction with many possible implementations. Let's visit a bit with a small but representative sample of these mechanisms to get a feeling for what they're like. The first will involve the use of collections of agents for the representation of concepts.

Agents can be active or not. Or they may have some activation level other than off or on. Active agents can represent properties or features, as illustrated in figure 10.2 Minsky's division—shape, substance, color, and size—are themselves collections of agents and may correspond to Ornstein's small minds. The gray blobs in the figure indicate inactive agents; the bold hexagons, active agents. The collection of active agents in the shape division may represent the shape "round." This representation is distributed as we've seen before in connectionist models. When attention

A small white rubber ball

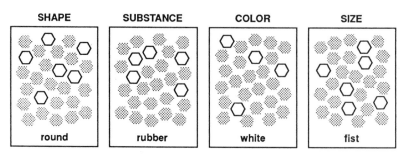

Some divisions of a mind-society

Figure 10.2
Agents' representation of concepts (adapted from Minsky 1985)

passes to some other object, a different collection within the shape division will become active, representing some other shape.

This mechanism employs configurations, patterns of activity, to represent objects, concepts, and so on (I, and others, have argued that objects are best viewed as special kinds of concepts rater than as privileged entities in the world.) Symbolic AI typically employs another familiar mechanism for representing a particular concept, a named data structure such as a frame (Minsky 1975) or a script (Schank and Abelson 1977). A third, and biologically motivated, mechanism for representing concepts has been proposed by Calvin (1992, 1993). Later we'll visit at some length with yet another mechanism for concepts, representation via attractor basins of a dynamical system (Skarda and Freeman 1987).

How are these representations retrieved? What is the mechanism for memory? We've heard Ornstein propose numerous specialized memories rather than a single all-purpose memory. Still, these many memories may all employ the same underlying mechanism. Minsky introduces the notion of a K-line as his basic mechanism for memory. He took this notion seriously enough to publish it in *Cognitive Science* (1980) instead of in a computer science journal. A K-line is a mental data structure and also an agent. What does it do? It connects other agents and awakens them when appropriate. Think of a K-line as a wirelike structure that attaches itself to agents that are active when the K-line is formed. Here is an entertaining example that Minsky attributes to one of his students. Suppose I am about to fix my bike. I get out my toolbox. I get out the red paint. I paint both hands red. In the process of repairing the bicycle, every tool that I used is marked with red paint. The next time I need to fix my bike, I can get out just the tools with red paint, thinking that they have a good chance of being used because they were used in a similar situation once before. The K-line activates those tools that are marked with red paint. An agent can be attached to several different K-lines.

K-lines are active agents of memory. We're not talking about declarative knowledge stored in propositional form but procedures for approximately reconstructing a prior mental state. And a prior mental state has to do with which agents are active. Memories, then, are dynamic procedural agents, not static data structures.

K-lines can be used to construct hierarchical memories. The upper image in figure 10.3 illustrates a K-line for the sentence "Jack flies a kite." That K-line is attached to many agents, some (male and young) helping to represent Jack, others (outside, wind, red, and paper) representing kite. K-lines can be hooked directly to agents in this way, or perhaps to other, preexisting, K-lines, as illustrated by the lower image. This version produces a hierarchical memory. It also tends to produce mental states based more on stereotypes and default assumptions than on actual perceptions, as also seems true of us humans.

Now that we've seen some of Minsky's mechanisms, it's reasonable to ask how they are controlled. (Questions of control will be visited at length on a later tour stop.) Minsky proposes a B-brain influencing an A-brain that, in turn, interacts with the world. Picture the A-brain as being comprised of agents that sense the outside world and of other, motor agents that act upon it. Picture the B-brain sitting atop in contact only with A's agents. The B-brain is composed of executives who direct, or at least influence, A's activity. Minsky gives several examples. If A seems disordered and confused, B makes A stop doing whatever it's doing. If A seems to be repeating itself, caught in an endless loop, B makes it try something new. If A does something B likes, B makes A remember it. If A is too much involved with detail, B makes it take a higher-level view, and conversely. The notion of a B-brain provides a high-level, abstract control mecha-

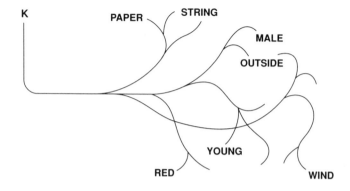

K-line attached to many agents

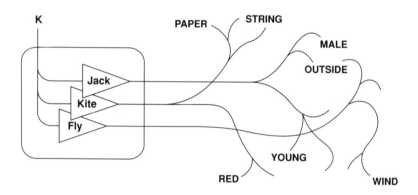

K-line attached to three K-lines

Figure 10.3
K-lines (redrawn from Minsky 1985)

nism. Soon we'll visit lower-level control mechanisms. In the context of one of these, Maes (1990) argues that B-brains, with their executives, are not needed for low-level minds, say for autonomous moon explorers.

But how are these brains composed? Hierarchically. At the bottom are the agents with their own hierarchy. At the next level up we find societies, organizations of agents.[12] Up another level you have layers of societies. Minds, according to Minsky, develop as sequences of layers of societies. Each new layer begins as a set of K-lines and learns to exploit whatever skills have been acquired by the previous layer. When a layer acquires some useful and substantial skill, it tends to stop learning and changing.[13] Suppose I'm a small child learning to walk in a straight line (creating an agent *walker*). Since I don't walk very well, if I want something badly, I'll probably get on my knees and crawl for it (use *crawler*). The better I get at walking that straight line, the more useful this skill is going to be, and the more *walker* will be called on by other agents that want to do things. At that point *walker* ceases to improve. Very carefully walking a very straight line, one foot in front of the other, would cause too much delay for all the agents that want to use *walker*. If a need occurs for that kind of skill (tightrope walking), it tends to develop as a new separate agent.

Minsky refers to another possible mechanism of mind, at least for some high-level agents, as a difference engine (see figure 10.4). A comparison of the current situation with a description of the goal it wants to reach provides a set of differences. Agents acting on the world so as to minimize these differences are then activated, thus moving the situation toward the goal. This strategy is referred to, in symbolic AI, as means–ends analysis. Means–ends analysis is a "weak" method in that it requires little domain knowledge to accomplish its objective (Laird et al. 1987). The General Problem Solver is an early symbolic AI program employing means–ends analysis (Simon 1981). You'll also recall our having met means–end analysis briefly during our earlier visit with SOAR.

Difference engines require goal descriptions. Goals must persist over some time, and require some image or description of a desired state. Can

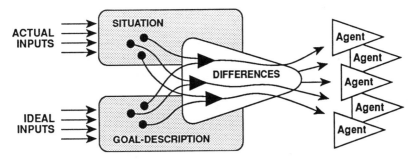

Figure 10.4
Difference engine (redrawn from Minsky 1985)

a machine have a desired state? Does Deep Thought "want" to win at chess?[14] Does a thermostat "want" the temperature to be at 72 degrees? Can you feel the mire rising above your ankles? Minsky helps to pull us free: "We need not force ourselves to decide questions like whether machines can have goals or not. Words should be our servants, not our masters. The notion of goal makes it easy to describe certain aspects of what people and machines can do" (p. 79). I think Minsky is led to this view not by difference engines requiring goal descriptions but by seeing the difference engine as a mechanism for goal-seeking behavior. He says, "The Difference-engine scheme remains the most useful conception of goal, purpose, or intention yet discovered" (p. 79). Note that the claim is "most useful." I tend to agree. We'll meet the issue of goals again when we visit Sloman's work once more later on the tour.

A favorite maxim of mine is "if it ain't broke, don't fix it." Minsky offers his version as a mechanism: if it is broke, don't fix it. Rather, suppress it. This dictum makes more sense that it seems to at first. Suppose a procedure has failed in a certain situation. What should I do? Fixing it might introduce errors in other situations where it now works perfectly well. Here's an example. IBM mainframe computers, the "big iron," employ a huge operating system, a massive piece of software that performs executive functions like scheduling tasks, allotting processor time slices, loading and saving files, and communicating with printers. Every year or so IBM produces a new version of the operating system that, in addition to offering some new features, fixes a few hundred of its known bugs.[15] In the process of fixing old bugs (and of introducing new features), they introduce new bugs. Conventional wisdom maintains that over the years, the number of bugs is essentially constant.

Well, if I don't fix the bug, what do I do? Minsky suggests inserting a censor that remembers some abstraction of the situation in which the procedure doesn't work. When that situation arises again, the censor suppresses the misbehaving procedure and calls on some other, special-purpose, procedure to do the job. This tactic reminds me once again of Brooks's subsumption architecture, which we'll visit next. I might conjecture that Brooks, a younger colleague of Minsky, was influenced by him, but I don't know that.

An autonomous creature,[16] like a person or a mouse, or maybe even a Mars lander, may need to learn some new behavior, say locomotion by walking or adding a column of figures by using a calculator. Such creatures must continue functioning as they learn. How to bring this about? You can't turn off a life-support system while learning to do it better. The trick is to keep the old system intact and operational while building the new as a detour around the old. Test the new system without letting it assume control. When satisfied, cut or suppress some of the connections to the older system. We'll see this approach illustrated in robots during our visit with subsumption architecture. I first encountered the idea in a different context. When consulting with small businesses moving to computer systems, one would carefully run the older manual system in parallel with the new computer system until all the bugs were flushed. The manual system was then discontinued (suppressed) but often remained available as a backup, at least for a while.

Suppression brings to mind another common mechanism employed by agents: mutual inhibition, or the "winner take all" strategy. In a group of agents, often only one can reasonably be active at a time, as a single-bodied organism can typically move in only one direction at a time. One way of accomplishing this is to have each member of the group send inhibitory signals to every other member: mutual inhibition. We encountered this idea, during our visit with connectionism. Recall that the connectionist model of word recognition of McCelland and Rumelhart (1981) made extensive use of the "winner take all" strategy.

Autonomous agents, by definition, pursue their own goals, multiple goals in all but the simplest cases. Any persistent goal can be expected eventually to conflict with other goals. Such conflict is likely to cause problems, since no longer-term project can hope to succeed, or even to persist, without some defense against these competing interests. Minsky claims that such conflicts among our most insistent goals produce strong emotional reactions. These emotions are needed to defend against competing goals. He concludes that "the question is not whether intelligent machines can have any emotions, but whether machines can be intelligent without any emotions" (p. 163). We'll hear from Sloman on the use and necessity of emotions later in the tour.

Note that real systems, like us, are remarkably robust, meaning that they perform reasonably well under widely varying circumstances. Minsky asks how such systems can be made robust. Duplication or redundancy is one possibility. For example, equipping your computer with two hard disks so that when you write to one, it writes to the other. Another techniques is to build your system so that it will repair itself. Some put this as a necessary condition for life itself. We saw yet another means during our visit with connectionism. Employ distributed processes so that each small agent can affect a large society of other agents, but will have only a mild effect on any one of them. Minsky favors still another way, accumulation. Each agency will accumulate under it a wide collection of little agents to do its bidding, so as to have several different ways of getting its job done. Some of these may be more efficient than others. But if one is lost in a particular circumstance, chances are there will be another way. This notion of robustness through accumulation is reminiscent of Edelman's selection of neuronal groups, to be visited at a later port of call.

After this brief sample of Minsky's mechanisms of mind, you may well conclude it's all a kludge, an ad hoc collection of mechanisms with no overall theme, no organizing order, no common thread. If so, I, and probably Minsky, would agree with you.

Perhaps the fault is actually mine, for failing to find a tidy base of neatly ordered principles. But I'm inclined to lay the blame upon the nature of the mind: much of its power seems to stem from just the messy ways it agents cross-connect. If so, that complication can't be helped; it's only what we must expect from evolution's countless tricks.

Maybe it's just a kludge, but it's a damn powerful one. What else do you know that's capable of delving into an understanding of its own mechanisms?

We've spent this tour stop with me trying to sell you, with the help of Ornstein and Minsky, on the multiplicity theory of mind, mind as aggregate rather than monolithic. Our next stop will focus on how minds can perform their primary function of choosing the next action. We'll also garner more support for multiplicity.

Notes

1. As did Freud with his ego, id, and superego.

2. The mystical branch of Islam.

3. Art Graesser reminds us here that much cognitive activity never reaches consciousness.

4. I got so upset by this seemingly outlandish statement that I called my friend Lloyd Partridge, who, after some effort, convinced me that even though the number may not be one trillionth, it's a very, very, very small number indeed.

5. That is, its graph approximates a straight line segment.

6. That is, it increases rapidly before tapering off and becoming almost flat, as does the logarithm function.

7. Exponential functions grow slowly for small values of their argument but extremely rapidly for large values.

8. Here's Dan Jones's view of this matter (with which I entirely agree): "I think at this point the 'localization vs. equipotentiality' debate in neuroscience is about as bankrupt as the 'nature vs. nuture' debate in developmental biology. There is now overwhelming evidence both for localization of function and diffuse integration of function. Any attempt at either/or categorization seems grossly misguided or naive."

9. I'm grateful to my friend Paul Byrne for calling this article to my attention.

10. Two humans sharing a common language and in physical proximity can be expected to have a broad bandwidth for communications. Without a common language, the bandwidth is narrowed to carry only gestures and sounds. A human and a dolphin must struggle with an even narrower bandwidth.

11. $1000 \times 10,000 = 10.^7$ But the brain has roughly 10^{11} neurons. The fraction is 1/10,000. Tiny indeed!

12. More technically of agencies. *Builder,* thought of as an agent, only knows how to call three other agents. *Builder,* thought of as an agency, knows how to build towers of blocks.

13. A fascinating evolutionary analogue to this idea is due to Kauffman (1993, chap. 3). Not very fit organisms tend to live in a very rugged fitness landscape where large mutations (changes) may well prove helpful. Fitter organisms, having climbed partway up some fitness peak, are likely to benefit only by quite small mutations (changes). This note is not intended to explain the idea but to tempt you to Kauffman's book.

14. Deep Thought is a computer system, based on symbolic AI and specialized hardware, that plays better chess than all but a few tens of humans. We met it briefly during Dennett's refutation of one of Penrose's arguments while touring the first AI debate.

15. In the early days of computing, Grace Murray Hopper, one of its pioneers, repaired a down computer by removing the corpse of an insect from between the contacts of a relay. Since then, a misbehaving computing system is said to have a "bug," the bug being the hardware or software cause of the misbehavior. The process of removing such bugs is called "debugging." Typically, more time is spent debugging a program than writing it.

16. I want to write "autonomous *agent*," equivocating on the use of the word "agent." An autonomous agent would not be an agent in Minsky's sense but an agent in that it senses and acts on its environment in pursuit of its own goals. Be warned. I may well lapse back into this usage.

11

What Do I Do Now?

A long while back, we explicitly, if tentatively, embraced the physicalist assumption that mind is what brain does. We've since devoted our tour to exploring mechanisms that brains, natural or artificial, may employ. We've been concerned with the "how" of mind. How does mind, the process, arise from brain, the material? For a moment only, I'd like to put the "how" question aside in favor of a "what for" question. What are minds for? What is their function? In stark contrast to the complexity and profundity of replies to the "how" question, the "what for" question is easily answered: *minds choose what to do next.*

Well, you might complain, that answer can be so simple because of its high level of abstraction. At a lower level, complex and profound functions appear. So what's so great about this simple answer? You're quite right, of course. Nonetheless, I found this high-level, easy answer both surprising and useful. Minds, particularly human minds, seem almost infinitely rich and complex, like some supernatural tapestry. That all this richness serves a single, easily stated goal amazes me.[1]

Think of an autonomous agent as a creature that senses its environment and acts on it so as to further its own agenda. Any such agent, be it a human or a thermostat, has a single, overriding concern—what to do next. And that's what minds are for—to address this concern by producing an appropriate action. In engineering terminology, minds are control systems. They balance all the mechanisms so that appropriate actions are continually generated in a timely fashion. (In humans, a jammed system is called a catatonic state.) And all our internal jabber—our feelings, beliefs, desires—subserve this single function of choosing what to do next.

Let's leave this brief digression and return to our concern with the "how" of minds. How do minds go about choosing the next action? We've already seen several possibilities. Although SOAR doesn't quite qualify as an autonomous agent, it offers definite possibilities as a control system. I'm looking forward to Robo-SOAR. Animat used a classifier system for control. I recall being astounded at the intricacies required for Animat to deal well with even the simplest environment. The agents of Ackley and Littman evolved their values as neural nets, and used them to train action nets to choose behaviors. Ornstein speculated on the internals of human control structures, and Minsky offered mechanisms for implementing specific control strategies. So we approach this port of call having been treated to several related sights that promise to clarify what we see here.

And what will that be? First we'll visit John Jackson's pandemonium theory of mind, which lies so close to Ornstein's work and Minsky's work that it could have well been visited from that port. After that, we'll see how Maes uses spreading activation to choose among possible symbolically controlled behaviors. Next, we'll visit with Brooks's robots, who have their behaviors built in, in layers. Finally, we'll think about something approaching a formal theory of autonomous systems, the work of Brustoloni. We should finish with a clearer concept of mind as a control structure.

Pandemonium Model of Mind

Selfridge (1959) proposed a pandemonium theory of perception built on primitive constructs called *demons*. What's a demon? It's a rule, a procedure, an agent in Minsky's sense, that responds at once when appropriately stimulated. In computer science, demons are processes that sit around and watch for something specific to happen, for example, for a keystroke on the keyboard or for an "out of paper" signal from the printer. When the awaited even occurs, POW, the demon jumps up and does its thing, such as printing a little box on the screen with "The printer is out of paper" written in it.[2]

In Selfridge's theory, demons serve to identify objects. On being presented with an object, a crowd of demons would stand around shouting,

Figure 11.1
Signal

each with a loudness proportional to how well its favored input matched the features of the presented object. The demon who shouts loudest is taken to identify the object. For example, a signal like that in figure 11.1 would stimulate the demon for R, because it sort of looks like an R, and the demon for O. But most of all, it would stimulate the demon for "Q," which would probably win out.

John Jackson (1987) wants to extend Selfridge's pandemonium theory to a theory of mind.[3] To this end he invites us to a thought experiment including not only demons involved with perception but also demons that cause external actions and demons that act internally on other demons. These classes need not be disjoint; a single demon may, for example, affect an action while influencing some other demon as a side effect. Think of Jackson's demons as abstract versions of Minsky's agents (dressed all in red and complete with horns, tail, and pitchfork).

Picture these demons living in a stadium, a sports arena of some kind. Almost all of them are up in the stands; they're the crowd cheering on the performers. A half dozen or so are down on the playing field, exciting the crowd in the stands. Demons in the stands respond selectively to these attempts to excite them. Some are more excited than others; some yell louder. Here's the punch line: The loudest demon in the stands gets to go down and join those on the field, displacing one of those currently performing back to the stands.

But why are some demons yelling louder than others? Are some just tired? No. A demon must excite other demons to which it is linked. If the Steelers are playing the Bears, the Steeler players are likely to excite Pittsburgh fans, the Chicago fans are moved by the Bears, and not so much vice versa. And individual fans will respond more strongly to favorite players. Stronger links produce louder responses.

So where do these links come from? The system starts off a certain number of initial demons and initial, built-in links between them. New links are made between demons and existing links are strengthened in proportion to the time they have been together on the field.[4] Demons on the field develop some sort of camaraderie, which results in links between them. Later, a demon on the field is able to excite his buddy in the stands.

The strength of the link between two demons depends not only upon the time they're together on the field but also upon the motivational level of the whole system at the time, the "gain," as Jackson calls it. You turn up the gain when things are going well; you turn it down, even to negative, when things are getting worse. The higher the gain, the more the links between performing demons are strengthened.

Under such a strategy, demons would tend to reappear on the playing field if they were associated with improved conditions. Improved conditions result in strengthened links between these demons. When one of them arrives once again on the playing field, its compatriots tend to be pulled in, too, because of the added strength of the links between them. The system's behavior, Jackson claims, would then tend to steer toward its goals, the goals being the basis on which the system decides things are improving.

Typically, improved conditions result not from a single action but from a coordinated sequence of actions. Suppose we make the links from demons on the playing field to new arrivals stronger than those from new arrivals to incumbents. Uphill links would tend to be stronger than downhill links, as illustrated in figure 11.2.

And suppose we also have demons gradually fade from the playing field. Instead of suddenly jumping up and heading for the stands, they

Figure 11.2
Dissimilar links

gradually lose activation as time passes. Habitual sequences could then be completed from memory simply by presenting an initial segment. Put the first demon in the sequence on the playing field. He has a strong link to the next one in the sequence, who, in turn, is strongly connected to the next, and so on. Once started, the system tends to redo that sequence.

Jackson calls a system of demons recirculating through a playing field, as we've just described, an *association engine*. More precisely, an association engine is a mechanism that chooses one demon from the stands, brings him down to the playing field, sends somebody else back up, and continues in this way. I suppose Jackson chose "association" because the whole system is based on the association that occurs between demons when they are together on the playing field. Now comes the tricky part. How does it work?

Although the spotlight is on the playing field, much of the really important activity takes place below ground (subconsciously?) in the *subarena*. What can the subarena do? For one thing, it measures the system's well-being so that "improved conditions" can be discerned. On this basis, the subarena adjusts the gain on changes in link strengths through association. In terms of how the well-being is doing, it turns the gain up or down. The subarena performs sensory input by sending demons representing low-level input to the playing field, providing an interface between the actual sensory input and whatever the system does with it. Demons also represent low-level actions that are carried out by the subarena at the command of action demons on the playing field. Any such system must come equipped with some primitive sensory capabilities and some primitive actions built in, so it's not surprising that Jackson chooses to postulate such.

Just a bit ago I speculated parenthetically that Jackson's playing field might correspond to the conscious mind, and the subarena acted as the subconscious. Since both primitive sensory items and primitive actions take their place at center stage, this conjecture would depend on the level of primitive sensing and acting. We are not typically conscious of individual retinal cell firings or motor cell firings. On the other hand, in a pandemonium-controlled Animat, demons recognizing trees and food, and demons pushing for movement in the eight directions, would all seem to be "conscious."

Concepts via Pandemonium

Jackson also allows for the creation of concepts in his system. Demons that have appeared together frequently—that is, those that have very strong links—can be merged into a single concept demon. (This calls to mind chunking à la SOAR.) When concept demons are created, their component demons survive and continue to do their things. Like the central processing unit in a von Neumann computer, the playing field here is a major bottleneck because so few demons appear on the playing field at any one time. Concept demons help relieve this bottleneck. Also, when compacted into a concept demon, higher-level features of one problem enable the transfer of solutions to another. Jackson notes that this might give the impression of creativity. (I think he means misimpression, because all of this is quite mechanical. We won't be so quick to jump to the conclusion that "mechanical" rules out "creative" after visiting with Hofstader's work at a later port of call.) Jackson also cautions that explicit concept demons are not always needed, since similar objects may well arouse similar responses because of their similar features.

We can have not only concept demons but also *compound concept demons* that result from merging concept demons. These again help to overcome the playing field bottleneck. They also link demons who don't usually share the playing field, who typically aren't there at the same time. I think this notion is critical to the whole enterprise. Without it the capability of the association engine would be relatively trivial. Everything would depend on sequences of primitive sensations and primitive actions. Common human abstractions, say mathematics, would be impossible. With compound concept demons, on the other hand, a hierarchy of concepts at various levels of abstraction is possible. Jackson also suggests that higher-level concept demons might well linger on the playing field longer than low-level demons. He doesn't suggest a mechanism for merging demons. The paper is intended as a high-level outline of his idea for a mind. On a subsequent stop we'll visit Kanerva's sparse distributed memory, which might be used to implement compound concept demons.

Meanwhile, can this pandemonium mind think? Jackson talks about dreaming, but either thinking or dreaming could be accomplished by much the same mechanism: turn off the subarena interference, especially the external sensory channels. Don't allow any sensory input from below; just let the association engine freewheel above. Demons are then brought together only by association with other demons, not by association with external inputs. Links between memory demons will tend to be formed over longer distances due to additional available space on the playing field. Without sensory demons crowding the work space, there's more room for demons that might not normally interact.

Jackson also builds decay into his pandemonium mind. Unused links decay, or lose strength, at some background rate. Negative links may decay at a different rate. High-level demons enjoy a slower decay rate. As a consequence, sufficiently rarely used links disappear, and recent associations count more than older ones. (This reminds me of Ornstein's "What have you done for me lately?")

Links have strengths. Demons also have their strengths, the strength of voice of those in the crowd yelling, and the strength of signal of those on the playing field trying to stimulate the crowd to yell. I think of all this from a connectionist point of view, the strengths of links being weights and the strengths of demons being activations. (Don't conclude that Jackson's model is implemented as an artificial neural network, but only that it could be.) Demons enter the playing field with a strength determined by their strength of summoning. The demon that yells the loudest goes to the playing field. How strong will he be when he gets there? As strong as he was when he was summoned.

Typically, the playing field is a small place, harboring only a half-dozen to a dozen demons at once. One might want to vary its size. For example, the playing field might shrink to allow a well-learned process to execute reliably, that is, with less chance of other demons distracting it from its course.

A Computing Perspective on Pandemonium

Jackson claims that his pandemonium system avoids the major pitfalls of parallel and serial computing by combining their better features. Serial machines are often too slow, and at any given time are actively using only a fraction of their available hardware. As I type this into a microcomputer, most of the computer's chips are doing nothing at all, except possibly refreshing themselves. Parallel machines, on the other hand, can be faster and can make more efficient use of their hardware. But they often spend much of their time communicating between one processor and another. Having more processors working doesn't necessarily mean more output. (Note that all of the multiple agent systems we've visited postulate narrow communication bandwidths between the agents. Most pairs don't speak to one another. Those that do, say very little.) This system, according to Jackson, captures the best of both worlds. First, it scans the demons in the crowd in parallel to determine the loudest. In the parallel processing world, this scanning would be called perfect parallelism. Imagine a processor for each of the demons in the stands. All that processor has to do is decide how loud his demon should scream. He doesn't care what his neighbors are doing; he doesn't have to communicate with them at all. That's perfect parallelism. The tasks are divided up so that the various processors can perform them without any communication whatsoever. Next Jackson talks of spinning the selected demons "into a single thread" on the playing field, which gives back some of the advantages of the serial machine. From a computational point of view, it looks like not a bad system.[5]

Jackson's pandemonium model can also be seen from a computing point of view as a database. From this vantage point, it consists almost entirely of pointers,[6] namely, the links. In implementing a pandemonium model, links will constitute most of the data. From a demon on the playing field, the next demon appears almost immediately. The implementation has only to look at where the link is pointing. No search is required. Of course, this assumes that "the system or its trainer, must ensure that the next demon is an appropriate one." That doesn't come free.

A pandemonium model is an inductive system, an example of machine learning. It learns rules through repeated observation. The learning procedure seems connectionist; it strengthens links between demons. With a half-dozen demons on the playing field at once, thirty such links get adjusted per cycle. (Each demon is connected to five others, and there are six of them.) So a lot of learning goes on. A typical connectionist system learns a while and then runs a while. If it doesn't run well enough, it gets stopped and trained some more. A pandemonium model works more like us, running and learning at the same time. This is clearly an advantage, since autonomous agents typically can't afford to stop acting in order to learn, or to stop learning in order to act.

An Implementation of Pandemonium

We've noted before that no intelligent agent can begin life from a tabula rasa. Each must come provided from the start with some innate knowledge, be the provider evolution or a designer. A pandemonium model must come equipped with its association engine. Its subarena must have built-in abilities to control the links, to control the gain, to control the sensing mechanisms and the motor mechanisms. From the point of view of a lot of people, particularly the computational neuroethologists, the subarena does all the interesting stuff. The system must also have some initial demons together with their links. Jackson worries that you might think everything of interest is built in. He responds with "If the feeling that 'it has too much of a mind of its own' persists, it should be noted that behavior tends to get less predictable as it becomes more advanced" (1987, p. 25). It seems to me that even at lower levels it's fairly unpredictable.[7]

Jackson tells of a software simulation on a personal computer. The association engine required only six pages of Pascal code,[8] and each demon was described in about a thousand characters (1k). Requirements for the subarena vary greatly, depending on how the system perceives and acts. Jackson ran his version on a machine with only 500k of memory.

Problems, Comments, and Questions

Jackson is concerned about how his system can distinguish remembered stimuli or imagined actions from real ones. Perhaps the answer lies with some mechanism that knows when sensory input is turned off and notes that stimuli during those periods are imagined, or dreamed, or thought, rather than real. Any autonomous agent that plans explicitly must face this problem. Some autonomous agents avoid the problem by planning implicitly. We'll meet one such at our very next attraction in this port.

Jackson is also concerned about how to control the gain when the system is doing, or has done, a purely mental "generate and test" routine.

Suppose it's creating tentative actions and trying a new sequence to see if it works. Does the gain control work exactly as if the actions were really performed and the imagined stimuli were their results? Or must the gain control behave in some modified fashion in increasing or decreasing connection strengths?

These are only two particular problems. Since Jackson's paper is only two and a half pages in length, you could probably come up with a dozen others. I view each of these problems as a design decision to be made during implementation. I would expect tens, maybe hundreds, of such design decisions.

Jackson's pandemonium system leaves much room for expansion. For example, the gain control seems fairly crude. How about a demon for each of several emotions, each one affecting the gain enforced when a given link is modified? I think that in humans and animals, emotional states determine the changes of strengths of these connections. An event accompanied by rampant emotions is not easily forgotten. The new connections are strong.

Jackson has included many numeric variables that allow for fine-tuning the system. One is the length of time the demons stay in the arena. The number of arena occupants could be varied, as could the decay rate of the links. Some such variable could control the way that dreaming or thinking is allowed to happen. Or perhaps the parameters themselves can vary, but slowly.

Note that pandemonium theory is not about a single system but about a whole range of systems under a single architecture. Systems with different parameters might well exhibit quite different behaviors even when otherwise begun with exactly the same initial conditions.

Note also that a pandemonium systems combines features of both symbolic AI and connectionist systems. Each demon can be implemented by a finite-state machine or a production system. On the other hand, each demon has its own activation that spreads from one to another. (Our next attraction will present another such hybrid system.) Learning by strengthening links also reminds me of connectionist systems.

The pandemonium model is certainly a multiplicity of mind model, much in the spirit of Minsky's "Society of Mind," but at a higher level of abstraction. We'll next visit Maes's model, which lives at a slightly lower level of abstraction. All of these systems speak to the issue of control— what shall I do next?

As is typical of a useful theory, Jackson's pandemonium theory seems to raise as many questions as it answers. Here are a couple to chew on.

How does the system decide when to dream, when to think, or when to act in its world? (This is a different question than the one we previously considered, about distinguishing thought products from the world.) Should there be a demon that acts on the subarena to abort sensory input? Perhaps two such, one for thinking and one for dreaming? Or could the amount of attention devoted to external input be an emerging property of the whole system? Even if attention to externals is an emerging property, there's still going to be a mechanism under it. The issue here seems to be one of providing a local mechanism out of which the global property of attention to externals emerges.

A more general form of our original question (if you can remember what it was) asks how much of the subarena's duties could be taken over by demons. How much can be accomplished with just the association engine itself?

My second question concerns the mechanisms for producing new demons. Pandemonium systems come equipped with initial demons, and some new ones are obtained by chunking the actions in a sequence (as we first saw while visiting SOAR). Chunking mechanisms aren't hard to imagine, even for demons. But what about concept demons? Whenever you learn something like juggling, or patting your stomach and rubbing your head at the same time, you're creating a concept demon. And what about yet higher-level demons?

Another form of this question concerns the possibility of replacing the notion of producing new demons with one of selecting from existing (pre-existing) but unassigned demons. Edelman postulates such selection of neuronal groups.

But here I go jumping ahead again. We won't meet Edelman's work until our next port of call. These mechanisms of mind just don't seem to lend themselves well to a linear ordering. Like Jackson's demons, they seem to be linked to one another in complex ways. Let's go on to view another fascinating hybrid (symbolic and connectionist) system, one that employs multiple agents and has its action selection procedure spelled out.

Behavior Networks—the Design Criteria

Most often a tour guide must lead his or her group along an itinerary designed by someone else. On occasion, one is lucky enough to be allowed to choose the itinerary, so that almost every attraction is one of his or her favorites. On this tour, I'm one of those lucky ones, and I must say I'm enjoying visiting and displaying many of my favorites immensely. But even on a tour of favorites, some are more favorite than others. This next attraction, due to Maes, is one of my most favorite. I'm telling you all this so that you can defend yourself against any overly euphoric descriptions.

The paper describing this work is titled "How to Do the Right Thing" (1990). This title is a rephrasing of the major question faced by minds: what to do next. The "right thing" here refers to the correct action, or perhaps *a* correct action, in the current context. This work is about behavior selection, that is, a control system.

To motivate the constraints and objectives of her design, Maes asks us to imagine an autonomous agent, perhaps a Mars rover used to collect soil samples,[9] with distinct, and maybe independent, global goals. Suppose it's operating in a complex, dynamic environment that's changing all the time. How should its actions be controlled?

To control actions is too general. The real issue is how to control actions subject to constraints. Here are the constraints that Maes sets for her design: It should work well

- in a world that's not entirely predictable
- with limited computational and time resources.

These are certainly reasonable constraints. Worlds typically aren't predictable. I don't know of any that are, except mathematical worlds. And in a changing environment, you don't have all day to ponder. It's not like my writing this sentence, which is done off-line. If I cogitate a while to get it right, nothing drastic happens. A Mars rover must take some decision, and the consequent action, before it gets to the edge of the cliff. These constraints imply that behavior selection cannot be optimal. Optimal actions are simply impossible in a complex dynamic world under computational and time constraints. We must settle for actions that are good enough, that is, good enough to get us by.

Maes also presents a long list of desired characteristics for her autonomous agent. It should be goal oriented, opportunistic, persistent, able to plan ahead, robust, reactive, and fast. These bear some discussion because there are clearly some trade-offs to be made. Having several goals, our agent, Rover, should act so as to further these goals, or at least some of them. If, while pursuing one goal, something happens that makes it easy to fulfill another, we'd like Rover to stop what he's doing and take advantage of the opportunity. But we'd also like Rover not to flit from goal to goal, never accomplishing any of them. Imagine an artificial herbivore who walks to South Lake to slake his thirst. After a couple of swigs, thirst subsides a little and hunger takes over. He then walks to North Plain, where, after grazing a few moments, hunger subsides a little and the remaining thirst, augmented by the walk to North Plain, takes over. He then walks to South Lake. After a few times around this loop, our herbivore probably drops dead. Clearly, some persistence is needed. So there's a trade-off between opportunism and persistence.

Maes sees virtue in Rover's planning ahead. But he must still be reactive, that is, responsive to the current situation, which may well not be what was planned for. And he must be fast. (Often the alternative is to be dead.) Here we have two trade-offs, since planning takes time, and planned actions and unplanned reactions are at opposite ends of the scale. Finally, Rover should be robust, meaning he ought to behave reasonably well in circumstances a little different from what he's previously encountered. He shouldn't be brittle, and just crash.

If all this seem like a tall order to you, it does to me, too. Let's see how Maes pulls it off.

Behavior Networks—the Mechanism

Maes's system, like those of Ornstein, Minsky, and Jackson, relies on the multiplicity of mind. She calls her multiple agents (demons, talents) *competence modules*. They are interactive, mindless agents, each with a specific competence. Imagine Rover having competencies called `pick-up-rock`, `put-rock-in-bag`, `back-up`, `turn-left`, `signal-base`, and so on. `Pick-up-rock` might rely on `grasp` and other lower-level competencies. Or imagine me with the competence `ride-a bicycle`. Now the question is how to control the behavior of these competencies. When does a competence become active and do its thing?

There are several standard approaches to answering this question. One possibility is to hardwire or hand-code the control. Whoever designs the system decides exactly who's in charge and when. Priorities are set by the designer, who must have anticipated the relevant environmental configurations the system will encounter. Ah, but that anticipation is the rub. This strategy works well only for systems with simple, nonconflicting goals in a relatively static and not too complex environment, like a thermostat, an assembly line robot, or a toy AI system playing tick tack toe.

The military, government agencies, and corporations most often rely on a hierarchical control structure, a decision tree. Symbolic AI systems sometimes employ this strategy also. Some expert system shells[10] implement algorithms that, given a set of input–output pairs as exemplars, produce an appropriate decision tree. Even in a multiple agent setting, Ornstein postulates a governing self, one of his talents who governs as chief executive from the top of a hierarchy. A hierarchical strategy often suffers from rigidity, working well until an unusual circumstance is encountered, and then crashing. Such systems are said to be brittle.[11]

In his pandemonium theory, John Jackson suggests a distributed system of control, in which the authority to act passes from agent (demon) to agent over time. His control system could be implemented as an integrated symbolic, connectionist algorithm. Individual agents, implemented as finite-state machines, provide the actions, and strengths (activations) decide who gets to act. Whereas Jackson's work allows this interpretation, Maes insists on it. She doesn't attempt nearly as much, but what she does, she fills out in a lot more detail. Let's have a look.

A competence module looks very much like a production rule.[12] Each has some preconditions. You can think of them as statements about the environment or environmental variables that have to hold before the competence can be performed. Each also contains lists of additions and of deletions, that is, statements the module wants to add to the global data-base or statements it wants to delete. A competence module is distin-guished from a production rule by the presence of an activation, a number indicating some kind of strength level. Now competence modules look more like the classifiers we met while visiting Wilson's Animat.

Think of each competence module as occupying a node of a digraph, a structure we met during our visit with connectionism. But a digraph must have links. In this case the links are completely determined by the compe-tence modules. Here's how they are formed. If a competence module X will add a proposition b, which is on competence Y's precondition list, then put a successor link from X to Y (figure 11.3). There may be several such propositions resulting in several links between the same nodes. Next, whenever you put a successor going one way, put a predecessor going the other (figure 11.4). Finally, suppose you have a proposition m on compe-tence Y's delete list that is also a precondition for competence X. In other

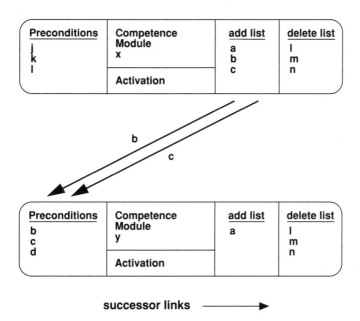

Figure 11.3
Successor links

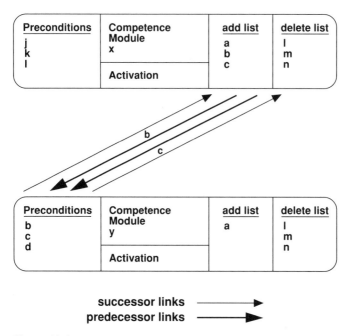

Figure 11.4
Predecessor links

words, X wants m and Y wants to get rid of m. In such a case, draw a conflictor link from X to Y, which is to be inhibitory rather than excitatory (figure 11.5). Note that the diagram should also contain a conflictor link for 1. Sometimes a competence X will want to delete one of its own preconditions. For example `hand-empty` may be a precondition for `pick-up-rock` but should also appear on the delete list as a result of the rock's being picked up.

We now know how to construct a digraph corresponding to a collection of competence modules, but we don't know what it's for. As in connectionist models, the underlying digraph spreads activation. But where does the activation come from? From activation stored by the competence modules themselves, from the environment, and from goals.

Every autonomous system must have goals to guide its actions. Some are built in, and others are created subgoals, as in SOAR. Maes's system has only built-in global goals. Some are once-only goals to be achieved

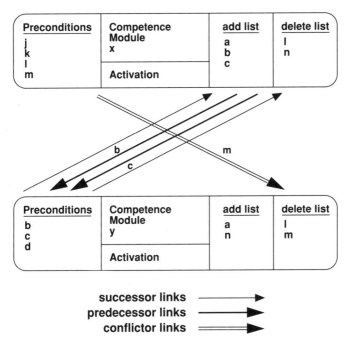

Figure 11.5
Conflictor links

one time, like `find-and-test-a-rock sample`. Others are permanent goals (drives) to be achieved continuously, like `no-self-damage`.

We are now ready to describe the sources of spreading activation in the system. The environment awards activation to a competence module for each of its true preconditions. The more true preconditions a competence has, that is, the more relevant it is to the current situation, the more activation it's going to receive from the environment. This source of activation allows the system to be opportunistic. (At this point you may recall my discomfort, during our visit with Animat, with reinforcement coming from the environment. I'm no more comfortable here, again preferring to think of environmental activation as being supplied by the system in response to conditions in the environment.)

Next, each goal awards activation to each competence that, by being active, will satisfy that goal. In other words, if the competence includes a proposition on its add list that satisfies a goal, then this goal will send activation to that competence. This source of activation tends to make the system goal-directed. The system also allows for protected goals. A completed goal inhibits any competence that will undo it.

Finally, activation is spread from competence to competence along links. Along successor links, one competence strengthens those competences whose preconditions it can help fulfill. It does so by sending them activation along successor links. Along predecessor links, one competence strengthens any other competence whose add list fulfills one of its own preconditions. A competence sends inhibition along a conflictor link to any other competence that can delete one of its true preconditions, thereby weakening it. Every conflictor link is inhibitory.

Thus, a competence that can satisfy some goal gets activation from that goal, and passes it backward to other competences that can satisfy one of its preconditions, that is, can help it become active. On the other hand, a competence that has many of its preconditions satisfied is awarded activation from the environment and passes some of it forward to other competences it can help activate. Activation spreads both ways. A fascinating idea. I like it.

Call a competence module *executable* if all of its preconditions can be satisfied. In other words, the competence is ready to shoot, although it may not. With this last concept in place, we're ready to see Maes's algorithm for the system. Here's a pseudocode version:

Loop forever

1. Add activation from environment and goals

2. Spread activation forward and backward among the competence modules

3. Decay—total activation remains constant

4. Competence module fires if

i.   it's executable and

ii. it's over threshold and

iii. it's the maximum such

5. If one competence module fires, its activation goes to 0, and all thresholds return to their normal value

6. If none fires, reduce all thresholds by 10%.

The point of such an algorithm is to tell you how the system works. First, note that, once started, there's no stopping. The system continues to attempt to choose an action time and time again, just like you and me. Also note that each step in the algorithm operates in parallel over all competence modules. The first two steps, and step 5, are local, requiring no information as to global state.

Let's trace through the cycle of choice from the point of view of a single competence. First it updates its activation, adding that arriving from the environment, or from any goal, or from a protected goal that may be inhibiting it. Then it adds in whatever spreading activation arrives from other competence modules, including possible inhibition over conflictor links. Next, its activation decays, that is, it decreases proportionally with respect to all competences so as to keep the total activation in the system constant. The decay is to compensate for what the environment and the goals add in; otherwise, the activation of the system would grow without bound. The total activation is one of the system's global parameters.

At this point, our competence knows its activation for this particular cycle. It fires—that is, its action is taken—if three conditions hold. First, it must be executable, that is, all of its preconditions must be met. Second, its activation must be above threshold. There's a uniform threshold for the whole system that must be exceeded. And third, this competence must have the maximum activation among executable competences over threshold. Ties are broken randomly. If our competence fires, its activation drops to 0. A competence using all its activation to fire prevents an action from being repeated over and over. If no competence can fire, reduce the threshold by 10 percent. Think of the cycle with no action taken as the system considering what it wants to do but reaching no conclusion. Reducing the threshold makes it more likely that some competence can fire on the next cycle. This reduction prevents the system from thinking and thinking, and never acting. The normal threshold is a system parameter.

A comparison with Jackson's pandemonium theory seems in order. The algorithm we've just described corresponds to choosing a demon to descend to the playing field. Not every demon can perform at a given time. You can't ride a bicycle when there's no bicycle around. In a pandemonium model, presumably only executable demons are yelling. If there's no bicycle available—that is, no bicycle-recognizing demon on the playing field—the bicycle-riding demon won't be excited. Jackson doesn't postulate a threshold for yelling strength. Maes uses the threshold for planning. Jackson employs some unspecified mechanism to shut down outside sensory input and motor action so that planning (dreaming) can take place. Perhaps that mechanism could be a threshold on yelling strength. And the threshold could decrease over time. The last condition for selection, maximum loudness, seems the same in both systems. One might well use Maes's behavior network as a mechanism for implementing Jackson's pandemonium model.

Maes's behavior networks are tunable via global parameters. The normal activation threshold for a competence to become active is one such. Raising it makes the system more thoughtful, and lowering makes it more reactive. Another is the amount of activation added to a competence for each satisfied precondition. Increasing this one makes the system more opportunistic. The counterpoint to this parameter is the amount of activation a competence receives for being able to satisfy a goal. Increasing this one leads to more goal-oriented behavior. These last two parameters trade off with one another, since goal orientation and opportunism are at opposite ends a single scale. The user decides on values for these and other parameters. The values remain constant during a run. Deciding on optimal or good enough values for these parameters is a search problem in parameter space,[13] which depends heavily on the problem at hand.

Planning in Behavior Networks

Now that we've seen how behavior networks are implemented, let's take brief looks at their operating features. Many of these have been introduced before. Here we'll both summarize and add some detail.

Behavior networks can create and follow a plan. Suppose there exists a sequence of competencies whose actions transform the present situation into a desired one. In other words, this path solves a problem. (Keep in mind that there may well be several independent goals, and the system must decide which one to act toward at any given time.) The sequence can become highly activated via forward spreading from the current state and backward spreading from the goal state. If the goal is *ride-bicycle*, the sequence of competencies might be `find-bicycle`, `recognize-bicycle`, `move-to-bicycle`, `mount-bicycle`, `ride-bicycle`. When the preconditions of *find-bicycle* are met, activation begins to spread forward along the sequence while, at the same time, activation spreads backward from `ride-bicycle`. Eventually enough activation may be available to `find-bicycle` activate it, starting the plan in motion. Of course, all this may be happening in competition with other sequences striving toward other goals. With activations under threshold, the system considers effects before executing a sequence of actions. The forward spreading of activation promotes situations relevance and opportunistic behavior. At the same time, the system is biased toward ongoing plans because of a shorter distance between current state and goal.

Although this sequence certainly seems like a plan, there is no obvious representation of such a plan anywhere in the system. An outside observer might well look at such a sequence and call it a plan, but the system doesn't use it as a plan to be consulted.[14] Rather, the plan seems to exist only in the propensity for activation of its competences. Also, no centralized preprogrammed search process builds a search tree. This avoids the typical combinatorial explosion of conventional symbolic planning, resulting in cheaper operation than traditional planning methods. The system seems less rational, less brittle, and faster; less rational in that it's hard to explain its action by rules, less brittle in that getting a bit beyond what the system is expected to do doesn't crash it. All this, of course, is meant in the context of controlling autonomous agents.

Behavior Network Features

Let's spend a few minutes summarizing some useful features arising from Maes's behavior network architecture. Such a system should be goal oriented, situation relevant, adaptive, fault tolerant, biased toward ongoing plans, thoughtful, and fast. In addition, it should avoid goal conflicts. Let's take each of these individually.

Given the goal, activation flows to competences that achieve that goal, and then spreads backward to competences yielding its preconditions, and so on. Competences contributing to several goals get activation from each one. Competences contributing to close goals are favored, because the backward spread of activation dilutes. Competences with little competition are favored. *Goal orientedness* can be tuned via a global variable controlling how much activation comes from goals. For a more goal-oriented system, raise its value.

The forward spreading of activation promotes *situation relevance.* What's happening in the environment makes a big difference because it controls a major source of activation. This biases the search for the next action in favor of those relevant to the current situation. It also allows the system to exploit opportunities that present themselves. Also, situation relevance can be tuned by the parameter controlling the activation resulting from true preconditions.

At each step a behavior network reevaluates what's going on, which allows it to adapt easily to changing or unforeseen circumstances. This *adaptivity* presents a trade-off with the bias toward ongoing plans. If one competence module fails, the system will try to find an alternative solution. This will happen automatically. A certain amount of *fault tolerance* is built in.

A behavior network is *biased toward ongoing plans,* since distance between the current state and the goal is typically shorter than that of other plans. If several competence modules in a sequence have been fired, the system may be fairly close to its goal, so that backward-spreading activation will be strong. This property tends to *prevent goal conflicts,* such as oscillation between two goals. Note the trade-off between this feature and opportunism.

There's also a trade-off between *thoughtfulness* and *speed* that can be tuned by the normal threshold parameter. Ideally, thoughtfulness should vary inversely with the changeableness of the environment. If you're playing chess, the environment that you're interested in doesn't change very much, only an occasional move. In this case a lot of thoughtfulness seems called for. On the other hand, if you're leading the fast break in a basketball game, you don't want to think long about anything. That environment changes very rapidly indeed. Note that a strong argument has just been made for having this threshold parameter under the control of the system so that both situations can be accommodated.

Faster action is less thoughtful, less goal oriented, less situation oriented. The speed of the system, however, is enhanced by several features of its architecture. It evaluates different paths in parallel. Also, it doesn't replan at each time step, as symbolic planners are wont to do. For example, if `ride-bicycle` gains some activation, it's not lost until the module actually fires, at which time it goes to 0. There's a kind of memory in the system that makes it faster.

Maes predicts that real world autonomous agents will be "larger" rather than "longer." That is, they will need shallow knowledge more than deep knowledge, and will need a number of different kinds of shallow knowledge. In terms of the system architecture, this means that, typically, lengths of paths to the goal will be relatively short.

Maes also points out that local links and uniform spreading activation allow for massively parallel implementation of these behavior networks. On the other hand, she notes some limits. Three are the lack of variables and of memory, and the difficulty of selecting the global parameters well.

To me, Maes's system has a decided connectionist flavor due to its spreading activation over an underlying digraph.[15] Her links have no weights (or all have weight 1, if you prefer). In a later paper (1991b), she adds weights to the links to implement a connectionist form of learning. This latter implementation also has more of an artificial life flavor.

As a tour guide, I'm often faced with the unpleasant choice of moving on, or of staying longer with the current attraction and omitting some subsequent place of interest. In this case, I've reluctantly chosen to leave Maes's second paper to you as an optional side trip, and to move on to visit with a fascinating roboticist.

Nouvelle AI

In an article titled "Elephants Don't Play Chess" (1990c), Brooks, a roboticist, takes on the symbolic AI community. Why that title? Because knowing that elephants don't play chess is no reason to think that they're not intelligent. It's an argument against the sufficiency of the Turing test. And it's an argument for a new brand of AI that attempts to simulate the kind of intelligence exemplified by elephant behavior rather than that of the more abstract human behaviors (games, speech recognition, problem solving, etc.) that have been favored by the symbolic AI people.

"Artificial Intelligence research has floundered in a sea of incrementalism" (p. 3). As you can see, Brooks is not overly tactful as he argues for his new brand of AI. Another example: "the symbol system hypothesis upon which classical AI is based is fundamentally flawed" (p. 3). If tactfulness isn't a problem, neither is modesty: "we believe that in principle we have uncovered the fundamental foundation of intelligence" (p. 13).

Brooks refers to his alternative brand of AI as "Nouvelle AI," calling it a strengthened form of situated activity, and bases it on the "physical grounding hypothesis," of which more in a bit.

Brooks points out that classical AI decomposes intelligence into functional information-processing modules, where each module has a specific function to carry out. The combination of these modules provides the overall system behavior. One module, by itself, typically can't do much. Brook's nouvelle AI, by contrast, decomposes intelligence into individual behavior-generating modules. Each module, by itself, actually generates some behavior. The coexistence of these behavior-generating modules and their cooperation allows more complex behaviors to emerge.

Classical AI systems combine many modules, each one performing some function that, when combined, produces behavior. System competence is improved by improving individual modules. Computer programs are typically written with little procedures, each serving a particular function and each requiring others in order to act. Brooks, in contrast, wants each of his modules to operate on its own, and to do something from start to finish by itself. In such a system, you improve system competence by adding new modules. This idea initiates his subsumption architecture, which we'll soon visit in detail.

Again for contrast, Brooks summarizes the symbol system hypothesis as follows: Intelligence operates by means of a system of symbols. Perception and motor interfaces are sets of symbols on which central intelligence acts. The meanings of the symbols are unimportant. Central intelligence acts on them domain independently. The executive, reasoning engine can operate equally well in one domain or another. Coherence emerges for an observer who grounds the symbols within his or her own experience. Without the observer, the human in the loop, there isn't much meaning. To the observer, symbols represent entities in the world: individual objects, properties, concepts, desires, emotions, nations, colors, and so on. Furthermore, symbols typically represent named entities, such as chair3 or block38.

Central intelligence must be fed symbols by perception. Creating a correct symbolic description of the world must be task dependent. Suppose I want to stack blocks. My concern would be for shape. Is the block a cube or a rectangular solid or a pyramid? For this task, I'm not concerned with its surface area. If, on the other hand, the task is to paint blocks, I will be concerned with surface area, which isn't part of the previous description. Perception must provide relevant descriptions. Descriptions are delivered in terms of typed, named individuals and their relationships. For another task a different representation may be important.

Brooks claims that simple symbols are inadequate. In pure form, symbol systems assume a knowable objective truth. Not only must we assume that there is a world out there, which we are perfectly willing to do from our physicalist assumption, but we must also assume that objects exist per se and relationships exist between them. We also must assume that some relationships are true and some are not, and that which is which can be known. Brooks questions these assumptions, as do I, and as will others whom we'll meet later on the tour. To glean beliefs from partial views of a chaotic world requires added complexity, such as modal logics[16] or nonmonotone logics. Simple methods just don't get it. A commitment to symbol systems requires more and more complex and cumbersome systems in pursuit of objectivity. This leads to the frame problem, which, you'll recall, is how to know which propositions remain true when some fact changes. As we've noted, all proposed solutions leave much to be desired. Finally, Brooks points out, determining the truth of a proposition under reasonable conditions is NP-hard[17] (Chapman 1987). As Brooks mentions, this isn't as damaging as it would appear, since "good enough" solutions may be well be available.

If Brooks doesn't think much of the symbol system hypothesis, what does he offer instead? The previously mentioned *physical grounding hypothesis*. "To build a system that is intelligent, it is necessary to have its representations grounded in the physical world" (p. 5). The symbol system hypothesis is "fundamentally flawed" because its symbols are not thus grounded. As long as the system's representations are not grounded in the world, it must cope with these complexity problems. Brooks really means the physical world, since he's building robots. Taking an artificial life point of view, I suspect that grounding representations in the agent's environment, whatever that is, will do nicely. But why ground representations in the real world? For one thing, the world is always up to date. For another, it always contains every detail there is to be known. The trick, according to Brooks, is to sense it appropriately and often enough. The idea is clear; if you want to know where you are, look around you. Don't look at the global database of your production systems.

To build a system based on the physical grounding hypothesis, one must connect it to the world by its sensors and its actuators. This almost entails a bottom-up construction. High-level abstractions must grow from concrete representations. The system must express all its goals as physical actions and must extract all its knowledge from physical sensors. Every known intelligent system, including us, does so. The forms of low-level interfaces have consequences that ripple through the entire system.

If you're going to build a typical symbolic AI system, what do you do? You assume that the vision guys are going to give you good vision routines, and they are going to find objects for you. You also depend on them to give you relationships between objects. All of this is to arrive as input, already done. Some would say you've just assumed the hardest part of the problem, the part that requires the most intelligence. On the other end, you assume that your output is going to a screen to be interpreted by a convenient human. So what have we done? We've cut the problem down to size by palming off these low-level interfaces on some (usually imaginary) colleague, so we don't have to worry about them. It's a reasonable approach because we're dealing with hard problems. Brooks maintains, though, that not dealing with these two interfaces undermines the whole endeavor. Low-level interfaces are so important to what goes on higher up, that simplifying assumptions about them leave you not really knowing what you're doing.

Symbol-based mobile robots have not performed well in comparison with physically grounded robots. Brooks's robots do things that other people have not been able to get theirs to do. Not that his are that good, mind you. They are not. But they're a lot better than those based on symbolic AI—as autonomous agents, anyway. With a view of Brooks's philosophy in hand, let's see how he deals with low-level interfaces.

Subsumption Architecture

Brooks refers to his key idea as *subsumption architecture*. It's a computational architecture that enables a tight connection of perception to action. This is accomplished by building a series of incremental layers, each layer connecting perception to action, that is, it has a competence. Each layer, by itself, does something. Layers are implemented as finite-state machines with timing elements. Finite-state machines, as the term is used here, are much like those we've visited several times already. In addition to a finite input alphabet, a finite set of states, and a transition function, these machines have a finite output alphabet. The transition function takes a given state and some input, and returns a (possibly) different state and an output.

An augmented finite-state machine (AFSM) is the basic building block for the subsumption architecture (see figure 11.6). An AFSM starts with a finite-state machine. Add a collection of registers,[18] each of which collects an input for the finite-state machine. Finally, there's a set of timers. The finite-state machine can change state or emit an output when the timer goes off. Input messages are delivered to registers. A change of state may be triggered by a message arriving in a register or by the expiration of a timer. Messages are generated on the output wires of some AFSM.

Registers are written to by input wires from some AFSM. A message written to a register replaces its existing contents. Sensors also deposit

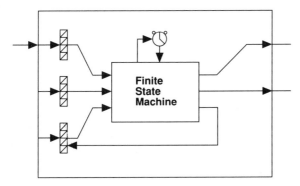

Figure 11.6
Augmented finite-state machine (redrawn from Brooks 1990b)

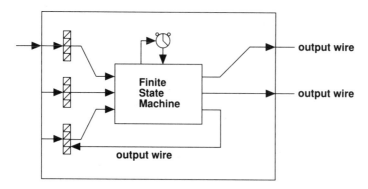

Figure 11.7
AFSM output (adapted from Brooks 1990b)

their values in registers. The finite-state machine reads its registers as input.

Output from some AFSM can provide input to a register of some AFSM, possibly itself (figure 11.7). Or it can attach directly to an actuator, turning a motor on or off. Finally, it can attach directly to an input or an output of some AFSM, inhibiting or suppressing it, as we shall see.

An AFSM seems a rather simple device. What can one do? It can wait for some event to occur, that is, wait for some specific message to arrive in one of its registers, or it can wait until its timer fires. It can change to either of two states, depending on the contents of a register. It can perform an if-then-else operation,[19] depending on the contents of a register. Finally, it can compute some function of the registers and deliver it as output. Not bad for such a simple device.

An AFSM can also inhibit existing outputs and suppress existing inputs (figure 11.8). What's the difference? Why the two distinct terms? Suppressing messages are gated through to replace the original message, whereas inhibiting messages only prevent output. When suppression occurs, the original message on the line is waylaid and the suppressing message usurps its place. These inhibiting and suppressing messages gate, but only briefly. They are the essential mechanisms of conflict resolution in a subsumption architecture. Priorities are hardwired into the system via suppression or inhibition.

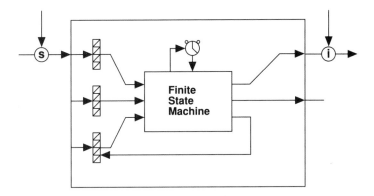

Figure 11.8
Inhibition and suppression (redrawn from Brooks 1990b)

Brooks imposes some interesting systemwide constraints. AFSMs cannot share state. One of these machines cannot look inside another and tell what is gong on. In particular, one can't read another's registers or timer. Thus, what little information passes back and forth travels over outputs and inputs. Brooks considers this crucial to keeping things simple enough to work. Both timers and messages act asynchronously. They act when they act, and not according to a clock. The timers do share a uniform tick period, but only as an artifact of purchasing. It is just easier to buy all the timers at the same place.

A group of coordinated AFSMs (processes) forms a behavior, for example, *to-grasp*. Message passing, suppression, and inhibition can occur between the processes in a behavior or between distinct behaviors. Behaviors act as abstraction barriers. Like AFSMs, one behavior cannot reach inside another. With all this as background, let's look at a couple of Brooks's robots.

Allen

Let's meet Allen—named after Allen Newell, I assume—who was Brooks's first physically grounded robot. Allen has sonar range sensors and an odometer to tell him how far he's gone. He's controlled. via a cable, by an off-board special-purpose computer, a LISP machine, that simulates his subsumption architecture. Allen has three layers of control. The first layer simply avoids obstacles, either stationary (static) or moving (dynamic). Allen will happily sit in the middle of a room until approached, then scurry away, avoiding collisions as he goes. That's what's to be expected. If your only behavior is to avoid obstacles, what else are you going to do?

How does Allen work? Each sonar return is taken as a repulsive force falling off as the square of the distance. A reflex halts Allen when he's moving forward and something is just in front of him. Rather than bump into it, he will come right up to it and stop. That's the first layer. It's a prototypical competence or behavior.

If layer 1 is working properly, adding a second layer requires no change to layer 1 except possibly hooking suppressors and inhibitors onto some of its wires. Allen's second layer wanders randomly about. The urge to move in a random direction is generated about every ten seconds. The obstacle avoidance of layer 1 is not suppressed or inhibited. The wander urge couples with obstacle avoidance by vector addition.[20] Keep in mind that Allen has no internal state. He remembers almost nothing, and builds no models about what is happening out there in the world. He has no symbolic rules but is simply hardwired. The summed vector suppresses layer 1 obstacle avoidance, substituting its own direction.

What happens if layer 2 breaks down? Suppose it just dies. Allen goes right back to simply avoiding again. He finds the middle of the room and stays there. Even if layer 1 breaks down, he'll probably get in front of something and stop, at least for a while. The halt reflex of layer 1 operates autonomously and unchanged. Robustness seems built in.

Layer 3 looks for distant places and heads for them. Whereas layer 2 wanders in some random direction with no goal in mind, layer 3 uses sonar to look for distant places and odometry to monitor progress. The sonar tells Allen not only which direction it's in but also how far it is. Hence the usefulness of the odometer.

That's Allen. I wanted to describe him to you not only because he was the first but also because he's the most basic in terms of behavior. Let's meet one of Allen's more complex relatives.

Herbert

Herbert, presumably named in honor of Herbert Simon, is more sophisticated. He's a one-trick pony who wanders about a typically cluttered office environment picking up empty soda cans and returning them to his starting point.

His twenty-four-processor onboard computer, made of 8-bit CMOS processors,[21] is light and requires little onboard battery power. The processors communicate via serial port[22] interfaces that are both slow and unsophisticated. The connections between processors are along copper wires. Altogether, Herbert employs a simplistic distributed processing system.

Sensing is done via 30 infrared ports and a laser light striping system that looks out at a 60 degree angle over a range of 12 feet and provides 3-dimensional depth data. All this is supported by a high-performance visual algorithm. His actuators consist of motors driving wheels, and an onboard manipulator arm with several simple sensors.

Herbert's subsumption architecture demonstrates obstacle avoidance, wall following, and real time recognition of soda can-type objects. Fifteen different behaviors drive the arm alone as it searches for a soda can, locates it, and picks it up.

Herbert uses the world as its own best model, and has no internal communication between behavior-generating modules other than suppression or inhibition. Each behavior is connected to sensors and to an arbitration network. The arbitration network decides which of competing actions are taken. Many simple animals seem to operate in just this kind of way.

Here's a brief description of Herbert in action. While following a wall, the vision algorithm spots a soda can. Herbert, sometimes with considerable effort, squares up in front of it. When the wheels stop moving, arm motion begins. After several behaviors, the soda can is located with sensors local to the arm (Why is all this needed? To home in on a soda can requires a great deal more coordination and exact positioning than to look out and see the can from a distance.) The hand now moves so that the soda can breaks a beam between two appendages, thus triggering the grasping reflex.

Brooks claims several advantages for Herbert's architecture. Herbert has no expectations as to what will happen next, which allows him to be naturally opportunistic. If Herbert is wandering around looking for soda cans and someone puts one in his hand, he immediately quits looking and returns to his starting point. More generally, Herbert easily responds to changed circumstances. He successfully finds soda cans on a variety of cluttered desktops, although he may never have seen a particular desktop before and has no internal knowledge of desktops. Herbert is opportunistic but not that smart.

Brooks doesn't advocate all robots being built this way. Rather, his point is that a lot more can be done without internal representations than we have thought. He attempts to do as much as he can without internal representations, which are costly in both computing time and memory space. This approach seems perfectly reasonable to me.

Let's wind up our visit with Brooks's robots with his comparison of traditional vs. nouvelle AI. Traditional AI, he says, demonstrates sophisticated reasoning in rather impoverished domains and hopes to generalize, or scale up, to robust behavior in more complex domains. SOAR, for example, employs sophisticated reasoning to play tic-tac-toe, an impoverished domain compared with navigating around a cluttered room. One can describe VAX configurations with a thousand or so rules, but can hardly so describe a cluttered room for navigational purposes. Nouvelle AI, on the other hand, demonstrates less sophisticated tasks operating in more complex domains and hopes to generalize, or scale up, to more sophisticated tasks.

Although this endeavor has enjoyed some success, there are still problems, as Brooks points out. How can more than a dozen or so behaviors be combined productively? It may well turn out that the nouvelle AI strategy won't scale up. How can multiple perceptual sources be fused when necessary? The simple situations explored so far haven't needed fusion, but more complex situations certainly will. How can we automate the building of interfaces between behaviors? Handcrafting is difficult and time consuming.

Recall that during our introductory visit, even before the itinerary was discussed, I presented a two-dimensional diagram with the synthetic vs. analytic dimension laid out on the horizontal axis and the top-down vs.

bottom-up dimension on the vertical. Brooks's approach falls on the lower right of that diagram, being synthetic and bottom up. Symbolic AI is synthetic and top down, as is much of connectionism. Cognitive psychology is analytic and top down, and neuroscience occupies the analytic and bottom-up slot. I think all of these approaches, including Brooks's, will be needed to make sense of mind. But for now, let's concentrate on making sense of autonomous agents.

Autonomous Agents

Our next visit will be with the work of Brustoloni (1991), who has spent some time thinking abstractly about autonomous agents and has produced the beginnings of a theory. First, what are we talking about? What is an autonomous agent? According to Brustoloni, it's a system capable of autonomous, purposeful, real world action that responds to external stimuli in a timely fashion.

Let's pick this definition apart. Certainly an autonomous agent should be autonomous, that is, not under the control of some other agent. Allen is under the control of the LISP machine to which it is tethered. Or is that LISP machine a part of Allen? Since the mobile part of Allen consults the LISP machine to produce each action, either the LISP machine is part of Allen or Allen isn't autonomous after all. But consulting can't be all of it. Suppose I'm assembling a bicycle for one of my twins. For each step, I consult the directions. Must those directions be part of me before I can be considered autonomous? Probably not, since I'm pursuing my own agenda and the paper is consulted only in support of this agenda.

That's the purposeful action Brustoloni talks about. But it must be my purpose. On a later tour stop, we'll see what Newell and Simon have to say about purposeful action. In the meantime, let's consider whether a thermostat has a purpose. Why, of course, I might say. Its purpose is to maintain room temperature at 68 degree. But, you say, that's the purpose of whoever set the thermostat, not of the thermostat itself. All right. But what about me? Aren't all my basic drives decreed by evolution? Aren't all my goals subsidiary to one or more of these drives? But within the constraints imposed by these built-in drives, I have my own agenda and am autonomous. Isn't that the best we can hope of any agent? If so, doesn't a thermostat have its own agenda within the confines of its single built-in drive? But a thermostat's drive isn't built in, you say. It's controlled from without. Suppose I'm a sex offender whose sex drive is controlled by drugs under a court order. Am I still autonomous? But I have other drives, you say, while the thermostat has only the one. What if the thermostat also controlled lighting via motion sensors? What then? As you can see, the matter of autonomy isn't a simple one. I'm inclined to return to Sloman's discussion of free will and conclude that there must be degrees of autonomy, with the thermostat close to one end of the scale and us closer to the other.

I'm not so sure about Brustoloni's "real world" requirement. I can imagine artificial life agents that act within a computer world that's "real" for them. And I can image them being reactive, that is, responding to external stimuli in a timely fashion. "External stimuli" here means external to the agent but within its computer world environment. With these caveats, let's provisionally accept Brustoloni's definition.

Agents have drives, such as hunger, thirst, homeostasis (say of temperature). Drives may be independent of one another. I can be hungry without being thirsty and vice versa. Perhaps they may be derivative—the drive to succeed may, for some people, be subsidiary to their sex drive. And drives, or at least the means of satisfying them, may conflict. When scrumptious Memphis barbecue is available, my hunger drive may well conflict with my drive for self-preservation via clear arteries. Where do drives come from? Do we learn new drives? I doubt it. I suspect drives come with the hardware or are derived in the service of drives that do.

And agents devote their resources to satisfying their drives. This gives the appearance of purpose to their actions. Or is it in fact purpose, and not just appearance? Does the thermostat turn on the furnace purposefully? Do I regulate my heart rate purposely? Purpose can be observed in the actions of agents. But this is purpose imposed from without, laid on by an outside observer. The thermostat just does what it is does. Animat just does what it does. It wanders in search of food, and it eats. Any purpose that's present seems to come from the outside. If that's the case, why do we humans seem to have internal purposes? I've often been accused of having ulterior motives (wrongly, of course). I suspect that our internal purpose most often results from our being both actor and observer. Most often, as actor, I just act. And then, as observer, I step outside of myself and explain my action, often only to myself. All this seems to be in the service of a drive to explain.

Still, I do at times plan, say, my route along city streets to a particular destination. It seems only reasonable to call the action of following that plan purposeful, the purpose being to reach the destination. Here the plan is conscious. Can I act purposefully but not be conscious of the purpose? Of course, all this discussion is only about how to use the word "purpose." Perhaps we should agree to refer to any action that serves to satisfy some drive as being purposeful. Some actions would then be consciously purposeful.

Which brings us to goals. All goals are ultimately in the service of the drives, though many are not directly so. Goals have subgoals, subgoals have sub-subgoals, and so on. At any of the several tops of this hierarchy,[23] you'll find a drive. Different goals may satisfy the same drive. Hunger may be satisfied by eating at a restaurant, by cooking and eating at home, or need not be satisfied at all if the agent is satiated. Satisfaction of hunger may be postponed if the house is on fire or if you're on a diet. In this case, some other drive suppresses the hunger drive, as in Brooks's subsumption architecture.

And the same goal may serve different drives. I may study out of sheer intellectual curiosity. Or I may study, thinking it will help me predict the stock market, thus serving the derivative drive of amassing wealth. Or maybe I want to impress the young lady sitting next to me, in service of my reproductive drive. On the other hand, maybe her father is sinfully rich. Among humans, it's hard to tell which drive is being served. When this is also true of our artificial agents, we will have made real progress.

Various subgoals and their satisfying actions may accomplish higher-level goals. At the bottom of the tree are primitive actions supported by the architecture. There are limits to my free will. I may want to burrow in the ground, but my architecture doesn't support that action. As a means of locomotion, I may choose to walk or to run, but not to burrow.

Drives may compete for resources, giving birth to incompatible goals. I want to stay longer and finish this chapter, but the Steelers are on "Monday Night Football." How can I allocate resources so as to avoid starvation of some drive? In our society some drives often get starved. As artificial agents gain in complexity, they'll face "allocation of resources" issues.

So agents achieve goals to satisfy drives. They act to achieve goals. But how do they know what actions achieve which goals? How do they answer the only question there is: What do I do now? An agent must either know or find out how to satisfy drives or to achieve goals. Either the agents is born or constructed knowing how to achieve some goal or it must search to find a way. It's either reflexes or problem solving. The more you know, the less you need to search. The less you know, the more you have to search. We're back once again to the duality between knowledge and search. Storing values of the sine function in a lookup table is accumulating knowledge; calculating each value anew when needed is search.

But we can't rely solely on search. Some minimal knowledge must be built in, in the form of primitive actions. In animals, individual muscle contractions, or even muscle fiber contractions, may be considered primitive actions, whereas those of artificial agents tend to be at a higher level of abstraction, that is, move one square to the right. An agent can search for composite actions to achieve goals beyond any simple action. In humans, as in some robots, walking is a composite action. Of course there may be no one correct way of assigning primitive actions to a system. After all, we're building a theory here. It's not a question of what's right or wrong but of what's useful.

Knowledge can be embedded in an agent either structurally or symbolically. The architecture of an agent uses structurally embedded knowledge to process a stimulus and generate an action. Real neural networks, artificial neural networks, and Brooks's subsumption architecture are examples of structurally embedded knowledge. The stimulus is related causally to the action it produces. Don't confuse this view with simple behaviorism. The action depends both on the stimulus and on the internal state of the agent. If I'm not hungry, I'll likely pass right by that restaurant. If I am hungry, I may go in.

With symbolically embedded knowledge, stimuli are first transformed into symbols, and symbol manipulation leads to the action. SOAR is an example, as is a human doing long division. Symbolic AI is based on this paradigm. Structural embedding is often faster and more reactive, whereas symbolic embedding is often more flexible, says Brustoloni.

As with so many dichotomies, we face the problem of where to draw the line. Clearly a thermostat uses embedded knowledge, and SOAR is based on symbolic knowledge. But drawing the line is difficult. Maes's behavior networks seem to use both types of embedding. And what of Allen, where the structural subsumption architecture is simulated symbolically on a LISP machine? Brustoloni asserts that stimuli are always transferred into some internal representation, be it an electrical pulse, a voltage, a string of bits or characters. The internal representation of temperature in the thermostat may be the relative lengths of two pieces of metal. Symbolic and structural representations are functionally equivalent, Brustoloni says, so the problem of drawing the line isn't crucial.

In any nontrivial autonomous agent, one must expect to find much knowledge structurally embedded in its input/output system. That's certainly true of all the artificial life agents we've encountered so far, and it's true of us and our animal relations. Our whole world, as opposed to the "real" world, is determined by the way our senses operate, by built-in, sensory knowledge of what's important. Cells in our retinas respond most strongly to line segments at particular angles, to movement, and so on, all examples of built-in sensory knowledge. Reflex withdrawal from extreme heat demonstrates knowledge built into our output system. Both sensors and affectors are either designed or evolved for specific tasks. Having evolved from arboreal insectivores, primates typically have superior sight but weak olfaction. Apes, being forest dwellers and more or less arboreal, tend to have large arms and small legs, whereas humans, evolved as runners in the savannas, have small arms and large legs.

Classification of Agents

The study of autonomous agents, whether real world robots or artificial life agents, is not yet blessed with a useful taxonomy. Brustoloni makes a stab in that direction, defining several different types of autonomous agents.

He first talks about a *regulation agent,* regulation not in the sense of rule governed but in the sense of keeping something regulated, as a thermostat regulates temperature. A regulation agent has plenty of built-in knowledge and typically knows what to do next. Its prescribed actions tend to satisfy its drives. Regulation agents are capable of quite complex actions. Recall from our visit with animal minds the mama wasp performing an elaborate ritual of digging a burrow, closing it with tiny stones, finding and stinging a suitable cricket, bringing the cricket to the burrow, opening the burrow, entering and inspecting the burrow, inserting the paralyzed cricket, laying her egg, and closing the burrow. How do we know she's a regulation agent? Interrupting her routine leads to what seems to us inappropriate actions. If the cricket is moved away a bit while she's inspecting the burrow, she'll bring it back and then reinspect. This needless loop has been observed to happen forty times. How does mama wasp come by this complex sequence of actions? Since she dies before the new wasp hatches, she never saw *her* mama do it. She probably never saw any other wasp do it. She comes equipped with this prescribed action sequence to help satisfy her reproductive drive.

Mama wasp doesn't have to plan her sequence of actions because she has a complete plan built in. In principle, on-the-spot planning can be avoided by a designer, or evolution, providing the agent with complete, built-in plans. In practice, the sheer number of possible situations and goals may well preclude this. Prior analysis sufficient to allow recovery from error may well be impossible. Mama wasp's ancestors never had to deal with entomologists shoving their crickets away. Still, this is a rare event. For mama wasp, the built-in sequence works often enough.

Brustoloni asserts that a regulation agent is the implementation of choice when actions are reliable in their effects. We will hear more of reliability when we visit Drescher's schema mechanism, and will see exactly what is meant by actions being reliable. But actions are not always reliable. Sometimes, on saying hello, I'm greeted like a long lost friend. At another time, the same person may give me a dirty look and walk off. Actions are often not reliable among social animals.

Brustoloni next introduces the class of *planning agents*. They are like regulation agents but have the additional ability to plan a sequence of actions and execute the plan. He identifies four distinct types of planning agents: *problem-solving* agents, *case-based agents,* OR (operations research) agents, and *randomizing* agents. We'll meet each of these individually. Keep in mind that planning is terribly expensive. As was mentioned earlier, Chapman (1987) has shown planning to be NP-hard under reasonable conditions. It's particularly hard to do in real time.

Problem-solving agents model each primitive action by pre- and post-conditions. They are likely to be based on a rule-based system, a production system, a classifier system, and so on. The agent searches for a sequence of actions, the preconditions of the first action being currently satisfied and the last action's post-condition satisfying a goal. He searches for a path to a goal, paths being sequences of actions represented in some problem space, as we've seen before. Some problem-solving agents may look for optimal solutions, and others may be satisfied with good enough solutions. A problem-solving agent may remember its plans and chunk them into a single complex action. (Recall that Wilson and others, including your tour guide, believe that some such capability to combine sequences of simple actions into a single complex action is necessary for any agent with more than modest abilities. Later we'll visit with Agre and Chapman's routines, a related notion.) Problem-solving agents must maintain a world model, and so must face the frame problem, nonmonotonic logics, and other such hassles. Brustoloni asserts that problem-solving agents are not well suited as a general model of intelligence.

Of the agents we've visited, SOAR (or at least Robo-SOAR, being autonomous) is surely a problem-solving agent. Agents based on Maes's behavior networks also may be problem-solving agents. Although no internal structure explicitly represents a plan, planning does seem to occur. The learning version of these agents could remember plans. Whether or not a behavior network constitutes a model of the world is debatable. And chunking seems not to be part of their armament as yet. Such considerations suggest possible refinements of Brustoloni's taxonomy.

A case-based agent decides what to do next by search and analogy. It keeps a library of cases, of plans that have been tried before and that worked in specific circumstances. If the new situation is sufficiently similar, perhaps an existing plan will work again. Recall Dreyfus's assertion that experts simply do what usually works, and it usually works. To solve a problem, a case-based agent finds the most suitable plan; tweaks it if necessary, because the conditions may not be exactly the same; and then uses the tweaked plan. Not a bad strategy. I suspect that you and I do exactly that most of the time.

We usually have little difficulty in deciding on the most similar case or one sufficiently similar to use. But computationally, the issue of how to retrieve the solution to the most similar problem is not yet well studied and is likely hard. Brustoloni claims that finding the most similar problem solution should be computationally less expensive than the kind of search problem-solving agents do. I think his idea is that consulting a lookup table should be easier than searching a whole problem space. Somehow, I'm not completely convinced.

On a later tour stop, we'll visit with Hofstadter and Mitchell's Copycat program, which reasons by analogy. It might be an example of a control structure for a case-based agent. None of the agents we've met so far seem to be case based.

An OR agent uses a mathematical model, such as queuing theory, to provide its control. This requires an accurate model of both the agent and the agent's world. Again, such control is not computationally cheap. A basic principle seems to say that even relatively simple autonomous agents require vast amounts of computation. Neither Brustoloni nor I know of any agents of this sort, but he points out that one could readily be built and experimented with.

Finally, he briefly mentions randomizing agents that simply work by trial and error. Ackley and Litman (1992) have experimented briefly with such.

Another major category contains *adaptive agents* that can acquire domain knowledge, allow them to perform actions they were not previously capable of. Brustoloni contrasts such agents with those that learn by chunking or similar devices. Making a single complex action out of a sequence of primitive actions doesn't yield any new domain knowledge. The agent can't accomplish anything it couldn't have done previously. It can only speed up its response. Adaptive agents should fare relatively well in a dynamically changing environment, he says. If such can be developed, much of the notoriously difficult and tedious knowledge engineering problem[24] would be eliminated.

I'm a little concerned about Brustoloni's claim for this category of agent. All any agent can do is string together sequences of primitive actions. Our seemingly infinite possibilities in language production, for example, are all based on some finite (and fixed?) number of primitive muscle fiber contractions. Haven't I learned something new about the environment when I learn to string together primitive actions so as to ride a bicycle? Doesn't Animat learn something new if he evolves a classifier telling him to eat food when next to it? Certainly, he could have performed the action before, but didn't always know to.

Combining categories yields *adaptive planning agents,* which discover and model the results of their primitive actions, thereby forming concepts for modeling their world. On a later tour stop, we'll meet Drescher's schema mechanism and Edleman's Darwin III, both of which claim to create concepts. Adaptive planning agents engage in problem solving—searching the problem space. Further, they adapt—search the space of problem spaces, which Brustoloni refers to as "extraordinarily hard to do."

He then introduces *adaptive case-based agents,* which learn by storing new cases, and speculates that they should be easier to do than adaptive planning agents. One could go on. And there is certainly much more to understand as we create a useful taxonomy of autonomous agents. Brustoloni's hierarchy of behaviors, which we'll visit next, should prove helpful.

Hierarchy of Behaviors

Brustoloni also offers a first stab at a potentially useful hierarchy of behaviors. Most basic are the *instinctive behaviors,* which maintain invariants important to the agent. In humans, the endocrine system and much of the neural system are devoted to instinctive behaviors. At the bottom of the autonomous agent chain, a thermostat does nothing but maintain a temperature. Herbert's avoidance of obstacles is a higher-order example. Instinctive behaviors are implemented by regulation agents. Here, Brustoloni implicitly assumes a multiplicity of mind approach, with internal agents responsible for various behaviors. Regulation agents performing instinctive behaviors must operate continuously, and be both reliable and sufficiently fast.

Next up the behavioral ladder is what Brustoloni calls *habitual behavior,* the following of patterns previously known to yield desired results. Examples in humans and other animals include procedures, routines, and rituals. (Presumably he intends these to be learned, which leaves me in something of a quandary about the sand wasp's egg-laying behavior. Although clearly a ritual, the behavior appears to be instinctive. A finer classification seems called for.) Habitual behavior is implemented by case-based agents and appears most frequently in a stable environment. Such behavior is effortless in that it requires no thought. It arises from problems previously solved, imitation, operant conditioning, and so on.

Less frequent than habitual action is *problem-solving behavior.* Implemented by problem-solving agents, and requiring longer response time, it's rarely used in a situation with a habit available. Examples abound in humans: chess playing, mathematics, route planning, interior decorating, and so on. Problem-solving behavior is still rare in artificial agents, with the coming Robo-SOAR the only example that comes to mind. Do other animals problem solve? I suspect so, but have no convincing example to offer. Griffin (1984, pp. 134–43) offers support for this position.

Next up in Brustoloni's hierarchy of behaviors is *playing,* by which he means experimentation for its own sake. Though relatively rare in adults, playing occupies a central role in early human development. Once knowledge for habitual and problem-solving behaviors is acquired, playing assumes a less important role. Implemented by randomizing agents, playing can be "disastrously expensive." Playing has been built into several artificial creatures, for example, Johnson and Scanlon's Packrat (1987).

At the top of Brustoloni's behavior chain is *theory making.* This infrequent behavior typically takes a long time to produce results and is implemented by adaptive agents. Among humans, one finds theory making indulged in by mathematicians, philosophers, scientists, social scientists, historians, literary critics, theologians, screenwriters, astrologers, football coaches, and, at a low level, all the rest of us. Theory making seems to be a quintessential human trait. Do other animals make theories? I suspect some do, but I have no evidence to support this suspicion. To my knowledge, no artificial agent has shown signs of theory making. Animat evolves rules at too low a level to constitute theory. There have, however, been symbolic AI systems (not agents) that rediscover laws of physics, Langley's BACON being one such (1977, 1980).

Note the progression in the amount of knowledge embedded in agents as the level of behavior ascends. For instinctive behavior, all needed knowledge is built in. At the other end of the chain, theory making, nothing is known.

Note also that each level of behavior acts through the next lower level, using it rather than replacing it. This leads Brustoloni to suggest implementing agents as hierarchies of simpler agents, each specialized in its behavior, with agents on one level acting through those at lower levels. This is very much in the spirit of multiplicity of mind and smacks of the philosophy behind Brooks's subsumption architecture, Minsky's society of mind, and so on.

As we've seen, minds decide what to do now. This continual decision is based not only on internal state but also on what's going on in the world. In a sense, though, we create not *the* world, but *our* world, our version of the world. Our next major stop will explore mechanisms for that creation.

Notes

1. And reminds me of Simon's parable of the ant (1981, pp. 63–65). Having observed an ant zigzagging across a beach, he observed: "An ant, viewed as a behaving system, is quite simple. The apparent complexity of its behavior over time is largely a reflection of the complexity of the environment in which it finds itself." Simon goes on to replace "ant" by "man" and to argue for the same resulting statement.

2. I'm tickled at writing about demons just now. Last night was Halloween. I was visited by witches, goblins, and, yes, demons. Such a demon responds to the sound of candy dropping into its bag with a well coached "Thank you."

3. Though full of fascinating ideas, this paper has hardly been noticed. I have never seen a reference to it, although, in my opinion, it richly deserves to be well known.

4. This sounds a lot like Hebb's rule from our connectionist stop. Recall that Hebb says the synapse between two neurons is strengthened when they both fire essentially simultaneously.

5. All this reminds me of an algorithm used on a massively parallel machine (a connection machine) for retrieving text (Stanfill and Kahle 1986). Each of 16,000 processors is responsible for some news story from Rueters. To retrieve stories about attacks by pit bulls, first find one such story, using traditional key words. Then use all the words in that article as key words. Broadcast this list to all the processors. Each processor checks its text and reports the number of matches. The processors with the most matches (those that yell the loudest) are allowed to supply their text. This account is greatly oversimplified, but the idea's right.

6. We met the notion of a pointer (usually the address of the next data item) during our interlude with the second AI debate.

7. Joe Stinnett a student at the University of Memphis is currently working on a pandemonium controller for an Animat. We'll see how predictable it turns out to be. ,

8. Pascal, in addition to referring to a famous French mathematician, is the name of a computer language. I'm surprised that such a small program could implement so complex a structure.

9. If you're going to do this kind of research, surely you want to find something fundable to aim it at. Somebody might put up funds for a Mars rover.

10. Expert systems are most often symbolic AI products that use knowledge, represented internally by production rules, to solve problems in diagnosis, classification, and so on. An expert system shell is a software system into which knowledge can be infused to create an expert system.

11. Art Graesser suggests that *all* systems may be brittle. He may be right.

12. If you're afflicted with a leaky mind like mine, you might want to reread the section on production systems in chapter 4.

13. Points in parameter space are vectors of parameters.

14. This issues of what's a representation and what's not will return to plague us when we visit the third AI debate.

15. Technically, Maes's system is an instance of an automata network (Fogelman Soulie and Tchuente 1987; Garzon and Franklin 1994), which consists of an underlying digraph whose nodes are populated by finite-state machines. Each finite-state machine takes its inputs from the incoming links and sends its outputs along outgoing links. Automata networks are quite general, massively parallel computation devices; artificial neural networks, cellular automata, and the Boolean networks of Kauffman (1993) are special cases.

16. Modal logics include provisions for reasoning about beliefs, desires, and so on.

17. For an NP-hard problem only exponential time solutions are known or are expected to be known. That is, the length of time required to solve an NP-hard problem increases exponentially with the size of the problem. As a consequence, optimal solutions become impossible for reasonably sized problems. Heuristics must be relied upon to find suboptimal, but good enough, solutions.

18. Each visible numeral on a pocket calculator occupies a register, for instance.

19. For example, if the input is an S, then change to state q^2 and output a T, else remain in the current state and output a W.

20. Think of Allen's direction as being represented by the direction of an arrow (vector) and his speed by its length. If layer 1 produces one such vector to avoid an obstacle, and layer 2 produces another randomly for wandering, vector addition produces the diagonal of a parallelogram derived from the two vectors.

21. CMOS refers to a particular process of manufacturing VLSI chips (very large scale integrated circuits). The internal registers of these processors contain eight 0's or 1's; hence 8 bit.

22. A serial port translates parallel signals (all abreast) into serial signals (single file) and vice versa.

23. To a computer scientist, a hierarchy with a single "top" is a tree. A computer scientist's tree stands on its leaves with its single root in the air. A hierarchy with several such roots is called a forest.

24. The most commercially successful product of symbolic AI is the expert system, a program that incorporates expert human knowledge of some narrow domain, say diagnosing faults in a diesel locomotive, and makes humanlike decisions. The difficult part of creating an expert system is transferring expert human knowledge to the system. This process is called knowledge engineering.

12

What's Out There?

It is clear that the notion of information preexisting in the world must be rejected.
—George N. Reeke, Jr., and Gerald Edelman, "Real Brains and Artificial Intelligence"

A little mathematics is good for the soul.
—Stan Franklin

Several times we've encountered the notion of a paradigm shift for viewing mind, intelligence, cognition. This new paradigm includes such strange ideas as degrees of mind and multiple minds in a single agent. Perhaps the most unsettling of all notions in this new paradigm is that of information being created by mind rather than as existing in the outside world for processing by mind. During this tour stop we'll explore a mechanism by which animals can discriminate between stimuli, that is, can categorize their input. We'll also meet two mechanisms for creating those categories in the first place, for creating information. But to appreciate our first major attraction, we need a brief excursion into dynamical systems theory—for the sake of our souls, of course.

Dynamical Systems

A decade or so ago I had a systems theorist as a colleague. I asked him to tell me what a system was. After all, if you're going to study systems theory, you ought to know what a system is. He replied by asking me to tell him what a set was. "No one defines a set," I told him. "'Set' is a primitive undefined term in mathematics." "So it is with a system," he told me. If "system" and "set" are undefined terms, how do we come to know about them? By examples. Here are some examples of systems: the solar system, an automobile, the weather, your desktop computer, an animal's nervous system, the secretary's chair I'm sitting on (with all its adjustments). Typically systems are composed of parts or subsystems, and these subsystems generate the behavior of the system.

A system is said to be *static* with respect to a given time frame if it is essentially unchanged during that time. The Himalayas, for example, can be assumed to be static over a human life span. But over geologic eons they are not static at all. Here we want to meet dynamical systems, systems that change in significant ways in a given time frame. Examples? All those of the last paragraph, and so many more. It's hard to find anything that isn't an example. Essentially everything we think of that's of any interest can be interpreted as a dynamical system. The concept seems so broad as to be useless. There's not much point in talking about a concept that doesn't discriminate at all.[1] But strangely enough, if you make the notion precise in a mathematical way, it turns out to be useful. So let's look at a mathematical formulation of the notion of dynamical system.

An abstract *dynamical system* is a mathematical object[2] consisting of a set that we'll name X, together with a self-map[3] of X that we'll call T. X is called the *state space* of the dynamical system. Think of a point (element) in the state space of a system as a snapshot of the system at a particular moment in time. Each point of the state space of the solar system might contain the positions and velocities of each of the nine planets and of each of their many moons. A point in the state space of your desktop computer might contain the contents of each of the memory cells and each of the registers in the central processing unit as well as some additional items. The self-map, T, is called the *dynamics* of the system (sometimes the *global dynamics*). For the moment, let's suppose our dynamical system is *discrete,* that is, time passing is measured in discrete steps. If at a particular moment the system is in state x, its state at the next moment is T(x). The global dynamics transforms the state of the dynamical system.[4] During a single time step (clock cycle) of a desktop computer, the contents of a register or of a memory location may change. In the cases that will interest us most, X will be a space of vectors—finite sequences of numbers, like the three-dimensional space we live in, only with some large number of dimensions. In the desktop computer example, there will be at least as many dimensions as there are registers and memory locations.

Discrete dynamical systems give rise to *iterative systems.* Suppose an initial state, x_0, of the system is given. As time passes discretely, the global dynamics, T, generates a sequence of subsequent states. From x_0, the state of the system at time 0, applying T yields $T(x_0) = x_1$, the state of the system at time 1. Another application of T yields $T(x_1) = x_2$, the state of the system at time 2. In general, T operating on the state of the system at time $t-1$ yields the state of the system at time t. The (possibly infinite) sequence of systems states so generated, x_0, x_1, x_2, x_3, x_4, . . . is called the *orbit* of the point x_0. Orbits are sometimes called *itineraries* in the discrete case and *trajectories* in continuous systems, which we'll soon encounter. Dynamical systems theory is concerned with the long-range behavior of orbits. How does this sequence of system states develop as you go further and further out? How will the system behave in the fullness of time? Does it stabilize on some fixed state? Does it endlessly repeat some small pattern of states? Does it just go off wildly, like an epileptic seizure? Let's digress a bit to explore possible long-range behaviors.

Our digression takes us to the real numbers between 0 and 1, that is, to infinite decimals with nothing to the left of the decimal point. Think of these numbers as sequences of digits. What's the long-term behavior of the infinite sequence .33333333 . . . ? This sequence starts at state 3 and continues in that same state at each time step. Its long-range behavior is described as converging to a *fixed point,* as would the sequence .123333333 . . . , or the sequence .9876543211111. . . . Converging to a fixed point is one kind of long-term behavior of a sequence. The latter two sequences go through a transient time before settling onto a fixed point.

Another type of long-term behavior is illustrated by the sequence .123123123123. . . . This sequence starts in state 1, goes to state 2, goes to state 3, returns to state 1, and continues in this fashion forever. Such behavior is called *periodic.* This particular sequence has period 3. (Fixed points can be thought of as periodic with period 1.) A periodic sequence can also have some transient time. Here is one, .68459012121212 . . . , which starts out doing some wild stuff and then suddenly settles into a pattern of period 2.

The sequence .41421256 . . . illustrates yet another type of long-range behavior. You may recognize it as the decimal expansion of $\sqrt{2} - 1$. As an irrational number, it's never periodic of any period.[5] Its long-term behavior is, in principle, unpredictable, even though its short-term behavior, the next digit, is easily gotten by an algorithm. Such behavior is often called *chaotic*.[6]

Thus we have seen three types of long-term behavior: converging to a fixed state and remaining there (fixed point); continually traversing some periodic track of states (periodic); and unpredictable (chaotic).

With some of the jargon for long-range behavior in hand, let's talk about limit points. To make the process more concrete, let's explore the dynamics of a particularly simple abstract dynamical system. Let the state space, X, be the real numbers, thought of as the points on a two-way infinite line, with a point at infinity, ∞, on the positive end. A thermometer provides an example of a dynamical system with a single number, the temperature, as its current state. It would not, however, allow an infinite value. (My mathematician side is sneaking out again.) With state space in hand, we must define the global dynamics of the system. Let T be the function that squares whatever number you give it, that is, $T(x) = x^2$.

Let's look at the behavior of the orbits of various initial states (points) of this system. Since $T(0) = 0$, we've found a fixed point. The point 1 is also a fixed point. What happens to the orbit of any number greater than 1, say 2? The orbit looks like 2, 4, 16, 256, ... It gets arbitrarily large as you go arbitrarily far out in the sequence; it converges to infinity. If we start with a point between 0 and 1, its square is smaller than itself. The orbit goes downward and converges to 0. Suppose an initial state lies between -1 and 0, say -0.5. One application of T yields .25 and the orbit again converges to 0. The orbit of the initial state -1 goes directly to the fixed point 1. It has a transient of length 1. An initial state less than -1 is immediately bounced above 1 so that its orbit converges to infinity. Thus 0, 1, and infinity are limit points of this system, that is, states to which orbits converge.

Notice that 0 and infinity are *attractors* in the sense that the orbits of states close to them converge to them. On the other hand, 1 is a *repeller*, since the orbits of initial states close to 1 move away from 1.

The set of all initial states whose orbits converge to a limit point is called the *basin of attraction* of that limit point. The basin of attraction of 0 in this system includes all real numbers strictly between −1 and 1. The basin of infinity includes all points strictly less than −1 or strictly greater than 1. The limit point 1 has a two-point basin, −1 and 1. Basins of attractions partition[7] the state space. Figure 12.1 gives a visual version of all this.

So far we have seen only basins of point attractors. Let's look at a periodic orbit as well. Take the state space X to be the real numbers plus

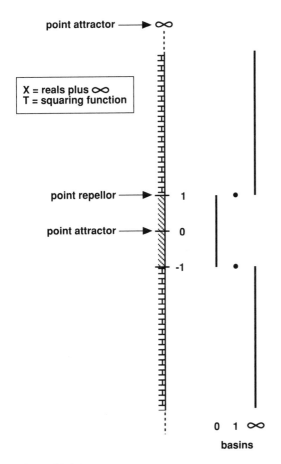

Figure 12.1
Basins of attraction

infinity, as before. Change the global dynamics to be the squaring function minus 1, that is, $T(x) = x^2 - 1$. Now we can see some periodic behavior. $T(-1) = 0$ and $T(0) = -1$. Thus the orbit of -1 looks like 0, $-1, 0, -1, \ldots$, while that of 0 looks like $-1, 0, -1, 0, \ldots$. Thus, each of the initial states 0 and -1 has a periodic orbit of period 2. The orbit of the initial state 1 also has period 2 after a transient time of 1. For those of you with a mathematical bent, here's the first (and probably the only) exercise of the tour: What does the orbit of a state close to 0 look like? Determine the basins of attraction of this system.

For an example of an orbit with period 4, we can call on our high school algebra. Let the state space, X, of our new dynamic system be the set of all complex numbers, $z = x + iy$, that you met while solving quadratic equations.[8] Define the new global dynamics by $T(z) = iz$. Then $T(1) = i$, $T(i) = -1$, $T(-1) = -i$ and $T(-i) = 1$, so that the orbit of any of the initial states $1, i, -1, -i$ has period 4, and bounces infinitely often on each of these four states.

Finally, let's look at chaotic orbits. Let the state space, X, be the real numbers again, and take T to be defined by the logistic equation, $T(x) = \alpha x(1-x)$, where α is some real number parameter. This time let's pick some initial state, say 0.1, and fix it. The long-term behavior of this system is going to depend on the value the parameter α. Figure 12.2 shows a graph of the orbits of 0.1 as α varies, roughly between 2.8 and 4.

For a value of α, say 2.9, picked along the x-axis, the vertical line through 2.9 contains the orbit of our initial state, 0.1, when α is 2.9. In this case, the orbit is a fixed point near 0.65. The program that drew this graph throws away the first 100 or so states of the orbit, trying to get past the transients. It then plots the next 300 states as points, all on the single vertical line through α. In the case of $\alpha = 2.9$, these 300 points are plotted one on top of another; the orbit has converged to a fixed point. If $\alpha = 3.2$, the 300 points alternate between roughly 0.5 and roughly 0.8, a periodic orbit of period 2. At $\alpha = 3.5$ we get a periodic orbit of period 4.

For $\alpha = 3.7$ a chaotic orbit emerges. The 300 points are all different, and unpredictable. Note carefully that this orbit, although unpredictable, is completely deterministic. Any state in an orbit can be found by applying the logistic equation to the preceding state; that's certainly deterministic. Then in what sense is the orbit unpredictable? In the sense that there is

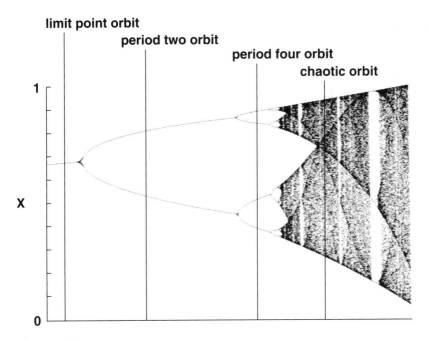

limit point orbit

period two orbit

period four orbit

chaotic orbit

Figure 12.2
Chaotic orbits of the logistic function

no quicker way to determine the behavior of a chaotic orbit than to calculate it state by state. Note also that changing the parameter α just a little bit results in very different long-term behavior of the orbit. There's much more of interest to be said about this last dynamical system[9] (see Devaney 1987, where it is referred to as the quadratic map).

Think of the state x(t), of a system at time t, as a snapshot of those important features of the system at that time. If you are defining the system, you need to decide what features are relevant to your purposes.[10] Often an individual feature can be described as a real number. In that case, the state of a system with, say, six salient features can be described by a list of numbers (a vector) of length 6. In general, the state of a system is given by an n-vector where n is the number of salient features. The state space, X, of the system—that is, the set of all possible states—can then be represented as a subset of some Euclidean n-space.[11] I say "subset" because of possible constraints on the values that can describe a given feature. Some feature, for example, might take on only the values 0 and 1, that is, be present or absent. As an example, take an artificial neural network with N nodes. Consider the vector of activation of the nodes at some given point in time as the state of the system at that particular time. We've previously called the state space of such a system its activation space. For a biological example, take some neural structure in the nervous system of some animal. A vector containing the firing rates of each of its neurons at a given time represents a state of that system.

Both artificial and biological neural networks are massively parallel devices. Each little unit, or neuron, is itself a computational device. It computes its next state, or value. These devices update their state locally and in parallel. One unit or neuron need only know the states of its neighbors in order to compute its own next state. It doesn't need to know the states of units or neurons with which it has no direct contact. In that sense the updating is local. These local dynamics operating in parallel give rise to the new state of the entire system. Local dynamics of individual units or neurons, operating in parallel, define the global dynamics of the entire system. Instead of T being defined by a single equation, as we've seen before, it's defined by the local updating of each individual feature, in these cases of units or neurons. These simple local rules frequently give rise to complex emergent, global properties, which often are not easily predictable from knowledge of the local activity. Though most of the dynamical systems that have interested us are defined locally in this way, not every dynamical system is. There are theorems, for example, that show under exactly what conditions a given dynamical system can be produced locally by some cellular automaton (Richardson 1972) or by some artificial neural network (Franklin and Garzon 1989; Garzon and Franklin 1990).

To complete our preparation for a visit to Freeman's work, we must briefly talk about continuous dynamical systems. In the discrete dynamical systems we've seen so far, time is measured in discrete ticks, like a clock. After each time step there is a next one. The system updates in discrete steps; the global dynamics are described by difference equations like $x(t + 1) = T(x(t))$. SOAR, Animat, and the artificial neural network we've seen are examples of discrete dynamical systems. In continuous dynamical systems, on the other hand, time is measured continuously. The system updates continuously, not in a stepwise fashion. The local dynamics are described as solutions of differential equations. The solar system and biological neural networks are examples of continuous dynamical systems. Continuous systems are often approximated by discrete systems by sampling their state every so often. If the sample period is short enough, a pretty good approximation typically results.

Figure 12.3 represents a continuous dynamical system as a vector field. The lopsided donut represents the underlying state space of the system. At each state there is a vector that gives the direction and the velocity of the instantaneous movement of that state under the global dynamics. Taken together, these vectors constitute a vector field.

Why do we want to know about vector fields? Because of limit cycle attractors.

Figure 12.4 depicts a continuous dynamical system with a single *limit cycle* attractor denoted by the heavy line. The trajectory (orbit)[12] of any state eventually ends up on the limit cycle or approaching it arbitrarily closely. Its basin of attraction is the whole space. A limit cycle is another kind of attractor that appears only in continuous systems. Think of it as a continuous version of a periodic attractor.

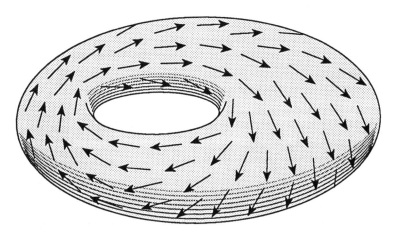

Figure 12.3
Continuous dynamical system

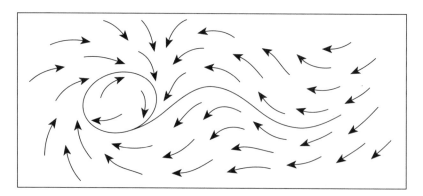

Figure 12.4
A limit cycle attractor

Well, so much for our whirlwind tour of some of the fundamental concepts of dynamical systems. Let's see how Freeman and company apply them to perception.

Perceptual Categories

Chaotic behavior serves as the essential ground state for the neural perceptual apparatus
—Christine Skarda and Walter Freeman, "How Brains Make Chaos . . ."

Yesterday at lunch, the conversation rolled around to our next attraction, Freeman's theory of basins of attraction as the mechanism for recognition. My friend Paul Byrne allowed as how (as we are wont to say down South), for him, the essence of Freeman's work was to make semantics palpable. (This is my transliteration of Paul's comment.)[13] The question of how symbols relate to their referents becomes no longer a subject of endless debate among philosophers. Rather, we'll see that it has a surprising and satisfying answer,[14] at least in some important cases.

To a rabbit, for instance, rapid and accurate recognition is often of crucial importance. It can be a matter of life or death that he distinguish quickly and correctly between the smell of a carrot and the smell of a fox. And a typical rabbit does so quite nicely. But *how* does he do it? That's a question that has occupied Walter Freeman and his colleagues at Berkeley for some years (Skarda and Freeman 1987). To understand Freeman's theory, we'll first need a tad of neuroanatomy.

The anatomy of olfaction (figure 12.5) begins with receptors inside the nose. These receptors send messages to the olfactory bulb. Neurons in the bulb also communicate with one another. The bulb exchanges information with the olfactory cortex. Cells within the cortex exchange information with one another, and the cortex exchanges information with the limbic system (attention, arousal, motivation) and the motor system. The receptors are chemoreceptor neurons, each with a docking place for a molecule with a protuberance of a shape complementary to its own. Apparently we are born with receptors keyed to many differently shaped molecules. Since these receptors inhabit interior surfaces of a nostril, they can be thought of as occupying a sheet, a two-dimensional array. Odor-specific data are encoded as patterns of activity, both spatial and temporal, on this sheet. Receptor cells sensitive to a particular odorant are clustered nonuniformly about the nostril.

With this sketchy picture of olfactory structure, what about its function? Here's my speculation as to how olfaction might work.[15] Molecules of smoke, sucked into my nostrils with an incoming breath, dock at some of the receptors. The pattern of activity on the receptor sheet is changed. This pattern is forwarded to the olfactory bulb, where it is recognized as "smoke." A "smoke" signal passes to the olfactory cortex, which may become alarmed and signal to the motor cortex to "get me out of here." Let's pick at the pieces of this hypothetical scenario.

Smoke is composed of many types of molecules. Smoke from different types of fires may differ greatly, stimulating very different receptors. Also, the pattern of receptors stimulated during a particular inhalation depends so on the vagaries of air currents and the geometry of nostrils as to appear random. The particular pattern stimulated would be harder to predict than numbers resulting from rolling dice. A particular pattern might occur only once in the lifetime of the individual. In spite of all this variation, each of the resulting patterns must be recognized as smoke.

Different patterns on the receptor sheet result in different patterns on the olfactory bulb, where recognition appears to take place. The recogni-

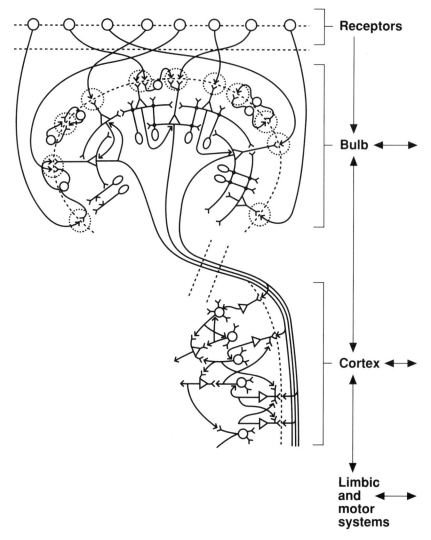

Figure 12.5
Anatomy of olfaction (adapted from Skarda and Freeman 1987)

tion problem is transferred from one piece of nervous tissue to another. So how does it happen? Freeman's answer is via attractor basins. But more on that later, after we've finished picking.

Once it is recognized, the signal goes on to succeeding areas of cortex, which presumably decide how to react and send instructions to the motor cortex. Here context becomes all important. Being awakened from sleep by smoke would provoke a very different reaction than smelling a little smoke just after having lit a fire in the fireplace. The internal context also plays a causal role. I may find the smell of cigarette smoke distasteful, or nostalgic of my younger days as a smoker. If I'm allergic to cigarette smoke, I may beat a hasty retreat.

Recall that signals run both ways between several of these structures. If I'm hungry, the hickory smoke of Memphis barbecue will be easier to detect. Presumably, this means a change in the olfactory bulb produced by signals from the olfactory cortex. (Keep in mind that all this is, no doubt, greatly oversimplified.) Freeman's theory will account for this. Let's get on with it.

Freeman maintains that odor-specific information must exist in the olfactory bulb. Somehow this information must be created. He claims it appears as spatial patterns of amplitude of an oscillation of EEG potential[16] over the olfactory bulb. Let's see what he's talking about. Consider a device with an 8 X 8 array of electrodes, 64 all together. Each electrode is embedded in the olfactory bulb of a rabbit, where it reads an EEG trace. The presumption is that these sixty-four readings provide a fairly reliable sample of what is happening all over the bulb. Each lead records an oscillation of EEG potential at its location. The activity at one of these electrodes, over the short time interval of a sniff, appears as a wavy squiggle on Freeman's oscilloscope (figure 12.6). The average amplitude, or height, of the squiggle varies from electrode to electrode. A contour map, created by drawing isobars (lines) connecting neighboring points of equal amplitude, depicts a pattern of activity over the bulb. This pattern of activity, this spatial configuration, is what, according to Freeman, characterizes the odor(s) present during the sniff. The contour map displays *average* intensity in both a temporal and a spatial sense. Each mapped point records the average over an event time window measured by the length of

EEG

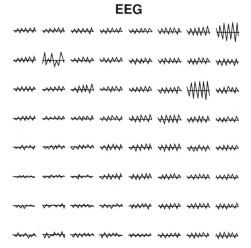

TRIAL SET 3

Figure 12.6
Sniff activity (redrawn from Skarda and Freeman 1987)

the corresponding squiggle. Each point also depicts output from one electrode that is measuring average intensity over a group of neurons.

How did Freeman come to this conclusion that patterns of activity over the whole olfactory bulb encode the needed information? By the hardest! He spent a decade looking for internal representations of odors in phase variation, amplitude modulation, frequency modulation, and a jillion other variables that didn't work before discovering the only thing that counts, the topographical map.

Notice the distributed representation. Every neuron in the bulb participates in every olfactory discriminative response; each plays its role in creating the contour map. This is the "distributed representation" we spoke of during our visit to artificial neural nets. But Freeman doesn't want to call these patterns representations at all. He maintains this topographical map is no internal representation. Why not? Because an odorant does not lead to an odor-specific pattern being formed. A single odorant can produce different patterns.

For example, the stereotypical patterns of which we've spoken form only in motivated animals. Some intention, attention, or expectation must be present before the patterns form. Without such, the bulb remains chaotic.

Odor-specific patterns also depend on behavioral response. A rabbit that has learned to follow a particular odor with an associated behavior may reliably produce, under controlled conditions in the lab, a certain pattern on the bulb. If it is subsequently taught a different behavior to follow that same odor, the corresponding pattern will be different. Thus, the patterns seem to be mediated not only by signals from the receptors but also by feedback from the cortex.

Patterns also differ in the same animal as a result of learning to respond to new odors. Suppose our rabbit has ten odors in its repertoire, corresponding to ten behaviors and to ten stereotypical patterns on the bulb. Now you train it to recognize and respond to one more odor. A new stereotypical patterns appears, and *all the old ones change*. Thought it still performs the old actions in response to the old odors, the patterns on the bulb, which had been relatively constant before, are now different. Nothing has been unlearned, but the patterns change.

Freeman claims this dynamic process isn't representational until an observer intrudes. These patterns may represent specific odors to us but not to the rabbit. The kinds of things one would want to do with a representation simply don't work—for example, comparing two patterns to determine if they represent the same odor. I couldn't agree more.

The existence of and/or the need for internal representation, that is, an internal model of the world, was discussed during our visit with Brooks on our last major stop, and will arise several more times before the end of our tour. Resolution will, of course, depend on our emerging with an understanding of what it is to be a representation. Typically a symbol is said to represent an object. Further, the symbol is assumed to be conventional, somewhat arbitrary, and the object is assumed to exist "out there." The pattern on the olfactory bulb during a sniff can be an arbitrary point in some basin of attraction. To me, that's not arbitrary enough to call it a symbol. And, as you know by now, I view information, including objects, as being created by autonomous agents for their own use, and not "out there" at all. This view doesn't conflict with our physicalist assumption that "out there" is both real and causative. Let's see how Freeman views information and other important concepts.

Information, Order, and Entropy

Information is a difference that makes a difference.
—David Chalmers, "Consciousness and Cognition" [17]

Yes, indeed! Information must be useful, must make a difference. And it must result from some distinction that is created from sensory stimulus. All this gives rise to a behavioral response. Something is distinguished sensorially, which makes a difference because it gives rise to a different behavioral response. Not all sensory stimuli convey information in this sense. I'm completely ignoring most of what is coming in to me at this instant. Almost all sensory input never achieves informational status; it is excluded by attention and habituation. That sensory input to which we do attend, affords the creation of information resulting in an increase in order.

What follows is by Prigogine out of Freeman (Prigogine and Stengers 1984). The second law of thermodynamics insists that everything gets more and more disordered (increased entropy). If this is so, how is it that we see things all around us that seem to get more and more ordered? Examples abound: atmospheric storms, dividing cells in embryos, neurons comprising the nervous system. When microscopic particles interact in large numbers, a macroscopic entity forms. Atoms are ordered into molecules, molecules into cells, cells into insects, insects into hives, nests, colonies, and so on. Neurons order themselves into nervous systems, which especially interest us here. How does all this happen in the face of the second law? "Why, of course," you say, "the second law applies only to closed systems." Exactly! We don't have a closed system. With a source of free energy, like our sun, and a sink for entropy (heat), like outer space, patterns of energy exchange emerge. As long as the sun radiates, and doesn't expand too much or blow up, we can expect pattern (order) to emerge. These patterns grow and evolve toward ever-increasing complexity. Material systems in their natural settings tend toward order, not disorder. The law of entropy is not repealed, but it is dethroned. Order emerges without an external prescription (self-organization).

Freeman views our nervous system as an open system with blood supplying free energy, from the brain's point of view, and carrying off waste heat (entropy). Thus Prigogine's notions lead us to expect emerging order that grows toward ever increasing complexity.

Conventional wisdom has the environment delivering complete information to the nervous system, information that is then degraded by noise. Not so, says Freeman (and your tour guide as well). Brains are self-organizing physicochemical machines whose business it is to choose the next action. In the service of this business, they internally create information. Stimuli from this page enter your visual system via your retinas. Subsequent processing creates information depending partly on what's printed on the page and, in large measure, on your prior knowledge, experience, and understanding. Recall Chalmers, on an earlier tour stop, talking about the duality of pattern and information. Here's a case in point. These patterns of energy first become stimuli, and then become information when they make a difference to the sensing agent.

Well, enough of background. Let's see how Freeman thinks this recognition of odors really happens.

Signals and Chaos

When one first encounters a working brain, I once heard Freeman say, the ceaseless activity of the background state is astounding. Conventional wisdom attributes it to noise. Again, not so, says Freeman. The background state of a neural system is chaotic. Against this chaotic background, signal starts when the system bifurcates from chaos to "burst activity." Chaotic activity stops and signal starts. In an alert animal, burst activity begins with inhalation. Freeman provides us with a diagram of his view of olfactory dynamics. In figure 12.7, the z-axis represents the level of arousal of the system, rising from coma (deep anesthesia) to seizure. In the center we see the exhalation/inhalation cycle depicted. During exhalation, the bulb remains chaotic. During inhalation, the system bifurcates to burst activity in the form of limit cycles, each enabling a particular classification of an odorant.

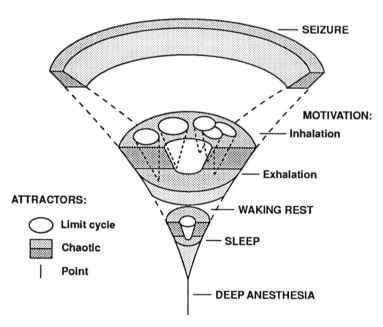

Figure 12.7
Olfactory dynamics (adapted from Skarda and Freeman 1987)

Freeman offers us yet another diagram depicting his view of the various "phase portraits" of the system, maps of the basins of attraction, as arousal increases (figure 12.8). At the coma level we see a point attractor. Any signal experienced goes nowhere. During exhalation, there's a single chaotic attractor into which every signal rolls. But during inhalation, the dynamical landscape is more complex, containing limit cycle attractors as well as a single chaotic attractor.

But what does all this mean? you ask. What indeed? According to Freeman, it means recognition. The basin of attraction of each limit cycle is the set of all those bulb patterns that lead to the recognition of a particular odor. On inhalation of one of the learned odors, a particular limit cycle attractor is selected by the input, placing the system within its basin. Which basin determines which odor. Thus many different patterns of activity on the olfactory bulb can result in the recognition of the same

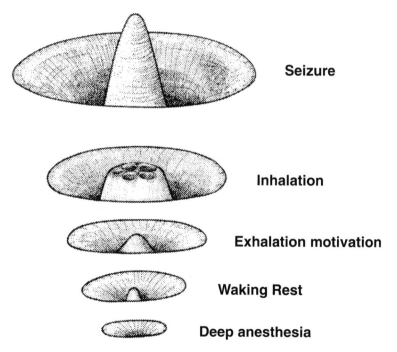

Seizure

Inhalation

Exhalation motivation

Waking Rest

Deep anesthesia

Figure 12.8
Maps of basins of attraction (adapted from Skarda and Freeman 1987)

odor—namely, all those in a particular basin. It's a slick way Mother Nature has found to recognize a single odor from any of a multitude of varied inputs.

Now I'm at least a little clear about what role the limit cycles play, you say, but why chaos? I thought chaos was to be avoided. Freeman offers several answers. Like muscle cells, neurons wither and die if unused. Chaotic activity exercises neurons.

Equally important, chaotic activity doesn't lead to cyclic entrainment (periodic or oscillatory behavior) or to spatially structured activity. Thus the system enjoys rapid and unbiased access to every limit cycle on every inhalation. The entire repertoire of learned smells is always instantly available. The system doesn't have to search through a memory store.

Finally, chaotic wells provide a catch basin for failure, allowing a "novel smell" classification. A new odor without reinforcement leads to habituation followed by a status quo activity. It's simply ignored. The system may run into all sorts of new odors, but if they are not a difference that makes a difference, there is no information, and hence no reinforcement.

A new odor with reinforcement leads to a chaotic state, allowing avoidance of all previously learned activity. A new activity can take place and, if successful, can be learned. The chaotic state, by keeping the system away from learned responses, gives it a chance to come up with a novel response to a novel smell. This new response may or may not be learned.

But minds are in the business of figuring out what to do next. Controlling action is what they are all about. According to Freeman, action comes via destabilization. Suppose an alert, motivated animal. During exhalation, its olfactory bulb is stabilized in its chaotic attractor. As inhalation occurs, input from the receptor sheet destabilizes the system, knocking it out of its chaotic state. If the stimulus is new, it may fall back into the chaotic attractor. If it's a known smell, the signal will fall into the appropriate basin of attraction. The system has bifurcated, and the odorant is thereby recognized. Convergence to an attractor in one system (the bulb) may destabilize other systems (the motor system, the olfactory cortex), leading to further state changes and, ultimately, to action.

What are we to conclude from all this? Freeman proposes a mechanism of mind accounting for categorization, a mechanism other than the information-processing metaphor that has held sway for so long. He conjectures, far beyond his data, that

> the dynamics of basins and attractors can suffice to account for behavior without recourse to mechanisms for symbol storage and invariant retrieval, "teachers" in learning devices, error-correcting feedback, comparators, correlators, associators, and the fine-grain point-to-point topographic connectionism that is required for their effectuation. (Skarda and Freeman 1987, p. 184)

I suspect, almost believe, he'll be proved right. All this will serve to fuel the flames of the third AI debate, about the need for representation, which we'll encounter before ending our tour.

But there are attractions left on this tour stop. Let's now visit another opponent of the information-processing metaphor and meet Darwin III.

Neural Darwinism

Among the most relentless pursuers of mechanisms of mind is Edelman. After winning a Nobel Prize for work in immunology, he successively took on categorization (1987), morphology of the nervous system (1988), and consciousness (1989).[18] As you can see, he's not easily deterred by hard problems. Here we'll visit briefly with his views on categories and their formation, and later meet their robotic embodiment, Darwin III.

Edelman contrasts the information-processing model of mind with what he calls the "evolutionary paradigm." Instead of information from the environment being perceived through the senses, we have *stimuli arriving* from the environment in "polymorphous sets," that is, in many different forms and in several sensory modes. While I'm writing this line, I'm aware not only of the cursor and text on the screen but also of the boundaries of the screen, the telephone in view to the right, the feel of depressing the keys, the sound of a fan, the lingering smell of an orange I ate a little bit ago, and a host of other stimuli less attended to. This last sentence blurs the distinction Edelman wants to make. The stimuli composed of a mostly black blob surrounding a silver patch embossed with little squares arrive through the senses, not yet identified as a telephone. These stimuli result not only from the present condition of the environment but also from prior *action,* movement of the head, saccades, fingers pressing, a hand tracing edges of a tactile pattern, inhalation. The stimuli, reflecting both the environmental state and the actions, *select* among *pre-existing nervous system states*. Activity of some states is enhanced, of others is suppressed. Edelman will refer to the neural substrates of these "nervous system states" as neuronal groups. We can think of them as biological embodiments of Minsky's agents, Jackson's demons, Ornstein's talents, and Maes's competences.

Such stimulus sets constitute information only after selection (recognition), after we work on them. Information is constructed; we build it. Sure, my dining room table is an object "out there" for me, but not for the tiny mite that lives in the carpet beneath it. The mite has no use for that particular way of partitioning its environment. In the same way, Inuit languages sport words for snow in many different forms, reflecting real world distinctions useful in the arctic environment but of no use to me because I live in an almost snowless clime:

the world, with its "objects," is an unlabeled place; the number of ways in which macroscopic boundaries in an animal's environment can be partitioned by that animal into objects is very large, if not infinite. Any assignment of boundaries made by an animal is relative, not absolute, and depends on its adaptive or intended needs. (Edelman 1992, p. 28)

Not only objects but, more generally, categories are not present in the environment. Things don't come with bar codes so I can tell that what I'm sitting on is a chair. Neither do categories such as water, clouds, calculus class, quarks. Categories must be constructed by each individual according to what is adaptive for its species in its environment. Tools for categorization—senses, neuronal groups, bones, and muscle tissue—evolved with the species. What categories are useful to this individual at this time depends on the environment. For example, pigeons have learned to distinguish photographs containing images of water, or of human faces, from those that don't. Their environment provided both the photographs and rewards for correct categorization. (See Barber 1993, p. 8, for an account and further references.) The complexity, the variability, and the unpredictability of the world preclude generally applicable, a priori rules of categorization. Categories must constantly change due to new experiences, and can be validated only by constant coupling to the world by behavior (shades of Brooks and of the computational neuroethologists). Each individual must go it alone.

How does each individual do it? How does a pigeon do it? How do you and I do it?

How can an animal [or an artificial autonomous agent] initially confront a small number of "events" or "objects" and after this exposure adaptively categorize or recognize an indefinite number of novel objects (even in a variety of contexts) as being similar or identical to the small set that it first encountered? How can an animal, in the absence of a teacher, recognize an object at all? How can it then generalize and "construct a universal" in the absence of that object or even in its presence? (Edelman 1992, p. 28)

These are questions Edelman wants to answer by finding and explicating their mechanisms. Assuming prerecognized and represented information, as AI systems typically do, won't satisfy. He wants to start earlier, with how information comes to exist in an unlabeled world, with the relationship between signals in the nervous system and the categories it has constructed. After accomplishing this daunting task to his satisfaction, he wants to know how interactions of those signals yield behavior without prearranged codes to give them meaning, and without prearranged algorithms to process them. The constraints are no labels in the world, no external semantics, and no internal, unexplained homunculus in the loop to provide meaning.

All this certainly explicates the questions, but where are the answers? Edelman presents his answers, conjectural in my view, in terms of several key concepts: neuronal groups, mappings, classification couples, global functions, global mappings.

Neuronal groups are collections of 50 to 10,000 neurons, formed during development and prior to experience, whose intraconnections allow them to respond to particular patterns of synaptic activity. Inputs originate at the sense organs but may be relayed through other neuronal groups. My mathematician self bridles a bit at this description. Why wouldn't any set of an appropriate number of neurons be a neuronal group? I suspect the answer has to do with proximity and interconnectedness. Cells within a group would be relatively close to one another and should show a high degree of interconnected activity. Two cells picked at random, on the other hand, would almost never connect.

A *primary repertoire* of neuronal groups occurs epigenetically (outside of genetic control) during development. These neuronal groups result from several selective mechanical-chemical events that govern morphology (Edelman 1988), controlling when a cell divides, how it moves, how it differentiates (neuron or muscle cell or some other kind). Some cells die. Connections are formed, and sometimes are lost. No two individual animals are likely to have identical neural connectivity, not even identical twins with identical genetic material.

The neuronal groups that process incoming stimuli, although perhaps algorithmic, are not prearranged in that they are *selected* by the stimuli in a way that's not prearranged. A vaguely remembered experiment makes this more plausible to me. Using probes, the mapping of a monkey's hand onto a tactile region of its cortex was charted. Everything was as expected. Next to the thumb area was the forefinger area, next to the forefinger was the middle finger, and so on. Nerves serving one of the fingers were then severed,[19] so that the corresponding area received no signals. Inspection at a later time found that the area that had served this finger was now being used for some other purpose. Yet another example is reported in *Science News* (April 9, 1994, pp. 229–30) under the headline "Nursing Mother Rats Show Brain Changes." The brain area sensitive to the underbelly increases in size after nursing commences.

A *secondary repertoire* forms as a result of this postnatal interaction with the environment via synaptic modifications both within and between neuronal groups. Connectivity—that is, where the axons terminate—doesn't change.[20] Selection occurs within the primary repertoire. The primary repertoire, according to Edelman, contains all the neuronal groups you are ever going to get.[21] Combinations of groups are selected when their activities are correlated with various signals arising from adaptive behavior.

We now have all the pieces of what Edelman calls a *selective system.* The three requirements are a diverse population from which to select, opportunities for selection, and differential reproduction or amplification of selected entities. Sources of variation must be causally unrelated to subsequent selection. The primary repertoire, evolving into a secondary repertoire and continuing to evolve, serves as the needed diverse population. Interaction with the environment provides opportunities for selection. Modification of synapses of selected neuronal groups constitutes amplification. Edelman concludes that the brain is a selective system operating in somatic time.[22]

In my view, the function of this particular selective system is to decide what to do next. In the service of this function, instances of categories must be recognized. If the recognition system is too specific, makes too many distinctions, there can't be enough categories for all the stimuli, and certainly not enough useful categories. If recognition is too broad, confusion of stimuli with significant differences may occur. The zebra out on the savanna has to be able to distinguish between a lioness that is hunting and a lioness that has just eaten. Recognition must occur at an intermediate level, allowing several neuronal groups to respond more or less well to any stimulus. Selection is between these groups.

Edelman dignifies the notion of multiple neuronal groups with different structures, each capable of performing the same function more or less well, with a name: *degeneracy*. In this degenerate selective system, with several neuronal groups responding more or less well to a given set of stimuli, any perceptual problem has several possible solutions. Context determines which groups respond and which are selected for synapse enhancement or suppression. Note that this system is fail-safe against the loss of an individual group. If you lose one group to a blow on the head or to a ruptured capillary, others will do the same job more or less well.

A few paragraphs back we saw described a map—or mapping, as Edelman is wont to call it—of a monkey's hand into its motor cortex. Such mappings are building blocks of Edelman's mechanism of characterization. Some map the retina into areas of the visual cortex. Locations close together on the retina have images that are close together in the visual cortex. Yet another maps motor actuators into areas of the motor cortex. Edelman speaks of a mapping as being an "ordered arrangement and activity of groups of neurons and large fiber tracts projecting onto laminae and nuclei with defined delimitations of functions" (1987, p. 107) (figure 12.9).

Beside each mapping in one direction typically lies another in the opposite direction. Edelman refers to this as *reentry*, the exchange of output signals between repertoires, usually in a mapped arrangement. Connectionists would call such networks recurrent (as opposed to the feed-

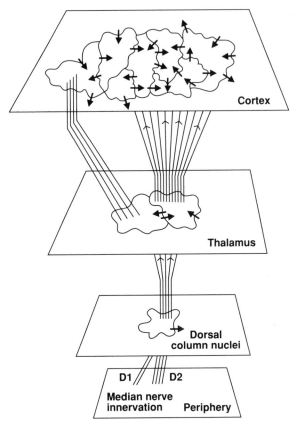

Figure 12.9
Mappings (redrawn from Edelman 1989)

forward nets we've already encountered). Let's take his description apart. Signals between repertoires? Recall that repertoires are collections of neuronal groups, probably of neuronal groups performing similar functions, and typically are physically located near one another. Thus a mapping makes sense. Reentry correlates responses of corresponding positions and related maps. Information passes back and forth. Each repertoire's responses depends to some extent on what the other is doing. Reentry is ubiquitous in the nervous system. Edelman has taken a lot of flack for introducing "reentry" when "feedback" with its broad meaning would

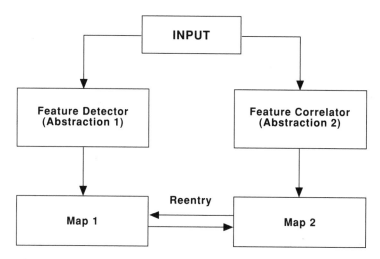

Figure 12.10
Classification couple (redrawn from Edelman 1987)

do as well. The notion encompasses feedback but is more general than a single feedback loop.

Edelman calls his basic mechanism for categorization a *classification couple* (see figure 12.10). Input is detected or correlated by distinct initial processing repertoires, one detecting features, the other correlating features, with no reentry between the repertoires. Each outputs to its following map, and there's reentry between these maps. Edelman claims that this sort of mechanism can classify where neither side could do so independently. Classification couples are modeled in Darwin III, whom we'll meet shortly.

Edelman refers to activities leading to categorization, memory, and learning as global functions enabling adaptation and survival. Such global functions, he claims, require the concerted functioning of multiple areas in large parts of the brain and also employ the sensorimotor apparatus.

Implementing a global function requires a global mapping, a dynamic structure containing multiple reentrant local maps, both motor and sensory. These interact with nonmapped regions to form a "spatiotemporally continuous representation of objects or events." A global mapping, Edelman claims, is the minimal unit capable of such function.

Another key point is that perceptual categorization depends upon the interplay between local cortical sensory maps and local motor maps. Global mappings permit the definition of objects via continual motor activity. This is how, according to Edelman, objects come into existence as objects. Categorization cannot be a property of one small portion of the nervous system.

The accepted view postulates independent categorization by the sensory areas. Some sensory information arrives, resulting in activity that causes some change in the environment. This leads to more sensory information, more processing of it, further motor activity, and so on, the whole process controlled by feedback loops. Edelman is selling a different view: selection among movements by a reentrant system provides for categorization and motor learning. The results of motor activity are an integral part of the original perceptual categorization. We'll see this same view again shortly, when we visit with Drescher's schema mechanism.

Perceptual categorization, memory, and learning are not properties of molecules, of synapses, or even of small numbers of neurons. Nor are they species faculties independent of development. Rather, each individual builds these faculties in somewhat different ways. They reflect the concerted workings, in each of us, "of motor and sensory ensembles correlating neuronal group selection events occurring in a rich and distributed fashion over global mappings." These global mappings are our objects and our events.

Edelman has produced a theory. Its utility (correctness?) is an empirical matter yet to be decided, though he does present evidence in favor in his various writings. Edelman and company have also produced models of parts of the theory. One such, Darwin III, will be our next attraction.

Darwin III

Edelman and colleagues have constructed a series of computer models referred to as *selective recognition automata*. Since they are networks of simulated neuronlike units, we can think of them as artificial neural networks similar to those we've met previously. Selection enables simple categorization and association in a world full of novelty. Since no categories are predefined, we have a pure example of the Zen notion of "beginner's mind."[23] The computer simulates neuronal units, the functions of which are not programmed. What does that mean? Certainly these units are programmed to yield specified outputs to particular inputs. Of course, but there is no built-in connection between the construction of the units and the role they eventually play vis-à-vis the outside world. The selective recognition will depend on sensory input from the environment. That's built in, as receptor organs are built into every animal species, every autonomous agent. The key point is that built-ins don't include categories of objects or of events.

Three such selective recognition automata have been constructed.[24] Darwin I dealt with recognition of binary strings. Darwin II recognizes and classifies two-dimensional patterns based on a retinalike array. Darwin III adds motor circuits and effectors to Darwin II, and thus is capable of autonomous behavior. Ah, it's time to put on our artificial life hats. Darwin III lives on the edge of a two-dimensional world of moving or stationary objects of different shapes, contours, and textures. Objects to the experimenter may differ from objects to Darwin III. A human experimenter controls the movement of objects, which makes the "artificial life" sobriquet more doubtful. Although he can't change his position, Darwin III has a movable head supporting a single eye, and a multijointed arm. Figure 12.11 is a drawing of Darwin III in his impoverished world, as it would appear on the computer's screen.

Darwin III has both peripheral and foveal vision. The motions of his eye effect only the perceived positions of objects. He senses light touch, distinguishing textures (light vs. dark) and shapes by tracing their contours. He also has a proprioceptive (kinesthetic) sense; he knows where his arm is, or at least the angles involved. Darwin III can move his arm, and thus affect objects, but he doesn't control them.

So what does Darwin III do? He learns to track and fixate particular objects, watching them move across the screen. He must learn this, since he doesn't even know what an object is. He will reach out, touch the object, and trace its outline. Darwin III learns to characterize a set of stimuli as an object, more or less, if it has a closed contour.

Edelman provides a functional schematic diagram to help us understand how Darwin III does what he does (figure 12.12). Though it won't take us even near full understanding, it's still useful. Take time for a slow,

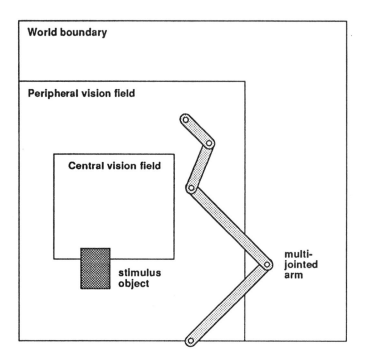

Figure 12.11
Darwin III's world (redrawn from Edelman 1989)

top-down look. Some items to note: First, there's a built-in classification couple; its feature detector is called Darwin, and its feature correlator is called Wallace. (Now you know why I've resisted shortening Darwin III to Darwin in the paragraphs above.) Second, simple motor actions required for sensing are distinguished from motor actions in response to the environment. Sensing is not passive reception; it requires active sampling. I suspect this may prove to be a generally useful mechanism of mind when designing autonomous agents. Third, learning doesn't appear as a separate module but is incorporated in the neural structure. Fourth, memory as continual recategorization needs explanation. Think of memory not as having stored an image somewhere but as an enhanced ability to react in a certain way to a certain stimulus.[25] And finally, Darwin III responds in Boolean fashion; he grasps the object (how, I'm not quite sure) if he likes it, and rejects it (knocks it away) if he doesn't. But how does he know if he likes it or not?

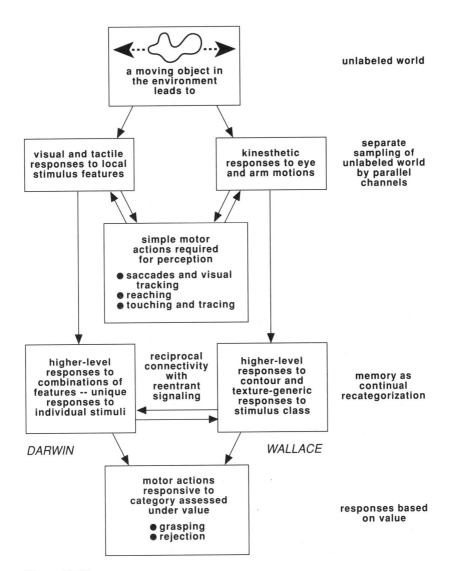

Figure 12.12
Functional schematic (adapted from Edelman 1989)

Darwin III has built-in adaptive values, specialized networks that reflect what he thinks of actions and sensations, what hurts and what feels good. These values drive the selection process, the modification of synapses, in a kind of reinforcement learning with internal reinforcement. Hebb's rule or some other learning mechanism is operating with parameters determined by values. All this reminds me of the evaluation networks of Ackley and Littman that we visited awhile back. The two architectures differ in that Darwin III isn't part of an evolving population. I conjecture that every adaptive autonomous agent must have some such built-in set of values upon which to base learning and action selection. Values prior to experience seem necessary.

The *Darwin subsystem* responds uniquely to individual stimulus patterns. It corresponds loosely to "matching to exemplars" but does not store feature patterns. How can this be? How do you match exemplars when there's no stored pattern to match? Here's my speculation. A feature pattern close to one previously seen has a better chance of being recognized, that is, reacted to more strongly. The pattern with the very best chance of being recognized could be considered the exemplar. Darwin behaves as if it were matching exemplars but consults no data structures encoding particular patterns. We, as observers, might be tempted to interpret Darwin's pattern of connection weights as such a data structure, but Darwin doesn't consult it as such.[26] What is stored is a tendency to react in a certain way to a given stimulus pattern.

The Darwin subsystem, by itself, cannot define an object because it is sensitive only to what it sees now, not to continuity in time or space. Objects are defined in terms of their contours. Thus, something more is required. The *Wallace subsystem* responds in the same way to different objects in a class by correlating a variety of features, making up classes as it goes. Its operation corresponds loosely to a probabilistic approach to categorization, and is dependent on the arm's ability to trace contours of stimulus objects. This allows objects to be distinguished from the background by connectedness. Wallace is insensitive to both rigid and nonrigid transformations of stimulus objects. It cannot distinguish individuals.

Both Darwin and Wallace are made up of neuronal groups, each an artificial neural network with its own inputs and outputs. One such neuronal group may output to others. A given neuronal group will respond strongly when the most active inputs are connected via strong synapses. Each responds optimally to some particular pattern of inputs, and more or less well to other patterns. More than one group responds in its own way to a given input. These overlapping responses provide the variation needed for selection.

Selective amplification occurs when connection strengths within and among groups are modified. All this is purely local, depending on parameters that can reasonably influence real synapses. Hebb's rule is the most common learning algorithm, strengthening a synapse if the neurons leading to it and from it are active at roughly the same time. Connection strengths can also be weakened. (Note that the line between selection and learning is blurred here.)

Categorization in Darwin III involves not naming but similarity of response. (I suspect this is what every animal does. We certainly use categories that we don't name, my favorite example being the paper strips with holes torn from the sides of computer paper.[27]) Categories are defined implicitly by responses to them. Particular categories depend on the kinesthetic trace correlations responded to by Wallace's groups. They may or may not correspond to the experimenter's categories.

Edelman speaks of recognition as the enhancement of meaningful response to a previously experienced stimulus. Groups with stronger responses are strengthened, those with weaker responses are weakened, those not involved are unchanged. This view of recognition jibes with categorization by similarity of response.

Darwin III generalizes by responding to novel shapes similarly to previously encountered shapes in the same class. Wallace is the instigator by means of feature correlating. Reentrant connections allow Wallace to bias Darwin's amplification according to class membership. Eventually, Darwin's responses become more alike within each class.

Association occurs when individual Darwin responses are linked as different stimuli in the same class via Wallace. Then presentation of one of these stimuli may evoke in Darwin elements of the response to the other one.

Much ado has been made about Darwin III not being given objects, as objects, "out there." How does he come to recognize, or create, objects at all? As human infants do, Darwin III conceives objects as spatially connected and continuously movable. Coherent motion provides a critical clue that the world can be parsed in a useful way into separate objects.

Let's see how Darwin III goes about tracking an object. In the beginning he doesn't know much because he hasn't had much experience. Imagine visual layers in his "brain" mapped to the "retina" of his eye, and also connected to motor layers that control the position of the eye. These connections are to motor neuronal groups capable of eye movements in all possible directions. Motor skills are not prearranged; he doesn't know how to track an object, for example. Exploration results from spontaneous movements generated by pairs of mutually inhibitory motor layers. Connections between sensory and motor areas are modified as a result of values favoring activity in a peripheral vision region and activity in the central visual region, the fovea. Connections will tend to be strengthened when motor activity leads to foveation (centering the activity in the visual field), and weakened otherwise. After experience with moving stimuli, Darwin III begins to make appropriate saccades and fine motor movements. The value scheme rewards trying to follow something.

After sufficient experience, Darwin III scans at random when no stimulus is visible, saccades rapidly to any stimulus appearing within his visual field, and finely tracks any successfully foveated stimulus. He categorizes the now centered object independently of position. After following this object for a while, he gets bored, and occasionally saccades to other parts of the visual field. He'll then track a new target if one shows up.

Darwin III learns to do all this. Of course, the motor and sensory mechanisms allowing tracking must be built in, as must the values. But they weren't singled out for that purpose from the beginning. A baby, given a rattle, may simply hold it and look around until spontaneous movement results in some sound. A built-in value kicks in, and the baby soon learns to shake the rattle to make the sound. Similarly, Darwin III learns to track. How much and how fast Darwin III learns also depends on the richness of the environment. With lots of things to track, he would learn quickly.

Next Darwin III learns to reach out and touch someone, or at least something. His multijointed arm can reach for and touch objects. This entails coordination of motions involving the joints.[28] As with tracking moving objects, this requires experience. Well, enough of all this talking about it. Let's have a look at Darwin III in action (figure 12.13).

What happens? He notices a stimulus in his peripheral vision (1) and moves his visual field so as to foveate it (2). While tracking the stimulus, he begins to trace its outline with his arm (1–2). As he goes around, proprioception of the arm joints is interpreted as bumpiness, and visual cues are construed as stripedness. Thus the stimulus is categorized as a striped, bumpy object. A built-in value to reject such a thing causes Darwin III first to pull his arm away (3), and then pop it down (4), swatting the offending object away (5). At this point Darwin III is still tracking (6).

Darwin III exemplifies a self-organized system; it learns without a teacher and without external reinforcement. As every self-organized system must, its actions are reinforced by built-in, internal values. Its selective system capitalizes on experience within its environment to develop functional capabilities. Initially it cannot track, reach, grasp, or swat. Though equipped with primitive sensing and actions, it lacks preprogrammed functions; the machinery doesn't know what it's for.[29] Apparently this is also true to some extent of the human nervous system. People recover from strokes with different parts of the nervous system taking over functions previously performed by now damaged parts. In Darwin III, a particular network or neuronal group can accomplish various tasks, depending upon what is found to be adaptive, that is, depending on value and circumstance. The necessity of values to any autonomous agent, particularly to an adaptive agent, becomes ever clearer.

As we conclude our all too brief visit with Edelman's work, I'm left with the feeling of excitement that is so often engendered by important work. I'm also left with some frustration, and an image of smoke and mirrors, brought about by my not having had access to the details of these particular mechanisms of mind. And the ideas themselves aren't easy. Ah, well, relativity theory, quantum mechanics, and even my own work in categorical topology and in neural computability aren't easy going either.

What we've just seen is Edelman's answer to the crucial question of semantics, of how meaning occurs in agents faced with an unlabeled world. Let's next look at yet another answer.

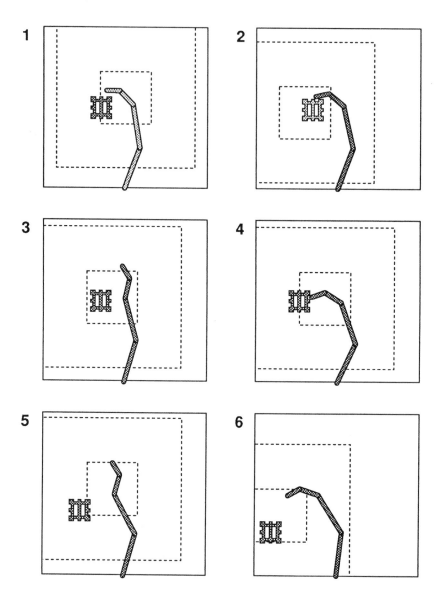

Figure 12.13
Darwin III in action (adapted from Edelman 1989)

Schema Mechanism

First, a few remarks to set the stage for this visit. Drescher (1986, 1987, 1988, 1991) views his work as a computational model or implementation of the early stages of Piaget's theory of child development: "I take Piagetian development as a working hypothesis: trying to implement it is a way to test and refine the hypothesis" (1987, p. 290). Sometimes on our tour it's been hard to identify a mechanism of mind as a mechanism, for example, Freeman's basins of attraction as a mechanism for categorizing. Here we'll encounter no such difficulty. What Drescher proposes is clearly a mechanism.

It is, however, a computationally expensive mechanism. To this charge, Drescher retorts, "There is no good reason to be confident that human intelligence can be implemented with vastly less computational power than the human brain." He argues, in his 1988 paper, that we have sufficient computational power in our wetware to implement his mechanism. The later work of Foner and Maes (1994) drastically reduces the computational needs of Drescher's mechanism by adding selective attention. Keep your eyes peeled for computational costs during this visit.

One could imply from the last quote that intelligence is inherently computationally expensive. This certainly seems true to me. Recall that Wilson went through all sorts of contortions to get Animat to find food efficiently in a relatively simple environment. Think of the computational costs of scaling up that system. Adding an attention mechanism à la Foner and Maes, however, might well mitigate them.

The quote might also be misread as asserting that sufficient computational power gives us at least a chance of implementing human intelligence. As we've seen, some would deny that any amount of computational power would do, and maintain that computation is not the right model for doing it in any case. Drescher's step toward proving them wrong is earlier work than some we've visited, beginning in 1986 or before, and is more in the symbolic AI mode.

Let's start our visit with Drescher's take on Piaget's constructivist theory of mind as it applies to objects. Mental representations are not innately supplied but must be constructed afresh by each individual, even representations of physical objects. It's a do-it-yourself project, for each of us must build our own objects. Though I, and perhaps not Drescher or Piaget, am seriously questioning the notion that objects are "out there" in any real sense, the idea is probably less strange to you after encountering Edelman and Darwin III. Anyway, the basic idea is that we create our objects by using mental representations. We've argued before, and will again, about how necessary representations are, even for the creation of objects.

Drescher samples Piaget's theory in the following scenario. Infants at first enjoy the world as solopsists, representing it only in terms of sensory impressions and motor actions. Later they become aware that some actions effect some sensations. Still later, the infant invents for itself the idea of a physical object, independent of sensory input. At this point you cover a ball with a cloth and the kid still knows there is a ball under there. She constructs this concept of ball gradually. Intermediate representations become less subjective, less tied to the internal perspective. The ball is still the ball at a different distance, against a different background, partially obscured, and even when it rolls behind the couch.

Drescher designed a mechanism that models this behavior. He calls it the *schema mechanism*. "Schema," as he uses it, is singular, the plural being "schemas." His schema mechanism controls a body in a microworld, much like Darwin III. The mechanism interacts with this microworld, accumulating and organizing knowledge about it. It uses that knowledge to select actions in pursuit of goals. One primary goal is to acquire more knowledge.

The schema mechanism uses three kinds of data structures: items, actions, and schemas. Items are binary state holders; they're either on or off. Actions can produce state in the environment. In particular, an action might turn an item on or off. Schemas designate the effects of actions on states. Take "designate" seriously. Schemas designate effects; they don't perform any actions. Let's meet each of these structures individually and also look at the relation between them. They will eventually be recursively intertwined, one defined in terms of another.

What kinds of *items* are there? To begin with, there are primitive items, corresponding to sensory inputs. We'll see shortly what senses this thing has. Later we'll see other synthetic items, autonomously constructed by the mechanism. The concept of a table might be synthetically constructed by the mechanism in an appropriate environment and with appropriate goals (values). These synthetic items designate states at higher levels of abstraction.

Actions include primitive actions, motor outputs, and composite actions constructed autonomously by the mechanism. The latter designate transitions at higher levels of abstraction. A composite action chains a sequence of less abstract actions, eventually backing down to primitive actions. A composite action might reach an arm under a table and lift it.

Schemas are defined in terms of items and actions. We'll see how in a moment. Synthetic items and composite actions are defined in terms of schemas. So here we start with some items and some actions, and define some schemas. These schemas then help define further items and further actions, and hence also further schemas. Subsequent schemas may have schemas as elements, a recursive definition.

Such recursive definitions can move from rather simple things to much more complex entities. Spin-off schemas are constructed each time a relation between items and actions is discovered. Composite actions are implemented by schemas and coordinated to achieve some goal. A synthetic item designates a state that may be inexpressible by any combination of the current state of other items, a new concept, something novel. Synthetic items permit the invention of radically new concepts, for example, conservation.

What does an individual schema look like? It consists of a context, an action, and a result. The context is a set of items. The action is an action. The result is also a set of items. The schema asserts that if the context is satisfied (all its items are on) and the action is taken, then the result becomes more likely (more likely that all its items are on). A schema designates a possible result of a given action within a given context.

A schema is not a production rule. Rather, it's a statement of likelihood, a stochastic statement. It asserts that the specified action, taken in this context, makes the result more likely than if it isn't taken. Perhaps not very likely, but more likely. The context also is not a precondition; its action may well be performed in another context, or it may not be performed in this one. A schema is a bit of knowledge of the effects of a specific action in a specific context. But it's not very reliable knowledge.

The action of a *reliable* schema makes the result not just more likely but likely, that is, more likely than not. Schemas keep track empirically of their reliability. (This is our first indication of the computational cost discussed earlier.) A *plan* is a set of schemas coordinated to achieve a specified result. Only reliable schemas are permitted to participate in a plan. We'll see how unreliable schemas are stepping-stones to finding reliable schemas. This schema mechanism is an intricately intermeshed system, and so, dear to my mathematician's heart.

Drescher's implementation of his schema mechanism lives in a simple microworld populated by objects that can be seen, felt, grasped, and moved. The schema mechanism controls a hand that can feel, grasp, and move, and an eye that can see.

Primitive items are of four types: visual (input from various places in the microworld), tactile (input from around the hand), visual proprioceptive (the direction the eye is looking), and tactile proprioceptive (how far out the hand is reaching and in what direction). Primitive actions are of three types: the hand can move forward, back, left, and right. Four actions change the visual field, and the hand can open and close.

Schemas with satisfied contexts compete to have their action performed. How does this happen? Part of the time, schemas compete on the basis of how well their results contribute to some goal expressed as a set of items. The mechanism chooses at random among the more qualified schemas. But most of the time schemas compete via their exploratory value. Recently activated schemas are likely to be activated again until habituation occurs, reducing their likelihood of activation. Schemas leading to undesirable results can be suppressed.

Drescher talks of built-in, mundane goals such as eating, and curiosity-based goals that appeal to heuristic assessments of a schema's value for learning. States can become valued as goals because of strategic facilitation of other things of value. I might want a job in order to earn money in order to eat. I also might lead a tour of the mechanisms of mind in order to earn money in order to eat, but that's probably not as good an idea.

Unreliable schemas are not particularly useful in themselves. What you want is reliable schemas that tell you what to expect if their action is taken within a certain context. The schema mechanism looks for results that follow from actions, reliably or not. If a result follows unreliably, the mechanism looks for conditions (added context) to improve that reliability. When successful, the mechanism doesn't simply add new context items to the schema to make it more reliable. Rather, it spins off a new schema, adding the newly discovered context to a copy of the old schema. A reliable schema usually evolves in this way from a sequence of less reliable schemas.

This process gives rise to a "chicken or egg"-type problem. A result that follows reliably when certain conditions are met rarely happens when they aren't. If my hand is next to an object to its left, and I move my hand to my left, I'm likely to touch something. On the other hand, just moving my hand to the left isn't likely to touch something in some other context. Even when the result does follow, it is likely to be hidden among hundreds of other events. All sorts of other things are happening in the environment besides my touching something to the left. Which ones are relevant? Until relevant conditions are known, it's hard to recognize what's an appropriate result and what isn't. On the other hand, until the result is recognized, the search for conditions can't begin. That's the "chicken or egg" problem. Drescher intends to tell us how to get around it.

How's he going to do this? One way would be to ignore relevance and use the British Museum method.[30] Keep track of everything. Exhaustively monitor the result of each action with respect to all conjunctions of items. Clearly, the computational burden of such a strategy increases exponentially with the complexity of the environment and the number of actions. It won't scale up. Knowledge engineers building expert systems solve this problem by incorporating enough prior knowledge to drastically curtail the search. Another approach, used in many of the microworlds we've visited, is to simplify the environment so as to reduce the number of possibly relevant conditions to a manageable size. Neither of these is of much help to an autonomous agent in a complex, dynamic environment. The dynamic part rules out the first solution. The designer typically can't predict circumstances well enough to build in behaviors to cope with all of them. The complex part obviously rules out the second. So what to do? Let's watch Drescher's solution unfold, but keep in mind the issue of computational burden.

The schema mechanism begins with one primitive schema for each primitive action. Each such schema sports an empty context and an empty result, and thus asserts nothing whatever about its action. What earthly use can this be? It's like the empty set in mathematics, serving as a point of departure, in this case for building schemas *with* context and result. Out of these schemas, new schemas are spun off by adding new items of context or result to copies of the existing schema, and continuing the process recursively. Note that the original schema remains. Once a schema, always a schema. Think about how that is going to affect computations.

How will the schema mechanism know when and what new schema to spin off? Statistically, by keeping track of frequencies. Each schema comes equipped with both an extended context and an extended result. Each extended context includes a slot for every item. Every item! So does each extended result. Every time a new item is created, a slot for it is added to each extended context and extended result. You might visualize a schema with its extensions as in figure 12.14.

Each extended result slot keeps track of whether its item turns on more often if the schema has just been activated or not. Is there some correlation between this action and one of these items as a result? If it finds one, the mechanism spins off a new schema with that item added to its result. If an item is more likely to turn off, the spin-off schema is created with the negative of the item in its result. Keep in mind that a result must only be more likely after the schema action than without the action. The result may still be arbitrarily unlikely, may have only a tiny probability of oc-

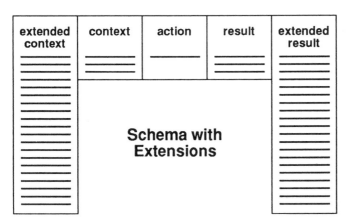

Figure 12.14
Schema with extensions

curring. A schema may be arbitrarily unreliable. Similarly, each extended context slot keeps track of whether the schema is more reliable when its item is on. If so, a new schema spins off with that item as part of its context. If it's more reliable with that item off, the context of the spin-off schema contains the negative of the item.

By now you're no doubt beginning to understand why Drescher asks for the computational capability of the human brain for his system. He's going to need it, although the work of Foner and Maes (1994) helps.

Let's see if we can get a better grasp of what's going on by looking once again at our simple example. Suppose a primitive schema is activated whose action is glancing to the left. If a frog was noticed to the left before, the action results in a frog in the center of the field. This result follows that action infrequently without the condition but frequently with it. But not always. Maybe the frog jumps right the moment you look left. The same action in other contexts may have quite different results. If there was nothing just to your left, glancing left is not likely to find anything.[31] But it might. The friendly frog might jump there at just the right moment. Let's continue. The initial glance-left schema identifies an item, something in the visual field center. That item is turned on. The mechanism then identifies this item as a tentative result, prompting a spin-off schema with an action and a result. Eventually its extended context finds conditions that yield reliability, that something had been left center just before. A reliable schema is spun off.

Drescher refers to this statistical learning process as *marginal attribution*. It uses built-in and constructed representational elements to express regularity in the world. It requires no prior knowledge of the world. (It starts too far back to be a good model of Piaget's theory. Human infants are born knowing more than this system does.) Drescher allows as how the exhaustive cross-connectivity between schemas and items seems an expensive solution to our chicken or egg problem. It certainly does. He claims it's a bargain compared with searching the space of all expressible schemas. He further argues that it's neurologically possible, if not plausible (1988), that we've got plenty of neurons to do the job. I'll spare you the details.

We've seen how schemas yield new schemas. Schemas also give rise to *composite actions*. Any newly achievable result can lead to a new composite action. A composite action, unlike primitive actions, will have a goal state. The conjunction of items constituting the new result comprises the goal state of the new composite action. The composite action identifies schemas that can help achieve its goal state, that is, schemas that chain to the goal state. Schemas chain when they're in a sequence so that the results of the first one help to establish the context for the next one, and so on down the line. When activated, a composite action coordinates the successive activation of its schemas. These schemas need not compete independently to become active. Once the composite action is started, the actions in its sequence of subschemas get performed. (It's a chunking condition, as we saw when visiting with SOAR, a way of compiling actions. I suspect every adaptive autonomous agent in a complex dynamic environment needs some such mechanism.) With a new composite action in hand, it creates a schema with empty context and result around it. As before, this bare schema starts the process of finding results of the new action, and then finding conditions that lead reliably to those results.

The Constructivist's Challenge

At long last we come to what is, in my view, the major achievement of Drescher's work. We see what all this machinery will yield. Here's how he puts it: "a constructivist system's greatest challenge is to synthesize new elements of representation, to designate what had been inexpressible" (1987, p. 292). I would prefer to say "unrepresentable" rather than "inexpressible," since this doesn't have to do with expression in a language or anything of that sort. Otherwise, I couldn't agree more. We're about to see a mechanism by means of which concepts are born. We've seen spinoff schemas. We've seen composite actions. Now we'll see *synthetic items*, by means of which objects and, in principle, other concepts can be constructed.

A synthetic item is based on some schema that essentially suggests how to recover a manifestation that is no longer present. We're heading toward object permanence. How do you get the ball back when it rolls behind the couch? The synthetic item reifies this recoverability. The potential to recover is construed as a thing in itself. With the introduction of a synthetic item, the ontology of the system changes.

Let's look at a simple example to motivate this construction. Suppose the schema mechanism moves its hand away from some object[32] directly in front of it while looking away from it. The object now has no manifestation in the state of any primitive item. Hence the object no longer exists for the schema mechanism because there is no way to represent it. The mechanism is oblivious to the possibility of reaching to touch the object again or of glancing toward it. Now suppose some schema, without context, says, "If I reach directly in front of me, I'll touch something." Its context is empty; its action is to reach directly forward; its result is touching something, tactile stimulation. This schema is unreliable. Mostly reaching forward won't touch anything. It works only when some object is there.

On the other hand, it is *locally consistent*. If it reaches out and touches an object, draws back, and reaches out again, it's likely to touch something again. If it works once, it's likely to continue to work for the next little while. Objects tend to stay put awhile. The schema mechanism tracks the local consistency of each schema. Local consistency provides the key to building synthetic items. If a schema is unreliable but locally consistent, the mechanism builds a synthetic item for it. The new item designates whatever unknown condition in the world governs the schema's success or failure.

Now that we've got it, what do we do with it? Why, spin off a new schema, its host schema, from the locally consistent one, with the new synthetic item as its context. When the synthetic item is on, the mechanism regards it host schema as being reliable, at least for the next little bit. But when is the new synthetic item on? An item says that something is true or that something is false. Items are useful only if they are reasonably accurate, only if their on or off state corresponds correctly to the truth or falsity of the condition it designates. Hence it's important to get on/off right. For primitive items, this isn't a problem. Each is hardwired to some sensory apparatus that maintains its state. But what about synthetic objects?

Some machinery will be needed to keep the state of synthetic items updated. Here are the rules the schema mechanism uses. Successful activation of its host schema turns the synthetic item on; unsuccessful activation turns it off. A synthetic item turns off after its time period of local consistency. The schema mechanism keeps track of this period. A synthetic item turns on or off together with any strongly correlated item. Again, the schema mechanism must keep track of such. And finally, a synthetic item can be turned on or off as a result of a subsequently created reliable schema.

Note that the schema mechanism must learn when a new synthetic item is on or off. It has constructed a new, and one hopes useful, concept and must discover the conditions under which it's applicable. Note also that a synthetic item is not some combination of primitive items. Rather, it's something fundamentally different from what we started with, "a new element of representation."

Drescher describes this process of concept formation as one of synthesis and abstraction. A new concept forms as a synthesis of various fragments of itself. At first the fragments include details of a particular perspective and of particular actions. By abstraction, the synthesis becomes independent of these details, producing something that can be used in another, very different schema. He claims that this process of synthesis and abstraction is central to constructing concepts that are fundamentally different from their precursors. In his view, this is how new ideas come about. His schema mechanism is a mechanism of mind designed to produce new concepts.

As you no doubt can tell, I'm quite enamored of Drescher's work. My major concern is for its enormous computational requirements. Yes, it is a "bargain" compared with a British Museum algorithm. But, in an absolute sense, it keeps track of too much. A partial solution to this problem is provided by Foner and Maes (1994), who drastically reduce computational requirements by focusing the attention of the schema mechanism, both perceptually and cognitively. Their version updates only statistics for sensory items that have changed recently and only for schemas making predictions about them. When deciding about spinning off new schemas, they consider only recently changed sensory items, and only schemas whose statistics have recently changed.

On this stop we've met basins of attractions offered as mechanisms for categorization, classification couples proposed as a mechanism for creating the categories, and the schema mechanism suggested as a means of creating the very objects to be categorized. From the constructivist point of view, all these are mechanisms for constructing our own individual version of reality, for deciding what's out there. Yes, deciding. The constructivist view is very much a part of the new paradigm. It maintains that we partition our environment in ways that prove useful, creating objects. From these we iteratively create categories and ever higher-level concepts. Our physicalist assumption postulates a real world out there, but the semantics of that world lies in our hands, either by species or individually. And so, says the new paradigm of mind, it must be for any adaptive autonomous agent.

Suppose we've created our version of the world. Where is it? What's the mechanism for representing it? Our next major stop will begin with these questions and move on to higher-level generation of actions.

Notes

1. This sentence asserts a thoroughly Western point of view. Eastern philosophy views it differently, talking at length about the Tao, which certainly doesn't discriminate (Lao-Tzu 1988).

2. Mathematics is best thought of as an art form whose medium is composed of concepts. A mathematical object is a conceptual structure typically composed of a set with some additional structure, that is, special subsets, mappings, axioms, and so on.

3. A self-map of a set, X, is a function, T, that assigns to each element, x, of X some other element, T(x), of X. Don't take that "other" too seriously. T(x) may be x itself, in which case x is called a *fixed point* of T.

4. What you've just seen is the simplest and most abstract version of a dynamical system. Typically more constraints are put on X and T, say, assuming that X is a topological space and that T is continuous, or that X is a manifold and that T is infinitely differentiable. If these terms are strange to you, please ignore this note altogether. Doing so won't hinder your understanding of what follows.

5. In the jargon of mathematics, rational numbers are those that can be represented by fractions. The decimal expansion of any rational number is periodic, and every periodic decimal represents a rational. Thus the irrational numbers, those real numbers that are not rational, are represented by decimal expansions that never repeat themselves. I find it hard not to include a proof that $\sqrt{2}$ is irrational.

6. Bob Sweeney reminds me to include a caution at this point. Chaotic dynamical systems, though unpredictable in the long run, do have structure, pattern. The digits of $\sqrt{2} - 1$, while exhibiting the unpredictability of a chaotic system, may well be truly random, with no structure whatever.

7. That is, distinct basins have no common points and, together, the basins fill up the state space.

8. Recall that $i^2 = -1$.

9. For example, as α varies, orbits of all possible integer periods occur. Also, values of α with periodic orbits are dense; between any two α's with chaotic orbits is another α with a periodic orbit. It's a simply described system that behaves with incredible complexity.

10. Such decisions are not easy, and are crucial for biological systems (see S. Edelman 1993).

11. We live in Euclidean 3-space because the position of a point can be described by three numbers. Or, taking an Einsteinian point of view, we live in 4-space, with the fourth dimension being time.

12. Note that arrows in this diagram represent the beginnings of orbits, whereas arrows in the previous diagram were vectors giving direction and speed of motion.

13. I'm sad to report that Paul passed away before having formally taken this tour. He's sorely missed.

14. Some philosophers would no doubt retort that I've simply missed the point of the semantics issue altogether, and perhaps they'd be right.

15. Remember that it's always amateur night on the artificial minds tour. I'm particularly conscious of that right now.

16. "Potential" as in "voltage." EEG stands for electroencephalograph, a machine that records "brain waves."

17. Both Brian Rotman and Nick Herbert tell me that this assertion dates back to Gregory Bateson. (In press, Chalmers also pointed this out to me.)

18. I found all three of these books hard going. If you're intent on reading Edelman, start with his more recent *Bright Air, Brilliant Fire* (1992), which gives an abbreviated and more readable account of much of his recent work.

19. I have decidedly mixed feelings about this experiment.

20. This is Edelman's assertion, as well as conventional wisdom in the field. However, I've recently seen speculation that we actually grow new neurons, and certainly we grow additional axons right along. Some songbirds grow new nervous tissue in the process of learning new songs.

21. This is closely analogous to the immune system—you are born with all the various kinds of antibodies you'll ever have.

22. We've encountered, or at least mentioned, three other selective systems: natural selection à la Darwin, the immune system, and Holland's genetic algorithms.

23. Zen practitioners cultivate "beginner's mind," pure awareness uncontaminated by expectations, judgments, or distractions, as in the phrase "be here now."

24. I've heard tales of Darwin IV but haven't yet found a reference.

25. This view blurs the psychologist's distinction between procedural memory (riding a bicycle) and episodic memory (of what I had for breakfast). I suspect

Edelman would claim that the underlying mechanism is of the same type for both, and that episodic memory requires active reconstruction. I certainly lean toward that view.

26. This brings us to an issue I have struggled long and hard with, the distinction between rule-describable behavior and rule-governed behavior. I'd say that Darwin's behavior, at the low level of individual units, is rule governed, while at a higher level it is only rule describable.

27. Though they are typically unnamed, some call them "perfs."

28. Remember that Brooks's Herbert required fifteen different motions to grasp a soda can.

29. I'm tickled to note how the gender of the pronoun I use for Darwin III has changed in this paragraph. In prior paragraphs, when he was acting on an environment, he was "he." In this one, the discussion is about its self-organization, and it has become an "it." The difference seems to be one of animate or not.

30. Rumor has it that the acquisition policy at the British Museum is a simple one: collect everything. Although no doubt apocryphal, this tale has led AI workers to refer to exhaustive search as the "British Museum method."

31. I've never experienced glancing left and finding nothing. This can occur in a microworld but not in our world. On the other hand, I've often glanced left and found nothing of interest, which leads us once more to the work of Foner and Maes (1994) on attention.

32. An object to us, not yet to the schema mechanism.

13

Remembering and Creating

There is a popular cliché . . . which says that you cannot get out of computers any more than you have put in . . . , that computers only do exactly what you tell them to, and that therefore computers are never creative. This cliché is true only in a crashingly trivial sense, the same sense in which Shakespeare never wrote anything except what his first schoolteacher taught him to write—words.
—Richard Dawkins, *The Blind Watchmaker*

On this tour stop we'll be concerned with getting out of a computer—or a human, for that matter—both what was put in (memory) and more than what was put in (creativity?). We'll enjoy an extended stay with Kanerva's sparse distributed memory (1988a), a brief encounter with Calvin's Darwin machine (1990) and his hexagonal mosaics (1992), and finally, a leisurely visit with Hofstadter and Mitchell's Copycat (Hofstadter 1984; Mitchell 1993).

Our last major stops were designed to sell features of the emerging new paradigm of mind I've been pushing. One supported mind as a control device, its function being to produce the next action. Our last stop emphasized information as being created internally by minds in the service of the control function of mind. This one will be concerned with state of mind, "state" being used in the technical sense of the state of a system as we've used it before. Think of the mind assuming a certain state in forming some internal model of what's going on outside, or what has gone on. State (of mind) changes when information is created.

Whereas Brooks's Herbert had state lasting no longer than three sections, we humans can have state—that is, the ability to remember—lasting almost a lifetime. I can easily conjure up memories of fifty-year-old events. How does this magical production of images happen? Do I perform the mental equivalent of taking a photograph from a folder in a filing cabinet and looking at it? That seems to be the way memory is tacitly thought of. Our newly emerging paradigm proposes that we view memory, instead, as an active process of reconstruction. It's this proposal, and its implications about creativity, that the attractions of this stop are intended to support.

Let's first meet some of Kanerva's assumptions about memory.

Memory

Cognitive scientists work with memory in action, modeling its function. As scientists, they've had some success explaining and predicting memory, at least in laboratory contexts. Kanerva takes an engineer's view. He wants to build a memory. That's not quite right. He doesn't actually want to make one; he wants to make a theory about making one. A theory? What for? Here's Kanerva's answer:

The usefulness of a theory is measured by its ability to explain observations, to simplify old explanations, to predict, and to inspire discovery. . . . A theory can be beneficial without even being correct, for it can stimulate the discovery of a better theory.[1] (1988a, p. 90)

As I once heard from an unremembered source, "there's nothing so practical as a good theory."

Kanerva hopes to base his theory of memory on a series of assumptions, or high-level design decisions, that will constrain its development. Here they are, mostly in his own words (1988a, pp. 80–81): "appropriate behavior entails successful prediction. . . . The function of memory is . . . to make relevant information available rapidly enough." This of course resonates with the view of mind as fundamentally a control system and puts memory in a supporting role. The implied constraints are speed and relevance, the latter being addressed more explicitly in the following assumptions:

The present is predicted best by the most recent past and by earlier events similar to it. . . . memory should allow the present situation to act as a retrieval cue, and, when presented with a situation that is similar to some previously encountered situation, it should retrieve the consequences of that previous situation. (1988a, p. 81)

That the present is best predicted by the recent past is almost a truism. If you want to predict the weather without going to a lot of trouble, just say that tomorrow is going to be like today. More often than not, you are going to be right. Of course, determining what's recent is an important, and probably nontrivial, issue.

Predicting by earlier, similar events is even trickier. I might predict snow tomorrow even though it didn't snow today, if today was similar to an earlier day preceding a snowfall. But how can one know what's similar? Well, we do it all the time, and so must Kanerva's memory, at least in theory. We'll see how he proposes to recognize similarity.

The assumptions made so far have been at a high level of abstraction. Moving down the abstraction ladder, Kanerva provides a few more, each constraining his system. Think of all the memory items in your head. *Most pairs of such items are unrelated.* However, *most pairs can be associated via one or two intermediate items.* (Kanerva argues convincingly by example at this point. I'll leave it as an exercise for the reader.) *Many associations between items are learned explicitly; many others occur automatically.* If I describe a tree to you as a "sap pipe," the association therein probably makes quite good sense, though you may never have learned it explicitly. Note that this association did not occur automatically until you read the two words on the page. The association was *constructed* automatically. *Memory capacity is limited.* Certainly this is true in all the real systems I know about, but it's an arbitrary assumption in a theoretical memory.[2] Kanerva must want his theory to be applicable. Of course, *sequences of events must be remembered.* And, further, the system must be able to *find and continue some sequence from a part.*

As we proceed further down the abstraction ladder, assumptions blend more clearly into design decisions:

> ... patterns are to serve as addresses to memory—and not just previously encountered patterns, but new patterns as well. In other words, the memory has a permanent addressing framework that is independent of what we have learned so far, and the record is stored in and retrieved from the addressed parts of the memory. (1988a, p. 3)

We'll soon see how all this works. Also, *sequences must be stored and retrieved, and even continued on the basis of some part of the sequence.* In spite of their importance, time and space constraints dictate that we

meet sequences only briefly. Here's what Kanerva refers to as the "unify-
ing idea of the theory": "there is no fundamental distinction between addresses to memory and the data stored in the storage locations; the data
stored in memory are addresses to the memory" (1988a, p. 5).

Having had a preview of this coming attraction, we need, for the second time in as many major tour stops, a brief excursion into mathematics.
This time we'll visit Boolean geometry. I hope it continues to be good for
the soul.

Boolean Geometry

Boolean geometry is the geometry of Boolean space. What's Boolean
space?[3] It's the set of all Boolean vectors of some fixed length, n, called
the dimension of the space. Points in Boolean space are Boolean vectors.
A few examples should get the idea across. One-dimensional Boolean
space consists of Boolean vectors of length 1. There are only two of them,
(0) and (1). Two-dimensional Boolean space is the four-element set {(0,0),
(0,1), (1,0), (1,1)}. Three-dimensional Boolean space has eight elements,
each of 0-1-vector of length 3. Note that Boolean space of dimension n
contains 2^n Boolean vectors of length n. The number of points increases
exponentially as the dimension increases. Though this model of memory
is more general, Kanerva uses 1,000-dimensional Boolean space, the
space of Boolean vectors of length 1000, as his running example. We'll
follow this lead.

Two-dimensional Boolean space can be visualized as the corner points
of the unit square in two-dimensional Euclidean space (figure 13.1). Similarly, three-dimensional Boolean space maps to the corners of the unit
cube in Euclidean three-space. Kanerva's example space maps to the corners of the unit hypercube in 1000-dimension Euclidean space, a little
harder to visualize.

We could use ordinary Euclidean distance for our foray into Boolean
geometry but will find it more useful to use the *Hamming distance*, where
the distance between two points is the number of coordinates at which
they differ. Thus d((1,0,0,1,0), (1,0,1,1,1)) = 2. The distance between
two points will measure the similarity between two memory items in Kanerva's model, closer points being more similar. Or we might think of these

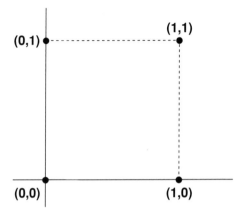

Figure 13.1
Two-dimensional Boolean space

Boolean vectors as feature vectors where each feature can be only on (1) or off (0). Two such feature vectors are closer together if more of their features are the same.

Kanerva calls a Boolean vector, x, *indifferent* to another, y, if they differ at precisely half their coordinates, that is if $d(x,y) = n/2$, where n is the dimension of the Boolean space. He calls $n/2$ the *indifference distance* and proves that almost all of any Boolean space is *almost* indifferent to any given point. For $n = 1000$, 99.9999 percent of the space lies between distance 422 and distance 578 from a given vector. Almost all the space is far away from any given vector. Boolean space of high dimension is thinly populated, an important property for the construction of the model.

A sphere is defined as usual as the locus of points at some fixed distance, the radius, from its center. The sphere of radius r with center x is formally expressed by $O(r,x) = \{y \mid d(x,y) \leq r\}$. Spheres in Boolean space are quite different in one respect from the Euclidean spheres we're used to. Points of a Euclidean sphere are uniformly distributed throughout. For $r \leq n/2$ (the indifference distance) most of the points in the sphere $O(r,x)$ lie close to its boundary. For $n/3 < r < n/2$ most points of $O(r,x)$ are nearly indifferent to x.

This is enough Boolean geometry to get started. Let's see how Kanerva uses it to build his model.

A Sparse Distributed Random Access Memory

An old-fashioned audio turntable, complete with tone arm and record, is a random access device, whereas a tape deck with head and tape is a sequential access device. A user can reach any chosen location[4] on the record in essentially the same time it would take to reach any other, simply by placing the tone arm at the desired location. This essentially constant time to reach any location on the medium is decidedly not true of the tape deck system, where some locations are much closer to the current head position than others. To move from one location on the medium to another, the random access device can "jump over" intervening locations, whereas a sequential access device must pass by each of them. A memory is called random access if any storage location can be reached in essentially the same length of time that it takes to reach any other.

Kanerva constructs a model of a random access memory capable, in principle, of being implemented on a sufficiently powerful digital computer, and also implementable via artificial neural networks. Here, at last, is how he does it.

This memory, like my city, has an address space, a set of allowable addresses, each of which specifies a location. A memory address specifies a storage location; a city address specifies a place. Kanerva's address space is Boolean space of dimension 1000. Thus allowable addresses are Boolean vectors of length 1000, henceforth to be called *bit vectors* in deference to both the computing context and brevity.

This address space is enormous. It contains 2^{1000} locations, probably more points than the number of elementary particles in the entire universe. One cannot hope for such a vast memory. When I first thought about bit vectors (feature vectors) of length 1000, it seemed a lot of features, that a lot could be done with so many features. But thinking about incoming sensory data made me reconsider. A thousand features wouldn't deal with human visual input until a high level of abstraction had been reached. A dimension of 1000 may not be all that much; it may even be unrealistically small.

Kanerva proposes to deal with this vast address space by choosing a uniform random sample, size 2^{20}, of locations—that is, about a million of them. These he calls *hard locations*. With 2^{20} hard locations out of a possible 2^{1000} locations, the density (ratio) is 2^{-980}—very sparse indeed. In addition, 98 percent of the time the distance from a random location in the entire address space to the nearest hard location will fall between 411 and 430, with the median distance being 424. The hard locations are certainly sparse.

We've seen in what sense this memory is to be random access, and in what sense sparse. How is it to be distributed? If many hard locations participate in storing and retrieving each datum, and if one hard location can be involved in the storage and retrieval of many data, we call the memory *distributed*. This is a very different beast than the store-one-datum-in-one-location type of memory to which we're accustomed. Let's see how this is done.

Each hard location, itself a bit vector of length 1000, stores data in 1000 counters, each with range −40 to 40. We now have a million hard locations, each with a thousand counters, totaling a billion counters in all. Numbers in the range −40 to 40 will take most of a byte to store. Thus we're talking about a billion bytes, a gigabyte, of memory. Quite a lot, but not out of the question. How do these counters work? Writing a 1 to the counter increments it; writing a 0 decrements it. A datum, η, to be written is a bit vector of length 1000.[5] To write η at a given hard location x, write each coordinate of η to the corresponding counter in x, either incrementing it or decrementing it. Thus, if η = (1, 0, 1, 1, 1, 0, . . .), x's first counter will be incremented, its second decremented, its third incremented, and so on, until a thousand counters are changed.

We now know how to write to one location. But this memory is to be distributed. To which locations shall we write? Call the sphere of radius 451 centered at location ξ the access sphere of that location. An access sphere typically contains about a thousand hard locations, with the closest to ξ usually some 424 bits away and the median distance from ξ to hard locations in its access sphere about 448. Any hard location in the access sphere of ξ is *accessible* from ξ. With this machinery in hand, we can now write distributively to any location, hard or not. To write a datum η to a location ξ, simply write η to each of the roughly 1000 hard locations accessible from ξ. Distributed storage.

With our datum distributively stored, the next question is how to retrieve it. With this in mind, let's ask how one reads from a hard location,

x. Compute η, the bit vector read at x, by assigning its ith bit the value 1 or 0, according as x's ith counter is positive or negative. Thus, if x's counters look like $-1, 1, 4, 14, 3, -5, -2, \ldots$, then $\eta = (0, 1, 1, 1, 1, 0, 0, \ldots)$. Thus, each bit of η results from a majority rule decision of all the data that have been written on x. The read datum, η, is an archetype of the data that have been written to x but may not be any one of them. From another point of view, η is the datum with smallest mean distance from all data that have been written to x.

Knowing how to read from a hard location allows us to read from any of the 2^{1000} arbitrary locations. Suppose ζ is any location. The bit vector, η, to be read at ζ is formed by pooling the data read from each hard location accessible from ζ. Each bit of η results from a majority rule decision over the pooled data. Specifically, to get the ith bit of η, add together the ith bits of the data read from hard locations accessible from ζ and use half the number of such hard locations as a threshold. At or over threshold, assign a 1. Below threshold, assign a 0. Put another way, pool the bit vectors read from hard locations accessible from ζ, and let each of their ith bits vote on the ith bit of η.

We now know how to write items into memory and how to read them out. But what's the relation between the datum in and the datum out? Are these two bit vectors the same, as we'd hope? Let's first look at the special case where the datum ζ is written at the location ζ. This makes sense because both are bit vectors of length 1000. One copy of ζ is then written at each of approximately 1000 hard locations. Reading from ζ then recovers archetypes from each of these hard locations and takes a vote. The voting is influenced by the ∼1000 stored copies of ζ and, typically, by about 10,000 other stored data items. The voting comes out as we would like it. Since the intersection of two access spheres is typically quite small, these other data items influence a given coordinate only in small groups of ones or twos or threes. The thousand copies of ζ drown out this slight noise and ζ is successfully reconstructed. Kanerva offers a mathematical proof that the process works.

Thus, items that have been read in (with themselves as address) can be retrieved (actually reconstructed). That seems to be the very definition of memory, and not to justify all this mathematical machinery. Ah, but this memory is content addressable. Not all of the stored item is needed to recover it. Let's see what happens if we try to read with a noisy version of what's been stored or with an arbitrary bit vector.

For this task we'll need iterated reading. Here's how it works. First read at ζ to obtain a bit vector ζ_1. Then read at ζ_1 to obtain a bit vector ζ_2. Next read at ζ_2 to obtain a bit vector ζ_3, and so on. If the sequence ζ_1, ζ_2, ζ_3, . . . , converges[6] to ξ, then ξ is the result of iterated reading at ζ.

Suppose ζ is any test datum, perhaps a noisy version of something already stored, and suppose ξ is the item retrievable from memory that is most similar to ζ. If the distance between ζ and ξ is not too great, say <200 bits, and if the memory is not too full, say <10,000 items stored, then reading at ζ yields a bit vector closer to ξ than ζ is. Thus iterated reading at ζ converges to ξ. Again Kanerva provides mathematical proofs. Since convergent sequences of iterates converge very rapidly, whereas divergent sequences of iterates bounce about seemingly at random, comparison of adjacent items in the sequence quickly tells whether a sequence converges. Thus, this memory is content addressable, provided we write each datum with itself as address. In this case, starting with a bit vector, ζ, if some retrievable item is sufficiently close to ζ, iterated reading will find it. That is, if the content of some reconstructable item is sufficiently similar to that of ζ, the item can be recovered by iterated reading starting at the content of ζ.

Kanerva lists several similarities between properties of his sparse distributed memory and of human memory. One such has to do with the human property of knowing what one does or doesn't know. If asked for a telephone number I've once known, I may search for it. When asked for one I've never known, an immediate "I don't know" response ensues. Sparse distributed memory could make such decisions based on the speed of initial convergence. If it's slow, I don't know. The "on the tip of my tongue phenomenon" is another such. In sparse distributed memory, this could correspond to the cue having content just at the threshold of being similar enough for reconstruction. Yet another is the power of rehearsal, during which an item would be written many times, each time to a thousand locations. A well rehearsed item would be retrieved with fewer cues. Finally, forgetting would tend to increase over time as a result of other writes to memory.

The above discussion, based on the identity of datum and address, produced a content addressable memory with many pleasing properties. It works well for reconstructing individual memories. However, more is needed. We, and our autonomous agents, must also remember sequences of events or actions. Kanerva shows how the machinery we've just seen can be modified to provide this capability. The basic idea is something like this. The cue for a sequence of patterns serves as the address for the first pattern of the sequence. Thereafter, the content of each pattern in the sequence is the address of the next pattern. Due to the finite length of our tour, we'll skip lightly past this attraction. Any of you who would like a side trip at this point should consult chapter 8 of Kanerva's *Sparse Distributed Memory* (1990). For the rest of our visit with Kanerva's memory, we'll assume that remembering sequences is possible.

Cognition à la Kanerva

Just a bit back we saw similarities between properties of this memory and those of human memory. Let's now look at artificial versions of other cognitive functions. When many similar patterns have been used as write addresses, individual patterns can no longer be recovered. Rather, an average of patterns written is reconstructed, an *abstraction* of what was put in.

Objects, typically viewed many times from different angles and distances, produce similar patterns, each written to itself as address. Reading any of these will yield a composite that *recognizes the object*. A region of pattern space, with poorly defined boundaries, represents the object abstractly. I tend to view objects as particularly simple concepts. Thus *concepts* may also be formed by writing similar patterns to themselves as addresses. A concept, then, is a fuzzy region of pattern space. Memory will produce aggregate patterns representing the concept, some features of which will be significant and others unimportant.

Kanerva contends that understanding is to be measured by the ability to predict.[7] In the service of this need to predict, intelligent agents rely on an internal modeling mechanism that constructs objects and concepts, and captures and reproduces statistical regularities of the world. This internal model profoundly affects its (and our) perception of the world, relying on sensory scans for overall cues but filling in detail from the model.

Sparse distributed memory can serve as such an internal model mechanism (figure 13.2). The key item in the figure is the *focus,* a part of the modeling mechanism fed by both senses and memory. Sensors extract features from incoming environmental signals and pass them to the focus, a combined address-datum register with additional machinery. Memory is addressed by the focus and the contents of the focus written to memory. The current contents of memory at the addressed location, more accurately the reconstructed datum, is simultaneously fed back to the focus. The way into memory and the way out of memory are through the focus.

Think of the current contents read from memory into the focus as the model's prediction of the next sensory input. These contents are then compared with the actual sensory input, and a resulting new datum is

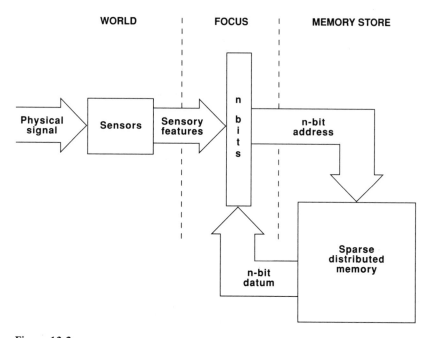

Figure 13.2
Sparse distributed memory as an internal model mechanism (redrawn from Kanerva 1988)

created in the focus. If the prediction proves accurate, this new datum is the same as the previous one. If the prediction is in error at some features, a corrected datum is created in the focus and afterward written to memory. The system learns.

The sequence of patterns in the focus comprises the agent's ongoing experience.[8] When the present situation resembles a past situation, the senses create patterns in the focus that resemble stored patterns. These patterns, addressing memory, reconstruct what consequences were in the past. A comparison of these past consequences with what actually occurs is the basis for updating the internal world model. Pretty neat. All that's lacking is the ability to act.

An Adaptive Autonomous Agent

An autonomous agent must not only sense, remember, recall, and predict but also act upon its environment so as to affect subsequent sensory input. In animals (robots), actions are mostly produced by sequences of neural (computational) patterns driving muscles (motors). Actions are included in the world model by storing these motor sequences in memory.

Kanerva provides for such action by allowing his system's motors to be driven from the focus. Thus deliberate action becomes part of the system's experience. How is this implemented?

In figure 13.3, we see that motors have been added whose actions affect not only the outside world but also the system's sensory mechanism. Perception becomes active, as it should be, instead of passive. The motors are controlled by signals from the focus. How can this be? By allotting some portion, say a fifth, of the components of each datum in the focus to controlling motor activity. (Keep, say, half of the components for sensory data, and the rest for internal activity, including values.) Reconstructed data from memory in the motor part of the focus result in action.

Kanerva supplies a thought experiment, omitted here, that shows the power of expectation in his system. "Sometimes a system will respond properly to a cue only if it is waiting for the cue." The system continually monitors the effects of its actions. When these effects don't confirm its expectations, the sequence of actions it has embarked on stops, and it tries something else.

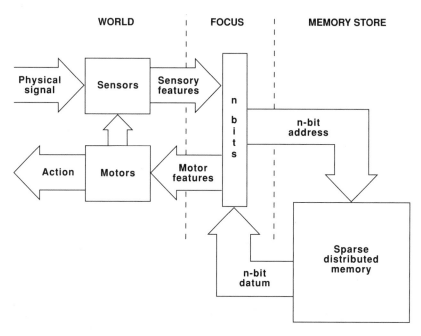

Figure 13.3
Sparse distributed memory control for an autonomous agent (redrawn from Kanerva 1988)

Since the system's actions and their effects can be part of the internal model, planning seems possible. Suppose the system shuts down sensory input but otherwise runs as usual. We could say that "thought" occurs in the focus and that planning results. We've met this notion of shutting down sensory input to allow for thought in John Jackson's pandemonium theory. It also occurs in the work of Johnson and Scanlon on Packrat (1987). I suspect it must occur in any sufficiently intelligent autonomous agent.

Similarly, some sort of initial values (needs, drives, preferences, dislikes, evaluation function à la Ackley-Littman) must be built in, present "at birth," for an autonomous agent to learn. In this system some patterns in the focus must be inherently good, others inherently bad, and most indifferent. Indifferent patterns must acquire value if they lead to other desirable or undesirable patterns. We'd want the system to choose actions leading to desirable patterns and to avoid actions leading to undesirable patterns. Learning to act is the process of storing sequences in memory that are likely to find desirable patterns and to avoid undesirable patterns.

Kanerva proposes to build values into his system by means of a preference function that assigns a number to each pattern in the focus. How will he implement this function? By means of a preference register at each hard location that reads positive for desirable patterns, negative for undesirable patterns, and 0 for indifferent patterns. But this memory is distributed over roughly a thousand hard locations. How is the reconstructed pattern valued? No problem. Just add up the contents of the preference registers at those hard locations accessible to the pattern at which we're reading. Does this mean additional machinery to accommodate preference registers? Not at all. Just allot a fixed but small number of components of each datum to values. (This ignores some easily managed technical details.)

Preference registers then have built-in values, the initial values the system is born with. Most would be modifiable, but some may not be. The kung fu master may deliberately lift the dragon pot and thus brand his forearms, but you can be sure he's never going to like it.

In addition to some built-in initial values, Kanerva postulates some initial built-in action sequences. Some of these sequences could contain random thrashing movements to provide an initial repertoire for selection à la Edelman. Others may be reflex actions.

Not only must these sequences be stored in memory, but values must also be stored. Action sequences, as well as patterns, must have their values. Again Kanerva provides a mechanism. Suppose an action sequence leads to a desirable pattern in the focus. Positive preference is propagated back down the sequence with decreasing force. The immediately preceding pattern gets a raise in preference value. The pattern just before that gets a somewhat smaller raise, and the process continues for a few more steps. I'm reminded of Holland's bucket brigade algorithm whose acquaintance we made while visiting Wilson's Animat. The algorithm allowed learning in classifier systems.

Kanerva produces hypothetical situations demonstrating the system learning in various ways: classical conditioning, learning from failure, learning from meaningful events, and learning by imitation. The first we'll omit. The second has already been discussed—failure means expectations weren't met. Let's look at the other two.

Call an event meaningful if it results in a highly positive or highly negative preference value. "Emotionally charged" might be another term. A sequence leading to a meaningful event is stored in memory, and its large (in absolute value) preference is extended back a few steps. Learning should be quite rapid in this case. A good prediction, or a bad one, can be a meaningful event, and thus trigger rapid learning.

Learning by imitation can also take place in a system provided there's an internal reward mechanism and the ability to model the behavior of other systems. The idea is to store an image of the other's behavior, then map this image to one's own actions. The results of one's own actions are compared with the stored image of the other's behavior, and the internal value system provides a reward mechanism to perfect the match. Kanerva speculates that this type of learning is primarily responsible for complicated social learning.

How does a sparse distributed memory agent compare with symbolic AI systems? Kanerva claims one major advantage: the frame problem never arises. You may recall the frame problem from an early tour stop. It's the problem of keeping track of the many side effects of actions. For example, suppose a mobile robot is built from a cart. It has a tool in its hand, and a telephone sits on its cart. A symbolic AI database knows that the robot, the tool, and the telephone are all in this room. Now the robot rolls itself out the door and down the hall to the next room. What must the system know to change in the database? Clearly, the position of the robot must be changed. It must also remember to change the location of the tool in the robot's hand. This is a side effect. There was no action on the part of the tool. What about the telephone? Should its location be changed? That depends on whether it is a cordless phone or is attached by a cord to the wall and it is now bouncing around on the floor in the same room. The frame problem is still an unsolved one for symbolic AI.

Kanerva's internal model is built from exposure to the world. The side effects of an action and its main effect are stored in memory. His system already knows, automatically, whether the telephone is attached to the wall. When the system moves, the model is checked against the world. The frame problem never arises.

All that we've seen thus far of sparse distributed memory is theory and thought experiment. How does it work in practice? Dimitri Kaznachey, in work as yet unpublished and in progress, has implemented a small version controlling an Animat in the WOODS7 environment we met previously. Here the bit vector length was chosen as 100 rather than 1000, reflecting the relative simplicity of the environment and of the agent's single goal, to eat. This choice puts the system at the lower end of the range for which Kanerva's proofs are valid. How did it work? Not well at all. The environment was so simple that almost any bit vector that arose during a run was accessible from any other. The Animat couldn't reliably distinguish desirable actions from undesirable. Adding artificial landmarks in the form of integers in the blank squares helped somewhat. Our impression is that much more complexity of both the environment and the agent's drives will be needed to adequately test a sparse distributed controller.

As you've no doubt discerned, your tour guide is inordinately fond of Kanerva's work. It speaks to me. And not only to me. Hofstadter (Kanerva 1988a, p. xviii) wrote:

> Pentti Kanerva's memory model was a revelation for me: it was the very first piece of research I had ever run across that made me feel I could glimpse the distant goal of understanding how the brain works as a whole. It gave me a concrete sense for how familiar mental phenomena could be thought of as distributed patterns of micro-events, thanks to beautiful mathematics.

Hofstadter chose his words carefully. It's only a "glimpse," but a glimpse nevertheless. Kanerva's mechanisms do evoke in me a "concrete sense" of how mind, even a sophisticated mind, could arise from a physical system.

Kanerva has provided a mechanism potentially capable of reconstructing, or perhaps creating, images, actions, plans, narratives, plays, paintings, concerti, poems, mathematics. The line between memory and creativity has become blurred. Stepping across this blurry line, let's visit with Calvin and his Darwin machine.

The Darwin Machine

> Darwinism shows that the product of trial and error can be quite fancy, when shaped by many rounds of selection against memories.
> —Calvin, *The Cerebral Symphony*

During a recent semester, our cognitive science seminar[9] devoted itself to creativity in humans, in other animals, and in machines. We were exposed to psychological models, anecdotes, philosophical arguments, software systems purporting to create, and introspection. For me the most vivid common thread through all this was the notion of *generate and test*.[10] Using a problem-solving metaphor for creativity, various solutions are generated, perhaps randomly or with the aid of heuristics, and then tested against internal values. In humans, these values have emerged from our genetic makeup, our development, and our culture. Presumably the same is true of animals. The machines we looked at had their values imposed by their designers.

We saw one example of generate and test while visiting with sparse distributed memory. The contents of the focus prodded memory to generate a pattern that was then tested against incoming sensory data. In this case, the value was accuracy of prediction. In symbolic AI programs, testing is typically done against some internal criterion. And you'll recall genetic algorithms as an example of parallel generate and test.

Calvin (1990) offers a parallel generate and test "minimalist model for mind," calling it a Darwin machine (in contrast to a computer model, a von Neumann machine).[11] Shades of Edelman's Darwin III. Calvin's Darwin machine is to be our next attraction. Since Calvin is a neurobiologist, interpret what you see as a high-level description of underlying neural processes.

In devising this model, Calvin is concerned with sequences: sequences of words forming a sentence, sequences of notes forming a melody, sequences of actions forming a plan, sequences of events forming a scenario, sequences of muscle contractions and relaxations forming a throwing motion.[12] For the most part, he's concerned with the production of such sequences. How, for example, am I producing this sentence as I type it into the computer? Let's use Calvin's vivid analogy of a railroad marshaling yard as a bridge to his answer.

Imagine a dozen or so parallel spurs funneling into a single output track. Each spur contains a string of cars (words in the sentence sequence) chosen randomly or heuristically from recently used words (short-term memory) and from associations with current context (long-term memory). Assign the contents of each spur a numerical value based on the utility of similar past utterances in similar context and on appropriate syntax. Next replace some of the lower-valued sequences with copies of higher-valued sequences, with some randomness in the choices and with some replacement of words by synonyms or by other mutations. When some level of agreement is reached among the spurs, or when some value threshold is reached, the winning train rolls onto the single track to consciousness. This winning sentence may only be a thought, or it may be expressed in speech, sign language, handwriting, or typed into a computer. Voila, a Darwin machine. Similar mechanisms, or perhaps the same neural mechanism, could produce plans, scenarios, throwing motions, melodies, and so on.

The likeness to genetic algorithms is striking. Words correspond to genes, sequences of words to strings of genes, the contents of the spurs to the population, and value to fitness. Calvin's Darwin machine can be fairly described as a neural genetic algorithm.

I'm also struck with the analogy between the single output track and Kanerva's focus. Calvin calls the contents of the single track the contents of consciousness, whereas Kanerva terms the contents of the focus "subjective experience."[13] This analogy tails off rapidly because of two key issues. Kanerva's model is inherently serial, whereas Calvin's is decidedly parallel. Further, Kanerva's model explicitly accounts for the current context via sensory input.

Imagine an amalgam of the two systems with a marshaling yard inserted between memory output and the focus (= single track). The sparse distributed memory serves as long-term memory. Some short-term memory must be added. Many questions arise, seemingly in parallel. How can memory feed the individual spurs? Or should it feed into short-term memory as a buffer? These issues might become simpler if we could implement it all by using Boolean geometry. Is that possible? But let's get back to the Darwin machine.

The brief description of a Darwin machine given above leaves out almost all detail. One issue is how to assign values. It's easy for me to visualize assigning a value to a throwing sequence based on past experience with a projectile of the given size, shape, and weight; on past experience with targets in the given direction and at the given distance; and on the intention of the thrower. Assigning a value to a plan, a sequence of actions, can use past experience with each given action in its updated context, as well as the desirability of the final outcome. Notice how these assignments depend on intention and desirability, as must be the case for an autonomous agent. Assigning a value to a sequence of words on the basis of grammar seems straightforward enough. Including the utility of past experiences with such utterances is less clear to me but within the range of what I may accept provisionally. So let's assume values can indeed be assigned.

How will the choice of a copy of one sequence to replace another be made? Calvin gives us general guidelines but no specifics. How about borrowing the selection procedure from genetic algorithms? That should work well.

Then there's the issue of when to send a winner to the single track. Calvin distinguishes several different modes in which a Darwin machine can function. In its "choral mode," precision is the goal, and a winner isn't declared until there's virtual unanimity on the spurs. Throwing, he says, requires this mode. In the "variations-on-a-theme mode," a winner is sent forward when near-clones of a highly valued sequence have replaced most of the lower-valued sequences. The idea here is to maintain some variation in output. Finally, there's the "random thoughts mode" characteristic of dreams and daydreams, and perhaps of songwriting or other creative activity. Here the valuation scheme is changing, and what comes out is much less predictable.

Among the many questions left, that of how to implement a Darwin machine stands out. One possibility, as suggested above, is to use Boolean geometry à la Kanerva. Calvin, as a neurophysiologist should, suggests a neural approach via hexagonal mosaics of neurons and their axons (1992, 1993).

Having thought about remembering and sentence building, our next attraction makes analogies. Our first two attractions of this stop were about recalling and planning or speaking; the next one is about understanding.

Copycat

You'll no doubt recall encountering Searle's Chinese Room thought experiment on one of our early tour stops. With it, Searle hopes to make patently clear the absurdity of a computer understanding anything. As you've seen from my "quadratic understanding" tale, I view understanding as a matter of degree. Therefore, even a computer program that can solve quadratic equations understands quadratics at a minimal level. Searle would agree about levels of understanding but would put the level of such a program at 0.

We'll next visit a program that, in my view, understands the making of one kind of analogy at a level clearly above 0. Let's have a look at it and see what you think. To that end we'll visit the Copycat project of Hofstadter and Mitchell (Hofstadter 1984; Mitchell and Hofstadter 1990; Mitchell 1993).

In order to get in the right mood for this visit, why don't you pretend you're taking an IQ test? Get out paper and pencil, and write your answers to these analogy questions.

1. abc → abd   ijk → ?
2. abc → abd   xyz → ?
3. abc → abd   iijjkk → ?
4. abc → abd   srqp → ?

Most people answer question 1 with ijl, replacing the rightmost letter with its successor. There are other possibilities, say ijd, replacing the rightmost letter by d. Question 2 is a little trickier, since z has no successor. We could, of course fall back on xyd, but many people prefer to let the alphabet wrap and answer xya. Question 3 offers several possibilities: iijjll, iijjkl, iijjkd, iikjkk, at least. Question 4 seems to require a little more mental agility. Many people respond with srqo by slipping from successor to predecessor. Again there are other possibilities. What rule would yield srpp? srqd? srdp? srrp?

And what would you say about a computer program that would sometimes answer question 2 with wyz? Copycat is such a program. Now that we're in the mood, let's look first at the assumptions underlying Copycat's design, and then at its architecture and operation.

Hofstadter and Mitchell consider analogy making, along with recognition and categorization, as an example of high-level perception—that is, a deep, abstract, multimodel form of perception rather than a low-level, concrete, unimodel form. Copycat is intended to model this kind of high-level perception. Its design assumes that high-level perception emerges from the activity of many independent processes, running in parallel, sometimes competing, sometimes cooperating. Copycat is the most fleshed-out example of the multiplicity of mind concept of Ornstein, Minsky, and John Jackson that I've encountered. These independent processes, here called *codelets,* create and destroy temporary perceptual constructs, trying out variations in the spirit of Calvin's Darwin machine, if not in its form. The codelets rely on an associative network knowledge base with blurry conceptual boundaries. The associative networks evolve to the problem by changing activation levels and by changing degrees of conceptual overlap. There is no central executive, no one in charge. Decisions are made by codelets independently and probabilistically. The system self-organizes; analogy making emerges.

Copycat's architecture is tripartite, consisting of a slipnet, a working area, and a population of codelets. The slipnet, an associative network comprised of nodes and links, contains permanent concepts and relations between then. That's what Copycat knows. It does not learn. The slipnet is its long-term memory. The system has a connectionist flavor by virtue of spreading activation in the slipnet. All of this is explicitly encoded. The working area—working memory, if you like—is where perceptual structures are built and modified, sometimes by being torn down. The population of codelets (Ornstein's small minds, Minsky's agents, Jackson's demons) are perceptual and higher-level structuring agents. As demons should, they wait until the situation is right for them to run, and then jump into the fray.

Let's have a closer look at each of the three pieces. The slipnet is composed of nodes, each the core of a concept, and labeled links, each indicating some relationship between concepts. That relationship is named by the label. Note that nodes are meant to represent not a concept but the core of a concept. More on this in a bit. Figure 13.4 diagrams a small piece of Copycat's slipnet.

Note that each relationship, each type of association, is labeled, and that each such label is represented by a node—to some finite depth, of course, to avoid infinite regress.

How does the slipnet work? Nodes are activated by codelets when they seem relevant. A codelet whose job its to watch for an "a" in the input will activate the "A" node in the slipnet if it finds one. Activation decays,

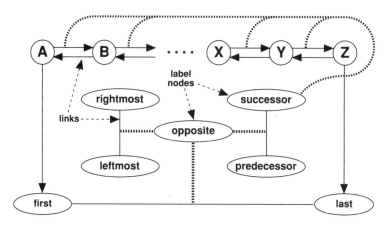

Figure 13.4
Portion of Copycat's Slipnet (adapted from Mitchell 1993)

and so goes to 0 over time, if not reactivated. A node may become inactive as a temporary structure containing it disappears from the work area. Nodes spread activation to their neighbors, starting with the nearer neighbors. Thus, concepts closely associated to relevant concepts become relevant themselves. Decisions about slippage—for example, from successor to predecessor, as we saw earlier—are made probabilistically, as is almost every decision. Copycat is a highly nondeterministic model.

Perhaps the most important single concept involved with this model is the notion of fluid concepts. Hofstadter has written about it separately (1985), arguing that concepts must be fluid to do the things humans do. In the Copycat model a concept is a region of the slipnet centered at its core node and has blurry boundaries. Neighboring nodes are included probabilistically by similarity, which is context dependent. The similarity between two nodes shrinks or expands according to what's happening down in the working area. Fluid concepts vary over time. They are emergent phenomena and are not explicitly represented anywhere in the system.

Perceptual structures are built in the working area. Copycat starts with three initial strings, say "abc," "abd," and "xyz." It knows the category of each letter, recognizing that "a" in the working area corresponds to the core node in the slipnet of the letter "A." More accurately, some codelet(s) knows this and acts to activate the proper node. Others know about leftmost, successor, and so on. High-level perceptual structures are gradually built of parts (nodes, links, labels) copied from the slipnet by codelets. At each moment the content of the working area represents Copycat's current perception of the problem at hand.

The problem-solving process is highly interactive. Low-level perception of what's going on in the working area exerts bottom-up influence by activating relevant nodes in the slipnet. Spreading activation identifies other relevant nodes. This produces top-down influence from the slipnet that guides low-level perception by enabling additional, appropriate codelets. The process continues until some codelets decide on a satisfactory answer. Don't let this fool you. There really is no top-level executive in this model.

We've talked of perceptual structures being built in the working area. Of what do they consist? There are four major components. Objects are described. The first "a" in figure 13.5 is *described* as being the leftmost in its string. The other three are explicitly illustrated in the figure.
Relations between objects are drawn, say the successor arc from "a" to "b." Objects are *grouped* together as "jj" and "kk" are in the figure. Such grouping may or may not emerge. If it doesn't, Copycat might answer "ijjkl" instead of the more common "iijjll." Finally, *correspondences* are drawn between objects, such as that between "c" and the group "kk" in the figure.

Having viewed the slipnet and the working area, let's move on to the third section of Copycat's architecture, codelets. Each codelet is a small piece of code, originally LISP code. I think of them as acting like Jackson's demons, each hanging around (in the stands) watching the work area, and jumping into action (into the arena) when the conditions are right. Each codelet carries out some relatively simple local task. One might estimate the importance of the "a" in the string "abc" as being the alphabetic first. Is that crucial here, or would starting with "bcd" instead do as well? Another codelet might notice the role of "a" as the first of that string. Still another might note that the "b" in the string "abc" succeeds its left neighbor. Yet another one might build the structure representing this last fact. The idea is to keep the action of a codelet so small and so local that it doesn't make a great deal of difference whether one acts at a given moment. Some other one might do a similar job, or the same one might have a chance later.

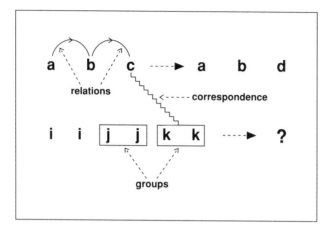

Figure 13.5
Perceptual structures (adapted from Mitchell 1993)

For each type of structure, "musing" codelets consider the possibility of building such a structure, whereas "building" codelets wait in the wings ready to construct it. Other codelets calculate the *strength* of an existing structure, that is, how well it contributes to an understanding of the current situation. This strength value serves a decision, by some other codelet, as to whether to continue the structure. Every structure, then, is built by a sequence of codelets, some deciding probabilistically to continue or to abandon it. Such decisions are made according to strength assigned by other codelets. If the structure is to be continued, another codelet assigns an *urgency* value to subsequent codelets. If the structure is not abandoned, the sequence ends with a builder codelet, which adds it to the work space, where it possibly competes with existing incompatible structures, such as a successor link competing with a predecessor link.

How do codelets become active? First, codelets are selected from the population of codelets and added to a single pool of relevant codelets by currently running codelets and by active slipnet nodes. A codelet returning a high strength for a given structure might well select a builder of that structure as relevant. A node in the slipnet that has recently been the beneficiary of spreading activation may select codelets that evaluate structures of which it's a part for inclusion in the pool. Codelets are then chosen from the pool to run, the choice being probabilistically based on urgency. An active codelet is removed from the pool.

Copycat begins "life" with an initial population of codelets that does not change. Codelets are predetermined by the designers. However, the speed of each codelet, and computational resources, are dynamically regulated by moment-to-moment evaluations of their relevance to the current overall structure. A process, such as one building a particular structure, consists of many codelets and is not predetermined. Rather, it's postdetermined, becoming visible to an outside observer. Within Copycat, such processes are emergent entities with no formal representation.

In Copycat, all activity is performed by codelets: "many possible courses of action are explored simultaneously, each at a speed and to a depth proportional to moment-to-moment estimates of its promise" (Mitchell and Hofstadter, p. 328 of reprint). Hofstadter and Mitchell refer to such an operation as a *parallel terraced scan.*

Only one more key idea is needed. Computational *temperature* is intended to measure the "disorganization ('entropy') in the system's understanding of the situation." Temperature starts high and falls as more and better structures are built, reflecting a better understanding of the system. As the total strength of the existing structures increases, the temperature decreases. The temperature at a particular instant controls the degree of randomness in the system, both in the choosing of active codelets and in the decisions of individual codelets. At high temperatures such choices and decisions are more random; at lower temperatures they are more deterministic.[14] Note that temperature is a global concept in the midst of an otherwise entirely local system. To calculate it, strengths must be summed over all existing structures.

With all this machinery of mind in hand, let's see Copycat in action.

A Copycat Run

Mitchell and Hofstadter (1990) graciously provided sample screen dumps from a run of Copycat, giving us an opportunity to watch mechanisms of mind in action. We'll go through the screens, picking out some high points. I urge you to come back and spend more time exploring. This one is an exceedingly rich attraction.

The initial input for our sample run (figure 13.6) was "abc => abd" as "xyz => ?" Keep in mind that what you'll be seeing are sample screen dumps with much happening in between.

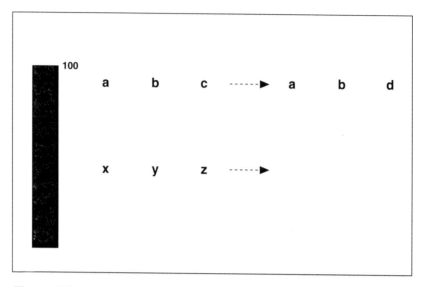

Figure 13.6
Sample run, screen 1 (redrawn from Mitchell 1993)

Note that the initial temperature, depicted by the bar at the left, is 100, reflecting the lack of structure (understanding) in the working area. The screen shows neither slipnet nor codelets.

In figure 13.7 solid lines reflect identity relations already constructed. The dotted lines depict relations and one correspondence ("a" to "x") being considered. Note the competing predecessor and successor relations between "b" and "c."

In figure 13.8 we see more structure and, hence, a lower temperature. The "c" to "z" correspondence is in place and labeled (rightmost to rightmost); the "a" to "x" is still being considered.

For the first time, a group is being considered in figure 13.9.

In figure 13.10 the successor group "abc" has been built, a second correspondence put in place, and a rule proposed, by filling in a template (Replace _____ by _____). This rule describes what Copycat now thinks is happening on the first line of the input. As a result of the additional structure, temperature has taken a sizable hit. Note the predecessor relation "c" to "b" still competing.

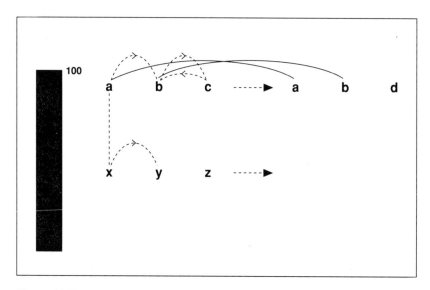

Figure 13.7
Sample run, screen 2 (redrawn from Mitchell 1993)

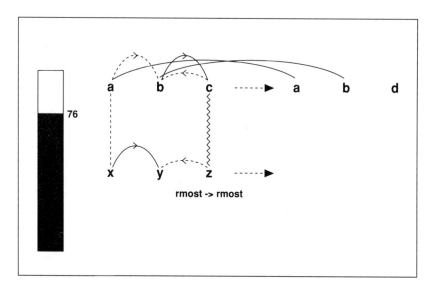

Figure 13.8
Sample run, screen 3 (redrawn from Mitchell 1993)

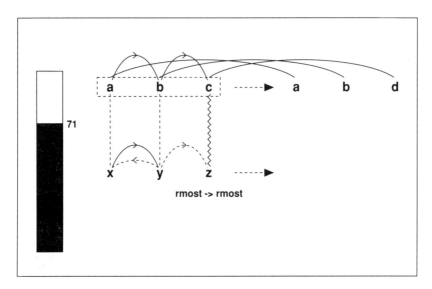

Figure 13.9
Sample run, screen 4 (redrawn from Mitchell 1993)

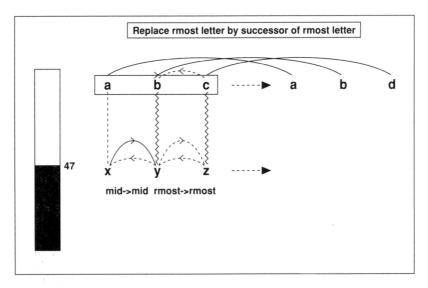

Figure 13.10
Sample run, screen 5 (redrawn from Mitchell 1993)

Copycat is becoming ever more confident in figure 13.11. Another successor group has been identified. Three correspondences have been built, and a group correspondence is being considered. Another hit to temperature.

Everything is looking rosy in figure 13.12. The correspondences are in place and are listed ("sgrp => sgrp" says that a successor group corresponds to a successor group.) The listed correspondences are applied to the top rule to produce the bottom rule, the one Copycat intends to apply to create an answer. In this case, the rules are the same. Temperature has dropped almost to 0. Now an answer-building codelet goes looking for a successor to "z" and finds none. The slipnet not only has no successor to "z" but purposely has been given no relation from "z" back to "a." The bottom has dropped out. This line of reasoning won't work. What to do now?

Copycat decides that its current understanding of this situation leaves something to be desired (see figure 13.13). Temperature shoots up, and as a result, structures begin to break down. Copycat is starting afresh, but not completely afresh. You may well ask how the temperature can be

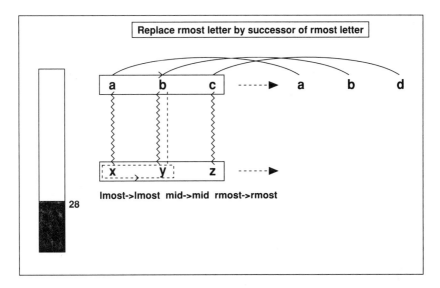

Figure 13.11
Sample run, screen 6 (redrawn from Mitchell 1993)

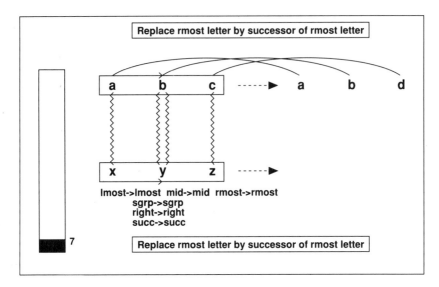

Figure 13.12
Sample run, screen 7 (redrawn from Mitchell 1993)

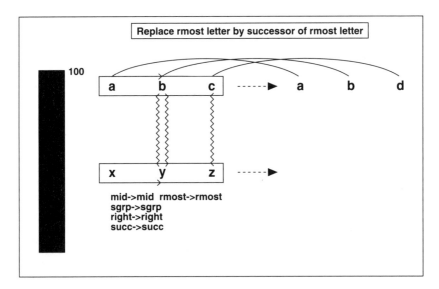

Figure 13.13
Sample run, screen 8 (redrawn from Mitchell 1993)

so high with so much structure left. Remember, it's the total strength of structure that is inversely related to temperature. The strengths of these structures suffered mightily when the rule couldn't be applied.

In Figure 13.14 we see more structure down the tubes, along with all rules. And a possible "a" to "z" correspondence.

The top rule has returned in figure 13.15, and all sorts of structures are being tried. The "a" to "z" correspondence is in place, and with it a first-to-last *slippage*. The temperature is dropping.

Two groups have formed in figure 13.16, a successor group on top and a predecessor group on bottom. Temperature more than halves, showing Copycat's confidence in the newly formed structures.

Correspondences are now complete in figure 13.17. The resulting slippages are listed, by means of which the top rule is transformed into the bottom rule. Answer-building codelets are now able to implement this last rule, arriving at "wyz" as an answer. Not bad for a computer system.

The rather creative answer arrived at by Copycat during this run happens occasionally with this input. More often Copycat falls back on the

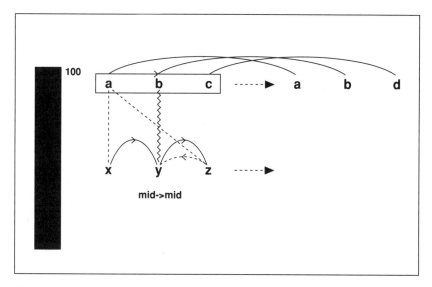

Figure 13.14
Sample run, screen 9 (redrawn from Mitchell 1993)

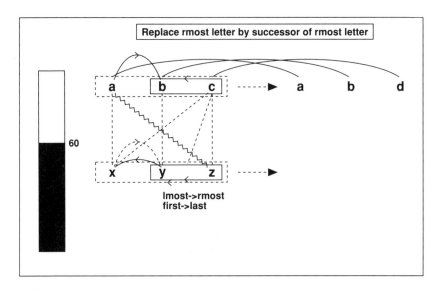

Figure 13.15
Sample run, screen 10 (redrawn from Mitchell 1993)

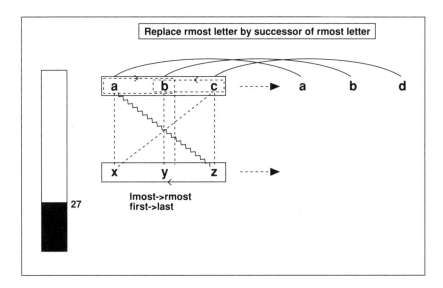

Figure 13.16
Sample run, screen 11 (redrawn from Mitchell 1993)

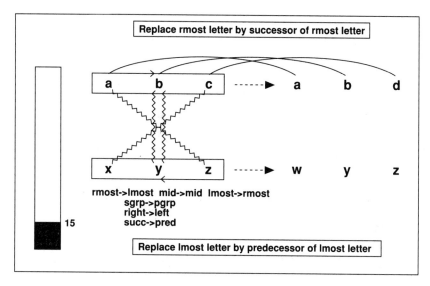

Figure 13.17
Sample run, screen 12 (redrawn from Mitchell 1993)

more humdrum rule *replace rmost letter by "d."* Well, none of us can be creative all the time.

Copycat's parallel terraced scan strategy uses information as it's obtained, thus speeding up convergence to a solution. It biases its choices probabilistically and never absolutely rules out any path. (Note the similarity to the notion of maintaining genetic diversity in genetic algorithms.) Mitchell and Hofstadter speculate that this type of strategy "is optimal in any situation where an intractable number of paths are to be explored in a limited time." I wouldn't be surprised.

They make a further, perhaps even more ambitious, claim: "temperature-controlled parallel terraced scan is a plausible description of how perception takes place in humans" (Mitchell and Hofstadter 1990, p. 329 of reprint). During a talk on Copycat to our cognitive science seminar, I relayed this assertion to an audience liberally sprinkled with cognitive psychologists and their students, expecting a howl of protest. To my amazement, all I saw was a nodding of heads. It seems that, to some at least, Copycat's architecture embodies plausible mechanisms of mind.

The Copycat system could be viewed as a more filled-out version of Calvin's Darwin machine, with the spurs all superimposed on one another in the working area and the single track corresponding to the answer area within the working area.[15] I suspect that in writing the last sentence, the idea of comparing the two and of the specific correspondences was produced in a Copycat-like fashion, whereas my actual sentence was generated in a Darwin machine-like way. Copycat seems more concerned with content; a Darwin machine, more with form. For a Darwin machine, form and content are ultimately determined by assigned values. Could a Copycat-like architecture take part in this assignment? I suspect so. And, as long as we're speculating, I can imagine a system integrating sparse distributed memories with Darwin machines and with Copycat architectures.

The three attractions of this tour stop, on top of the many other mechanisms of mind we've encountered, tend to support the idea that *mind is enabled by a multitude of disparate mechanisms,* one of the tenets of the new paradigm of mind I'm trying to sell. On our next stop we'll explore further the idea of situated action, the world as its own best model, that we met earlier while visiting the work of Brooks.

Notes

1. When I tried this out on my neurophysiologist friend Lloyd Partridge, he promptly explained that no scientific theory is correct.

2. In my previous incarnation as a topologist, only infinite topological spaces were of interest to me.

3. For the mathematically more sophisticated, Boolean space refers to some vector space over the two-element field Z_2.

4. In this case a location is an almost circular arc of spiral groove.

5. I will try to adhere to Kanerva's convention of using lowercase Greek letters for locations and for data, and lowercase Roman letters for hard locations. The Greek letters will include ξ (xi), η (eta), and ζ (zeta).

6. "Convergence" here means that for sufficiently large n, $\zeta_n = \xi$, that is, far enough out in the sequence all bit vectors are, in fact, ξ.

7. Although there's certainly truth in this view, it omits a vital aspect of understanding, the number and complexity of associative connections. You'll recall our earlier visit with "quadratic understanding."

8. Kanerva uses the term "subjective experience." I've avoided it in order not to become embroiled in issues of qualia and first-person consciousness.

9. One of the interdisciplinary seminars sponsored by the Institute for Intelligent Systems at the University of Memphis.

10. "Generate and test" is the term commonly used in symbolic AI for this idea. It denotes a somewhat more sophisticated approach than does "trial and error."

11. The Hungarian-American mathematician John von Neumann is credited with the idea of storing programs as well as data in memory. Such computers, almost all of ours today, are in this sense von Neumann machines.

12. Calvin has been long concerned with the question of encephalization. What caused a fourfold enlargement of homind brains in a mere, by paleontological standards, 2.5 million years? Part of Calvin's answer is "projectile predation" enabled by sequences of muscle contractions and relaxations forming a throwing motion (1991).

13. I'd be interested to hear if Dennett (1991) would consider Calvin's single track or Kanerva's focus Cartesian Theaters to be avoided. Dennett's multiple drafts model otherwise seems in line with a Darwin machine.

14. Temperature seems analogous to learning rate in an artificial neural network, which, when high, allows large jumps, perhaps out of local minima, and when small, moves steadily toward a solution.

15. One mustn't carry this analogy too far. Whereas Copycat certainly works in a parallel fashion, a Darwin machine is more massively parallel, having tens or hundreds of candidate solutions.

14

Representation and the Third AI Debate

The much greater perspicuity and the inherent thinking advantages of powerful representations enable progress that would be impossibly difficult with anything less adequate. . . . [A good representation] makes the important things explicit [and] exposes the natural constraints inherent in the problem.
—Patrick Henry Winston, *Artificial Intelligence*

Winston is right. Once an appropriate representation is available, many problems do become amenable to automatic solution. In our view, however, the problem requiring intelligence is the original one of finding a representation. To place this problem in the domain of the system designer rather than in that of the designed system is to beg the question and reduce intelligence to symbol manipulation
—George Reeke and Gerald Edelman "Real Brains and Artificial Intelligence"

Symbolic AI researchers stress the importance of choosing a "powerful" representation for a computing system to use while solving a problem. Others maintain that finding a powerful representation is what requires intelligence in the first place, and that what comes after is *only* symbol crunching.[1] Still others (Agre and Chapman 1987a, 1988) contend that we often choose the wrong *type* of representation. And there are those, several of whom we've met, who think that the need for representations at all is highly exaggerated (Brooks 1990c; Freeman and Skarda 1990; Agre and Chapman 1987a). This last is the bone of contention of what I call the third AI debate.

Let's begin with a brief visit to one powerful representation. I'll present it in the context of a problem and its solution. Please don't turn the page until you've read the statement of the problem and thought a few moments about possible methods of solution.

The problem: Can an 8 × 8 grid missing two corners, as illustrated in figure 14.1, be covered exactly by nonoverlapping dominos?[2]

What, exactly, does the problem ask for? A positive solution would consist of a pattern of dominoes, nonoverlapping, each covering two squares, with no square uncovered (or of a proof that such exists).

How might we go about trying to solve this problem? Buy several boxes of dominoes and proceed by trial and error to find a covering? Unlikely to work. Try an exhaustive computer search of all possible such coverings? Too time consuming. Use a temperature-controlled, parallel terraced scan à la Hofstadter and Mitchell? That's a lot of machinery to construct. How about a powerful representation? What?

Well, here a representation. Think of the grid as a checkerboard with white and black squares (figure 14.2).

It is powerful? You bet. Since each domino covers one square of each color (a natural constraint exposed by the representation), any exact nonoverlapping covering must cover an equal number of squares of each color (an important thing made explicit). But white squares number thirty-two, and black squares only thirty. Hence, there is no such covering of this board. A powerful representation made the negative solution almost trivial.

All this is by way of focusing our attention on representations, which along with goals and motives, provide the conceptual underpinnings of the attractions of this tour stop. Our first attraction will introduce us to a different kind of representation.

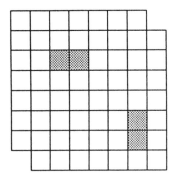

Figure 14.1
Domino covering problem

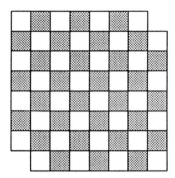

Figure 14.2
A powerful representation

Deictic Representations

Life is a continual improvisation.
—Philip Agre and David Chapman, Pengi

... state is less necessary and less important than is often assumed.
—Philip Agre and David Chapman, Pengi

Our first major attraction of this tour stop introduces us to the work of Agre and Chapman (1987a, 1988; Chapman and Agre 1987; Chapman 1991; Agre 1995) on *deictic* representations, sometimes known as indexical-functional representations.[3]

Two central themes of this work are set out in the quotes above. "Life is a continual improvisation." Think about improvising music as opposed to following the score. We make immediate decisions in response to immediate situations much more often than we follow detailed plans. We don't plan as much as we improvise.

Equally important is "state is less necessary and less important than is often assumed." Here "state" is used in the sense of the internal state of a system, in this case an internal model of the world. We don't have to use internal representations when we can look out and see the world as its own best data structure. Agre and Chapman are coming down on one side of the third AI debate.

Agre and Chapman distinguish between capital-P Planning and little-p planning. During the former a smart planner constructs a plan, as a

programmer writes a program, and a dumb executive carries it out mechanically. The plan must be readily interpretable by the executive, that
is, no creativity or originality, or even much thought, should be needed
in order to know what to do next. Instructions should be immediately
meaningful to the executive. This kind of Planning entails problem solving and reasoning with representations, as is common among symbolic
AI systems. There's a large literature on Planning in an artificial intelligence context.

Little-p planning is introduced via prototypes: following a recipe for
spring onion soup, following directions on getting from here to the airport, or using a reference manual for Microsoft Word. In this type of
planning, being a dumb executive won't cut it. Some rearrangement might
be called for, doing things in a different order. The task may involve inter-
polation. In going from here to the airport, I might have to stop and inter-
polate the changing of a flat tire. And disambiguation may well be
needed, though ambiguous commands are prohibited by definition in
Planning. And I might substitute skim milk for whole milk in a recipe.
Improvising while following a plan is the essence of planning. Note that
planning doesn't require following someone else's recipe, directions, or
whatever. I may mentally lay out my own rough route to the airport from
an unfamiliar starting point and improvise my way through it. That's
also planning.

Agre and Chapman are critical of Planning, not in all cases but as a
basis for daily activities. Why? Because real situations are complex, uncertain, and immediate. Planning is combinatorially explosive (Chapman
1987),[4] and thus unlikely to scale up to the complex situations we and
other interesting autonomous agents may face. There are simply too many
details to consider. The complexity also implies that real situations cannot be completely represented. Again there are too many details. There is
neither time nor space to represent a given real situation completely. Thus
complexity leads to uncertainty, creating difficulties for Planning. Also,
the actions of other agents and processes cannot be predicted. (Ethologists have claimed that the most difficult problem a chimp faces is to predict what another chimp in the band is going to do next.) One reason is
that we typically don't know enough to predict actions with much confidence. Another is that other agents may well be complex systems exhibiting sensitive dependence on initial conditions, and are thus inherently

unpredictable. Planning can be a problem. Finally, real situations are immediate: "Life is fired at you point blank: when the rock you step on pivots unexpectedly, you have only milliseconds to react. Proving theorems is out of the question." (Agre and Chapman 1987a, p. 268)

Well, if we mostly don't plan, what do we do? Activity, they say, is mostly derived from simple machinery that exploits regularities in previously encountered situations similar to the present one. (Shades of Kanerva's agent. I'm beginning to detect some convergence of ideas.) This machinery engages in "complex and apparently planful activity without requiring explicit models of the world." Agre and Chapman are not opposed to internal models of the world. They simply claim, along with Brooks and others, that a lot can be done without them. But how can simple machinery produce such complex behavior? Recall Simon's ant tracing a complex path among the pebbles on a beach, the complexity due to the pattern of the pebbles. With autonomous agents in general, complex action likely arises from the situation rather than from the machinery choosing for the agent.

So much for the general ideas. What have Agre and Chapman actually done by way of mechanisms of minds? They've played games. At least one game, Pengo (see figure 14.3).

Pengo is played on a two-dimensional maze of ice blocks. The player navigates a penguin icon with a joystick. Bees chase and try to kill the penguin. Both penguin and bees can kick ice blocks, making them slide. Sliding blocks kill bees or penguin on contact.

But what does Pengo have to do with deictic representation? Agre and Chapman take Pengo as a simple model of reality because, like reality, it's complex, uncertain, and immediate. Pengo is complex in that the several hundred objects would require a thousand propositions, too much for any current Planner. Bee behavior is not fully predictable because of a built-in random component. Finally, real-time response is required; if you're the penguin, you'd better get out of the way. Pengo, then, models the situation in which real autonomous agents typically find themselves.

And playing Pengo requires certain skills. A player would run to escape the bees, would hunt down bees when he had an advantage, might build traps and escape routes, could maneuver bees into corners. So much for a background in playing Pengo. Let's meet Pengi.

Figure 14.3
The Pengo Board (redrawn from Agre and Chapman 1987)

Pengi is an autonomous agent, a software agent, who plays Pengo. As you would expect, given the buildup, he follows no rigid Plan but acts upon the immediate circumstances. It's situated activity. Pengi uses a set of goals and a stock of skills. He takes advantage of opportunities and deals with unexpected contingencies as best he can. He, like you and me, follows routines.

Routines are patterns of interactions between an agent and its world. I have a routine for cutting a banana into my cereal, another for toweling dry after a shower. My routine for each of these is probably different from those of other people. Don't mistake a routine for a Plan or a procedure.

Nor for a data structure. An agent doesn't typically represent its routines at all. Rather, routines emerge from local behavior. Pengi, for example, when running from a bee, typically runs as far as he can or until he hits an ice wall. In the latter case he kicks through it and continues running until he meets the next wall, and continues in this way. Note that "routine" is a concept useful to us, the observers, but not a concept used by Pengi.

Since the concept of routine is an important one for this work, let's look at it a little more closely. The routine of running from a bee seems as if it were implemented by a pair of rules, the first being to run away when you are being chased, the second to kick through a wall if you run into it while running away. When the situation changes—say the chasing bee is crushed by a block kicked by another bee—the "being chased" rules no longer apply. There is no need even to represent that event internally. Pengi can just forget that bee. He doesn't have to know that the chasing bee was killed. He doesn't care. Other responses become applicable. Pengi can do things now that he couldn't do while being chased by the bee. Routines are opportunistic. Responses can be simple, allowing real-time activity: "Causality flows into this system from the world, drives the rules, which choose what to do, resulting in action which changes the world, and back again into the system, which responds to the changes." (Agre and Chapman 1987a, p. 269)

OK, if you were going to write a program to implement Pengi, how would you do it? The obvious way to us old-time procedural programmers (or even functional programmers[5]) would be with object relation representation.[6] A LISP form (AT BLOCK-213 197, 52) would represent a relation AT holding between BLOCK-213 and a position on the board given by the pair of numbers 197, 52. The form (IS-A BLOCK-213 BLOCK) would assert that BLOCK-213 is a member of the category BLOCK. (NEXT-TO BLOCK-213 BLOCK-23) would tell us that two blocks are neighbors. Keep in mind that a Pengo board contains roughly 25×25 squares and over 100 ice blocks. A traditional Planner would use probably thousands of such forms to represent each board situation, since it must know where each block is, which ones are its neighbors, where the bees are, their relations to neighboring blocks, their direction, and so on. With this type of representation, each form names some individual block or bee or penguin. None refers to the penguin's situation or goals. They are situation independent and goal independent.

Agre and Chapman want to offer us another way. They introduce the notion of an *indexical-functional entity*. Some examples: the-block-I'm-kicking, the-corridor-I'm-running-along, the-bee-on-the-other-side-of-the-block-next-to-me, the-block-that-the-block-I-just-kicked-will-collide-with. Pengi doesn't name these entities and doesn't manipulate them directly. He doesn't care which block he's pushing. Typically he's pushing just one block, so that the-block-I'm-pushing really distinguishes a block. Entities are intermediate between logical individuals and categories. BLOCK-213 is a logical individual. The set of blocks being pushed is a category. The-block-I'm-pushing is neither but something in between. Well, if Pengi doesn't name or manipulate these entities, how are they used? They are embedded in *aspects*. What is an aspect?

An indexical-functional aspect is some aspect of the current Pengo situation in the way we normally use the word. Here are some examples: The-block-I'm-going-to-kick-at-the-bee-is-behind-me (so I have to backtrack). I've-run-into-the-edge-of-the-screen (better turn and run along it). The-bee-I-intend-to-clobber-is-closer-to-the-projectile-than-I-am (dangerous). . . . -but-it's-heading-away-from-it (which is OK). I'm-adjacent-to-my-chosen-projectile (so kick it). Aspects are properties of the situation in which Pengi finds himself that are relevant to his current goals. He uses them to help select the next action. They're a mechanism of mind.

We've spoken of indexical-functional entities and aspects. Entities and aspects are functional representations in that they are relative to Pengi's purposes, goals, or motives. When running away, Pengi should find the-bee-that-is-chasing-me and the-obstacle-to-my-flight. Aspects are not defined in terms of specific individuals (BEE 70) but in terms of function in the current situation. The-bee-that-is-chasing-me may be a different individual from moment to moment. Pengi can't tell the difference, and doesn't care. For his current purpose (getting out of harm's way), it doesn't matter. If a school bus is bearing down on me, I don't stop to ask from what school but simply get out of the way. A particular object may be different entities at different times, depending on function. The-bee-that-is-chasing-me might become the-bee-that-I-am-about-to-kick-a-projectile-at at a later time. Entities and aspects are indexical representations in that they are relative to the agent defining them. They depend on Pengi's circumstances at the moment.

Since changes propagate slowly over the Pengo board, Pengi can ignore most of the screen most of the time. To know where something is, Pengi simply looks at the screen rather than searching through some internal, and necessarily outdated, database. Hence much of the overhead of search, reasoning, and representation can be eliminated. Avoiding representation of individuals bypasses the binding of constants to variables. In order to kick some block (say SOME-BLOCK) at some bee (SOME-BEE), when representing individuals, these variables must be bound to (instantiated as) say BLOCK-23 and BEE-12. As in much of our moment-to-moment activity, there's simply no need to keep track of individuals. The result is simpler mechanisms.

And what do these simpler mechanisms look like? Here's a quick look. The high-level architecture, as you would expect, consists of peripheral systems responsible for perception and effector control, and a central system responsible for registering and acting on relevant aspects of the situation. Since entities and aspects avoid representation and reasoning, the central system can be relatively simple. You don't have to prove theorems in there. The central system is constructed as a combinational network, a connectionist-like network composed of digital circuits, each with many components (Boolean functions, gates). (The choice of this technology over artificial neural nets was dictated by engineering considerations. Either could do the job.) Inputs come from the perceptual system, and outputs go to the motor system. The central network decides on actions appropriate to the situation. Representation (as we spoke of it in the artificial neural net context) is distributed; many nodes, in conjunction, register particular aspects. As the world changes, perceptual inputs change, are propagated through the network, and drive appropriate actions. Pengi does all this without maintaining any internal state (memory) in the central system.

Keep in mind that aspects are not data structures but external descriptions of some aspect of the current situation as registered by the activity over a set of components in the central network. No variables are bound to symbols that represent objects. Aspects produce actions via output from the central system to the effector system. These actions, typically part of routines, change the world, and thus the perceptual systems, so that, perhaps, different aspects are seen.

Though the central system is relatively simple, one of the peripheral systems, the perceptual system, is a little more complex than we've indicated. There, a visual routines processor (VRP) operates in tandem with the central system, that is, there's input and output both ways between them (see figure 14.4). They exchange patterns of activity. The early vision part of the perceptual system produces a two-dimensional sketch of what it sees. The VRP creates and maintains internal copies of this sketch, each modified for the needs of its operations. The VRP can, often on command from the central system, color in regions, trace curves, track locations with visual markers, index interesting features, detect and track moving objects. This pretty powerful processor is based on the work of Ullman (1983).

The central network guides the VRP as to what operator is to be applied to what image. The outputs of the VRP are inputs to the central network. The central system gets no input directly from early vision. During a visual routine, the VRP, guided by the central network, finds entities in its images, registers aspects, and injects them as inputs into the central

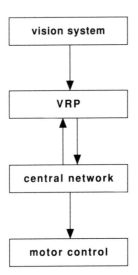

Figure 14.4
The VRP's place in the system

system. Much of the hard work is done here. This is another reason the central system gets away with simple machinery. The central network registers aspects using Boolean combinations of inputs from the VRP. Let's see an example or two.

Some visual routines run constantly. Pengi always wants to know if there's a bee chasing him. Some of them run under certain circumstances. After kicking the-block-that-is-in-my-way, it is useful to find the-block-that-the-block-I-just-kicked-will-collide-with. The central system directs the VRP to trace a ray from the kicked block until it hits something solid (figure 14.5). Then it's to mark that thing, and check to see if it's a block.

Here is another one.

The penguin is hiding behind a wall of bricks. A bee on the other side is heading toward the wall. To find the-block-to-kick-at-the-bee, what should the VRP do? First, extend a ray along the path of the bee and through the wall (figure 14.6). Then draw a ray along the wall, and drop a marker at the intersection. Note the necessity for exchange of patterns of activity between the central system and the VRP.

We've had a fairly good look at Pengi but have yet to encounter the most important issue: How does he decide what to do next? Each action is suggested by local plausibility in the current situation. There may be several plausible actions. Suppose a bee is closing in. Pengi could run

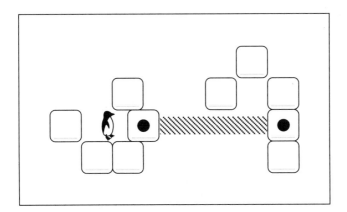

Figure 14.5
Finding a collision target (redrawn from Agre and Chapman 1987)

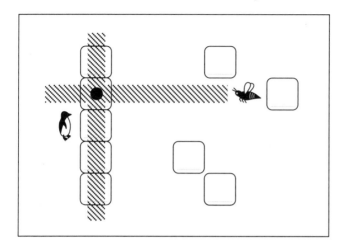

Figure 14.6
Finding the-block-to-kick-at-the-bee (redrawn from Agre and Chapman 1987)

away. Or he could run to a block and kick it at the bee. How does Pengi choose between these? He uses aspects of the situation and several levels of arbitration. There may be a general rule that *if you are being chased by a bee on the other side of a block, and you're closer to the block than the bee is, run to the block and kick it at him, or else turn tail and flee.* But there may be exceptions to the "or else" clause. *If you are in a narrow passage, then run toward the bee and hope for the best.* If you run away from the bee, it's going to kick the block, and there is no place for you to go. Your only chance is for something to happen to the bee. It might randomly stop chasing you. Or some other bee might squash it for you. A slim chance, but a chance. And the exception may have exceptions. *If there is time, kick a hole in the passage and escape.* An action may be proposed, discarded, resurrected, given up for another, and so on—an example of relatively simple machinery producing complex processes as a result of what's going on out in the world.

Agre and Chapman think highly of action arbitration, since it doesn't require internal representations in the usual sense, nor does it require search and prediction. Thus they claim—rightly, I expect—that it's more efficient than Planning. Action arbitration can produce sequences of actions and can resolve goal conflicts. Since Pengi's central system does all this with no state, they conclude that "state is less necessary and less important than is often assumed."

There's much for me to learn from this work. As Wilson pointed out to us earlier, most animals, and most interesting autonomous agents, exist in a sea of incoming sensory signals, almost all of which are irrelevant. It is not only inefficient, but usually impossible, to represent it all in an internal model. Here I mean objective representation via individual objects and relations between them. Agre and Chapman offer us deictic representations in terms of indexical-functional entities and indexical-functional aspects, representing not individuals but roles and conditions with respect to the defining agent. Action selection in real time becomes possible.

Action selection, at a high level, is emergent. The rules illustrating action arbitration, which we met a bit ago, are not written symbolically in somewhere memory. Rather, they arise in the mind of an observer watching the output of the circuits comprising the central system. One might say the rules are hardwired in. Somehow, I'm a little uncomfortable with that, and would prefer to say they emerge from the hardware. The source of my discomfort is the belief that more emerges than was intentionally built in by the designer.

This work also supports the notion of information as created rather than processed: "Because a deictic representation must be causally connected with its referent, part of its responsibility is to constitute an object. The real world is not neatly divided into discrete objects with identity labels on them. What counts as an object depends on the task" (Chapman 1991, p. 32). Chapman gives two examples. A window frame is part of the window to a carpenter nailing it into a wall, but not part of the window to a window cleaner squeegeeing it off. Similarly, the top of a can of paint is part of the paint can when it's being stored in a cabinet but a separate object when you want to dip a brush in.

Here's a philosopher's voice espousing this view: " 'Objects' do not exist independently of conceptual schemes. We cut up the world into objects when we introduce one or another scheme of description" (Putnam 1981, p. 52).

The work of Agre and Chapman provides a perfect introduction to the notion of structural coupling, which is central to our next attraction.

The Enactive Paradigm

We'll next visit with the work of Varela, Thompson, and Rosch (1991), a neuroscientist, a philosopher, and a cognitive scientist. They propound an enactive paradigm of mind that views mind as embodied action. To understand just what that means is my purpose for this visit.[7] Let's take a roundabout approach, comparing three different paradigms of mind: the cognitivist, the connectionist, and the enactive.

The cognitivist paradigm, embraced by symbolic AI and by traditional cognitive science, is motivated, as we've seen, by the computational model of mind. Mind can be likened to a virtual, von Neumann-like machine running on top of underlying neural mechanisms or on top of logic gates fabricated of silicon. Thought, then, consists of manipulating symbolic representations of both external and internal objects, concepts, and so on: "in addition to the levels of physics and neurobiology, cognitivism postulates a distinct, irreducible symbolic level in the explanation of cognition" (Varela et al. 1991, p.a 41).

Varela et al. (p. 42) summarize the cognitivist view by asking and giving cognitivist answers to three fundamental questions, as follows:

Question 1:   What is cognition?
Answer: Information processing as symbolic computation—rule-based manipulation of symbols.
Question 2:   How does it work?
Answer: Through any device that can support and manipulate discrete functional elements—the symbols. The system interacts only with the form of the symbols (their physical attributes), not their meaning.
Question 3:   How do I know when a cognitive system is functioning adequately?
Answer: When the symbols appropriately represent some aspect of the real world, and the information processing leads to a successful solution of the problem given to the system.

Note that the first answer, in prescribing rule-based manipulation of symbols, means *rule-governed* (rule-driven) rather than *rule-describable*. We'll meet this distinction again later. Recall the Horgan and Tienson contention that although representations are necessary, rule-governed processing over high-level representations can never produce real-time appropriate actions. The second answer brings the response from Searle and others that abstract symbol manipulation can never produce intelligence. We met some of them on our visit to the first AI debate. Embedded in the third answer is the assumption of information from the external world being processed by the system, a view we've seen opposed several times recently.

One consequence of the cognitivist approach is that "cognition can proceed without consciousness." It's quite consistent with consciousness being epiphenomenal, and thus seems unable to account for our intuition of consciousness being central to our idea of self. Some would reply, So what? Consciousness is only an illusion (Dennett 1991). The first answer above also assumes a central processor of some sort that manipulates symbols according to rules.

The connectionist paradigm, one of the names Varela et al. (p. 99) give it, dispenses not only with the symbol processor but also with the symbols themselves. Here, instead of a computer model of mind, we take a brain model of mind. From this perspective, the answers to the three fundamental questions look very different.

Question 1: What is cognition?
Answer: The emergence of global states in a network of simple components.
Question 2: How does it work?
Answer: Through local rules for individual operation and rules for changes in the connectivity among the elements.
Question 3: How do I know when a cognitive system is functioning adequately?
Answer: When the emergent properties (and resulting structure) can be seen to correspond to a specific cognitive capacity—a successful solution to a required task.

All this is, of course, familiar from our visit with artificial neural networks. To be interesting or useful, the network postulated in the first answer would typically contain *many* simple components *highly interconnected*. The emergent global states are patterns of activity of these components. Both artificial neural networks and the Boolean automata networks of Kauffman (1993) are examples. Some of the local rules of the second answer serve to update the activity (state) of the network, either synchronously or asynchronously, and others may enable a learning process, perhaps via changes in the strengths of connections. In the connectionist paradigm, meaning resides in emergent properties (global states) rather than in symbols.

As in the cognitivist paradigm, the quality of a connectionist system is relative to some "required task." Presumably the required task of an autonomous agent is to choose the next action so as to successfully satisfy its needs by interactions with its environment. This sounds a lot like Wilson's adaptation of van Heerdon's definition of intelligence, especially if we also require learning from experience, as allowed for in the second answer. This view leads us directly into the enactive paradigm.

The cognitivist answers to the three fundamental questions resonate with conventional wisdom in our culture, and so are easy to understand. The connectionist answers, I hope, present not much more difficulty, since we have visited with several connectionist or near-connectionist systems. The enactive answers, on the other hand, are couched in unfamiliar concepts and grounded in an exotic worldview. One possible course would be to meet the concepts and the worldview in preparation for the answers. I've chosen a different course: using the initially opaque answers as motivation to meet the concepts and worldview. Please bear with me. I hope clarity will prove to be an emergent property.

Here are the questions again, and the answers of the enactive paradigm (p. 206).

Question 1: What is cognition?
Answer: Enaction: a history of structural coupling that brings forth a world.
Question 2: How does it work?
Answer: Through a network consisting of multiple levels of interconnected, sensorimotor subnetworks.
Question 3: How do I know when a cognitive system is functioning adequately?
Answer: When it becomes part of an ongoing existing world (as the young of every species do) or shapes a new one (as happens in evolutionary history).

Wow! Where to begin? Let's let the answers guide us. "Enaction" is defined in terms of "structural coupling" and "bringing forth a world." Let's start with the second of these.

Our culture's dominant view has minds processing information from the world out there. I, and others, have tried to sell a different view: that minds create information for their own uses. Some Eastern religions view the outside world as *maya*, illusion created by mind. The enactive paradigm's "bringing forth a world" includes the view of information as created by mind, and goes a little farther: "mutual specification . . . enables us to negotiate a middle path between the Scylla of cognition as the recovery of a pregiven outer world (realism) and the Charybdis of cognition as the projection of a pregiven inner world (idealism)" (p. 172).

What is this middle path? Let's first consider another question. Which came first, the world or our experience of the world? Sounds ridiculous, doesn't it? Of course there has to be a world before I can experience it. Varela et al. propose an illuminating analogy. As one follows the flight of a bird, which comes first, a movement of the eyes or the registering of an image? Well, there must be an image of a bird flying before I can move my eyes to follow it. But I must move my eyes to a position to register the bird's image before that can happen. Ah, it seems impossible to say. It's the chicken or egg problem, each seeming to have the other as a prerequisite. Or, we might say, each mutually specifying the other, the image specifying where to look, the action specifying what image is seen: "Perception and action, sensorium and motorium, are linked together as successively emergent and mutually selecting patterns" (p. 163).

The enactive paradigm has the agent and its world mutually specifying each other. Note "*its* world" instead of "*the* world." An agent's world *is* the world of its experience. I don't experience radio waves per se, and experience sound rudimentarily. (Remember Dawkins's intelligent bats?) Both are out there, but the first is a part of my world only indirectly, and the second in a limited way. As for any autonomous agent, my sensorimotor apparatus specifies my world. Note "sensorimotor" rather than just "sensory." Could I fly, or swim deep and long in the sea, my world would be quite different.

But the world out there also specifies stimuli to my senses and constraints to my movements. These stimuli and constraints become part of my world. And I, as any autonomous agent must be, am myself a part of my world and am specified by it. Thus the circle is closed. Mutual specification, the middle path of the enactivists.

Varela et al. call the process that "brings forth a world" *structural coupling,* the coupling of the agent's structure to the *out there.* If the structure is changed, changing its relationship to the out there, the world changes. Their compelling example, from Sacks and Wasserman (1987), tells of an auto accident victim who, due to head injuries, lost his color vision. This change in structure literally changed his world. It became black, white, and shades of gray. Not only could he not see color, he coudn't imagine in color or dream in color. Behavior was also affected. Over time he became a "night person."

I love the nighttime. . . . I often wonder about people who work at night. They never see the sunlight. They prefer it. . . . It's a different world: there's a lot of space—you're not hemmed in by streets, people. . . . It's a whole new world. Gradually I am becoming a night person. At one time I felt kindly toward color, very happy about it. In the beginning, I felt very bad, losing it. Now I don't even know it exists—it's not even a phantom. (Varela et al. 1991 p. 164)

Our structure, and how it couples with the out there, determines our world.

But the first answer talks of a *history* of structural coupling bringing forth a world. Exactly. I am what I am because of a history of interactions with my world. My world is what it is because of its interaction with me, and with other agents, forces, and such. My world is determined not by my abstract sensorimotor structure but by the history of that structure's interaction with my world. There's good evidence that neural connections in the visual cortex depend on incoming stimuli (Crick 1994, p. 145). But which came first? Neither. They mutually specify each other.

And how does all this embodied action happen? The second answer talks of "a network consisting of multiple levels of interconnected, sensorimotor subnetworks." Where's the cognitive processor, the central system? Nowhere to be found. This is a whole other ball game. But we do have a model: Brooks's subsumption architecture. Herbert is constructed just as the second answer requires. And where are the representations? Again, nowhere to be found.

The third answer talks of the agent becoming "part on an ongoing existing world." Brooks's robots do just that. Varela et al. go on to talk of intelligence as "the capacity to enter into a shared world of significance." I presume they mean significance to the agent.

Significance to the agent triggers the issue of goals, motives, needs, drives, and so on, the content of our next attractions.

Goals

Human behavior, viewed externally, is clearly goal-directed.
—Allen Newell and Herbert Simon, Human Problem Solving

We've encountered before, and will soon again, the issue of rule-governed vs. rule-describable behavior. A related issue concerns goal behavior vs. directed behavior. We'll next visit briefly with Newell and Simon's views on this issue (1972, pp. 806–90).[8] In this work, they explicitly subscribe to the cognitivist view of mind as computation.

Newell and Simon define a goal as a symbol structure satisfying a couple of other requirements. To them, a goal must be some sort of data structure (list, string, etc.) populated with symbols, and hence a representation. It must be explicitly formulated for use within and by the system itself, and not merely a description of what's going on provided by some external observer. Recall that SOAR produced symbolic goals for its own use. Maes's action selection mechanism had built-in goals, but not in the Newell and Simon sense. Though they were within and used by the system, they weren't symbolic.

And what are the other requirements? First, the goal must specify some state to be attained, and some test to determine whether it has been attained. Second, the goal must have some causal power to evoke patterns of behavior. Newell and Simon call such behavior *goal behavior*. They refer to behavior resulting from other types of control structures as *directed behavior*. Note that Maes's system satisfies all this except for being symbolic.

Here's an example illustrating the distinction between goal behavior and directed behavior in the context of a cryptarithmetic problem. Suppose the system was trying to solve the following:

```
 DONALD
+GERALD
 ROBERT  D = 5
```

The system is asked to discover which letters correspond to which digits, thereby making this an accurate addition. Now suppose the system uses a production rule like this one:

P1: Given a new piece of information about a letter, find an occurrence of that letter and attempt to use the new information

To an external observer, the system may appear to have the goal of using new information; actually, however, no such goal is represented in the system. The behavior is directed by this single production rule. On the other hand, suppose the system use a different production rule:

P2: To get the value of a letter, go to a location of an occurrence of that letter and process the column containing it.   The precondition of this rule is "to get the value of a letter." This condition can be satisfied only if the system wants to get the value of a letter, that is, if some explicit goal embodies this desire of the system. A system containing P2 must use goals. The distinction between goal behavior and directed behavior can be pretty subtle to an outside observer.

Newell and Simon provide us with a list of named behavioral characteristics of goal behavior to aid us in recognizing it:

Interruptibility. When distracted, the agent later returns to the activity at the same point.

Subgoaling. Agent interrupts itself to pursue a means to its goal, and then returns.

Depth-first subgoaling. Several levels of subgoaling provide particularly conclusive evidence.

Equifinality. Failing with one method, the agent will attempt some other, perhaps quite different, method.

Avoidance of repetition. The agent operates with memory to avoid repetition of behavior.

Consummation. If the goal situation is attained, effort toward that goal is terminated.

Let's use a mama sand wasp's egg-laying behavior as a test case for these characteristics (Griffin 1984, pp. 101–2, 110). The question will be, is she or isn't she goal directed? Here's how she does it. First she digs a burrow in sandy ground, constructing an enlarged chamber at the lower end. Having closed the opening with small stones, perhaps brought from some distance, she goes hunting for a juicy caterpillar. After paralyzing the caterpillar with a sting, she carries it to the burrow, opens the entrance, and drags the caterpillar into the chamber. With preparations complete for feeding the hatchling on the living but immobilized flesh of the caterpillar, she lays an egg on him. Then she closes the entrance once again and goes her merry way, never to see her offspring.

Mama sand wasp's behavior certainly appears to be goal directed, but we've been warned of the subtlety of the distinction. Let's check Newell and Simon's characteristics of goal-directed behavior against what's known of the sand wasp's behavior.

Interruptibility. When distracted, the sand wasp later returns to her activity, but perhaps at a different point in the process.

Depth-first subgoaling. Here, the wasp's behavior apparently includes several levels of subgoaling. To lay an egg, first close the entrance (in preparation to hunting caterpillar). To close the entrance, bring pebbles. To bring pebbles, fly to pebbles, pick up pebble, and so on. Seem like particularly conclusive evidence?

Equifinality. When one method fails, the wasp will try again, but typically will attempt the same method once more.

Avoidance of repetition. If a paralyzed caterpillar is moved after the wasp has laid it down while opening the entrance, she often drags it back and repeats the digging even though the burrow is already open. This repetitious and unnecessary behavior may be repeated many times.

Consummation. When the egg is laid, mama wasp goes about her business.

What conclusion shall we reach? This may not be goal behavior à la Newell and Simon, even though a piece of the evidence, multiple subgoaling, is particularly conclusive. The repetition makes me suspicious. Or maybe mama wasp is indeed goal directed but not very smart.

And how about Maes's action selection system? Interruptibility seems likely due to the opportunism of the system. Depth-first subgoaling could well emerge from the spreading activation. Maes claims as much, calling it "sequences of actions." Equifinality is also built into her system. When one competence dies, a goal will continue to reward whatever other competences lead toward it. Avoidance of repetition results from the reward structure itself, and consummation is easily arranged for. It seems plausible to me that a system like Maes's could exhibit all the characteristics of goal behavior without symbolic representation. Some other characteristic will be needed to distinguish between them. Keep in mind that Newell and Simon had no system like Maes's to guide them in formulating the relevant characteristics. Two decades separate the work.

This meeting with goals à la Newell and Simon should warm us up for another visit with the work of Sloman, whom we met in chapter 2.

Motives and Goals

Our underlying concern during this major tour stop is with representation. There's been much discussion of representations of objects, of relations, of concepts. Our visit with Newell and Simon introduced representations of goals. Sloman (1987) goes even further and offers "a step towards a computational theory of emotions, attitudes, moods, character traits, and other aspects of mind so far not studied in Artificial Intelligence" (p. 217).

Yes, Sloman sounds like a cognitivist, but I'm not sure that's accurate. He explicitly asserts that the computations he postulates need not be implemented directly in physical processes; they may occur in a virtual machine[9] implemented in lower-level machines, either brainlike or computerlike. Thus he straddles the cognitivist–connectionist fence. Allowing for a virtual machine implementation, however, puts him squarely at odds with the enactive paradigm of mind. Of course, 1987 was a while back. Sloman may well think differently in light of newer evidence.

Sloman assumes the need for internal representations, saying that a theory of mechanisms of mind should "explain" how internal representations are created, stored, compared, and used for making inferences, formulating plans, and controlling actions. As we've seen, representations appear not to be biologically stored or compared in the sense we usually use these words. And some maintain we can go far without them; others, that we use no representations at all. Some of this disparity of opinion may result from different meanings attached to the word "representations." But that's a topic for our next attraction, not this one. In the meantime, I want to keep an open mind about Sloman's ideas, realizing that the meaning of "representation" needs to be clarified.

Sloman speaks of attitudes as dispositions to behave in certain ways. Love, in any of its incarnations, is an attitude. He sees emotions as episodes with dispositional elements: "Powerful motives respond to relevant beliefs by triggering mechanisms required by resource-limited intelligent systems" (p. 218). No new mechanisms are needed to account for emotions, he claims. Those underlying intelligence suffice. Further, emotions not only are not uniquely human but also are not confined to animals. Sloman expects intelligent machines to require emotions.

In addition to requiring emotions, what other constraints must be observed when designing a mind? One must allow for multiple sources of motivation, both internal and external. (I'm not at all clear about what constitutes external motivation.) One must count on speed limitations, on not having enough processing power to be profligate in the use of computation. One must expect gaps and errors to occur in the system's beliefs about the world. (Note "*the* world," as opposed to "*its* world.") One should build in degrees of urgency associated with motives to help with conflict resolution. And one must plan for resource limits: speed (as previously mentioned), memory, and external resources. As a consequence of limited resources and urgent goals, potentially unreliable heuristic, or "rule of thumb," strategies become almost mandatory.

Also, one will want to build in reflex actions, both in hardware and in software. Some may be modifiable by experience, some at least partly controlled by context-sensitive filters. These filters may rapidly assess priorities; may allow extremely important, urgent, or dangerous activities to proceed uninterrupted; but also may allow new, especially important, or urgent motives to interrupt what's going on. These filters implement conflict resolution on reflex actions. (In Brooks's robots, all actions are more or less reflex.) Sloman maintains that all intelligent systems, by necessity, will have fast but stupid subsystems that will sometimes let in undesirables.

He also claims that some sort of learning is required in order to cope with incomplete information and with long-term change in the agent's social or physical environment. This learning should extend to higher-level operators, not only the learning of generators and comparators of motives but also of generators and comparators of the generators and comparators, and so on. Sloman also advises building in "several independent subsystems that can execute plans in parallel, like eating and walking" (p. 219). Here Sloman embraces a multiplicity of mind view à la Minsky, Ornstein, and John Jackson. Though eating and walking may well result from plans about what to eat and where to walk, neither requires executable Plans. Overlearned, situational routines à la Agre and Chapman will suffice.

Pointing out that "conflicts among requirements can generate incompatible goals necessitating a decision-making mechanism" (p. 219). Sloman offers two main options: a democratic voting scheme and a centralized decision maker. Which to choose?

If subsystems do not all have access to the full store of available information or not all have equal reasoning powers, a "democratic" organization may be dangerous.
. . . a specialized central mechanism is required for major decisions (p. 219).

Is there really a central executive in humans? I doubt it. Must there be in other animals and machines? Not too likely. Other control mechanisms, such as those of Maes, Brooks, and Jackson, will probably work better.

At last we have seen enough of Sloman's constraints for the design of a mind to bring us to the issue of central interest to us here. Here's what he says about goals: "To have a goal is to use a symbolic structure represented in some formalism to describe a state of affairs to be produced, preserved or prevented" (p. 220). Sloman's definition is a little broader than that of Newell and Simon, but it doesn't require a test of completion. Sloman points out that his symbols need not be physical structures; they can be virtual, that is, emerging at a higher lever of abstraction from an underlying machine composed of neurons, or gates, or artificial neurons, or whatever.

He also points out that the same descriptive formalism, however the symbols arise, can be used for beliefs, hypotheses, instructions, rules, and hypothesized situations. They would be differentiated by context, by the roles they play. He compares goals with beliefs. A goal is a representation for producing behavior that changes the world to conform to it, whereas a belief is a representation that perceptual and reasoning processes alter to conform to the world. But must every goal be a representation? Certainly at a descriptive level. But what about a hardwired goal such as in Maes's action selection mechanism? Does a bacterium have goals?

Sloman distinguishes between a *derivative goal,* one generated by a planning process that subserves a prior goal, and a *nonderivative goal.* Some derivative goals may be triggered by a thought, an inference, or a recollection; others may be responses to new information, such as a loud noise or an awareness of hunger. Derivative goals are more readily abandoned and have fewer side effects. Nonderivative goals, when abandoned in favor of some higher goal, typically continue to clamor for attention. Some human nonderivative goals are bodily needs, a desire for approval, curiosity, and a desire to succeed. These, Sloman says, serve higher-level needs but are not derivative.

But what are these higher-level needs, and how are they implemented? Perhaps like the Ackley and Littman evaluation function (1992)? Recall that it evolves as an artificial neural network, is unchanging during the life of an individual agent, and provides reinforcement for learning by the agent's action function. Thus, needs must be generators of motives. Except for the lack of symbolic representation, the evaluation function would seem to be a primitive constructor of nonderivative motives.

Sloman views a motive as a disposition to produce certain effects or to resist changes, either internal or external. He goes on to distinguish several different quantitative dimensions, or measures, or motives. A motive's *insistence* measures its power to interrupt. A motive's *importance* measures its likelihood of adoption, of success in producing action. A motive's *urgency* measures the time left in which to act on it. A motive's *intensity* measures how vigorously it's pursued, how much energy is devoted to the pursuit. An agent's *distress* at failure to achieve and its *pleasure* at fulfillment can also be quantified.

Although a motive can be urgent (the plane leaves in four minutes), it need be neither insistent nor important nor intense (I'd rather stay with the later flight I'm booked on). A motive can be insistent (I'd like to tell off that guy who slighted me) without being important (I'll probably never see him again, so I don't want to cause a stir). Sloman, however, makes no claim that these properties of motives are independent of each other. He does suggest that motives may be needed in sophisticated robots and that they might have subjective correlates. (Does this mean a conscious machine?)

Sloman offers an extensive list of processes involving motives. On look-ing at it, my first thought was, What's missing? A brief search turned up nothing that didn't more or less fit into at least one of his sixteen catego-ries. Then a second thought hit. Of course, every action is the result of, among other things, a motive. Motives are, in principle, ubiquitous in the action selection mechanisms of autonomous agents. These motives need not be symbolic, as Sloman assumes; they may result from other types of control structures.

Sloman speaks of *emotions* as states produced by motives and beliefs, leading to the production of new motives, and offers anger as an example "X believes that there is something Y did or failed to do and, as a result, one of X's motives has been violated [frustrated]" (p. 224). Of course, X might only be disappointed. Anger, according to Sloman, requires a new motive to hurt Y. (I'm not sure I agree. In my experience, anger is most often expressed so as to frighten Y rather than to hurt him.) This new motive may not be acted on out of inculturation or fear of consequences. But more is required for anger. X's desire to hurt Y must be insistent, intense, and nonderivative.

Sloman claims that irrationality is inevitable:

The interruptions, disturbances, and departures from rationality that characterize some emotions are a natural consequence of the sorts of mechanisms arising from constraints on the design of intelligent systems, especially the inevitable stupidity of resource-limited interrupt filters that have to act quickly. (p. 228)

He goes on to discuss attitudes, moods, and personality, suggesting that all may be applicable not only to humans but also to animals and even to machines. Not all of these mechanisms are found in all animals. In some animals, for example, selection of a motive may always lead to acting on it. And it doesn't seem likely that all this richness of structure is present in young children. Learning and cognitive development occur in a frame-work of a complex and frequently changing collection of motivators. The complexity of these mechanisms provides enormous scope for bugs: "I conjecture that many emotionally disturbed people are experiencing . . . software 'bugs'" (p. 232).

Sloman has provided us with a rich and varied account of goals, mo-tives, emotions, and so on as high-level, perhaps virtual, mechanisms of mind. I suspect these concepts from human "folk psychology" will prove useful, and perhaps indispensable, in the design of sophisticated, adaptive, autonomous agents.

Sloman embedded his structures within the symbolic paradigm. Is this constraint critical to their usefulness? I suspect not. It's probably a result of this work having been done in the mid-1980s, before examples of other than symbolic control structures were common. Recall, however, that Sloman specifically points out the applicability of his theory within either the cognitivist or the connectionist paradigm. Thus representation, for him, must include connectionist representations, either local or distributed.

With the Agre and Chapman work, the enactive paradigm of Varela et al., and Sloman's theory as additional background, it's time to join the third AI debate.

The Third AI Debate

To represent, or not to represent? That's the question of the third AI debate.

In the first AI debate, scoffers maintained that the very idea of machine intelligence is ridiculous, while boosters claimed it's inevitable. The scoffers produced arguments supporting their position; the boosters said, "Just wait. We'll show you." Arguments were produced by one side, systems exhibiting some facet of intelligence by the other. In my view, the jury's still out, though if I had to bet, I'd side with the boosters.

The second AI debate had a similar form. Cognitivists produced arguments purporting to show that connectionist models can, at best, implement a virtual symbolic system, and can offer nothing new to the study of cognition. Connectionists responded that symbolic systems can, at best, approximate what's really going on in nervous systems and in useful cognitive models at a subsymbolic level. Both sides produced systems, the cognitivists typically at a more abstract functional level, the connectionists typically at a lower level. Again, I think the jury's still out. If pressured, this time I'd back the connectionists.

The third AI debate exhibits a rather different form. On one side a small but vocal coterie espouses versions of "representations aren't needed," or at least "are needed in only a minor way." On the other side is the overwhelming body of the culture, cognitive scientists, and AI researchers including connectionists, who, taking the need for representations as too obvious to talk about, simply ignore their critics. It's a band of Don Quixotes tilting at windmills. But I think they're right, just like the small group that once tilted with "the Earth is round" banners on their lances.

Let's visit the cast of characters, several of whom we've already met, and their ideas in roughly chronological order. (The history may be suspect. Keep in mind that your tour guide *is* an amateur and is *not* a scholar.)

Winograd and Flores (1986, p. 33) speak of the philosopher Martin Heidegger's "rejection of *mental representations*," which they paraphrase as follows:

> We do not relate to things primarily through having representations of them. . . . If we focus on concernful activity instead of on detached contemplation, the status of this representation is called into question. In driving a nail with a hammer (as opposed to thinking about a hammer), I need not make use of any explicit representation of the hammer. My ability to act comes from my familiarity with hammering, not my knowledge of a hammer.

Accepting this position forces us to conclude that hammering is not a rule-governed behavior.

Winograd and Flores also paraphrase the neuroscientist Maturana's argument against "the fallacy of instructive interaction" (p. 43):

> Instructive interaction is [Maturana's] term for the commonsense belief that in our interactions with our environment we acquire a direct representation of it—that properties of the medium are mapped onto (specify the states of) structures in the nervous system. He argues that because our interaction is always through the activity of the entire nervous system, the changes are not in the nature of a mapping. They are the results of patterns of activity which, although triggered by changes in the physical medium, are not representations of it. The correspondences between the structural changes and the patterns of events that caused them are historical, not structural. They cannot be explained as a kind of reference relation between neural structures and an external world.

If this view is correct, searching for representations in the nervous system would be fruitless. As we've seen, Freeman certainly found it so.

Noting a newborn's feeding behaviors—crying for mother's attention, rooting to position its mouth over a nipple, and sucking to express milk—

Winograd and Flores (1986, p. 52) assert: "The baby, like every organism, has a complex set of reflexes whose purposes can be explained in terms like those above, but whose functioning does not depend on representations, planning, or analysis." The behaviors may well be organized as prescribed in the enactive paradigm, or according to Brooks's subsumption architecture.

Earlier we visited with Skarda and Freeman's dynamical systems approach to understanding olfaction in rabbits. The article describing this work (1987) appeared in *Behavioral and Brain Sciences,* a journal whose enlightened policy allows for open peer commentary on each "target" article. Among the commentators was Gerhard Werner, who wrote of the "conceptual implications" of the Skarda and Freeman work as follows (1987, p. 183):

History is not represented as a stored image of the past; nor is the present a mirror of the environment. Instead, environmental events are specified by states of neural activity that are the result of the neuronal system's internal organization and dynamics. In this sense, the neural structure uses information to create its own internal states, which acquire meaning: The internal states are the neuronal system's own symbols, as these states stand in a regular relation to events in the world and signify potentials for action. This distinction highlights the departure from current cognitivism, for which meaning is assigned to symbols by an observer.

Once symbols are viewed as the system's own creations, any reference to representations becomes superfluous; Occam's razor can unburden us of the Trojan horse that was smuggled from the land of Artificial Intelligence into Neuroscience.

I'd rather say that the neural structure uses *stimuli* to create its own internal states, which constitute *information*. And recall that cognitivism does assert that a cognitive system interacts only with the form of the symbols (syntax), not with their meaning (semantics). In their rebuttal, Skarda and Freeman takes issue with Werner's "neuronal system's own symbols":

Our point is that the system can produce adaptive, ordered, cognitive behavior without using functional architecture based on rules and symbol manipulation. The neural patterns of our model are not symbols for the system because a distributed network doesn't require symbols to produce behavior. (1987, p. 186)

If anything about the rabbit's olfactory cortex looks like a symbol to me, it's the basin of attraction that categorizes the odorant. But that basin exists only in the mind of a mathematically inclined observer, and so can't be used as a symbol by the system itself. Unless, that is, it exists for the system as an emergent entity. Anyway, Werner used the term symbol to "highlight the departure from current cognitivism." Read "internal states" for "symbols," and Werner's argument seems cogent.

Freeman and Skarda take their own crack at representations in an article pugnaciously titled "Representations: Who Needs Them?" (1990):

Neural activity patterns in the olfactory bulb cannot be equated with internal representations of particular odorants to the brain for several reasons. First, simply presenting an odorant to the system does not lead to any odor-specific activity patterns being formed. Only in motivated animals, that is, only when the odorant is reinforced leading to a behavioral change, do these stereotypical patterns of neural activity take shape. Second, odor-specific activity patterns are dependent on the behavioral response; when we change the reinforcement contingency of a [conditioned response] we change the patterned activity. Third, patterned neural activity is context dependent: the introduction of a new reinforced odorant to the animal's repertoire leads to changes in the patterns associated with all previously learned odorants. Taken together these facts teach us that we who have looked at activity patterns as internal representations of events have misinterpreted the data. (p. 376)

If it doesn't look like a representation and doesn't act like a representation, it's probably not a representation.

Perhaps the most outspoken critic of representations is Brooks. In an article titled "Intelligence Without Representation" (1991), he castigates symbolic AI as follows:

Artificial intelligence research has foundered on the issue of representation. When intelligence is approached in an incremental manner, with strict reliance on interfacing to the real world through perception and action, reliance on representation disappears. . . . The fundamental decomposition of the intelligent system is not into independent information processing units which must interface with each other via representations. Instead, the intelligent system is decomposed in independent and parallel activity producers which all interface directly to the world through perception and action, rather than interface to each other particularly much. The notions of central and peripheral systems evaporate—everything is both central and peripheral. (p. 139)

Disclaiming any particular interest in neuroscience or cognitive science, in possible applications, or in philosophical implications, Brooks, as an engineering feat, simply wants to build "completely autonomous mobile agents [Creatures] that co-exist in the world with humans, and are seen by those humans as intelligent beings in their own right" (p. 145). Approaching the problem as an engineer, he lays down some requirements. A Creature must cope appropriately and robustly with its changing environment in a timely fashion. It must seek to satisfy multiple goals, switching among them according to circumstance. And it must do something. These constraints led Brooks to his subsumption architecture and to Creatures like Herbert, whom we've already met. Building such Creatures led Brooks to an "unexpected conclusion": "When we examine very simple level intelligence we find that explicit representations and models of the world simply get in the way. It turns out to be better to use the world as its own model" (1991, p. 140).

Brooks claims that his Creatures use no central representation, no world model, and that this efficiency allows them to react quickly enough to do their thing in the world. They substitute frequent sensing for an internal representation. And the individual layers of their structure attend only to relevant aspects (in the sense of Agre and Chapman) of the environment. Each layer has its own purpose, but there is no explicit representation of goals. The Creature is a "collection of competing behaviors." This "no representation" policy is carried to the lowest levels:

Even at a local level we do not have traditional AI representations. We never use tokens which have any semantics that can be attached to them. The best that can be said in our implementations is that one number is passed from a process to another. But it is only by looking at the state of both the first and second processes that that number can be given any interpretation at all. (1991, p. 149)

But isn't the very structure of Brooks's augmented finite-state machines and their interconnections within a single layer an implicit form of representation? Brooks feels they don't act enough like representations to be representations.

There are no variables . . . that need instantiation in reasoning processes. There are no rules which need to be selected through pattern matching. There are no choices to be made. To a large extent the state of the world determines the action of the Creature. . . . We hypothesize (following Agre and Chapman) that much of even human level activity is similarly a reflection of the world through very simple mechanisms without detailed representations. (1991, p. 149)

As to this last conjecture, I wouldn't be at all surprised.

Brooks's Creatures are simply hardwired, that is, causally constructed so as to do what they do. Their very structure can surely be interpreted as consisting of representations of their incoming stimuli, their goals, and their outgoing actions. (There's not much high-level cognition to require representation.) Every representation must be *of something* and *to some agent*. These representations are surely representations to an observer doing the interpreting, but are they representations to the Creature? That is, does the Creature use them as representations? In this last quote, Brooks argues not.

One way, perhaps the only way, to use representations is to consult them, say as a computer does its program. Certainly the cognitivist view leads to this analogy. My friend and colleague Daniel Chan (1994) gives an in-depth and nontrivial analysis of what it means for a physical system, say a layer in one of Brooks's Creatures, to consult in this sense. He distinguishes between a structure that actually performs an operation, like a screwdriver transferring torque, and a structure capable of several different operations that consults a representation to know which to perform, like a cook consulting a recipe. To me this seems the right distinction. A representation is consulted for its content, not simply used for its structure.

This distinction may be more subtle than it seems. An early model cash register, where you press the 5 button and levers open the drawer and raise the 5 flag, is to me a prototypical example of a hardwired structure using no representation in its operation. A computer program that writes 5 to the screen when the 5 key is pressed is a prototypical example of the use of representations, the program. What if I compile the program and run the machine code directly? Does it still use representations? What if I burn this compiled program into a PROM (programmable memory) and use it to build a calculator-type device with the same response? When, if ever, does it become hardwired? To Chan, the answer lies in the causal details of the functioning of the device. His article, though a struggle to read, is convincing. It also settles for me the rule-describable vs. rule-governed issue. Rule-governed requires consultation in Chan's technical sense.

Let's end our visit with the third AI debate by looking at the relation between high-level perception (mostly, but not entirely, missing in Brooks's Creatures) and representation. These ideas are from the work (1992) of Chalmers, French, and Hofstadter, two of whom we encountered earlier on our tour.

"Representations are the fruits of perception." Here they're talking about high-level perception, "extracting *meaning* from the raw material by accessing concepts, and making sense of situations at a conceptual level." High-level perception begins with concepts. Examples are recognizing objects, grasping relations, and the even more abstract comprehending of situations. A representation is the end product of this high-level perception. It's a structure that can be consulted, transformed, acted upon. My youth as a topologist was spent constructing just these kinds of representations from high-level perceptions about sequential spaces, quotient maps, epireflective hulls, and other such arcane mathematical concepts. It's certainly clear to me that representations are needed for sufficiently conceptual cognitive endeavors.

Chalmers and company take symbolic AI to task for bypassing high-level perception and taking representations as given. (They are not replying to the anti-representationists.) They claim, as did Edelman earlier, that finding the representations is the part requiring intelligence, and that to skip it amounts to stacking the deck. They go on to propose the Copycat architecture as a mechanism for high-level perception. Hear! Hear!

As with the other two AI debates, I think the jury's still out. Brooks, Edelman, Freeman, and the rest have convinced me that much of the activity of an autonomous agent, even one of us, can be accomplished without representations. On the other hand, my mathematician side refuses to dispense with them entirely. To what extent they're needed, and when they're just in the way, will become clearer as we design and build more autonomous agents. I suspect Chalmers et al. may have pointed to the dividing line; manipulation of concepts requires representation.

So much for representations. If you think each of our tour stops has shown a futuristic tinge, wait until you see the next one.

Notes

1. This calls to mind the very legitimate complaint of symbolic AI people about always having to shoot at a moving target. A century ago someone who could accurately and quickly add a column of figures was considered intelligent. But no more, since computers can do it. It's mere number crunching. The definition of intelligence is set just beyond what a computer can do.

2. I'm indebted to my colleague Cecil Rousseau for calling this problem and its solution to my attention.

3. Agre and Chapman originally used the term "indexical-functional representation," and later switched to "deictic representation." My linguist friend Leo Connolly tells me that "deictic," meaning "pointing to directly," is in fairly common use among linguists. I'll use both terms.

4. For the theoretical computer scientists among us, Chapman proved that Planning, under reasonable conditions, is NP hard. Thus we can never expect better than an exponential time algorithm. It won't scale up.

5. Most common programming languages are procedural, based on procedures that do things. They include FORTRAN, COBOL, C, and Pascal. LISP is a functional language, based on functions that take arguments and return values, and perhaps side effects as well.

6. Yes, of course, I'd prefer an object-oriented language (Smaltalk, CLOS, C++), but the difficulties would be similar and fewer of our fellow tour members would be familiar with it.

7. Let me caution you that our brief visit will be no substitute for a serious perusal of the work itself. Their purpose is much more than mine: "we propose to build a bridge between mind in science and mind in experience by articulating a dialogue between [the] two traditions of Western cognitive science and Buddhist meditative psychology" (p. xviii). Though I'm much interested in the second of these traditions also, having meditated regularly for some years, our mechanisms of mind agenda dictates involvement mostly with the first.

8. I'm endebted to my friend and colleague Art Graesser for pointing out the relevance of this work.

9. A chess-playing program running on your personal computer can be thought of as a virtual chess-playing machine running on top of your PC. Playing against it may be another virtual chess-playing machine running on top of a human nervous system.

15

Into the Future

Is it possible that consciousness is some sort of quantum effect?
—Nick Herbert, *Quantum Reality*

I believe that robots with human intelligence will be common within fifty years.
—Hans Moravec, *Mind Children*

Perhaps within the next few centuries, the universe will be full of intelligent life—silicon philosophers and planetary computers whose crude ancestors are evolving right now in our midst.
—Lynn Margulis and Dorion Sagan, *Microcosmos*

So far we've toured purported mechanisms of mind for which worked-out theories, or models, or even prototypes exist. Whether these mechanisms could be useful as mechanisms of actual minds may be doubted, but there's no doubt that they are mechanisms. On this, our final tour stop, we'll visit more speculative mechanisms and more speculation about the future of artificial minds.

The Quantum Connections

Surely the most mysterious theory of science today is quantum mechanics. Although spectacularly successful at predicting outcomes of experiments in physics, quantum mechanics is extraordinarily resistant to any kind of explanatory narrative. Any story that's told to explain it seems not to make sense somewhere. Some samples: Entities are routinely both particles and waves, and not waves in a real medium but probability waves. Parallel universes multiply at every observation, one universe realizing each possible outcome. Reality exists only in the presence of an observer. Reality is created by consciousness. (Note that creating reality is *not* the same as the creating of information about reality that I've been pushing.) My favorite layman's account of quantum mechanics is Herbert's *Quantum Reality* (1985), which demystifies the subject as much as seems humanly possible, and explores a variety of explanatory narratives, all more or less weird. The opening quote was taken from this book.

Quantum theory shines in the realm of the almost infinitesimally small, the world of subatomic entities like protons, neutrons, electrons, photons, quarks, and a host of others particles with yet stranger names. (I used to say "subatomic particles," but no more.) Each such quantum entity is associated with (or is?) its wave function. Suppose a photon is traveling through some medium toward a detector. Quantum mechanics has that photon traveling all its possible paths at once, with its wave function representing these possibilities. At a given location, the square of the amplitude (height) of the the wave function gives the probability of the photon's appearing at the location, should an observation be made. The shape of the wave represents attributes other than position (spin, mass, charge, momentum, etc.). If our photon's position is detected, say by its striking a phosphor screen, its wave function is said to collapse and its particle nature to emerge. All this must happen in relative isolation. If there is a chance encounter along the way, our photon's wave collapses before it reaches the screen.

In these days of digital everything, we've almost forgotten analog computing, using natural processes to compute for us directly. The simplest example I can think of is my old slide rule. By moving the slide appropriately, it would multiply two numbers for me. The speed was admirable, though the accuracy depended on the length of the rule and wasn't always what I wanted. Electronic analog computers could integrate in a jiffy, again with limited accuracy. The idea, like that of the slide rule, was to construct an electronic device whose operation, viewed mathematically, performed the operation you want. For example, Ohm's law says that in an electrical circuit the current flow equals the product of the voltage applied and the resistance. If I build a circuit whose voltage and resistance I can vary and whose current I can measure, that's an analog computer for multiplication. To multiply two numbers, a and b, set the voltage to a, the resistance to b, close the switch and measure the current, ab, the product of the two. An analog computer typically performs one specific task.

Over a decade ago the physicist Richard Feynman proposed building quantum analog computers for appropriate tasks. In an analog fashion, such a computer might perform a multitude of calculations in parallel and in an instant, as the wave function collapses to the desired answer. No such quantum computer has yet been built,[1] but the theory has been advanced (Deutsch 1985; Deutsch and Jozsa 1992). Shor (1994) has shown that a quantum computer could, in principle, be built to factor 100-digit numbers. Kak (1992) suggests building a quantum neural computer for solving AI problems. Caulfield and colleagues have shown that some optical processors can be "uniquely and truly quantum mechanical." They use such processors in the design of a quantum optical device to emulate human creativity.[2]

Is it just a short step from quantum computing to quantum consciousness? Can consciousness in humans (and other animals) be the result of quantum computing on the part of neurons? Recall that we saw such suggested by Penrose, a serious and respected scientist, who used it as an argument on the side of the scoffers in the first AI debate (1989). If intelligence is produced by nervous systems using quantum processors, ordinary computers might be hard pressed to duplicate it.

"But," you cry, "neurons aren't in the quantum realm, being several orders of magnitude too large." True. And this objection, of course, concerned Penrose until he was rescued by Hameroff. Hameroff proposed that the microtubules that act as an internal skeleton for each neuron (and any other cell as well) also serve as quantum information-processing devices (1987, in press; Jibu et al. 1994). He claims that certain properties of consciousness (unitary self, free will, subjective experience) resist non-quantum explanation, and that microtubules "are the best bets for structural bases for consciousness."[3] Penrose embraces this view in *Shadows of the Mind* (1994). Journalist accounts are also available (Freedman 1994; Horgan 1994).

As you no doubt expected, the notion of quantum consciousness via microtubles has been greeted with howls of protest. Microtubules are still orders of magnitude too large, are by no means isolated, operate at too high a temperature, and so on. Most critics are not yet ready to believe that consciousness, subjective experience, requires quantum explanation. They view Penrose and Hameroff's proposal as using an elephant gun to hunt an elusive mouse in a thicket. I suspect the critics might be right.

Right or wrong, quantum microtubles are now hypothesized mechanisms of mind, and thus bear watching. And hypothesized quantum computers are also intended as mechanisms of mind. Who knows what the future will bring?

Let's next visit with a respected roboticist, who may not know but is willing to stick his neck out and predict.

Mind Children

Moravec, a roboticist at Carnegie Mellon whom we met during our itinerary run, believes that intelligent robots, our *mind children,* will outstrip us.

Unleashed from the plodding pace of biological evolution, the children of our minds will be free to grow to confront immense and fundamental challenges in the larger universe.

We humans will benefit for a time from their labors, but sooner or later, like natural children, they will seek their own fortunes while we, their aged parents, silently fade away.

Very little need be lost in this passing of the torch—it will be in our artificial offspring's power, and to their benefit, to remember almost everything about us, even, perhaps, the detailed workings of individual human minds. (1988, p. 1)

A powerful prediction! Moravec is certainly not afraid to stick his neck out. And what's it based on? Projections, intuition, and an imagination that would do Robert Heinlein or Arthur C. Clark proud.

Moravec's projections flow from a couple of fascinating figures. The first plots power against capacity (figure 15.1).

Capacity is memory size measured in bits, and power is processing speed in bits per second. Note the log scale on each axis. Each labeled unit is a thousand times greater than the previous one. I'm particularly intrigued that a bee outperforms the computer I'm writing on, and that a single human can outdo the national telephone network. This figure sets the stage for Moravec's projections, and the next opens the curtains.

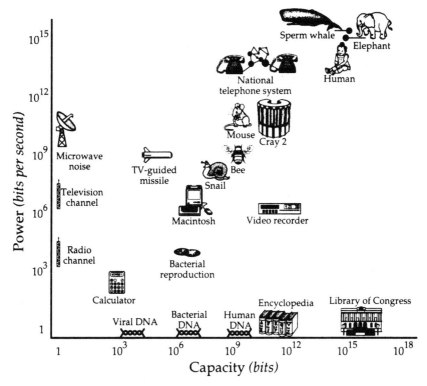

Figure 15.1
Computational speed and storage capacity (reprinted from Moravec 1988)

Figure 15.2 plots computing power per dollar against time. The result is essentially linear, with power per dollar increasing a thousandfold every twenty years. Extrapolation will yield tools with human computing power at a reasonable cost in forty years. Thus, Moravec's prediction. High-level artificial minds are just over the horizon, he says.

I'm a little skeptical. First, I'm doubtful about predictions in general. Thomas J. Watson, the founder of IBM, once predicted five machines as a worldwide market demand for computers. Second, every growth curve I've ever seen has eventually leveled off. The speed of an electron through a wire or chip is limited by the speed of light. The amazing development in recent years portrayed in this figure has resulted from chips more densely

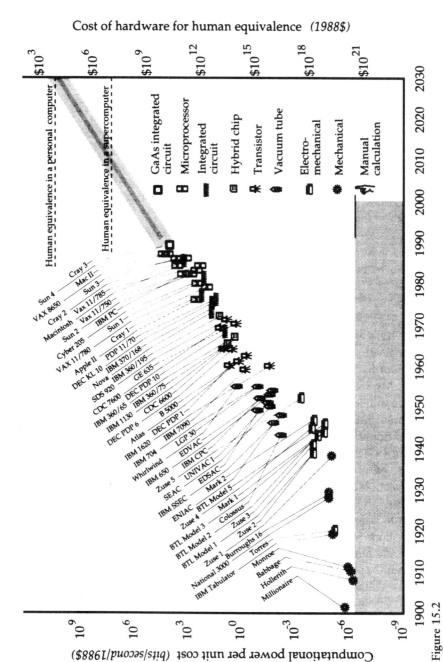

Figure 15.2
A century of computing (reprinted from Moravec 1988)

endowed with components, so that traveling distances are less. But we're approaching the quantum barrier. Much smaller distances and we're in the quantum realm, where computations may not be reliable. Maybe this curve is about to level off. Finally, even if computers as computationally powerful as a human nervous system do emerge, there's no assurance we'll be able to program human intelligence into them. Don't get me wrong, though. It's not that I disbelieve Moravec's prediction. It's that I wouldn't bet on his time frame.

Enough about projections. Let's go on to imagination. What would you say to a fractal, recursive robot? What? Well, let's take it slowly. Clouds are *fractal* in that they look much alike at any scale. A photograph of a square mile of clouds would be hard to distinguish from one of a square yard of the same clouds.[4] In computing, a recursive procedure is one that calls itself during its operation. Suppose I want a recursive procedure to find the length of a string of characters like abc. I might define the procedure so as to return 0 for the empty string, and to return 1 + the length of the rest of the string otherwise. The rest of abc is the string bc. This *length* procedure calls itself during its operation. It's recursive.

For our entire tour, we've visited mechanisms of mind. We'll now visit a mechanism of body, a fractal mechanism, a recursive mechanism. A strange body indeed. But why a mechanism of body on a mechanisms of mind tour? Because, as Varela et al. pointed out to us, minds are always embodied,[5] mind is constrained by structural coupling, that is by body, and how it meshes with the environment. So bear with me as we visit a wondrous body and speculate about possible minds for it.

Imagine a meter (yard)-long cylinder, ten centimeters (four inches) in diameter. Inside are a power supply and a control mechanism. Now imagine four half-length, half-diameter copies of it, including power supply and control mechanism, two attached at each end. The joints have at least the freedom of movement of a human wrist, and built-in sensors for position and force. Continue this recursive, robot building process twenty times, creating what Moravec calls a bush robot. Figure 15.3 shows his conception of what it might look like. After twenty halvings, the roughly 1 trillion last cylinders (cilia) would be about a micron (millionth of a meter) long. And, having so little inertia, they'd move a million times faster than the largest limbs. But what's the bush robot standing on?

Figure 15.3
A robot bush (reprinted from Moravec 1988)

These smallest limbs would be crushed by the weight. Well, it simply folds under enough sections to get to some strong enough to support it.

Moravec postulates remarkable sensing abilities for his bush robot. Since each joint can sense forces and motions applied to it, suppose each of the 1 trillion cilia senses movement of a tenth of a micron and forces of a few micrograms, all this at speeds up to a million changers per second. By comparison, the human eye distinguishes about a million parts, registering changes about 100 times per second. The bush robot would "look at" a photograph by caressing it with tiny cilia, sensing height variation in the developed silver. It could watch a movie by walking its cilia along the film as it moved by at high speed. Wild!

Cilia could also be sensitive to heat, light, and so on. An eye could be formed by holding up a lens and putting a few million cilia in the focal plane behind it. Or, without a lens, carefully spaced cilia could be used as a diffraction grating to form a holographic image. Wilder!

But try this one.

The bush robot could reach into a complicated piece of delicate mechanical equipment—or even a living organism—simultaneously sense the relative position of millions of parts, some possibly as small as molecules, and rearrange them for a near-instantaneous repair. In most cases the superior touch sense would totally substitute for vision, and the extreme dexterity would eliminate the need for special tools. (1988, p. 105)

There's more. Since each branch contains its own power supply and controller, the bush could break into a coordinated swarm of subbushes. They could communicate via sound vibrations of a few thousand cilia. The smaller the subbush, the less intelligent and less powerful it would be. Perhaps its home branch would send it on some mission. A light enough subbush would be able to walk on the ceiling, like geckos, using its cilia to hold to microscopic cracks. A sufficiently small subbush would have so much surface area for its weight, it would be able to fly like an insect, beating its cilia to provide propulsion. And what might a swarm of flying subbushes do? Dealing with killer bees might be one application.

But how might such a bush robot come into being? Moravec views it as self-constructing. Humans would build a few tiny bushes to start the process. These would cooperate to build bushes of the same size and one size larger, to which they would join themselves. The process would repeat until the largest branch was constructed. And the smallest branches?

It could make the smallest parts with methods similar to the micromachining techniques of current integrated circuitry. If its smallest branchlets were a few atoms in scale (with lengths measured in nanometers), a robot bush could grab individual atoms of raw material and assemble them one by one into new parts, in a variation of nanotechnology methods. (1988, p. 104)

And what about action selection for this bush robot? How is it to be controlled? Moravec suggests enough computing power in each branch to control routine activity, and to appeal one level higher when something unusual occurs: a hierarchical control structure. This places a severe burden on the largest branch. The buck stops there.

I'd picture each subbush as an autonomous agent with a built-in preference for being attached to the larger bush. Each subbush would select its own actions via some mechanism like those we've visited, say a pandemonium architecture. Such a strategy would make it much more reactive but might cause other problems. Imagine a subbush, away from the parent bush, whose own four largest subbushes decided to take a powder.

Why include such a thought experiment on our tour? Because it clearly highlights how much the action selection (controller) of an autonomous agent depends on its material form and function, that is, how much the mind depends on the body.

The Future Supercosm

Having just visited with physicists and roboticists, let's end this tour stop by visiting briefly with biologists. Margulis and Sagan, in their *Microcosmos* (1986), convinced me that I'm only an interloper living symbiotically with the bacteria in their domain. It was humbling for me to come to understand that this is the age of bacteria, that on Earth it's always been the age of bacteria, and that it's likely to be so until the sun blows. Unless, that is, it becomes the age of machines.

But let them tell their story:

That machines apparently depend on us for their construction and maintenance does not seem to be a serious argument against their viability. We depend on our organelles, such as mitochondria and chromosomes, for our life, yet no one ever argues that human beings are not really living. Are we simply containers for our living organelles? In the future humans may program machines to program and reproduce themselves more independently from human beings. (p. 259)

Margulis and Sagan share Moravec's view of the coming dominance of machines, and are, *sacre dieu,* even willing to consider including them among the living. But they do leave a ray of hope.

The most helpful note for human survival may be the fact that we are presently as necessary for the reproduction of our machines as mitochondria are for the reproduction of ourselves. But since economic forces will pressure machines to improve at everything, including the manufacture of machines with a minimum of human work, no one can say how long this hopeful note will last. (p. 259)

They even speculate on our roles should this ray of hope be realized.

Simply by extrapolating biospheric patterns, we may predict that humans will survive, if at all recognizably, as support systems connected to those forms of living organization with the greatest potential for perception and expansion, namely machines. The descendants of *Prochloron,* the chloroplasts, retained a much higher rate of growth inside plant cells than did *Prochloron,* their free-living green bacterial relatives patchily distributed in the Pacific Ocean. Analogously, human beings in association with machines already have a great selective advantage over those alienated from machines. (p. 260)

Viewed globally, domesticated cattle and sheep must be considered biologically successful. Their numbers are large and stable. They've a symbiotic relationship with humans by which they are provided food, reproductive assistance, protection from predators, and medical care. Nondomesticated cattle and sheep don't do so well by any of these measures. Perhaps we humans, as a species domesticated by our mind children, will do equally well in a world populated, perhaps dominated, by artificial minds, "silicon philosophers and planetary computers."

Thus our last and most speculative tour stop comes to a close. Before saying goodbye to the tour, let's recall some of what we've seen, and how the sights have supported the views of mind mentioned in the itinerary, if indeed they have.

Notes

1. My friend John Caulfield tells me that special-purpose quantum computers have been built, but I haven't yet been able to gather the specifics.

2. Personal communication.

3. From a message posted on Psyche-D, a disscussion group on the Internet, dated July 8, 1994.

4. A technical definition of fractal requires concepts that would take us too far afield, for instance, fractional Hausdorff dimension (Mandelbrot 1983; Barnsley 1988).

5. Moravec holds a diametrically opposite view, taking mind to be independent of body. Since this biased tour was designed to support a particular paradigm of mind, I won't take you to visit his speculations about transferring minds from body to body. But don't let my biases prevent you from making a side trip of your own to visit these wonders.

16

An Emerging New Paradigm of Mind?

The deliberate process we call reasoning is, I believe, the thinnest veneer of human thought.

—Hans Moravec, *Mind Children*

Alas (or Whew!), our tour of mechanisms of mind is winding down. As you can tell, your tour guide is both sad and relieved. We've visited with AIers, artificial lifers, cognitive scientists, computer scientists, connectionists, ethologists, evolutionary biologists, mathematicians, philosophers, physicists, neurophysiologists, roboticists, and probably some others I've forgotten. We've grappled with the mind–body problem and glimpsed three AI debates. We've encountered strange and wondrous architectures, models, strategies—all purported to be mechanisms of mind (by me, if not by their designers). Initially ridiculous-seeming ideas gradually became plausible or at least thinkable (I hope). And all the while, your tour guide was softly, and sometimes not so softly, selling an emerging new paradigm of mind. It's time to take stock. Exactly what is this supposed new paradigm? And is it really emerging?

Before embarking on this journey, I provided you a list of some seven assertions representing my biases. The attractions along the tour were chosen to support these biases. These assertions, taken together, constitute what seems to me to be the core of a new way of thinking about mind, a new paradigm. To begin our process of taking stock, let's review each of these assertions in the light of the problems, the debates, the architectures, the ideas we've encountered on our journey.

The most basic assertion of this new paradigm has to do with the function (purpose?) of mind.

The overriding task of Mind is to produce the next action. ("Producing" 'is used here in the sense that a producer "produces" a movie.) Minds are the control structures of autonomous agents. Note that "action" implies an environment on which to act. The agent is situated. The various cognitive functions—recognizing, categorizing, recalling, inferencing, planning—all ultimately serve what to do next. The senses do, too.

Actions are selected in the service of drives[1] built in by evolution or design. The evaluation nets of Ackley and Littman's agents, and the goals[2] to be built into Maes's hypothetical Mars rover illustrate built-in drives in artificial life agents. Brooks's hardwired subsumption architecture creatures do the same for robots. Examples from the animal world abound. Question: Do we humans have any built-in drives not found among our primate cousins, the great apes?

Agents select actions from among those allowed by their structure. I can't choose to flap my arms and fly. My structure won't allow it. This is part of what we've heard Maturana, and Varela et al., call structural coupling. Like drives, structure is determined by evolution or design, but unlike drives, also by interaction with the environment.

Viewing mind as action selection by autonomous agents has, as a corollary, another assertion of the new paradigm.

Mind is better viewed as continuous, as opposed to Boolean. It's more useful to allow degrees of mind than to demand either mind or no mind. We're likely to achieve a better and quicker understanding of our own minds by studying other minds. One can design autonomous agents with simple or complex control structures, agents with simple minds or complex minds, and a host of others in between. Still others may not be comparable with any of these. This assertion should not be interpreted as insisting on a *linear* continuum of minds.

This proposed use of "mind" does produce problems at a fuzzy boundary. A thermostat can be thought of as an autonomous agent sensing the world with its bimetallic strip and responding reflexively by tripping its relay, certainly a simple control structure. But do we want to call it a simple *mind?* Where are its built-in drives? Its single drive is surely to keep the temperature at a setting specified by the position of its lever or dial. But no such drive is explicitly represented in the thermostat. True.

But is my need to be appreciated explicitly represented by the mechanism my organism uses to try and satisfy it (say by conducting this tour)? I doubt it. To me, it's OK that this use of "mind" be fuzzy at the edges. That's in the nature of concepts other than mathematical concepts.

Structural coupling not only constrains actions, it constrains senses. I have no built-in senses allowing me to view an episode of "Star Trek: The Next Generation" directly. Yet an autonomous agent with such capability can surely be built. Senses come with structure that is determined by evolution or design, and by interaction with the environment. This brings us to the next assertion of the new paradigm.

Mind operates on sensations to <u>create</u> *information for its own use.* The widely accepted cognitivist paradigm views a mind as an information-processing machine, processing information taken in from the environment through the senses. We've heard Edelman, Freeman, and especially Varela et al. argue against this view of mind. We've met models of categorization by Edelman, and of prediction by Drescher, that illustrate, to my mind, the creating of information. Oyama (1985) gives the most thorough and persuasive account of information as created by mind. Recommended.

Maturana, and Varela et al., go further, arguing that information is created not from sensory *input* but from structural coupling. I agree. The information-processing view puts input in a three-part sequence: [input → processing → output]. In the context of animals, this suggests an independence of sensory and motor activity that doesn't exist. What I see depends heavily on what direction some set of muscles turns my head, and in what direction some other set turns my eyes. Sensory activity depending on motor activity. A loud noise off to my left will result in an almost automatic turning of my head to the left. Motor activity depending on sensory activity. Sensorimotor activity, the essence of structural couplings, cannot be easily teased into two.

Also, sensing and acting are not easily disentangled from cognition. All three are intricately interwoven. The phantom limb a person feels after amputation demonstrates that information (in this case misinformation) depends not only on what's out there but also what's in there. The Necker cube, a hologram, and the black and white disk that shows also red, blue, and green when spun, are other examples of this interconnection. And I haven't even mentioned how much expectation affects the information produced by high-level perception.

Ornstein points out that perception serves to filter, not to window. Only a minute fraction of available data becomes created information. Which fraction? That part the mind expects to be useful. We, as embodied autonomous agents structurally coupled to our environment, create our worlds to meet our needs.

An autonomous agent's creation of information is in the service of action selection, what to do next. Each such agent is designed or evolved with useful categories and schemas for action, or creates them as Darwin III and the schema mechanism did. Recall that Freeman's rabbit learned categories of odors, the desired response to which got him fed. Even with built-in categories, recognition is creation of information, as is enactment of routines à la Agre and Chapman. All these are part of structural coupling. Which categories, schemas, or routines will be useful depends on the structure of the agent and on the environment, that is, on the structural coupling of the agent with its environment. In a stable environment, more can be built in. In a dynamic environment, learning is a decided advantage. The creation of information from sensorimotor activity is always a must. And not only from sensorimotor activity, as the next assertion makes specific.

Mind re-creates prior information (memories) to help produce actions. Both filing cabinets and typical computer memories use a store-a-copy-and-retrieve-it-via-address strategy. For autonomous agents who must act on-line in real time, such memories are usually too slow and too costly in terms of space, especially when an agent doesn't know exactly what it's looking for and must search. Retrieval becomes problem solving. Acting on partial information and/or associative cues, a reconstructive strategy, as illustrated in Kanerva's sparse distributed memory, promises faster, more reliable action.

Although I do believe the previous statement, it's highly suspect. To my knowledge, such memory has not so far proved itself in any artificial autonomous agent. (When my posttour responsibilities are at an end, I hope to remedy this situation.) And, though I believe that we and many of our animal relatives use such a reconstructive strategy, hard evidence for such a view is scarce. And yet, it's beginning to be believed. My cognitive psychologist colleagues, although by no means ready to concur formally, no longer speak a word of opposition when I propose it or assume it. To me the appealing, if not convincing, argument comes from visual images. From either an actual view of my living room, or from a visual image of that same view, I can reconstruct much the same information. This includes recognition of objects, their categories, and their spatial relations. I strongly suspect the same constructive machinery is used in both cases. My admittedly weak case rests.

And how is this recognition, categorization, and relational machinery implemented? With dynamical system machinery. I believe that recognition, categorization, and such happen when some relevant pattern of (neural) activity falls into a particular basin of attraction in the appropriate state space. I'm *so* tempted to include this answer as another assertion of the new paradigm, but I don't dare. In spite of Freeman's seminal work, the evidence is too meager. "But," you reply, "that didn't stop you from making the last new paradigm assertion." Right you are, but there I was tempted by the tacit consent of colleagues. Here I have less such. Further, although I suspect it's often true of animals with nervous systems, I'm not sure it's always true. Probably some grandmother receptor cells do exist in simple animals, resulting in only a trivial dynamical system. And how about a single-cell organism? How does a paramecium swim down a temperature gradient? By the cilia on the warmer side being more active. Its global behavior emerges from multiple local actions, but not from a pattern of activity falling into some basin of attraction, as far as I can see.

The next assertion of our new paradigm, asserts the multiplicity of mind.

Minds tend to be embodied as collections of relatively independent modules, with little communication between them. This one is surely emerging. Its roots go back at least to Freud's id, ego, and superego. Fodor, in his *Modularity of Mind* (1983), suggests that human minds are formed of inborn, relatively independent, special-purpose modules. On our tour we've met such modules: Ornstein's talents, Minsky's agents, Jackson's demons, Maes's behaviors, Brooks's layers, Edelman's neuronal groups, Hofstadter and Mitchell's codelets, and probably others.

This assertion offers us a recursive view of mind. It looks as if the mind of each autonomous agent is composed of independent modules, each of which might be an autonomous agent itself. An infinite regress looms. It's time to remind ourselves of Minsky's warning: "Unless we can explain the mind in terms of things that have no thoughts or feelings of their own, we'll only have gone around in a circle" (1985, p. 18). Taking heed, our multiplicity of mind assertion must be understood as requiring a base of primitive modules that are not themselves autonomous agents, and hence have no mind. A mind may well be comprised of a hierarchy of modules, submodules, sub-submodules, and so on. Many may be autonomous, and thus have a mind of their own. But supporting the whole structure must be a collection of mindless waifs with no agenda of their own, doing only the bidding of others.

We still have the expected problems at the fuzzy boundary of the notion of an autonomous agent. Taken alone, a thermostat supports some argument that its action selection embodies a minimally simple mind. But suppose our thermostat is employed as the homeostatic temperature control of what the military would call an autonomous land vehicle (for the benefit of technical equipment, not humans). In this case, I'd be tempted to call the thermostat a mindless waif, especially if its temperature setting could be varied by the control system of the vehicle.

Just as a termite colony can build an amazing nest that no one of them could possibly know how to build, a collection of mindless modules can, by synergy, perform feats far beyond the capabilities of any one of them. As we've heard from Minsky before: "Each mental agent by itself can only do some simple thing that needs no mind or thought at all. Yet when we join these agents in societies . . . this leads to true intelligence" (1985, p. 17). As with termites, control is local, each module doing it own thing. From competition and cooperation between them, behaviors beyond any one of them emerge.

Emergent behavior is a corollary of the modularity of mind assertion, and in turn it implies the diversity of mind assertion.

Mind is enabled by a multitude of disparate mechanisms. Even among termites, there's a division of labor. At the very least the queen differs from the soldiers, who differ from the workers. It's hard for me to believe that much of a mind could be constructed from identical primitive modules. Edelman gave pride of place to the variability of his neuronal groups. In all the models of action selection we've visited, the modules have been diverse.

"But," the unified theory of cognition people would ask, "why can't identical modules perform different tasks, just as a computer runs different programs?" Here's the mind as computer analogy again, with minds being composed of a collection of identical modules performing different tasks. Which is correct, diversity or identity? It's the special-purpose device vs. the general-purpose device. Almost always, a device designed or evolved for a particular task can outperform a general-purpose device executing that same task.[3] Why? Because the flexibility of the general-purpose device comes at some cost. There's no free lunch. That's the source of my belief in the diversity theory. No designer would want to be limited, above a certain level of abstraction, to a single mechanism. When speed became an issue, as it inevitably would, the bottleneck modules would be replaced by special-purpose versions designed to operate faster.

That's not to say that there's no place for general-purpose devices. The computer I'm writing with will do much more than run a word processor. Flexibility is often worth a trade-off in speed. I'm also heavily involved in producing a general-purpose neurocomputer whose first application may well be to serve as brain for an artificial insect. But if it turns out to be too slow at some task, you can bet we'll try to introduce a faster special-purpose module.

As we've seen, Minsky is a great fan of diversity. Do spend a while with his *Society of Mind* (1985). There's much more there than we could visit on this tour. One mechanism of mind follows another. Diversity is rampant. And fascinating.

And finally, this new paradigm certainly takes sides in the first AI debate. If mind is the action selection mechanism of an autonomous agent, then surely some of Brooks's robots have simple minds. Thus: *Mind, to some degree, is implementable on machines.*

Well, there it is, all laid out in seven assertions. What shall we name this new infant?[4] The key idea seems to be expressed by the first assertion: mind as the action selection mechanism of an autonomous agent. So, how about the *action selection paradigm*[5] as a provisional moniker?

As we've seen, Varela et al. compared their enactive paradigms with two others via three basic questions. I propose to put the action selection paradigm in that perspective by composing answers to the same three questions. Here again, for your convenience and mine, are their answers to these basic questions for each of three paradigms.

Cognitivist answers

Question 1: What is cognition?
Answer: Information processing as symbolic computation—rule-based manipulation of symbols.

Question 2: How does it work?
Answer: Through any device that can support and manipulate discrete functional elements—the symbols. The system interacts only with the form of the symbols (their physical attributes), not their meaning.

Question 3: How do I know when a cognitive system is functioning adequately?
Answer: When the symbols appropriately represent some aspect of the real world, and the information processing leads to a successful solution of the problem given to the system.

Connectionist answers

Question 1: What is cognition?
Answer: The emergence of global states in a network of simple components.

Question 2: How does it work?
Answer: Through local rules for individual operation and rules for changes in the connectivity among the elements.

Question 3: How do I know when a cognitive system is functioning adequately?
Answer: When the emergent properties (and resulting structure) can be seen to correspond to a specific cognitive capacity—a successful solution to a required task.

Enactive answers

Question 1: What is cognition?
Answer: Enaction: a history of structural coupling that brings forth a world.

Question 2: How does it work?
Answer: Through a network consisting of multiple levels of interconnected, sensorimotor subnetworks.

Question 3: How do I know when a cognitive system is functioning adequately?
Answer: When it becomes part of an ongoing existing world (as the young of every species do) or shapes a new one (as happens in evolutionary history).

as to be almost indistinguishable. If we think of a long sequence of cognitive acts resulting in a history, we get the enactive formulation. If we think of a short sequence of cognitive acts resulting in selecting an action, we get the action selection formulation. Thus the first answers jibe, except for one emphasizing action selection and the other creation of a world via structural coupling. I'd be willing to expand my first answer to bring them even closer. *Revised answer to question 1: The process by which an autonomous agent selects actions, including those processes which by objectification, categorization, and so on create the agent's own world from its environment.* All this is surely part of the action selection paradigm.

The answers to the second question are a little easier to compare. Both paradigms embrace multiplicity of mind, with the action selection paradigm also including diversity and relative independence. Enaction specifies multiple levels, whereas action selection, remembering Maes's perfectly flat behavior selection network, does not. Also, enaction restricts itself to something like Brooks's subsumption architecture by insisting on sensorimotor subnetworks. Though quite fond of subsumption architectures, I don't believe they can do it all, and have framed the answer to question 2 so as to leave room for other types of mechanisms. The action selection paradigm also explicitly insists on action emerging from local cooperation and/or competition between these relatively independent modules.

The action selection answer to question 3 subsumes the first clause of the enactive answer; both require that the agent be embedded in its environment. To function adequately, the action selection paradigm further requires the agent to be successful in that environment, "successful" meaning "able to satisfy its needs over time." If our agent also learns, we may call it intelligent, according to van Heerden's definition as adapted by Wilson: "Intelligent behavior is to be repeatedly successful in satisfying one's psychological needs in diverse, observably different, situations on the basis of past experience" (1985). You may recall this definition from our visit with Wilson's Animat.

To sum up, the action selection paradigm seems to allow for cognitivist and connectionist mechanisms but to be both more restrictive and less restrictive, requiring an autonomous agent embedded in an environment

Though "minds" seems broader to me than "cognition," and the actic selection paradigm is meant as a paradigm of mind, I think "cognitio as used in the question above was meant to be taken broadly. So I'll sti with the questions as given. Here are some answers.

Action selection answers

Question 1:   What is cognition?
Answer: The process by which an autonomous agent selects actions.
Question 2:   How does it work?
Answer: Actions emerge from the interaction of multiple, diverse, rel tively independent modules.
Question 3:   How do I know when a cognitive system is functionir adequately?
Answer: When it successfully satisfies its needs within its environmen

With these answers in hand, let's see how the action selection paradig relates to the other three paradigms of mind.

Action Selection vs. Cognitivist Paradigm. Actions may certainly be s lected by rule-based manipulation of symbols. That's no problem. On th other hand, action selection requires an autonomous agent with no hu man in the loop to provide input and interpret output. Here we're sidin with the computational neuroethologists over symbolic AI. This positio also commits us to a stand on the first AI debate: "real" intelligence i possible only in an autonomous agent. Disembodied minds are out.

Action Selection vs. Connectionist Paradigm. Actions may, at leas equally well, be selected by connectionist modules, artificial neural net That's exactly what's intended for our proposed artificial insect. Bu there's still the need for an autonomous agent, which is required by th action selection paradigm but not by the connectionist.

The action selection paradigm seems almost to include both cognitiv ism and connectionism, but it differs from both of them in limiting min to autonomous agents. The situation vis-à-vis enaction is rather different I view the action selection paradigm as a further development of the en active paradigm.

Action Selection vs. Enactive Paradigm. In Varela et al.'s answer to th first question, whose history of structural coupling bringing forth a world are they talking about? The history of an embodied agent, presumably autonomous. Bringing forth a world is so close to creating information but allowing a diversity of mechanisms. It takes much of its meat from the enactive paradigm but changes the emphasis greatly and differs in how cognition is to be achieved.

Is the action selection paradigm actually emerging, or have I just made it up? Are we dealing with discovery or invention here? I don't know. Surely something is emerging. Critiques of the information-processing model of mind are blowing in the wind like leaves on a willow oak in the winter. We must have met half a dozen such critiques on this one tour. Artificial life conferences are held yearly now, and its first scholarly journal, *Artificial Life,* has appeared. Books are appearing with titles like *Emergent Computation* (Forrest 1991), *Designing Autonomous Agents* (Maes 1991a), and *Toward a Practice of Autonomous Systems* (Varela and Bourgine 1992). Conferences are springing up with names like "Adaptive Computing in Engineering Design and Control." Almost without effort I've accumulated several dozen references for an upcoming course on control of autonomous agents.

The work of ethologists on animal cognition (Griffin 1984; Cheney and Seyfarth 1990; Gallistel 1992; Barber 1993) lends strong support to degrees of mind. We've seen the notion of minds creating information pushed or supported by Maturana, Varela et al., Oyama, and Edelman. Memory as re-creation seems to have at least tacit support from many cognitive psychologists. We've seen the multiplicity and diversity of mind pushed by Fodor, Ornstein, Minsky, John Jackson, Edelman, Hofstadter and Mitchell, and probably others. This wide-ranging support comes from such diverse areas as philosophy, psychology, computer science, and neurophysiology. And we've seen first Moravec and then Margulis and Sagan predict superintelligent machines.

It's clear to me that the winds of change are blowing. It's not so clear that I've accurately gauged their directions. But that's not so important. These assertions, in context, raise a host of questions, and so may direct my research and that of my students for years to come. And if some prove false, discrediting them adds to our store of knowledge. I'm happy to have given the action selection paradigm a push, and will be eager to see if it flies or crashes. In either event I will have learned something.

Thus our tour of mechanisms of mind has come to an end, as all things must. For me, it's been rich and rewarding. I've learned a lot and have enjoyed almost every moment of it. I'm still awestruck by what we've seen. Maybe the mind–body problem will prove to have a solution after all. And maybe some of the attractions on this tour will contribute to it.

I hope you have found the tour entertaining and enlightening as well, and that it's lived up to its warning by expanding the concept of mind with which you started. I also hope that for many of you, the end of this tour is the beginning of further explorations through the references that follow or via other sources.

Ciao!

Notes

1. Drives are to be thought of as motivators serving built-in needs.

2. I've come to use "drive" to refer to built-in tendencies to pursue certain general ends, and "goal" as more specific and serving some drive or higher-level goal. Drives influence strategies, goals influence tactics.

3. Recall my surprise that general-purpose SOAR could emulate part of R1, and VAX configuring expert system, at two-thirds of R1's speed.

4. I've struggled mightily to find the right name, consulted others, stewed, stayed awake. Finally, I've consoled myself by realizing that the name I chose most probably wouldn't stick even if this newborn paradigm enjoys a long life. No doubt the PDP group struggled over "parallel distributed processing," which was soon superseded by "connectionism."

5. My thanks to Phil Franklin for jogging me into this name.

References

Ackley, David, and Littman, Michael. (1992). "Interactions Between Learning and Evolution." In Christopher Langton et al., ed., *Artificial Life II*. Redwood City, Calif.: Addison-Wesley. 487–509.

Agre, Philip E. (forthcoming 1995). *The Dynamic Structure of Everyday Life*. Cambridge: Cambridge University Press.

Agre, Philip E., and Chapman, David. (1987a). "Pengi: An Implementation of a Theory of Activity." *Proceedings of AAAI-87*. Menlo Park, CA: AAAI 268–72.

Agre, Philip E., and Chapman, David. (1987b), "From Reaction to Participation." MIT Artificial Intelligence Laboratory, p. 2.

Agre, Philip E. and Chapman, David. (1988). "Indexicality and the Binding Problem." *Proceedings of the AAAI Symposium on Parallel Models*. Menlo Park, CA: AAAI 1–9.

Almasi, George S., and Gottlieb, Allan. (1989). *Highly Parallel Computing*. Redwood City, Calif.: Benjamin/Cummings.

Anderson, J. A., and Rosenfeld, E., eds. (1988). *Neurocomputing: Foundations of Research*. Cambridge, Mass.: MIT Press.

Anderson, James R. (1983). *The Architecture of Cognition*. Cambridge, Mass.: Harvard University Press.

Andersson, R. L. (1988). *A Robot Ping-Pong Player*. Cambridge, Mass.: MIT Press.

Armstrong, D. M. (1987). "Mind–Body Problem: Philosophical Theories." In R. L. Gregory, ed., *The Oxford Companion to the Mind*. Oxford: Oxford University Press. 490–91.

Baggett, W. B., Graesser, A. C., Franklin, S. P., and Swamer, S. S. (1993). "Speech Act Prediction and Recursive Transition Networks." *Proceedings of the Society for Text and Discourse,* Boulder, Colo.

Barber, T. X. (1993). *The Human Nature of Birds*. New York: St. Martin's Press.

Barnsley, Michael. (1988). *Fractals Everywhere*. Boston: Academic Press.

Beer, Randall D. (1990). *Intelligence as Adaptive Behavior.* Boston: Academic Press.

Benedict, Ruth. (1934). *Patterns of Culture.* Boston: Houghton Mifflin.

Berlekamp, E. R., Conway, J. H., and Guy, R. K. (1982). *Winning Ways for Your Mathematical Plays.* London and New York: Academic Press.

Brooks, Rodney A. (1989). "A Robot That Walks: Emergent Behaviors from a Carefully Evolved Network." *Neural Computation,* 1: 253–62.

Brooks, Rodney A. (1990a). "A Robust Layered Control System for a Mobile Robot." In P. H. Winston, ed., *Artificial Intelligence at MIT,* vol. 2. Cambridge, Mass.: MIT Press.

Brooks, Rodney A. (1990b). "A Robot That Walks: Emergent Behaviors from a Carefully Evolved Network." In P. H. Winston, ed., *Artificial Intelligence at MIT,* vol. 2. Cambridge, Mass.: MIT Press.

Brooks, Rodney A. (1990c). "Elephants Don't Play Chess." In Pattie Maes, ed., *Designing Autonomous Agents.* Cambridge, Mass.: MIT Press.

Brooks, Rodney A. (1991). "Intelligence Without Representation." *Artificial Intelligence,* 47: 139–159.

Brown, Frank, M., ed. (1987). *The Frame Problem in Artificial Intelligence.* Los Altos, Calif.: Morgan Kaufman.

Brustoloni, Jose C. (1991). "Autonomous Agents: Characterization and Requirements." Carnegie Mellon Technical Report CMU-CS-91-204. Pittsburgh: Carnegie Mellon University.

Buchanan, B. G., and Shortliffe, E. H. (1984). *Rule Based Expert Systems.* Reading, Mass.: Addison-Wesley.

Calvin, William H. (1990). *The Cerebral Symphony.* New York: Bantam Books.

Calvin, William H. (1991). *The Ascent of Mind.* New York: Bantam Books.

Calvin, William H. (1992). "Association Cortex as a Darwinian Workspace: Corticocortical Axons Suggest Cloning from Hexagonal Engrams." *Society for Neuroscience Abstracts,* 18:214–18.

Calvin, William H. (1993). "Error-Correcting Codes: Coherent Hexagonal Copying from Fuzzy Neuroanatomy." *World Congress on Neural Networks Proceedings,* 1:101–104.

Caulfield, H. J., Garzon, M. H., Boyd, W. S., and Franklin, S. P. (submitted). "Acousto-optical Implementation of a General-Purpose Neurocomputer."

Chalmers, David J. (1990). "Syntactic Transformations on Distributed Representations." *Connection Science,* 2: 53–62.

Chalmers, David J. (1991). "Consciousness and Cognition." Center for Research on Concepts and Cognition, Indiana University. Preprint.

Chalmers, David J., French, Robert M., and Hofstadter, Douglas R. (1992). "High-Level Perception, Representation, and Analogy: A Critique of Artificial Intelligence Methodology." *Journal of Experimental and Theoretical Artificial Intelligence,* 185–212.

Chan, D. K. H. (1994). "Physical Realizations of Computational Models of Mind." Forthcoming.

Chapman, David. (1987). "Planning for Conjunctive Goals." *Artificial Intelligence,* 32: 333–77.

Chapman, David. (1991). *Vision, Instruction and Action.* Cambridge, Mass.: MIT Press.

Chapman, David, and Agre, Philip E. (1987). "Abstract Reasoning as Emergent from Concrete Activity." In M. P. Georgeff and A. L. Lansky, eds., *Reasoning About Actions and Plans.* Los Altos, Calif.: Morgan Kaufman. 411–24.

Cheney, Dorothy L., and Seyfarth, Robert M. (1990). *How Monkeys See the World.* Chicago: University of Chicago Press.

Cliff, D. T. (1991). "Computational Neuroethology: A Provisional Manifesto." in J.-A. Meyer and S. W. Wilson, eds., *From Animals to Animats.* Cambridge, Mass.: MIT Press. 29–39.

Cohn, Ronald, and Patterson, Francine. (1991). "Koko Speaks English Using Apple Computer." *Gorilla,* 15:1, 2–4.

Collins, Robert James. (1992). *Studies in Artificial Evolution.* Ann Arbor, Mich.: University Microfilms International.

Crevier, Daniel. (1993). *AI: The Tumultuous History of the Search for Artificial Intelligence.* New York: Basic Books.

Crick, Francis. (1981). *Life Itself.* New York: Simon and Schuster.

Crick, Francis. (1994). *The Astonishing Hypothesis.* New York: Scribner's.

Davies, Paul. (1988). *The Cosmic Blueprint.* New York: Simon and Schuster.

Dawkins, Richard. (1976). *The Selfish Gene.* Oxford: Oxford University Press.

Dawkins, Richard. (1982). *The Extended Phenotype.* Oxford: Oxford University Press.

Dawkins, Richard. (1987). *The Blind Watchmaker.* New York: Norton.

Dennett, Daniel. (1987). *The Intentional Stance.* Cambridge, Mass.: MIT Press.

Dennett, Daniel. (1989). "Murmurs in the Cathedral." *Times Literary Supplement,* September 29–October 5, 1055–56.

Dennett, Daniel. (1991). *Consciousness Explained.* Boston: Little Brown.

Dethie, V. G. (1986). "The Magic of Metamorphosis: Nature's Own Sleight of Hand." *Smithsonian,* 17: 122.

Deutsch, David. (1985). "Quantum Theory, the Church-Turing Principle, and the Universal Quantum Computer." *Proceedings of the Royal Society* (London), A400:97–117.

Deutsch, D., and Jozsa, R. (1992). "Rapid Solutions of Problems by Quantum Computation." *Proceedings of the Royal Society* (London) A439: 553.

Devaney, Robert L. (1987). *An Introduction to Chaotic Dynamical Systems.* Reading, Mass.: Addison-Wesley.

Diamond, Jarad. (1992). *The Third Chimpanzee*. New York: HarperCollins.

Drescher, Gary L. (1986). "Genetic AI: Translating Piaget into LISP." MIT AI Memo 890.

Drescher, Gary L. (1987). "A Mechanism for Early Piagetian Learning." *Proceedings of AAAI-87*. Menlo Park, CA: AAAI 290–94.

Drescher, Gary L. (1988). "Learning from Experience Without Prior Knowledge in a Complicated World." *Proceedings of the AAAI Symposium on Parallel Models*. Meno Park, CA: AAAI 96–96.

Drescher, Gary L. (1991). *Made-up Minds*. Cambridge, Mass.: MIT Press.

Dreyfus, Hubert L., and Dreyfus, Stuart E. (1987). "How to Stop Worrying About the Frame Problem even Though It's Computationally Insoluble." In Z. W. Pylyshyn, ed., *The Robot's Dilemma*. Norwood, NJ: Ablex.

Dreyfus, Hubert L., and Stuart E. Dreyfus. (1988). "Making a Mind Versus Modeling the Brain: Artificial Intelligence Back at a Branchpoint." In Stephen R. Graubard, ed., *The Artificial Intelligence Debate*. Cambridge, Mass.: MIT Press.

Dyer, Michael G. (1991). "A Society of Ideas on Cognition: Review of Marvin Minsky's *The Society of Mind*." *Artificial Intelligence*, 48:321–34.

Edelman, Gerald M. (1987). *Neural Darwinism: The Theory of Neuronal Group Selection*. New York: Basic Books.

Edelman, Gerald M. (1988). *Topobiology: An Introduction to Molecular Embryology*. New York: Basic Books.

Edelman, Gerald M. (1989). *The Remembered Present: A Biological Theory of Consciousness*. New York: Basic Books.

Edelman, Gerald M. (1992). *Bright Air, Brilliant Fire*. New York: Basic Books.

Edelman, Shimon. (1993). "Representation, Similarity, and the Chorus of Prototypes." Preprint, Dept. of Applied Mathematics and Computer Science, Weizmann Institute of Science, Rehovot 76100, Israel.

Fodor, J. A. (1975). *The Language of Thought*. New York: Crowell. Paperback, Cambridge, Mass.: Harvard University Press, 1979.

Fodor, J. A. (1983). *The Modularity of Mind*. Cambridge, Mass.: MIT Press.

Fodor, J. A., and McLaughlin, B. (1991). "What Is Wrong with Tensor Product Connectionism?" In T. Horgan and J. Tienson, eds., *Connectionism and the Philosophy of Mind*. Dordrecht, Netherlands, and Cambridge, Mass.: Kluwer.

Fodor, J. A., and Pylyshyn, A. (1988). "Connectionism and Cognitive Architecture: A Critical Analysis." *Cognition*, 28: 3–71.

Fogelman Soulie, F., Robert, Y., and Tchuente, M., eds. (1987). *Automata Networks in Computer Science*. Princeton: Princeton University Press.

Foner, L. N., and Maes, Pattie. (1994). "Paying Attention to What's Important: Using Focus of Attention to Improve Unsupervised Learning." *Proceedings of the Third International Conference on the Simulation of Adaptive Behavior*. Brighton, England.

Forgy, C., and McDermott, J. (1977). "OPS, a Domain-Independent Production System Language." *Proceedings of the Fifth International Joint Conference on AI.* 933–939.

Forrest, Stephanie. (1991). *Emergent Computation.* Cambridge, Mass.: MIT Press.

Franklin, Stan, and Garzon, Max. (1989). "Global Dynamics in Neural Networks." *Complex Systems,* 3: 29–36.

Franklin, Stan, and Garzon, Max. (1991). "Neural Computability." In O. M. Omidvar, ed., *Progress in Neural Networks,* vol. 1. Norwood, NJ: Ablex. 127–45.

Franklin, Stan, and Garzon, Max. (1992). "On Stability and Solvability (or, When Does a Neural Network Solve a Problem?)" *Minds and Machines,* 2: 71–83.

Franklin, Stan, and Garzon, Max. (to appear). "Computability via Discrete Neural Nets." In David Rumelhart, Paul Smolensky and M. C. Mozer, eds., *Mathematical Perspectives on Neural Networks.* Hillsdale, N.J.: Erlbaum.

Freedman, David H. (1991). "Invasion of the Insect Robots." *Discover,* March, 42–50.

Freedman, David H. (1994). "Quantum Consciousness." *Discover,* June, 89–98.

Freeman, Walter J. (1983). "The Physiological Basis of Mental Images." *Biological Psychiatry,* 18, 10: 1107–25.

Freeman, Walter J. (1987). "Why Neural Networks Don't Yet Fly: Inquiry into the Neurodynamics of Biological Intelligence." *Proceedings of the First International Conference on Neural Networks,* II, 1–7.

Freeman, W. J., and Skarda, C. A. (1990). "Representations: Who Needs Them?" In J. L. McGaugh, et al., eds., *Brain Organization and Memory Cells, System, & Circuits.* New York: Oxford University Press. 375–80.

Frege, Gottlob. (1893). *Grundgesetze der Arithmetik: Begriffsschriftlich abgeleitet,* vol. 1. Jena: Pohle. Reprinted Hildesheim, Germany: Olms, 1962. Partial English translation in Frege 1964.

Frege, Gottlob. (1903). *Grundgesetze der Arithmetik: Begriffsschriftlich abgeleitet,* vol. 2. Jena: Pohle. Reprinted Hildesheim, Germany: Olms, 1962. Partial English translation in Frege 1964.

Frege, Gottlob. (1964). *The Basic Laws of Arithmetic. Exposition of the System.* Translated and edited, with an introduction, by Montgomery Furth. Berkeley and Los Angeles: University of California Press.

Gallistel, C. R. (1992). *Animal Cognition.* Cambridge, Mass.: MIT Press.

Gallup, G. G., Jr. (1970). "Chimpanzees: Self-Recognition." *Science,* 167: 86–87.

Gallup, G. G., Jr. (1977a). "Absence of Self-Recognition in a Monkey (*Macaca fascicularis*) Following Prolonged Exposure to a Mirror." *Developmental Psychobiology,* 10: 281–84.

Gallup, G. G., Jr. (1977b). "Self-Recognition in Primates: A Comparative Approach to Bidirection Properties of Consciousness." *American Psychologist,* 32: 329–38.

Garzon, Max, and Franklin, Stan. (1990). "Global Dynamics in Neural Networks II." *Complex Systems*, 4: 509–18.

Garzon, Max, and Franklin, Stan. (1994). "Computation on Graphs: From Neural Networks to Cellular Automata." In O. M. Omidvar, ed., *Progress in Neural Networks*, vol. 2. Norwood, NJ: Ablex. 229–51.

Garzon, Max, Franklin, Stan, Baggett, William, Boyd, William, and Dickerson, Dinah. (1992). "Design and Testing of a General Purpose Neurocomputer." *Journal of Parallel and Distributed Computing*, 14: 203–20.

Gazzaniga, Michael S. (1985). *The Social Brain*. New York: Basic Books.

Gazzaniga, Michael S. (1988). *Mind Matters*. Boston: Houghton Mifflin.

Gazzaniga, Michael S. (1992). *Nature's Mind*. New York: Basic Books.

Gleick, James. (1987). *Chaos*. New York: Viking.

Gödel, Kurt. (1931). "Über formal unentscheidbare Sätze der *Principia mathematica* und verwandter Systeme I." *Monatshefte für Mathematik und Physik*, 38: 173–98. English translation in Gödel 1962.

Gödel, Kurt. (1962). *On Formally Undecidable Propositions of Principia mathematica and Related Systems*. Translated by B. Meltzer with an introduction by R. B. Braithwaite. Edinburgh and London: Oliver and Boyd.

Goldberg, Adele, and Robson, David. (1983). *Smalltalk-80: the Language and Its Implementation*. Reading, Mass.: Addison-Wesley.

Goldberg, David E. (1989). *Genetic Algorithms*. Reading, Mass.: Addison-Wesley.

Golden, Frederic. (1991). "Clever Kanzi." *Discover*, March, 20.

Goodall, Jane (1986). *The Chimpanzees of Gombe: Patterns of Behavior*. Cambridge, Mass.: Harvard University Press.

Gordon, Wendy, and Patterson, Penny. (1990). *Gorilla*, 14: 10.

Gould, Stephen Jay. (1989). *Wonderful Life*. New York: Norton.

Graesser, Arthur C., and Franklin, Stan. (1990). "QUEST: A Cognitive Model of Questioning Answering." *Discourse Processes*, 13, 3: 279–304.

Graubard, Stephen R., ed. (1988). *The Artificial Intelligence Debate*. Cambridge, Mass.: MIT Press.

Gregory, Richard, ed. (1987). *The Oxford Companion to the Mind*. Oxford: Oxford University Press.

Griffin, Donald R. (1984). *Animal Thinking*. Cambridge, Mass.: Harvard University Press.

Hameroff, S. R. (1987). *Ultimate Computing: Biomolecular Consciousness and Nanotechnology*. Amsterdam: Elsevier–North Holland.

Hameroff, S. R. (in press). "Quantum Coherence in Microtubules: An Intraneuronal Substrate for Emergent Consciousness." *Journal of Consciousness Studies*.

Harel, David. (1987). *Algorithmics*. Reading, Mass.: Addison-Wesley.

Haugeland, John. (1985). *Artificial Intelligence: The Very Idea*. Cambridge, Mass.: MIT Press.

Hebb, Donald O. (1949). *The Organization of Behavior*. New York: Wiley.

Herbert, Nick. (1985) *Quantum Reality*. Garden City, N.Y.: Anchor Press/ Doubleday.

Herman, Richards, and Wolz, (1984). "Comprehension of Sentences by Bottlenose Dolphins." *Cognition* 16: 129–219.

Hilbert, David. (1901). "Mathematische Probleme." Vortrag, gehalten auf dem Internationalen Mathematiker-Kongress zu Paris 1900. *Archiv der Mathematic und Physik*, 3rd ser. 1: 44–63, 213–37.

Hillis, W. Daniel. (1985). *The Connection Machine*. Cambridge, Mass.: MIT Press.

Hillis, W. Daniel. (1992). "Co-evolving Parasites Improve Simulated Evolution as an Optimization Procedure." In Christopher Langton et al., eds., *Artificial Life II*. Redwood City, Calif.: Addison-Wesley. 313–24.

Hillis, W. Daniel, and Steele, Guy L., Jr. (1986). "Data Parallel Algorithms." *Communications of the Association for Computing Machinery*, 29, 12: 1170–83.

Hinton, G. E. (1986). "Learning Distributed Representation of Concepts." In *Proceedings of the Eighth Annual Meeting of the Cognitive Science Society*. Hillsdale, N.J.: Erlbaum.

Hofstadter, Douglas R. (1979). *Gödel, Escher, Bach*. New York: Basic Books.

Hofstadter, Douglas R. (1984). "The Copycat Project: An Experiment in Nondeterminism and Creative Analogies." AI Memo 755. Artificial Intelligence Laboratory, Massachusetts Institute of Technology.

Hofstadter, Douglas R. (1985). "Analogies and Roles in Human and Machine Thinking." In *Metamagical Themas*. New York: Basic Books.

Hofstadter, Douglas R., and Dennett, Daniel C. (1981). *The Mind's I*. Toronto: Bantam Books.

Holland, John H. (1975). *Adaptation in Natural and Artificial Systems*. Ann Arbor: University of Michigan Press.

Holland, John H. (1992). "Genetic Algorithms." *Scientific American*, June, 66–72.

Holland, John H., Holyoak, K. J., Nisbett, R. E., and Thargard, P. R. (1986). *Induction*. Cambridge, Mass.: MIT Press.

Holland, J. H., and Reitman, J. S. (1979). "Cognitive Systems Based on Adaptive Algorithms." In Waterman and Hayes-Roth, eds., *Pattern-Directed Inference Systems*. New York: Academic Press.

Horgan, John. (1994). "Can Science Explain Consciousness?" *Scientific American*, July, 88–94.

Horgan, Terence, and Tienson, John. (1989). "Representations Without Rules." *Philosophical Topics*, 17 (Spring): 147–74.

Jackson, Frank. (1982). "Epiphenomenal Qualia." *Philosophical Quarterly,* 32: 127–36.

Jackson, John V. (1987). "Idea for a Mind." *SIGGART Newsletter,* no. 181 (July): 23–26.

Jibu, M., Hagan, S., Hameroff, S., Pribram, K., and Yasue, K. (1994). "Quantum Optical Coherence in Cytoskeletal Microtubule: Implications for Brain Function." *BioSystems* (in press).

Johnson, M., and Scanlon, R. (1987). "Experiences with a Feeling-Thinking Machine." *Proceedings of the IEEE First International Conference on Neural Networks, San Diego.* 71–77.

Just, M. A., and Carpenter, P. A. (1987). *The Psychology of Reading and Language Comprehension.* Boston: Allyn and Bacon.

Kak, Subsash. (1992). "Can We Build a Quantum Neural Computer?" Technical Report ECE/LSU 92-13. Baton Rouge: Louisiana State University Electrical and Computer Engineering Department.

Kanerva, Pentti. (1988a). *Sparse Distributed Memory.* Cambridge, Mass.: MIT Press.

Kanerva, Pentti. (1988b). "Computing with Very Large Patterns." In W. Daniel Hillis, ed., *Parallel Models of Intelligence.* Menlo Park, Calif.: AAAI. 163–69.

Kauffman, Stuart A. (1993). *The Origins of Order.* Oxford: Oxford University Press.

Kilman, David, Dickerson, Dinah, Franklin, Stan, and Wong, Seok. (1992). "Parallel Genetic Search via Clans." In C. H. Dagle et al., eds., *Intelligent Engineering Systems Through Artificial Neural Networks,* vol. 2. New York: ASME Press. 927–35.

Laird, John E., Newell, Allen, and Rosenbloom, Paul S. (1987). "SOAR: An Architecture for General Intelligence." *Artificial Intelligence,* 33: 1–64.

Laird, John E., Hucka, M., Yager, E. S., and Tuck, C. M. (in press). "Robo-Soar: An Integration of External Interaction, Planning and Learning Using Soar." *Robotics and Autonomus Systems.*

Laird, John E., and Rosenbloom, Paul S. (1990). "Integrating Planning, Execution and Learning in Soar for External Environments." In *Proceedings of the Eighth National Conference on Artificial Intelligence,* Menlo Park, Calif: AAAI Press. 1022–29.

Laird, John E., Yager, E. S., Tuck, C. M., and Hucka, M. (1989). "Learning in Autonomous Systems Using Soar." In *Proceedings of the NASA Conference on Space Telerobotics.* Pasadena, Calif.: Jet Propulsion Laboratory.

Langley, P. W. (1977). "Rediscovering Physics with BACON 3." In *Proceedings of the Sixth International Joint Conference on Artificial Intelligence.* Menlo Park, Calif.: AAAI. 505–7.

Langley, P. W. (1980). "Discriptive Discovery Processes: Experiments in Baconian Science." Report CS-80-121. Ph.D. diss., Computer Science Department, Carnegie-Mellon University.

Langton, Christopher. (1992a). "Life at the Edge of Chaos." In Christopher Langton et al., eds., *Artificial Life II*. Redwood City, Calif.: Addison-Wesley. 41–91.

Langton, Christopher, ed. (1989). *Artificial Life*. Redwood City, Calif.: Addison-Wesley.

Langton, Christopher, ed. (1992b). *Artificial Life II Video Proceedings*. Redwood City, Calif.: Addison-Wesley.

Langton, Christopher, ed. (1994). *Artificial Life III*. Redwood City, Calif.: Addison-Wesley.

Langton, Christopher, Taylor, C., Farmer, J. D., and Rasmussen, S., eds. (1992). *Artificial Life II*. Redwood City, Calif.: Addison-Wesley.

Lao-Tzu. (1988). *Tao Te Ching*. Translated by Stephen Mitchell. New York: Harper & Row.

Levy, Steven. (1992). *Artificial Life*. New York: Pantheon Books.

Lloyd, Dan. (1989). *Simple Minds*. Cambridge, Mass.: MIT Press.

Lucas, J. R. (1961). "Minds, Machines and Gödel." *Philosophy*, 36: 112–27.

MacKay, Donald M. (1965). "From Mechanism to Mind." In J. R. Smythies, ed., *Brain and Mind: Modern Conceptions of the Nature of Mind*. London: Routledge and Kegan Paul.

Maes, Pattie. (1990). "How to Do the Right Thing." *Connection Science*, 1:3.

Maes, Pattie. (1991a). *Designing Autonomous Agents*. Cambridge, Mass.: MIT Press.

Maes, Pattie. (1991b). "A Bottom-up Mechanism for Behavior Selection in an Artificial Creature." In J.-A. Meyer and S. W. Wilson, eds., *From Animals to Animals*. Cambridge, Mass.: MIT Press. 238–46.

Maes, Pattie, and Brooks, Rodney A. (1990). "Learning to Coordinate Behaviors." In *Proceedings of the Eighth National Conference on Artificial Intelligence*. Menlo Park, Calif.: AAAI. 796–802.

Mahowald, Misha A., and Douglas, Rodney J. (1991a). *Nature*, December 19–26.

Mahowald, Misha, and Douglas, Rodney J. (1991b). Described in *Science News*, 140, 25–26: 407.

Mahowald, Misha A., and Mead, Carver. (1991). "The Silicon Retina." *Scientific American*, May, 76–82.

Mandelbrot, Benoit B. (1983). *The Fractal Geometry of Nature*. New York: Freeman.

Margulis, Lynn, and Sagan, Dorion. (1986). *Microcosmos*. New York: Simon and Schuster.

Maturana, Humberto R. (1975). "The Organization of the Living: A Theory of the Living Organization." *International Journal of Man-Machine Studies*, 7:313–32.

Maturana, Humberto R., and Varela, Francisco. (1980). *Autopoiesis and Cognition: The Realization of the Living*. Dordrecht, Netherlands: Reidel.

McClelland, James L., and Rumelhart, David E. (1981). "An Interactive Activation Model of Context Effects in Letter Perception: Part 1. An Account of Basic Findings." *Pyschological Review,* 88: 375–407.

McClelland, James L., David E. Rumelhart, et al. (1988). *Explorations in Parallel Distributed Processing,* vol. 2. Cambridge, Mass.: MIT Press.

McClelland, James L., Rumelhart, David E., et al. (1986). *Parallel Distributed Processing,* vol. 1. Cambridge, Mass.: MIT Press.

McClelland, J. L., Rumelhart, D. E., and Hinton, G. E. (1986). "The Appeal of Parallel Distributed Processing." In David E. Rumelhart, James L. McClelland, et al., eds., *Parallel Distributed Processing,* vol. 1. Cambridge, Mass.: MIT Press.

McCulloch, W. S., and Pitts, Walter. (1943). "A Logical Calculus of the Ideas Immanent in Nervous Activity." *Bulletin of Mathematical Biophysics,* 5:115–33.

Mead, Carver. (1989). *Analog VLSI and Neural Systems.* Reading, Mass.: Addison-Wesley.

Minsky, Marvin. (1975). "A Framework for the Representation of Knowledge." In P. Winston, ed., *The Psychology of Computer Vision.* New York: McGraw-Hill.

Minsky, Marvin. (1980). "K-Lines: A Theory of Memory." *Cognitive Science,* 4:2.

Minsky, Marvin. (1985). *Society of Mind.* New York: Simon and Schuster.

Mitchell, Melanie. (1993). *Analogy-Making as Perception.* Cambridge, Mass.: MIT Press.

Mitchell, M., Crutchfield, J. P., and Hraber, P. T. (to appear). "Dynamics, Computation, and the 'Edge of Chaos': A Re-Examination." In G. Cowan et al., eds., *Integrative Themes.* Reading, Mass.: Addison-Wesley.

Mitchell, M., and Hofstadter, D. R. (1990). "The Emergence of Understanding in a Computer Model of Concepts and Analogy-making." *Physica* D 42: 322–34. Reprinted in S. Forrest, ed., *Emergent Computation.* Cambridge, Mass.: MIT Press, 1991.

Moravec, Hans. (1988). *Mind Children.* Cambridge, Mass.: Harvard University Press.

Nagel, Thomas. (1974). "What Is It like to Be a Bat?" *The Philosophical Review,* October. Reprinted in Hofstadter and Dennett (1981).

Newell, Allen. (1990). *Unified Theories of Cognition.* Cambridge, Mass.: Harvard University Press.

Newell, Allen, and Simon, Herbert A. (1972). *Human Problem Solving.* Englewood Cliffs, N.J.: Prentice-Hall.

Nilsson, Nils J. (1980). *Principles of Artificial Intelligence.* Palo Alto, Calif.: Tioga.

Ornstein, Robert. (1986). *Multimind.* Boston: Houghton Mifflin.

Oyama, Susan. (1985). *The Ontogeny of Information.* Cambridge: Cambridge University Press.

Patterson, Francine. (1991). "Self-Awareness in the Gorilla Koko." *Gorilla,* 14:2.

Penfield, Wilder. (1975). *The Mystery of the Mind.* Princeton: Princeton University Press.

Penrose, Roger. (1989). *The Emperor's New Mind.* Oxford: Oxford University Press.

Penrose, Roger. (1990). Precis of *The Emperor's New Mind. Behavioral and Brain Sciences,* 13: 643–705.

Penrose, Roger. (1994). *Shadows of the Mind.* Oxford: Oxford University Press.

Pepperberg, I. M. (1981). "Functional Vocalizations by an African Grey Parrot (*Psittacus erithacus*)." *Zeitschrift für Tierpsychologie,* 55: 139–60.

Pepperberg, I. M. (1983). "Cognition in the African Grey Parrot: Preliminary Evidence for Auditory/Vocal Comprehension of the Class Concept." *Animal Learning and Behavior,* 11: 179–85.

Pollack, Jordan. (1990). "Recursive Distributed Representations." *Artificial Intelligence,* 46: 77–106.

Post, E. (1934). "Formal Reductions of the General Combinatorial Problem." *American Journal of Mathematics* 65: 197–268.

Potts, Richard. (1991). "Untying the Knot: Evolution of Early Human Behavior." In M. H. Robinson and L. Tiger, eds., *Man and Beast Revisited.* Washington, DC: Smithsonian Institution Press.

Poundstone, William. (1985). *The Recursive Universe.* New York: Morrow.

Prigogine, I., and Stengers, I. (1984). *Order out of Chaos.* New York: Bantam Books.

Putnam, Hilary. (1981). *Reason, Truth and History.* Cambridge: Cambridge University Press.

Ray, Thomas S. (1992). "An Approach to the Synthesis of Life." In Christopher Langton et al., eds., *Artificial Life II.* Redwood City, Calif.: Addison-Wesley. 371–408.

Reeke, George N., Jr., and Edelman, Gerald M. (1988). "Real Brains and Artificial Intelligence." *Daedalus,* Winter, 143–73. Reprinted in S. R. Graubard, ed., *The Artificial Intelligence Debate.* Cambridge, Mass.: MIT Press, 1988.

Reynolds, C. W. (1987). "Flocks, Herds, and Schools: A Distributed Behavioral Model (Proceedings of SIGGRAPH '87)." *Computer Graphics* 21, 4: 24–34.

Rich, Elaine, and Knight, Kevin. (1991). *Artificial Intelligence.* 2nd ed. New York: McGraw-Hill.

Richardson, D. (1972). "Tessellation with Local Transformations." *Journal of Computation and System Science,* 6: 373–88.

Rosenbloom, Paul S., Newell, Allen, and Laird, John E. (1991). "Toward the Knowledge Level in Soar: The Role of the Architecture in the Use of Knowledge." In Kurt VanLehn, ed., *Architectures for Intelligence*. Hillsdale, N.J.: Erlbaum. 75–111.

Rowan, Andrew N. (1991). "The Human-Animal Interface." In M. H. Robinson and L. Tiger, eds., *Man and Beast Revisited*. Washington, DC: Smithsonian Institution Press.

Rumelhart, David E., Hinton, G. E., and Williams, R. J. (1986). "Learning Internal Representations by Error Propagation." In David E. Rumelhart, James L. McClelland, et al., eds., *Parallel Distributed Processing*, vol. 1. Cambridge, Mass.: MIT Press.

Rumelhart, David E., and McCelland, James L. (1982). "An Interactive Activation Model of Context Effects in Letter Perception: Part 2. The Contextual Enhancement Effect and Some Tests and Extensions of the Model." *Psychological Review*, 89: 60–94.

Rumelhart, David E., McCelland, James L., et al. (1986). *Parallel Distributed Processing*, vol. 1. Cambridge, Mass.: MIT Press.

Sacks, O., and Wasserman, R. (1987). "The Case of the Colorblind Painter." *New York Review of Books*, November 19, 25–34.

St. John, Mark F., and McCelland, James L. (1990). "Learning and Applying Contextual Constraints in Sentence Comprehension." *Artificial Intelligence*, 46: 217–57.

Schaller, George. (1972). *The Serengeti Lion*. Chicago: University of Chicago Press.

Schank, R. C. (1980). "Language and Memory." *Cognitive Science*, 4:243–84.

Schank, R. C., and Abelson, R. P. (1977). *Scripts, Plans, Goals and Understanding*. Hillsdale, N.J.: Erlbaum.

Schrödinger, E. (1935). "Die gegenwartige Situation in der Quantenmechanik." *Naturwissenchaften*, 23: 807–12, 823–28, 844–49. Translated by J. T. Trimmer in *Proceedings of the American Philosophical Society*, 124 (1980): 328–38. Also in J. A. Wheeler and W. H. Zurek, eds., *Quantum Theory and Measurement*. Princeton: Princeton University Press, 1983.

Searle, J. (1980). "Minds, Brains, and Programs." *Behavioral and Brain Sciences* 3:417–58.

Sejnowski, T., and Rosenberg, C. (1987). "Parallel Networks That Learn to Pronounce English Text." *Complex Systems*, 1:145–68.

Selfridge, O. G. (1959). "Pandemonium: A Paradigm for Learning." *Proceedings of the Symposium on Mechanisation of Thought Process*. National Physics Laboratory.

Shor, Peter. (1994). As reported in "Opening a Quantum Door on Computing." *Science News*, 145: 308.

Simon, Herbert. (1981). *The Sciences of the Artificial*, 2nd ed. Cambridge, Mass.: MIT Press.

Simon, Herbert, and Newell, Allen. (1958). "Heuristic Problem Solving: The Next Advance in Operations Research." *Operations Research*, 6: 1–10.

Simon, Herbert, and Newell, Allen. (1972). *Human Problem Solving*. Englewood Cliffs, N.J.: Prentice-Hall.

Skarda, C., and Freeman, W. J. (1987). "How Brains Make Chaos in Order to Make Sense of the World." *Behavioral and Brain Sciences,* 10, 2: 161–95.

Sloman, A. (1989). "A Personal View of Artificial Intelligence." In Sharples, M., Hogg, D., Hutchison, C., Torrance, S., and Young, D. eds. *Computers and Thought: A Practical Introduction to Artificial Intelligence*. Cambridge, Mass.: MIT Press.

Sloman, Aaron. (1987). "Motives, Mechanisms, and Emotions." *Cognition and Emotion,* 1, 3: 217–33.

Sloman, Aaron. (1988). "Disposing of the Free Will Issue." Connectionist List message on Internet, June 19.

Sloman, Aaron. (1992). "The Emperor's Real Mind." *Artificial Intelligence, 56:* 355–96.

Smit, Eefke. (1990). "Roger Penrose, the Mathematician: The Black Hole of Consciousness." In Janny Groen, Eefke Smit, and Juurd Eijsvoogel, eds., *The Discipline of Curiosity*. Amsterdam: Elsevier.

Smolensky, Paul. (1988). "On the Proper Treatment of Connectionism." *Behavioral and Brain Sciences,* 11, 1: 1–74.

Spafford, Eugene H. (1992). "Computer Viruses—A Form of Artificial Life." In Christopher Langton et al., eds., *Artificial Life II*. Redwood City, Calif.: Addison-Wesley. 727–45.

Stanfill, C., and Kahle, B. (1986). "Parallel Free-Text Search on the Connection Machine System." *Communications of the Association for Computing Machinery,* 29:1229–39.

Stubbs, Derek. (1989). "Genetic Algorithms and Neural Nets." *Neurocomputers,* 3:6, 8–9.

Suarez, Susan D., and Gallup, G. G., Jr. (1981). "Self-Recognition in Chimpanzees and Orangutans, but not Gorillas." *Journal of Human Evolution,* 10: 175–88.

Trivers, Robert. (1991). "Deceit and Self-Deception." In M. H. Robinson and L. Tiger, eds., *Man and Beast Revisited*. Washington, DC: Smithsonian Institution Press.

Turing, Alan M. (1937). "On Computable Numbers, with an Application to the Etscheidungsproblem." *Proceedings of the London Mathematical Society,* 2nd ser., 42: 230–65; correction, ibid., 43: 544–46.

Turing, Alan M. (1950). "Computing Machinery and Intelligence." *Mind, 59:* 434–60. Reprinted in E. Feigenbaum and J. Feldman, eds., *Computers and Thought*. New York: McGraw-Hill, 1963.

Twain, Mark. (1938). *Letters from the Earth*. Edited by Bernard DeVoto. Reprinted New York: Harper & Row, 1962.

Ullman, Shimon. (1983). "Visual Routines." MIT AI Memo 723.

van der Waerden, B. L. (1953). *Modern Algebra.* New York: Frederick Ungar.

van Gelder, T. (1990). "Compositionality: A Connectionist Variation on a Classical Theme." *Cognitive Science,* 14: 355–84.

van Gelder, T., and Port, R. (1993). "Beyond Symbolic: Prolegomena to a *Kama-Sutra* of Compositionality." In V. Honavar and L. Uhr, eds., *Symbol Processing and Connectionst Models in Artificial Intelligence and Cognition: Steps Toward Integration.* New York: Academic Press.

Varela, F. J., and Bourgine, P. (1992). *Toward a Practice of Autonomous Systems.* Cambridge, Mass.: MIT Press.

Varela, F. J.; Thompson, E.; and Rosch, E. (1991). *The Embodied Mind.* Cambridge, Mass.: MIT Press.

Washburn, David A., and Rumbaugh, Duane M. (1991). "Ordinal Judgements of Numerical Symbols by Macaques (*Macaca mulatta*)." *Psychological Science,* 2, 3: 190–93.

Werner, Gerhard. (1987). "Cognition as Self-Organizing Process." *Behavioral and Brain Sciences,* 10, 2: 183.

Whitehead, A. N., and Russell, B. (1910–1913). *Principia Mathematica.* 3 vols. Cambridge: Cambridge University Press. 2nd ed., 3 vols. Cambridge: Cambridge University Press, 1925–27.

Wilson, S. W. (1985). "Knowledge Growth in an Artificial Animal." In *Proceedings of the First International Conference on Genetic Agorithms and Their Applications.* Hillsdale, N.J.: Erlbaum. 16–23.

Wilson, S. W. (1991). "The Animat Path to AI." In J.-A. Meyer and S. W. Wilson, eds., *From Animals to Animals.* Cambridge, Mass.: MIT Press.

Winograd, Terry, and Flores, Fernando. (1986). *Understanding Computers and Cognition.* Norwood, N.J.: Ablex.

Winston, P. H. (1984). *Artificial Intelligence,* 2nd ed. Reading, Mass.: Addison-Wesley.

Winston, P. H. (1992). *Artificial Intelligence,* 3rd ed. Reading, Mass.: Addison-Wesley.

Wintsch, Susan. (1990). "You'd Think You Were Thinking." *Mosaic,* 21, 3:34–48.

Wooldridge, Dean. (1968). *The Mechanical Man: The Physical Basis of Intelligent Life.* New York: McGraw-Hill.

Zuckerman, Lord. (1991). "Apes R Not Us." *New York Review of Books,* May 30, 43–49.

Index